The First Amendment in
Cross-Cultural Perspective

CRITICAL AMERICA

General Editors: Richard Delgado and Jean Stefancic

The First Amendment in Cross-Cultural Perspective

*A Comparative Legal Analysis
of the Freedom of Speech*

Ronald J. Krotoszynski, Jr.

NEW YORK UNIVERSITY PRESS

New York and London

NEW YORK UNIVERSITY PRESS
New York and London
www.nyupress.org

Library of Congress Cataloging-in-Publication Data
Krotoszynski, Ronald J., 1967–
The First Amendment in cross-cultural perspective : a comparative legal
analysis of the freedom of speech / Ronald J. Krotoszynski, Jr.
p. cm.
Includes bibliographical references and index.
ISBN–13: 978–0–8147–4787–2 (cloth : alk. paper)
ISBN–10: 0–8147–4787–6 (cloth : alk. paper)
1. Freedom of speech—Cross-cultural studies.   2. Freedom of speech—
United States.   3. United States. Constitution. 1st Amendment.   I. Title.
K3254.K76   2006
342.08'53—dc22   2005037478

New York University Press books are printed on acid-free paper,
and their binding materials are chosen for strength and durability.

Manufactured in the United States of America
10 9 8 7 6 5 4 3 2 1

I dedicate this book to my students, past, present, and future, who consistently have challenged me to examine and then re-examine my understanding of the freedom of expression, including not only how it can best be protected but also how it can be reconciled with competing fundamental values, such as equality and human dignity. In particular, I want to thank Melanie Price, a former law student, for her consistent support and encouragement during the writing and revision process.

I also dedicate this book to my teachers and mentors. In particular, I want to acknowledge Professor Pam Hall, of the Emory University Department of Philosophy, who always pressed me to ask and answer hard questions, not merely to demand an answer but to seek the best answer (ideally one based on truth). In addition, I should recognize the impact that Judge Frank M. Johnson, Jr., for whom I served as a law clerk, has had on my professional development and research agenda. Judge Johnson's courage during the Civil Rights Movement demonstrated quite concretely the importance—and potential—of law as an agent of transformative social change. His lifelong commitment to protecting and enforcing fundamental human rights, including the freedom of expression, provides hope that law and justice need not be antithetical concepts.

Finally, I want to thank my immediate family—Ron, Sr., Barbara, James, David, and Roxanne—for their constant support and understanding.

Contents

Acknowledgments

Certain materials in this book first appeared in law review format. In all cases, I have substantially revised and updated the materials; nevertheless, I wish to acknowledge first publication of these materials as follows:

Chapters 2 and 5

Ronald J. Krotoszynski, Jr., "The Chrysanthemum, the Sword, and the First Amendment: Disentangling Culture, Community, and Freedom of Expression," 1998 *Wisconsin Law Review* 905, Copyright 2003 by The Board of Regents of the University of Wisconsin System; Reprinted by permission of the *Wisconsin Law Review*.

Chapter 2

S. Elizabeth Wilborn Malloy & Ronald J. Krotoszynski, Jr., "Recalibrating the Cost of Harm Advocacy: Getting Beyond *Brandenburg*," 41 *William and Mary Law Review* 1159 (2000). Copyright 2000 by the *William and Mary Law Review*.

Chapter 4

Ronald J. Krotoszynski, Jr., "A Comparative Perspective on the First Amendment: Free Speech, Militant Democracy, and the Primacy of Dignity as a Preferred Constitutional Value in Germany," 78 *Tulane Law Review* 1549 (2004). Reprinted with the permission of the Tulane Law Review Association, which holds the copyright.

Chapter 6

Ronald J. Krotoszynski, Jr., "*Brind & Rust v. Sullivan*: Free Speech and the Limits of a Written Constitution," 22 *Florida State University Law Review* 1 (1994). Reprinted with permission of the *Florida State University Law Review*.

Preface

Public comparative law has finally come into its own. After decades of relative obscurity, a variety of factors has led to an enhanced appreciation of the contributions that public comparative law can make to the understanding and enforcement of fundamental human rights, including the freedom of expression. The United States Supreme Court's public and self-conscious turn toward comparative law methodologies, including the "borrowing" of foreign legal precedents, arguably constitutes the main reason for the enhanced importance of comparative legal studies involving public law in general and constitutional law in particular.

Although enhanced judicial reliance on public comparative law has drawn needed (and welcome!) attention to the field, legal scholars have been working in the area for many years. For example, Dan Fenno Henderson's work on Japanese constitutional law spanned many decades and encompassed writings on both the substantive content of Japanese public law and the nature and operation of the judiciary in Japan, with particular attention to the role and workings of the Supreme Court of Japan. John O. Haley, of the Washington University School of Law, worked with Henderson prior to Henderson's death in 2001 and now carries on his tradition of comparative law scholarship.

In a similar fashion, Donald P. Kommers has worked to make the highly nuanced jurisprudence of the German Constitutional Court available to an audience of English-speaking lawyers, judges, and legal scholars outside Germany. His translations of the Federal Constitutional Court's decisions constitute an invaluable contribution to the comparative law field for non-German speaking students of the Federal Constitutional Court. Moreover, his books and law review articles, spanning three decades, represent a substantial contribution to both U.S. and German constitutional law.

In short, many legal scholars have made substantial contributions to the field of comparative public law over time—and particularly in the years following World War II. Although the focus of comparative legal studies traditionally has been on the private law side of the ledger, a small but dedicated corps of academics has used comparative law to better understand the operation of government, the nature of constitutionalism, and the substantive content and scope of fundamental human rights. This book constitutes but a small part of this larger, and crucially important, effort.

As citizens and governments confront common problems associated with new technologies and new social orderings, it stands to reason that we could benefit from considering how other nations have addressed the legal problems associated with these new realities. How should end-of-life controversies be decided? Who should enjoy decisional primacy? To what extent should assisted reproductive technologies be permitted? Should human cloning be legal? To what extent must society recognize and give formal recognition to nontraditional family structures? All of these questions present legal issues of profound importance; comparative legal studies can help to ensure that in domestic deliberations about these questions, and many others of similar complexity and difficulty, the issues are considered fully and carefully.

In my view, free speech law is a particularly appropriate area for comparative legal analysis. Virtually all constitutional democracies purport to respect the freedom of speech; moreover, all these polities face the same conflicts regarding the proper accommodation of competing social values when freedom of expression presents risks to other constitutional values, including equality, human dignity, and personal reputation. Consideration of how other nations have reconciled these competing—and conflicting—values can provide important insights into the compromises (some express, some implicit) that the constitutionally mandated free speech regime in the United States has struck.

For example, one need not necessarily agree with the differing approaches reflected in the free speech law of Canada (Chapter 3) or Germany (Chapter 4) in order to benefit from study of how these nations attempt to reconcile a deep commitment to the freedom of speech with an equally strong commitment to equality, in the case of Canada, and human dignity, in the case of Germany. The contrast between foreign and domestic free speech law can uncover implicit assumptions and provoke a domestic dialog about whether the social cost of a particular kind of speech is justified by its overall social benefits. In my experience, relatively few U.S. law students—or lawyers—appreciate the degree to which *New York*

Times Company v. Sullivan and its progeny depart from the approach to protecting both free speech and personal reputation prevailing in other nations. Indeed, *Sullivan* is a doctrinal outlier not only when compared to civil law nations such as France or Germany but even with respect to other common law nations, such as the United Kingdom and Australia.

To be clear, I am not suggesting that because other nations have rejected *Sullivan*'s approach, the United States courts automatically should conclude that the decision also is mistaken here. Rather, we should consider why *Sullivan* enjoys such iconic status: Why has such an unusual decision, in global terms, become such an important part of the fabric of U.S. efforts to safeguard the freedom of expression? Why does the United States place less value on dignity and reputation than Germany? Investigating and questioning the causes of differences in human rights law will not necessarily result in changes to domestic human rights law; it will result in a better understanding and articulation of the values that domestic human rights law serves and, conversely, those that it fails to advance effectively.

I hope that scholars and students of comparative public law will find the materials that follow helpful in advancing our shared understanding of the meaning and scope of the freedom of expression. Although I would not suggest wholesale adoption (or rejection) of foreign approaches to protecting the freedom of speech, I am convinced that domestic free speech doctrine and theory would benefit from the perspective afforded by consideration of free speech principles abroad (and particularly in nations sharing a common vision of democratic self-governance).

Finally, I would be remiss not to thank those persons who have assisted me with this project over the years in which I have been engaged in writing this book. First and foremost, I wish to acknowledge the support of the Frances Lewis Law Center, at the Washington and Lee University School of Law, which provided substantial research support for this project. My colleagues at W & L have been remarkably supportive; I owe them a collective debt of appreciation. In addition, a number of student research assistants made significant contributions to this project, including Mark Goldsmith (W & L class of '06), Dan Payne (W & L class of '04), Michael Dimitruk (W & L class of '03), and Allison Chock (Wm. & Mary class of '99).

I also should acknowledge and thank several individual scholars who offered incredibly useful comments on drafts of the various chapters; let me hasten to add, however, that the following persons do not necessarily endorse or agree in every respect with my interpretations or readings of particular cases or overall doctrinal approaches: on Canada, Mark Drumbl, Grant Huscroft, and Richard Moon; on Germany, Edward Eberle, Don Kommers, and Peter Quint; on Japan, John Haley, Dan Foote, Mark Levin, and Percy Luney, Jr.; and on the U.K., P. S. Atiyah. Each of these academics helped to keep me on track and, most important, within both the letter and the spirit of the decisions and reasoning of the foreign constitutional courts. I am deeply grateful for the time and effort that each of these individuals invested in this project. Finally, I should hasten to add that any errors or omissions are mine alone; at the end of the day, I am solely responsible for the ideas and the exposition of the ideas set forth in this book.

1

Comparative Law, Free Speech, and the "Central Meaning" of the First Amendment

I. The Utility of Comparative Law for Analyzing the Potential Costs and Benefits of Free Speech

Since Justices Oliver Wendell Holmes and Louis D. Brandeis began forcefully articulating a strong theory of the Free Speech Clause, judges, government officials, and legal scholars have struggled to reach a viable consensus regarding the "central meaning" of the Free Speech Clause of the First Amendment to the United States Constitution. The text of the First Amendment contains a mere forty-five words, only a few of which directly address the freedom of speech:

> Congress shall make no law respecting an establishment of religion, or prohibiting the free exercise thereof; or abridging the freedom of speech, or of the press; or the right of the people peaceably to assemble, and to petition the government for a redress of grievances.[1]

Although the Clause itself is sparingly worded, some of the nation's most talented legal thinkers have, over the years, expended tremendous intellectual capital in efforts to establish a persuasive theory that justifies protecting speech over other constitutional interests, such as equality or community, and that defines the metes and bounds of the free speech guarantee in a convincing fashion.

None of these efforts has succeeded in ending the ongoing debate, which rages on with a ferocity that seems only to build over time. Recent controversies involving laws against hostile workplaces, hate crimes, campus speech codes, and provocative Internet sites have only made the consideration of these issues more pressing. Should the state be permitted to criminalize, or impose civil liability, for "mere" speech, if the speech sufficiently degrades or alienates particular persons or groups within the community? Conversely, if one supposes that a meaningful commitment to equality mandates bright lines demarcating the limits of free speech, how far should one be willing to go in deciding what kinds of speech fall outside the bright lines? Is core political speech of a racist cast to go unprotected, even if some citizens sincerely and devoutly oppose policies aimed at creating an egalitarian society? Regardless of the point one occupies on the ideological compass, it is impossible to avoid wrestling with these issues in contemporary policy debates: free speech and equality are not merely on a collision course, they have in fact already collided. Legislators, judges, and academics are scrambling to put the pieces back together in some coherent fashion.[2]

Before proposing yet another meta-theory regarding the proper scope of the Free Speech Clause, domestic scholars of the First Amendment might find it useful to at least consider how other nations committed to democratic self-government have attempted to resolve the tension between freedom of speech and the project of securing equality of citizenship.[3] In particular, the free speech policies of Canada, Germany, Japan, and the United Kingdom might provide very useful insights and perspectives on domestic free speech theory. As Associate Justice Stephen Breyer has observed, even granting the relevance and importance of legal and cultural differences, comparative legal studies "may nonetheless cast an empirical light on the consequences of different solutions to a common legal problem."[4]

In fact, the United States Supreme Court has relied expressly on comparative law examples to support interpretations of the Constitution. When deciding whether the Eighth Amendment prohibits the execution of mentally retarded persons, the high court noted that "within the world community, the imposition of the death penalty for crimes committed by mentally retarded offenders is overwhelmingly disapproved."[5] Consideration of other countries' treatment of mentally retarded capital defendants did not go unnoticed by the dissenting Justices. Chief Justice Rehnquist, observing that the majority "adverts to the fact that other countries have disapproved imposition of the death penalty for crimes committed by mentally retarded offenders,"[6] questioned the relevance of the comparative law data: "[I]f it is evidence of a national consensus for which we are looking, then the viewpoints of other countries simply are not relevant."[7] The fact remains that a majority of six Justices of the Supreme Court of the United States held that comparative law considerations are relevant to interpreting the domestic Constitution on a question of considerable importance.

In much the same way, the Justices looked to comparative law to inform their decision in *Lawrence v. Texas*,[8] the case that invalidated a Texas criminal statute prohibiting same-sex sodomy. Writing for the majority, Justice Kennedy looked to the repeal of antisodomy statutes in Western Europe to support the Court's conclusion that such laws are fundamentally unjust and, hence, incompatible with "due process of law."[9] "To the extent that *Bowers* relied on values we share with a wider civilization, it should be noted that the reasoning and holding of *Bowers* have been rejected elsewhere."[10] Absent a showing "that in this country the governmental interest in circumscribing personal choice is somehow more legitimate or urgent,"[11] the content of U.S. human rights law should mirror that of Western Europe.

Justice Scalia, in dissent, referenced contemporary developments in the domestic law of Canada regarding same-sex marriage to support his argument that the majority's approach would have far-reaching and, in his view, highly undesirable, consequences.[12] The Supreme Court's self-conscious and strong turn to comparative law to aid in the elucidation of domestic constitutional norms makes the study of foreign human rights law a pressing field of inquiry not only for academics but also for practicing lawyers.

To be sure, any effort at understanding a legal rule outside its own particular cultural context is fraught with peril. This concern has led to a crisis of faith among comparative legal scholars in the United States, who recently have spent as much time and energy attempting to defend their discipline as they have actually spent *engaging* in their discipline.[13] As one commentator has observed, "[r]ecent times have seen comparative legal scholars, in a fashion unprecedented in other fields, turn their scholarly attentions to questions of their own academic self-worth and the future of their discipline."[14]

Of course, one must always recognize the dangers associated with simplistic comparative-law borrowing exercises that, utterly insensitive to cultural context, lay down legal rules side-by-side and purport to describe salient differences. Rules operate in cultural contexts, and a careful observer should never lose sight of this fact. Nevertheless, even if most lawyers in the United States understand a foreign legal system's resolution of a problem somewhat imperfectly, when an almost identical legal problem arises, the response to that problem in a different cultural milieu can provide a useful perspective for domestic consideration.

Consider, for example, Canada's constitutional free speech guarantee, which secures freedom of speech, subject to such controls as are "necessary in a democratic society."[15] Are rules against pornography that "degrades" or "subordinates" women as a class "necessary in a democratic society"? The Canadian conception of equal citizenship probably differs significantly from the predominant point of view in the United States; nevertheless, in constructing a jurisprudence of free speech, both the Canadian and United States Supreme Courts must decide largely identical questions:

> 1) Are sexually explicit materials "speech"?; 2) assuming that such materials constitute speech, should such speech be privileged over claims that it encourages attitudes and beliefs that prevent female citizens from enjoying a full measure of citizenship?; and 3) if some weight must be given to the equality project over the free speech project, how should a reviewing court balance the competing interests and the accommodation of these competing interests reflected in legislation that attempts to tilt the scales in favor of the equality project?

Given the ubiquity of these issues in contemporary Western-style democracies, any court of law charged with giving persuasive reasons to support a judgment will provide useful insights into the theoretical and jurisprudential axes on which such questions turn. Thus, one need not hold a terminal degree in sociology or anthropology in order to benefit from comparative legal studies.

Overt and self-conscious forms of transnational borrowing present yet another reason for pursuing comparative legal studies. Even if significant cognitive difficulties plague the project, the fact remains that judges are aware of major precedents in foreign jurisdictions addressing identical or highly similar legal questions. Members of the Supreme Courts of Canada, Germany, and Japan are quite familiar with landmark Supreme Court cases in the United States; they are similarly aware of well-known works of legal scholarship, such as Mari Matsuda's defense of campus hate speech codes,[16] Richard Delgado's arguments for valuing racial and gender equality more highly than freedom of speech,[17] and, perhaps most famously, Catharine MacKinnon's arguments in favor of protecting women from harassing speech in the work place.[18] Judges self-consciously borrow across national lines, even if they lack a perfect understanding of the legal culture that gave rise to a particular legal theory or judicial decision resolving a complex legal question. Because we know, empirically, that judges borrow from their colleagues in other countries, it would behoove legal academics to have some knowledge of the approaches that other nations sharing similar constitutional commitments have adopted in response to common legal problems.

Finally, the push to make human rights an enforceable part of international law will require a great deal of comparative legal scholarship.[19] As Professor Michael J. Perry has observed, "[t]hough there is significant transcultural agreement both that people have human rights and about what many of those rights are, there can be, and sometimes is, significant transcultural disagreement about whether a particular practice violates one or another human right, or more than one, that is transculturally agreed—and transculturally established, by international law—that people have."[20] Thus, to say that all nations must respect "equal rights for women" is nonsensical in the absence of a common understanding of what conditions will satisfy the requirement of "equal rights." If the international human rights community leaves the concept undefined, the effort to secure such rights universally will be little more than an empty rhetorical exercise. I agree with Perry that "[h]owever difficult it might be to achieve, productive moral discourse [about human rights] *is* possible interculturally as well as intraculturally."[21] Comparative legal studies can play a critical role in facilitating this discourse.

To be meaningful, rights must be understood to delimit government conduct; rights without corresponding duties on the part of governments are not rights at all.[22] Yet, if Western democracies committed to universal suffrage and free and fair elections do not have a shared understanding, much less a common definition, of "the freedom of speech," is it likely that efforts to promote an international consensus that "the freedom of speech" constitutes a basic human right that all just governments should be bound to respect will prove effective? To the extent that international human rights law fails to define with precision the content and scope of a particular right, nations like China and North Korea would be at least somewhat justified in asserting that they adequately respect the right in question (however much the available evidence might support a contrary conclusion). Simply put, the absence of a common understanding regarding the content and scope of a given human right makes the meaningful enforcement of international human rights norms very difficult, if not altogether impossible.

So, there are at least three reasons for supposing that a comparative law study of freedom of expression might prove helpful, if not essential, to domestic students of the subject: it provides a useful perspective with which to check one's baseline assumptions about the concept; judges routinely borrow across international lines, therefore making some knowledge of foreign legal systems helpful in understanding or predicting the behavior of domestic judges; and, finally, the push to incorporate basic human rights as part of the framework of public international law will require increased attention to and effort in comparative legal scholarship.

It is not my intention to attempt a comprehensive defense of comparative legal scholarship as a useful field of academic endeavor. Such an undertaking would constitute an entirely separate scholarly project and would potentially fill multiple volumes. Accordingly, if one doubts that any meaningful insights can be gained from such exercises and rejects out-of-hand the three rationales that I have advanced for valuing such work, there will be little of interest in the following pages. In my view, however, students of free speech theory can obtain important insights by considering basic jurisprudential understandings of the freedom of speech in nations sharing similar legal commitments.

Domestic free speech theory (and legal doctrine) could benefit significantly from a broader cultural perspective. As Professor Frederick Schauer has observed, in the United States "[o]nce the First Amendment shows up, much of the game is over."[23] He rightly suggests, however, that "the question whether the First Amendment shows up at all is rarely addressed, and the answer is too often simply assumed."[24] Schauer argues that "existing normative theories seem of little relevance to achieving a descriptive understanding of how the First Amendment [Free Speech Clause] came to look the way it does and how it came to include what it includes and exclude what it excludes."[25] He posits "that the most logical explanation of the actual boundaries of the First Amendment might come less from an underlying theory of the First Amendment and more from the political, sociological, cultural, psychological, and economic milieu in which the First Amendment exists and out of which it has developed."[26]

Thus, cultural factors might have as much prescriptive force on understanding and constructing "the freedom of speech" as do doctrinal rules and normative theories. Unpacking these cultural factors, however, is very difficult when one's vantage point is entirely situated within the culture itself—it is much like asking a fish to imagine existing in a world without water. Comparative legal studies, by changing the cultural and legal environment, can enable students of free speech to transcend, at least to some degree, the blinders of cultural familiarity. At least arguably, this represents one of the greatest potential benefits of engaging in comparative legal studies.

Perhaps most significantly, the illusion that there is a single way of framing, or thinking about, a particular legal question usually cannot survive the liberating realization that "the way things must be" is, in reality, quite contestable. Moreover, the recognition that free speech issues addressed one way in the constitutional jurisprudence of the United States are resolved very differently in legal systems sharing a common set of core values with the United States can lead to a much more nuanced understanding of the (often unstated) reasons that undergird our domestic constitutional free speech rules. In sum, the game should prove to be well worth the candle.

II. Searching for Common Themes

In the United States, competing theories regarding the scope of the Free Speech Clause have vied for influence in the federal and state courts (not to mention in the pages of leading national law reviews). Many, if not most, of these theories make extremely broad claims regarding the relationship of freedom of speech to particular social values, such as autonomy, community, self-realization, or the search for truth.[27] One way of testing the viability of these themes is to ask whether these rationales have transcultural significance.

Of course, it is possible for one society to understand free speech to facilitate individual autonomy while another society understands it to empower political groups but not individuals. If another legal system rejects personal autonomy as a rationale for protecting speech, this fact would not necessarily demonstrate the invalidity of such a theory domestically. Nevertheless, if no other legal system sharing a common commitment to protecting freedom of speech conceptualizes the free speech project in terms of autonomy, it would suggest that enhancing personal autonomy is not a necessary condition for a meaningful commitment to maintaining the freedom of speech. After all, it would require hubris of the highest magnitude to assert confidently that a theory of free speech has some inexorable persuasive force in light of compelling evidence to the contrary.

On the other hand, if facilitating democratic deliberation serves as a routine explanation for valuing the freedom of speech—and for incurring social costs associated with speech activity—then one could posit that democratic deliberation might bear some intrinsic association with the freedom of speech, at least as conceptualized in an industrial, Western-style democracy. Correlation is not causation, of course, but at some point one must acknowledge that more than mere simulacra exist.

After careful examination and consideration, no common themes may emerge from a comparative study of freedom of speech across national boundaries. This would not prove or disprove any particular jurisprudential theory but would lend support to the idea that freedom of speech in a democratic society does not have any intrinsic or immutable characteristics. If a comparative law study of the question demonstrates persuasively that diversity of approach is the rule rather than the exception, universalist assumptions about the proper scope of freedom of speech are, quite simply, untenable.

A comparative approach to the study of freedom of expression might also help to demonstrate the contestability of most propositions regarding the nature or scope of the right. That is to say, the fact that other industrial democracies sharing a commitment to freedom of speech do not equate money with speech, or do not view commercial speech as implicating serious free speech issues, or protect forms of erotica not protected in the United States while at the same time proscribing literature containing erotic themes that would enjoy domestic protections, would all suggest that contemporary understandings of freedom of speech in the United States could easily be other than as they currently are.

It necessarily follows that those who support contemporary free speech jurisprudence cannot simply rest on their laurels. Because different understandings of the freedom of speech are plausible, those who support the post-*Brandenburg*[28] free speech orthodoxy in the United States must be prepared to defend the absolutist faith. As will be shown in the pages that follow, free speech jurisprudence in other industrial democracies conclusively demonstrates that alternative conceptions of the free speech project are not merely possible but that they both exist and flourish in nations sharing a meaningful commitment to maintaining democratic self-government.

Moreover, most domestic observers probably would agree that the governments of Canada (Chapter 3), Germany (Chapter 4), Japan (Chapter 5), and the United Kingdom (Chapter 6) observe the Rule of Law and possess serious commitments to maintaining functional, participatory democracies. These nations all seek to facilitate democratic deliberation as an essential element of their polities. Accordingly, the constitutional courts in each have had to face and resolve serious questions regarding the definition and scope of free speech. Consideration of free speech jurisprudence in these nations should therefore be more useful than consideration of free speech principles in nations that lack similar political values (e.g., the People's Republic of China) or that face radically different economic circumstances (e.g., Albania).

Each of the chapters that follows advances, through a comparative law analysis, an understanding of how different political communities have come to define "freedom of speech." In Chapter 2, an examination of the free speech traditions in the United States begins the project and introduces important themes that will help to frame the project in the following chapters, each of which examines the free speech jurisprudence of a foreign constitutional court.

Chapters 3 and 4 consider freedom of speech in Canada and Germany. Both nations elevate concerns rooted in equality and the dignity of all persons above concerns associated with the protection of free speech. Chapter 3 examines free speech in Canada, where a concern for multiculturalism and pluralism—reflected in the Canadian Constitution itself—has led the Supreme Court of Canada to sustain laws that limit the means through which one may express ideas, but not the ideas themselves. Chapter 4 examines the free speech jurisprudence of the German Federal Constitutional Court, which presents an even stronger case than Canada of subordinating free speech concerns in order to advance the equality project.

Chapter 5 analyzes the free speech jurisprudence of the Supreme Court of Japan. The Japanese Constitution, like the United States Constitution, contains a facially unlimited free speech guarantee (unlike the Constitutions of either Canada or Germany). Accordingly, it should not be particularly surprising that one finds that the scope of free speech in Japan is significantly broader than in either Canada or Germany. Nevertheless, the Japanese conception of free speech is less broad than in the United States; it relates to political speech and does not extend to commercial speech or erotica. Chapter 5 suggests that even a nation strongly committed to the freedom of speech need not protect all forms of speech (a proposition that, at least arguably, should be self-evident, even to a student of exclusively domestic, U.S. free speech law, but evidently is not so).[29]

Chapter 6 uses the protection of free speech in the United Kingdom to test the limits of a textual guarantee of the freedom of speech (whether on a constitutional or merely statutory basis). Prior to the enactment and enforcement of the Human Rights Act of 1998, citizens of the United Kingdom did not enjoy any written guarantee of the freedom of speech. The House of Lords, the highest judicial body in the U.K., nevertheless showed considerable concern for a citizen's interest in free speech and managed to incorporate free speech values into the judicial review process. Chapter 6 offers a cautionary note about the limits of textual free speech guarantees and suggests that social traditions favoring free speech play an important role in the protection of this basic human right.

Finally, Chapter 7 reviews the major themes and trends reflected in the preceding six chapters and draws some preliminary conclusions about the nature of free speech in a democratic society. The radical differences reflected in the free speech jurisprudence of the United States, Canada, Germany, Japan, and the United Kingdom offer a strong cautionary note against unlimited universalist claims for any particular understanding of freedom of expression.

III. Setting the Stage for a Comparative Adventure

Before embarking on an examination of the foreign constitutional courts' various approaches to freedom of expression, a caveat or two about the limitations of comparative legal scholarship is in order. Every culture—including legal cultures—has its own *patois,* its own unique cadence. Those who grow up within the culture learn these shorthands and master the iconography of the legal landscape.[30] On the other hand, those from outside a particular legal culture do not possess this information; in a very real sense, they cannot effectively "talk the talk."[31]

Accordingly, any comparative law exercise comes with the inherent danger of reading culturally contingent meaning into legal terms of art. For example, if a foreign court uses the term "consideration" to describe a necessary prerequisite to the formation of a binding contract, an American lawyer is apt to read into that term a host of rules and ideas learned in the first semester of law school. Moreover, this conferral of specific meaning on an otherwise general term largely occurs subconsciously: The reader approaches the text and incorporates meaning reflexively, without, as it were, skipping a beat.[32] Of course, in a comparative context this assumed meaning may not—indeed probably does not—apply.

If it were possible to remove one's cultural blinders at will, these difficulties could be overcome quite easily.[33] Sadly, cultural blinders are not like sunglasses; one cannot simply remove them and store them in a convenient case. Instead, the comparativist must attempt to avoid doing that which comes naturally: assuming the universality of culturally contingent meaning.

Notwithstanding the potential pitfalls, it is possible to examine profitably a foreign legal system. The trick is to discern meaning by reference to the foreign texts themselves; one must double check unstated assumptions by reference to other materials from the relevant legal culture. In this fashion, one usually can avoid overreading, or underreading, foreign legal texts.

2

Freedom of Speech in the United States

Free speech theory in the United States is largely, although not entirely, a creation of the twentieth century.[1] To be sure, the very first Congress enacted the Bill of Rights, including the First Amendment, in its first session and the requisite supermajority of states quickly ratified virtually all of its provisions. Nevertheless, routine litigation of claims arising under the Free Speech Clause did not really exist prior to World War I.

Even after the Supreme Court began hearing and deciding free speech claims against both the federal and state governments, it was not until the Warren Court issued its landmark opinions in *New York Times Company v. Sullivan*[2] and *Brandenburg v. Ohio*[3] that the contemporary free speech orthodoxy took firm root in the collective consciousness of the legal and political communities. In more recent years, legal scholars, generally associated with Critical Legal Studies, Critical Race Theory, and Feminist Jurisprudence, have questioned the hierarchy of values advanced by free speech orthodoxy.[4] Those who support the Warren Court's expansive protection of the freedom of speech now face the challenge of justifying a judicial preference for free speech claims over efforts to promote social equality. Whether free speech should displace efforts to advance the project of creating and maintaining equal citizenship remains a hotly contested question.

One potentially useful way of thinking about the conflict between commitments to free speech and to equality would be to inquire into the first principles of free speech law; that is to say, why do we protect speech at all? Moreover, the question is even more complex than this rather simplistic formulation would suggest. The real question to be asked and answered is "Why do we protect some speech, but not other speech?" What leads courts to shield certain kinds of utterances from state suppression or from engendering civil or criminal liability, while withholding comparable protection from other sorts of speech? Ultimately, one must have a theory of free speech that draws lines around protected and unprotected discourse in a rational, principled fashion. A serious commitment to the Rule of Law demands nothing less.[5]

In the balance of this chapter, I will discuss the two principal domestic theories of the Free Speech Clause, with attention to case law showing these theories in action. Although trends exist, the United States Supreme Court generally has failed to pursue a single vision of the Free Speech Clause, applying one theory or the other as the circumstances seem to warrant. This has resulted in a highly nuanced, although arguably unprincipled, free speech jurisprudence.

I. Competing Theories of the Free Speech Clause

Over the course of twentieth century and continuing into the twenty-first, two basic models of the First Amendment's Free Speech Clause have emerged: the marketplace of ideas metaphor and the democratic self-government paradigm. Both models have appeared in decisions of the United States Supreme Court, and both models enjoy significant support within the academic community. There are, to be sure, other frameworks for theorizing the freedom of speech.

Professor Frederick Schauer has observed that "[p]rescriptive theories abound" and include "[t]heories based on self-government," the "[s]earch for truth," and theories premised on "[p]ersonal autonomy and self-expression."[6] He notes, correctly, that "if there exists a single theory that can explain the First Amendment's coverage, it has not yet been found."[7] All theories, however, ultimately assume either an openness or hostility toward the basic proposition that government efforts to regulate "free speech" (however narrowly or expansively defined) are either presumptively legitimate or presumptively illegitimate. The democratic self-government and marketplace theories provide useful paradigms for this bipolar choice. One's view of whether government presents the greatest threat or constitutes an essential midwife to free speech should prefigure the overall persuasive force of one paradigm (free markets with little or no government regulation/intervention) or the other (government regulation designed to facilitate and enhance deliberative discourse is both constitutional and desirable).

A. The Marketplace of Ideas

Justice Oliver Wendell Holmes's great dissents in *Abrams*[8] and *Gitlow*[9] evoked the metaphor of a "marketplace of ideas" in which various ideas compete for acceptance within the community as a framing device for the freedom of speech. Justice Holmes best expressed this iteration of the underlying values behind the First Amendment in *Abrams*:

> [W]hen men have realized that time has upset many fighting faiths, they may come to believe even more than they believe the very foundations of their own conduct that the ultimate good desired is better reached by free trade in ideas—that the best test of truth is the power of the thought to get itself accepted in the competition of the market, and that truth is the only ground upon which their wishes safely can be carried out. That at any rate is the theory of our Constitution.[10]

The marketplace of ideas understanding of the freedom of speech embraces an evolutionary process, not one predetermined by social, economic, or political results. As Justice Holmes explained, "[e]very idea is an incitement," and "[e]loquence may set fire to reason."[11]

The Holmesian marketplace of ideas conception of the Free Speech Clause broadly embraces John Stuart Mill's liberty ethic[12] and reflects an abiding faith in the capacity of reason to facilitate the sifting of wheat from chaff.[13] Citizens are free both to speak and to listen as they think best; truth is served by a free and full competition of ideas within the community, rather than by paternalistic state-sponsored efforts to protect citizens from the ill effects of bad ideas. At its best, the Holmesian view ensures that nondominant views are not squelched simply because they are different; thus, the Heaven's Gate cult[14] must enjoy the same right to hold and disseminate its beliefs as the Republican National Committee. Moreover, the competition of ideas within the marketplace of public opinion may result in virtually any set of social, economic, or political outcomes: "If in the long run the beliefs expressed in proletarian dictatorship are destined to be accepted by the dominant forces of the community, the only meaning of free speech is that they should be given their chance and have their way."[15]

The principal objection to this conception of the Free Speech Clause is that in practice it proves to be both overinclusive and underinclusive. It is overinclusive because it mandates the protection of "low value" speech, including both racist and sexually explicit speech.[16] The marketplace metaphor is also underinclusive because it permits the marginalization of speakers who lack the financial or political wherewithal to disseminate their views; market forces will drown out voices that deserve to be heard.[17]

These objections notwithstanding, the marketplace metaphor has proven durable, both at the Supreme Court and within the legal academy.[18] The theory has an intrinsic appeal because it is completely viewpoint neutral: The marketplace metaphor denies government the power to pick and choose which speakers shall be heard and which shall be silenced.[19] In a pluralistic nation populated by persons hailing from all points of the compass, government neutrality regarding the modalities and content of free expression arguably serves the citizenry very well.[20] The marketplace of ideas metaphor generally requires government to avoid making subjective value judgments about either the specific content of speech or the means of communication.[21] Alternative theories of the First Amendment require government officials (whether legislators, executive branch personnel, or judges) to make inherently subjective determinations about the nature of particular speech activity: For instance, is the speech political, and does it properly relate to the project of democratic self-governance?[22]

Of course, definitional difficulties haunt the marketplace metaphor too. Is flag burning speech or conduct?[23] Does nude dancing come within the protection of the First Amendment?[24] Should commercial speech enjoy the same First Amendment protection as noncommercial speech?[25] The resolution of these questions involves the exercise of judgment, which necessarily includes an element of subjectivity.[26] Even if one makes this concession, however, the marketplace metaphor offers a powerful and internally coherent account of the First Amendment and its role in facilitating the free exchange of ideas and information.[27]

B. Enhancing Democracy

Alexander Meiklejohn forcefully articulated the leading alternative account of the First Amendment.[28] In his view, the free speech guarantee of the First Amendment exists principally to facilitate democratic self-governance. Invoking the metaphor of the town hall, Professor Meiklejohn argued that the First Amendment required not that all opinions be heard but, rather, "that everything worth saying shall be said."[29] Meiklejohn's theory of the First Amendment has attracted a distinguished following of legal scholars, including Professors Harry Kalven, Owen Fiss, and Cass Sunstein.[30]

Meiklejohn's theory of the First Amendment tolerates government action aimed at ensuring that "everything worth saying" gets said. For example, if concentrations of wealth or limited access to the electronic media muzzled important voices within the community, the government could adopt measures aimed at leveling the playing field, including limitations on the use of wealth to disseminate a particular idea or advocate the election of a particular candidate.[31] Likewise, government could adopt regulations aimed at enhancing the relative voice of minorities within the community to ensure that citizens hear and consider all relevant viewpoints.[32]

The Meiklejohn theory of the First Amendment emphasizes Justice Brandeis's linkage of the Free Speech Clause to free and open democratic deliberation in his concurring opinion in *Whitney v. California*.[33] Unlike Justice Holmes, Justice Brandeis espoused a functional view of free speech:

> Those who won our independence believed that the final end of the State was to make men free to develop their faculties; and that in its government the deliberative forces should prevail over the arbitrary. They valued liberty both as an end and as a means. . . . They believed that freedom to think as you will and to speak as you think are means indispensable to the discovery and spread of political truth; that without free speech and assembly discussion would be futile; that with them, discussion affords ordinarily adequate protection against the dissemination of noxious doctrine; that the greatest menace to freedom is an inert people; that public discussion is a political duty; and that this should be a fundamental principle of the American government.[34]

For Justice Brandeis, "the path of safety lies in the opportunity to discuss freely supposed grievances and proposed remedies" and "the fitting remedy for evil counsels is good ones."[35] In Justice Brandeis's view, freedom of speech facilitates democratic self-government by generating open discussion of matters of public concern.[36]

Under the Brandeis approach, the deliberative process is a means toward the end of effective self-government. Accordingly, bad ideas or proposals should receive a full and free airing unless they present an immediate and palpable threat to the community. As Justice Brandeis puts it, "[i]f there be time to expose through discussion the falsehood and fallacies, to avert the evil by the processes of education, the remedy to be applied is more speech, not enforced silence."[37]

This instrumentalist view of freedom of speech differs significantly from the Holmesian marketplace paradigm.[38] For Justice Holmes, free speech is an end in itself, not a means to some other good.[39] Although Holmes's approach ostensibly seeks truth, "truth" in the Holmesian tradition is socially constructed by operation of the market; hence, if Marxist socialism proves sufficiently persuasive to enough voters, its tenets must be true.[40] In addition, socially constructed truth is valid only within a community that shares a common set of premises. Thus, for members of the Heaven's Gate cult, the Hale-Bopp Comet represented an intergalactic taxicab—although the general population did not concur in this assessment of the available data.

Under the Holmesian approach, the First Amendment requires tolerance of speech activity literally "fraught with death" absent a clear and present danger of serious harm, harm so grave that "an immediate check is required to save the country."[41] To the extent that Justice Holmes endorsed a functional role for free speech, it is the relation of free speech to the search for truth that is paramount, not the relation of free speech to good government.[42]

Although the primary exponents of the Meiklejohn theory of the First Amendment tend to be Civic Republicans (like Professor Cass Sunstein) or traditional liberals (like Professor Owen Fiss), the theory has attracted an eclectic following. For example, former Judge (and then-Professor) Robert Bork has embraced Meiklejohn's argument that the First Amendment should protect only political speech.[43] Needless to say, Bork is far from liberal in his views.[44]

The main attraction of Meiklejohn's theory is that it provides a plausible rationale for protecting speech over other important values, such as equality. When the Ku Klux Klan marches down the streets carrying banners proclaiming racist, sexist, or homophobic messages, the community's commitment to equality suffers.[45] The Meiklejohn theory supports the Klan's right to speak not on a libertarian basis (i.e., people have the right to be racists if they so choose) but rests, instead, on the notion that such activity assists the community in deciding who should govern and what rules should apply to the community (i.e., given the existence of these racist viewpoints, perhaps affirmative action remains a necessary social policy).

The Meiklejohn theory both recognizes and celebrates the inexorable connection between a functioning democracy and freedom of expression. As Professor Robert Reich has explained, representative government requires an active and ongoing debate to legitimate the public policy choices advanced by those holding office:

> Democracy requires deliberation and discussion. It entails public inquiry and discovery. Citizens need to be actively engaged. Political leaders must offer visions of the future and arguments to support the visions, and then must listen carefully for the response. A health-care plan devised by Plato's philosopher-king won't wash.[46]

The Meiklejohn theory is both optimistic (for it posits that meaningful self-government is possible) and pragmatic (for it acknowledges that achieving and maintaining a participatory democracy will not be an easy task).

The Meiklejohn theory's most significant drawback is its inability to provide a cogent rationale for protecting speech unrelated to politics or self-governance.[47] Meiklejohn himself argued that scientific and artistic expression is necessary to enable people to make wise political decisions and therefore should be deemed protected.[48] The arts and sciences, however, constitute positive social goods and ought to be (and are) valued for themselves.[49]

C. Other Competing Theories of the Free Speech Clause

In deciding particular cases, federal courts have relied on a variety of theories that help to explain or justify the protection of speech activity. Most of these theories can be traced to two basic frameworks. That is to say, free speech theories inevitably espouse either a market-based approach to the subject (Holmes) or a public-good-based approach (Meiklejohn and Brandeis).

Market-based theories tend to associate the freedom of speech with facilitating conditions conducive to the attainment of private goods by individual citizens without much regard for the social costs of such activities. The individual may exercise her free speech rights in the pursuit of truth, to enhance personal autonomy, or to facilitate self-realization. An individual citizen might well use free speech to advance truly awful substantive ends (such as racial discrimination) without transgressing the limits of the right.

Moreover, the state should not attempt to censor speakers absent extraordinary circumstances. The autonomy values advanced by the Free Speech Clause outweigh all other social concerns. If pressed, adherents of these approaches would probably concede that their faith in markets might be overstated, but they would argue that it represents a better alternative than faith in a censorial government. But, as Professor Martin Redish has explained, "[w]ere those in power able to selectively restrict private expression on the basis of the government's normative view of the positions expressed, the entire governing process would be seriously distorted and society's initial commitment to democracy threatened."[50]

Public-good-based approaches to the freedom of speech generally condition the protection of particular speech to a persuasive relationship between the expression and another governmental policy objective. Free speech is not an end in itself but merely a useful tool for advancing other, state-identified objectives (such as empowering subordinated groups within the community, or advancing "good governance").

Professor Redish aptly has observed that "[s]cholars and jurists have never achieved anything approaching unanimity on either the values served by the First Amendment guarantee of free expression or the doctrinal principles necessary to implement those values."[51] It is therefore not surprising to find that legal scholars (and sometimes courts) have offered up many variations on the basic marketplace and democratic self-governance theories of the Free Speech Clause. These include related, but distinct, theories such as libertarian approaches tying free speech to self-realization or personal autonomy,[52] theories that protect speech of a dissenting cast,[53] and more practically oriented theories that justify privileging free speech as a kind of social-safety valve that permits disgruntled political minorities to vent without resorting to acts of violence.[54] The degree to which particular speech activity advances these or other court-identified interests prefigures the amount of protection that the speech will receive.

Notwithstanding the prevalence of free speech theories relying on the content of the speech to determine the appropriate scope of First Amendment protection, some scholars and jurists have interpreted the First Amendment's free speech clause as representing a kind of absolute value that cannot be compromised.[55] These scholars take the position that free speech and the values it represents are a preferred freedom, a constitutional value that constitutes a "first among equals." From this perspective, free speech values cannot be compromised in order to serve other important values (even constitutional values), no matter how socially or politically desirable.

Most recently, these scholars have questioned campus speech codes and the recognition of hostile work environment claims under Title VII. They argue that such speech regulations have the effect of censoring free speech in the workplace and on college campuses and, therefore, should be deemed unconstitutional.[56] Based on the First Amendment values mentioned above, their basic argument is that the value of free speech trumps society's efforts to achieve racial and gender equality. They assert that the constitutional protection accorded to the freedom of speech simply reflects the benefits that society reaps from the free flow of information and exchange of ideas. Moreover, adherents of this approach to free speech questions believe that these benefits easily outweigh any costs that society incurs by permitting hurtful or even affirmatively dangerous ideas to circulate freely.[57]

A reasonable person might find it difficult to understand precisely *why* free speech concerns should always and routinely take precedence over society's efforts to eliminate various forms of discrimination. When weighing the social values implicated by permitting greater access to jobs on an equal basis to all members of society and the right to display the most graphic forms of pornography in the workplace, it hardly seems unreasonable to conclude that an individual's right to work might, under some circumstances, displace another individual's right to free expression.[58]

Similarly, informing a young college student that he cannot wear a T-shirt bearing a sexist message in the university library does not seem seriously to threaten core speech values. Such a conclusion appears eminently reasonable if, as a society, we value the ability of all students, male and female, to have an equal opportunity to receive an education and to use the university's library. After all, as authors like Professors Richard Delgado and Mari Matsuda have noted, equality is a constitutional value too, reflected in the text of both the Fourteenth and Thirteenth Amendments.[59] As a matter of logic and text, equality of the sexes and races stems from the Fourteenth Amendment, a later-in-time provision that modifies earlier constitutional provisions, presumably including the First Amendment.[60]

Despite the existence of a dedicated corps of free speech absolutists, most constitutional theorists agree that the government must be permitted to limit some forms of speech.[61] "[T]he First Amendment does not guarantee an absolute right to anyone to express their views any place, at any time, and in any way they want."[62] Indeed, even the Founding Fathers, in writing the Bill of Rights, probably envisioned some limits to the right of free expression.[63] This is not to say that not all statements are speech but, rather, that not all statements are protected speech. For example, even the relative absolutists would permit the criminalization of fraud, even though the fraud involves speech activity. Likewise, few would suggest that laws criminalizing threats against the life of the president violate the Free Speech Clause, or that the First Amendment protects your right to "joke" with airport security about explosive materials in your luggage.[64] As Professor Stanley Fish has explained, any plausible theory of free speech requires significant line drawing.[65] Whether the line drawing constitutes a principled or political exercise is largely in the eyes of the beholder.

II. The Supreme Court's Choice

Despite the ardor of the Meiklejohn adherents and the cogency of their arguments, the Supreme Court has, for the most part, rejected their vision of the First Amendment. Take, for example, the case of dial-a-porn services. It is difficult to fathom how the dial-a-porn industry or its services further democratic self-governance. On the contrary, one could make powerful arguments that pornography—regardless of its precise form— debases society and inhibits the creation of a polity capable of rational self-governance.[66]

Nevertheless, in *Sable Communications v. FCC*,[67] the Supreme Court held that dial-a-porn services enjoy significant First Amendment protection.[68] The outcome reflects the Supreme Court's rejection of the idea that entertainment lacks any serious claim on the Free Speech Clause.[69] This result is inconsistent with the Meiklejohn theory of the First Amendment, whether explicated by Fiss, Sunstein, Bork, or Meiklejohn himself.[70] On the other hand, the result comports nicely with the Holmesian marketplace of ideas model. If citizens wish to talk dirty to one another over the telephone, so be it; the government cannot prohibit such communications, however meager the civic value of such speech activity.[71]

The Meiklejohn theory of the First Amendment also is difficult to square with the result in *44 Liquormart, Inc. v. Rhode Island*.[72] In *44 Liquormart*, the Supreme Court held that the First Amendment protected the right of liquor stores to advertise their prices, notwithstanding Rhode

Island's objection that price-based advertising would tend to promote active price competition among retailers, result in lower prices to consumers, and thereby increase the consumption of alcohol among its citizens.[73]

Rhode Island asserted, reasonably enough, that the social ills associated with the consumption of alcohol justified restrictions on alcohol advertising.[74] Under the Meiklejohn theory of the First Amendment, Rhode Island should have prevailed: Advertising alcohol does nothing to enrich civic life, encourage active citizenship, or otherwise improve the overall state of well-being of the community. On the contrary, alcohol advertising, like cigarette advertising, is likely to impose significant social costs on the community. Advertising of this sort tends to generate increased consumption of alcohol because of both increased public awareness of its availability and lower prices.[75]

In this respect, the Supreme Court's decision in *Posadas de Puerto Rico Association v. Tourism Company,*[76] which sustained Puerto Rico's ban on casino advertising, better comported with the Meiklejohn theory of the First Amendment. Speech that does not directly or indirectly benefit the community by facilitating its ability to oversee the government is outside the First Amendment's free speech guarantee.[77]

Notwithstanding its earlier precedent in *Posadas,* the Supreme Court struck down the Rhode Island prohibition on price advertising, noting that Rhode Island could directly regulate the sale of alcohol but could not regulate speech associated with the sale of alcohol: "[A] state legislature does not have the broad discretion to suppress truthful, nonmisleading information for the paternalistic purposes that the *Posadas* majority was willing to tolerate."[78] Speaking for a plurality of four Justices, Justice Stevens emphasized that "the First Amendment directs that government may not suppress speech as easily as it may suppress conduct, and that speech restrictions cannot be treated as simply another means that the government may use to achieve its ends."[79] This approach to protecting commercial speech incorporates and reflects the Holmesian speech ethic.

Subsequent decisions have confirmed the Supreme Court's near-complete abandonment of *Posadas.*[80] The new general rule requires government to refrain from regulating speech if the government can achieve its objectives through the use of direct regulations or taxation.[81] Although the result in *Posadas* enjoyed substantial support in some quarters,[82] the Supreme Court's repudiation of the precedent reconfirms the ascendancy of the marketplace of ideas conception of the freedom of speech.

All of this is not to say that the Meiklejohn theory of the First Amendment has failed to influence the Supreme Court at all. On the contrary, the Supreme Court has embraced Meiklejohn's assertion that freedom of speech is intertwined inextricably with the project of democratic self-government; thus, the Supreme Court from time to time has noted that political speech is at the "center" or "core" of the First Amendment. In *New York Times Co. v. Sullivan,* for example, Justice Brennan's opinion for the majority essentially embraced Meiklejohn's argument that freedom to criticize the government is crucial to the proper functioning of a democracy.[83] Similarly, in cases involving "low value" speech, such as nude dancing or dial-a-porn, the Supreme Court has carefully distinguished marginal speech activities that lie at the "outer perimeters of the First Amendment"[84] from political, artistic, and scientific speech.

Finally, the Supreme Court's refusal to afford obscene materials[85] or materials featuring nude depictions of children[86] *any* First Amendment protection, and its decisions affording erotic nude dancing only minimal protection,[87] depart substantially from a pure market-based approach to enforcing the Free Speech Clause.[88] If the Justices were absolutely committed to the marketplace metaphor, graphic sexual depictions of children should be no less protected than a "Vote for Kerry" bumper sticker. The fact that government enjoys a relatively free hand when regulating child pornography precludes an unqualified claim that the Supreme Court invariably and reflexively abjures communitarian understandings of the Free Speech Clause. But these exceptions simply demonstrate the more general rule: in most cases, most of the time, the United States Supreme Court embraces and enforces the marketplace theory.[89]

Thus, the Supreme Court's approach essentially adopts aspects of both the Holmesian and Meiklejohn theories of the First Amendment. The Supreme Court has embraced both the marketplace metaphor and the notion that political speech is a special concern of the First Amendment. Its decisions also have recognized that the First Amendment protects individual autonomy, even when individuals or corporations elect to exercise that autonomy in ways inconsistent with the best interests of the community (or, for that matter, their own best interests). Cases like *Stanley v. Georgia,*[90] *Sable Communications,*[91] and *44 Liquormart*[92] reflect the Supreme Court's willingness to vindicate individual liberty, even at the expense of the community. The government, rather than self-interested private actors, presents the most pressing threat to free speech values.[93] In this way, it has maintained the Holmesian tradition of liberty.

At the same time, the Supreme Court has signaled its basic agreement with Meiklejohn's larger thesis. While embracing the marketplace metaphor, the Supreme Court has endorsed the proposition that political speech and speech that otherwise facilitates democratic self-governance enjoys the most robust First Amendment protection, a degree of protection more demanding than that applied to other forms of speech activity. Unlike Judge Alex Kozinski and some others in the law and economics movement,[94] the Justices have rejected the argument that all speech is of equal value for First Amendment purposes.

Under a pure market-based approach to the First Amendment, speech should be treated the same regardless of its content. Its success or failure would be a function of its ability to persuade. A flyer for a Macy's Labor Day sale, or an erotic picture of a six-year-old child, should receive no more, and no less, First Amendment protection than a flyer for a candidate for political office.[95] To date, however, the Supreme Court has maintained a dichotomy between political speech and other kinds of speech activity.[96]

There is, to be sure, a pronounced trend toward the marketplace metaphor in contemporary Supreme Court cases. Increasingly, the Holmesian view seems to be in ascendancy.[97] But the defenders of the Meiklejohn theory have not ceded the field just yet.[98]

III. Conclusion

As Professor Sunstein has noted, the Holmesian and Meiklejohn theories of free expression reflect a genuine dichotomy: results in concrete cases will differ depending on which theory the reviewing court embraces.[99] The United States Supreme Court's failure to make a firm choice may reflect an ambivalence about the proper role of the freedom of speech in a pluralistic society. At the same time, an examination of the free speech case law in other countries will demonstrate that a society's choice between the Holmesian and Meiklejohnian visions of the First Amendment may well be a function of its sense of community and shared values.

An examination of the free speech case law in Canada, Germany, Japan, and the United Kingdom should shed light on the relative strength of the Holmesian and Meiklejohnian accounts of freedom of speech. Moreover, this exercise should lead to a better understanding of the implicit values reflected in the United States Supreme Court's partial embrace of both theories. It might even suggest a proverbial "third way," an approach to freedom of speech that rejects both accounts in favor of some other set of values.

Socrates admonished that an unexamined life is not worth living.[100] So too, a circular jurisprudence that posits its own conclusions as justifications is intellectually indefensible. With the onslaught from both the left and the right,[101] traditional free speech advocates in the United States must be prepared to make their case persuasively within the academy, to the courts, and to the citizenry.[102] In the end, advocates of strong First Amendment protection for free expression will prevail only if we can offer compelling rationales for elevating speech over other important (constitutional) values, such as equality, civility, or comity within the community. Consideration of free speech traditions in other industrial democracies that have self-consciously embraced freedom of speech as a core social value will better prepare those who support freedom of speech here in the United States to meet both the present challenges and those that lie ahead.

3

Free Speech in Canada

Balancing Free Speech and a Commitment to Communitarian Values

The Canadian Supreme Court's approach to freedom of expression represents a marked—and quite intentional—break from the free speech tradition of the U.S. Supreme Court. Part of the explanation for this divergence relates to the text of the Canadian Charter of Rights and Freedoms, the document that secures fundamental rights in Canada.[1] The Charter provides an unqualified free speech guarantee but also contains two provisions that expressly save government action abridging the right. These limitations, in practice, justify government action designed to advance other social objectives, such as equality and cultural pluralism, sometimes at the cost of limiting free speech rights. The net result is reduced protection for free expression.[2]

The Supreme Court of Canada generally has upheld legislative efforts to promote equality by regulating or proscribing speech.[3] The Canadian Charter of Rights and Freedoms expressly protects freedom of expression, but it also protects both equality and multiculturalism. The Supreme Court of Canada has suggested that the constitutional values of pluralism and multiculturalism enjoy some degree of priority over the freedom of expression, at least when a legislative body acts to strike a balance favoring the equality project. As Professor Kathleen E. Mahoney puts the matter, "genuine democracies that respect the inherent dignity of the human person, social justice, and equality accept the fundamental principle that legislative protection and government regulation are required to protect the vulnerable," even at the expense of freedom of speech.[4]

Thus, in many cases raising serious free speech claims, the Canadian Justices have upheld government regulations that restrict speech in the name of equality. As Chief Justice Dickson explained in the landmark

Keegstra case, "[f]ew concerns can be as central to the concept of a free and democratic society as the dissipation of racism, and the especially strong value which Canadian society attaches to this goal must never be forgotten in assessing the effects of an impugned legislative measure."[5]

Moreover, the relative ranking of constitutional values is not entirely the product of judicial caprice. Section 27 of the Charter provides that "[t]his Charter shall be interpreted in a manner consistent with the preservation and enhancement of the multicultural heritage of Canadians."[6] Accordingly, the freedom of speech assumes a subordinated position relative to equality values in Canada because "the special role given equality and multiculturalism in the Canadian Constitution necessitate a departure from the view, reasonably prevalent in America at present, that the suppression of hate propaganda is incompatible with the guarantee of free expression."[7] As will be demonstrated in the materials that follow, Canadian free speech jurisprudence largely reflects and incorporates this approach.

I. Freedom of Expression and the Canadian Charter of Rights and Freedoms

Since 1982, Canadian citizens have enjoyed a constitutional right to the freedom of speech.[8] In relevant part, Section 2 of the Canadian Charter states:

> Everyone has the following fundamental freedoms:
> (a) freedom of conscience and religion;
> (b) freedom of thought, belief, opinion and expression, including freedom of the press and other media of communication;
> (c) freedom of peaceful assembly; and
> (d) freedom of association[9]

Section 2, on its face unlimited as to its scope, provides only part of the picture.[10] Other Charter provisions significantly qualify the scope of Section 2 rights—most notably Section 1, which saves legislation that violates certain Charter rights, and Section 33, which (at least in theory) authorizes direct legislative overrides of certain Charter rights. Similarly, Section 27, with its express reference to multiculturalism, also seems to inform the Canadian approach to evaluating free speech claims.

Although the textual guarantee of the freedom of speech does not differ significantly from the Free Speech Clause of the First Amendment, another provision of the Canadian Charter of Rights and Freedoms directly invites judicial balancing of rights against other social interests.[11] Section 1 of the Charter states:

> The Canadian Charter of Rights and Freedoms guarantees the rights and freedoms set out in it subject only to such reasonable limits prescribed by law as can be demonstrably justified in a free and democratic society.[12]

Since the adoption of the Charter, the Canadian Supreme Court has worked out a standard method of analysis for considering free speech claims (as well as other Charter claims). The landmark *Oakes* decision provides the general analytical framework that governs the adjudication of virtually all Charter claims.[13]

By way of contrast, the Free Speech Clause of the First Amendment makes no provision for direct rights balancing.[14] As noted in Chapter 2, however, the U.S. Supreme Court engages in a process of categorization that, in effect, balances free speech claims against other social interests. Such balancing also is implicit in the tests that the U.S. Supreme Court has created and employed in its free speech decisions.

Finally, one should note at the outset that the Charter maintains the principle of parliamentary supremacy (at least in theory, if not in actual practice) by authorizing legislative overrides of many Charter rights. Section 33 permits the federal and provincial legislatures to override certain Charter provisions, including Section 2, by enacting statutes containing a "notwithstanding" clause.[15] Such declarations can remain in force for up to five years, and may be reenacted, repeatedly, for additional periods of up to five years. A proper invocation of Section 33 effectively precludes judicial invalidation of the statute on Charter grounds. No corresponding legislative power exists in contemporary U.S. constitutional law. That said, the effect of Section 33 on constitutional rights may be more apparent than real—the federal Parliament has never invoked this power, and the provincial legislatures, with but two exceptions, have been equally reluctant legislatively to override Charter rights.[16]

A. The Constitutional Text, Judicial Interpretation, and the Scope of Freedom of Expression in Canada

The decisions of the Canadian Supreme Court demonstrate that Section 2 conveys very broad protection to expressive activities. The Supreme Court of Canada has defined the freedom of expression quite expansively; indeed, virtually any conduct, if intended to express a message (however inartfully or ineffectively) comes within the scope of Section 2's protection. As interpreted by the Supreme Court of Canada, the universe of "free expression" has almost no limits.

To a large extent, then, Section 2's facially unqualified language means what it seems to say—all expression, in whatever form and regarding whatever subject—enjoys constitutional protection. Professor Kent Greenawalt has noted aptly that "Canadian constitutional doctrine, up to the present, is less complicated than that of the United States."[17] Even though the scope of the right to freedom of expression is quite broad under Section 2, statutory enactments restricting its exercise can nevertheless pass constitutional muster, if saved by operation of Section 1.

Dolphin Delivery, a relatively early Charter case, established a general rule that courts should interpret Section 2 broadly.[18] The case involved an attempted picket of a courier business in Vancouver, British Columbia. Provincial labor authorities declined to intercede in the dispute between Dolphin Delivery and its employees; the employer, based on its existing common law rights, sought and obtained an injunction against employee pickets.[19] The employees, through their union, argued that the antipicketing injunction violated their Charter rights under Section 2(b) (freedom of expression) and 2(d) (freedom of association). The provincial court found that the trial court's injunction violated Section 2 but held that Section 1 saved the order as a legitimate means of preventing an unlawful breach of contract by the employees.[20]

After losing its initial appeal, the union took its case to the Supreme Court of Canada, where it argued only that the injunction infringed its rights under Section 2(b) and that, on the facts presented, Section 1 could not save the injunction.[21]

Writing for the majority, Justice McIntyre began his analysis of the Charter claim by noting that freedom of expression "is one of the fundamental concepts that has formed the basis for the historical development of the political, social, and educational institutions of western society."[22] He located the right to free expression as an essential corollary of the project of democratic self-government. "Representative democracy, as we know it today, which is in great part the product of free expression and discussion of varying ideas, depends upon its maintenance and protection."[23] Accordingly, "[t]he principle of freedom of speech and expression has been firmly accepted as a necessary feature of modern democracy" and "[t]he courts have recognized this fact."[24] He noted that Canadian constitutional jurisprudence recognized a citizen's interest in free speech long before this right received express recognition in the Charter and, in fact, has very deep roots in Canadian legal and political culture.[25]

The tone of the opinion, up to this point, strongly invokes the Meiklejohn vision of the freedom of speech: free speech merits special legal protection because it is an essential component of democratic self-government. Indeed, Justice McIntyre's language would fit comfortably in the writings of Meiklejohn himself. But the opinion then turns away from the democratic self-government model, toward a marketplace model, without providing any reason for preferring one model to the other.

The proposed picket sought, among other things, to induce others to honor the picket line. This, in turn, would necessitate the breach of numerous contractual undertakings by those who refused to cross the union's picket. The trial court intended the injunction to protect Dolphin Delivery's ability to enjoy the benefit of preexisting contracts with third parties. If free speech exists to facilitate democratic self-government, the relevant question for the Supreme Court should have been "To what extent, if any, would the union's proposed picket have advanced values associated with the project of democratic self-government?" But the Court never asks this question, much less does it purport to answer it.

The Court was "of the view that the picketing sought to be restrained would have involved the exercise of the right of freedom of expression."[26] Although the freedom of speech protected by the Charter "would not extend to protect threats of violence or acts of violence," or "the destruction of property, or assaults, or other clearly unlawful conduct,"[27] the proposed pickets would have been entirely peaceful, so this exception would not apply. Thus, even though the Court stated that the freedom of expression exists principally to facilitate self-government, it held that Section 2(b)'s scope encompasses a peaceful labor picket, without explaining how or why the labor union's proposed picket would have advanced democratic self-government.

As one commentator has observed, "[t]he Court's discussion of subsection 2(b) leaves unanswered important questions about the nature of freedom of expression."[28] The Meiklejohn theory would not support such a broad and all-encompassing construction of the freedom of speech. For speech or expressive conduct to merit protection, some plausible nexus between the speech activity and democratic self-government must be established.[29] In all probability, a labor dispute in which the provincial government had declined to become involved sufficiently implicates public policy to come within the scope of protected expression, but the Court does not establish this linkage.

If freedom of expression really is exclusively, or even principally, about the project of democratic self-government, however, Justice McIntyre's opinion has significantly overextended the definition of "the freedom of expression." A great deal of speech activity has very little to do with elections and oversight of the government; the scope of Section 2(b) should reflect this simple truth.

Even as it provided a remarkably expansive gloss to Section 2(b) rights, *Dolphin Delivery* also established an important limitation on the scope of Charter rights: only direct government action can violate the Charter. Indirect state action, such as a court order enforcing a common law right, does not usually implicate the Charter at all. "I am in agreement with the view that the *Charter* does not apply to private litigation."[30] Although the Charter applies to laws, including common law rules, the government itself must be a party to the litigation for Charter rights to attach: "We have concluded that the *Charter* applies to the common law but not between private parties."[31]

Nor, under *Dolphin Delivery*, does issuance of a court order implicate the government sufficiently to trigger the protection of the Charter. "To regard a court order as an element of governmental intervention necessary to invoke the *Charter* would, it seems to me, widen the scope of *Charter* application to virtually all private litigation."[32] Justice McIntyre strenuously argued that he could not "equate for the purposes of *Charter* application the order of a court with an element of governmental action."[33]

If a government agency participates in, or precipitates, litigation, the requisite level of government action will be met. "Where, however, private party 'A' sues private party 'B' relying on the common law and where no act of government is relied upon to support the action, the Charter will not apply."[34] This iteration of the state action requirement goes well beyond the approach currently embraced by the United States Supreme Court.[35]

Since *Dolphin Delivery*, the Supreme Court has expanded the scope of its state action doctrine to reach more broadly. If the case involves legislation, either directly or indirectly, the Charter applies.[36] Similarly, if an entity is governmental in nature, even at the local level, it must observe Charter limitations.[37] Finally, the Justices have taken the view that common law rules should be interpreted, whenever possible, in a fashion consistent with Charter values. So, even if the Charter itself does not have direct applicability in private law cases, it still has an indirect influence on the construction and interpretation of the common law.[38]

Even with these extensions of the state action doctrine, the Canadian approach to state action remains more restrictive than the prevailing state action doctrine in the United States. Moreover, state action doctrine in the United States is considerably more conservative in its scope than the German Constitutional Court's approach to the question of state complicity or responsibility for putatively "private" actions.[39] This is not to say that any particular approach to the problem of state action is demonstrably better than another.[40] Rather, it is to offer a brief cautionary note that, whatever the substantive scope of freedom of expression in a given polity, a careful observer should take care to factor in the potential effect of the presence (or absence) of a state action requirement. A broad protection, coupled with a strong state action requirement, might well provide less net protection of a constitutional right than a less robust protection broadly applicable to all interactions in the society.

Three years after *Dolphin Delivery,* in the landmark *Irwin Toy* decision,[41] the Justices reaffirmed and restated their expansive definition of "the freedom of expression" guaranteed under Section 2(b). In *Irwin Toy,* the Supreme Court faced a challenge to a Quebec provincial statute that prohibited advertising targeted at children.

Section 248 of the Consumer Protection Act provided that "no person may make use of commercial advertising directed at persons under thirteen years of age."[42] In determining whether an advertisement was directed at a child, section 249 of the statute required consideration of "the context of its presentation," "the nature and purpose of the goods advertised," "the manner of presenting such advertisement," and "the time and place it is shown."[43] Irwin Toy wished to advertise its products in periodicals subject to the prohibition against advertising targeted at children; accordingly, it sought judicial invalidation of the ban on grounds that it violated Section 2(b) of the Charter and was not saved by operation of Section 1.

Chief Justice Dickson, writing for the majority, began his analysis of the free speech question by inquiring into whether commercial speech should enjoy any Section 2 protection: "Does advertising aimed at children fall within the scope of freedom of expression?"[44] The freedom of speech, he suggested, has concrete limits. "Clearly, not all activity is protected by freedom of expression, and governmental action restricting this form of advertising only limits the guarantee if the activity in issue was protected in the first place."[45]

The Chief Justice explained that " 'expression' has both a content and form, and the two can be inextricably connected" and he noted that the concept encompasses "thoughts, opinions, beliefs, indeed all expressions of the heart and mind, however unpopular, distasteful or contrary to the mainstream."[46] Expression has value because "we prize a diversity of ideas and opinions for their inherent value both to the community and the individual" and free speech is "little less vital to man's mind and spirit than breathing is to his physical existence."[47]

Expression may be conveyed in myriad forms, which Chief Justice Dickson described as "infinite" in their variety.[48] Forms coming within the scope of Section 2 include "the written or spoken word, the arts, and even physical gestures or acts."[49] He declined to define the limits of the concept with any precision, noting only that "[i]t is not necessary here to delineate precisely when and on what basis a *form* of expression chosen to convey a meaning falls outside the sphere of the guarantee."[50]

Violence, and perhaps threats of violence, are the only matters plainly falling outside the scope of Section 2: "While the guarantee of free expression protects all content of expression, certainly violence as a form of expression receives no such protection."[51] Even if violence communicates a message, the social costs associated with violence justify categorically excluding it from the scope of Section 2's protection. Thus, "it is clear, for example, that a murderer or rapist cannot invoke freedom of expression in justification of the form of expression he has chosen."[52]

As a matter of logic, a great deal of speech falling well short of violence might well be excluded from Section 2's protections. If free speech exists to facilitate democratic self-government, the need for protecting commercial speech is far from self-evident.[53] As Professor Moon has noted, "[d]espite the Supreme Court's stated commitment to interpret Charter rights purposively, the court has defined expression without any explicit reference to the values said to underlie freedom of expression."[54]

Given earlier precedents holding that commercial speech, in general, enjoys Section 2 protection, Chief Justice Dickson concluded that the subcategory of commercial speech targeted at children under 13 years of age also enjoyed protected status. "Surely, it aims to convey a meaning, and cannot be excluded as having no expressive content."[55] But, under this test, why shouldn't politically motivated acts or threats of violence count as "expression"? Ted Kaczynski, the Unabomber, certainly "aimed to convey a meaning" and his murders and attempted murders contained serious expressive content.[56]

Obviously, one could distinguish acts of violence from advertising directed at children on the basis of social cost—although Chief Justice Dickson does not offer this distinction in his majority opinion. Even if one could distinguish advertising aimed at children from violence, however, the question remains as to how commercial speech advances the social values that the Court identified earlier in its opinion as underlying the Charter's protection of freedom of expression.

Chief Justice Dickson helpfully noted that, in addition to conveying a meaning and possessing a modicum of expressive content, the Supreme Court lacked "any basis for excluding the form of expression chosen from the sphere of protected activity."[57] But this is to substitute a conclusion for a reason. Precisely *why* is commercial speech targeting young children worthy of constitutional protection? Is it because children are thought to possess agency as potential consumers? Is it, rather, that adults might benefit from advertising aimed at children? That companies, like Irwin Toy, would attempt to manipulate children might provoke some wider public discussion of consumerism and the dangers of materialism? Despite these nagging questions, the majority never explains precisely why advertising aimed at children comes within the rubric of "the freedom of speech."[58]

Having found the speech protected, Chief Justice Dickson proceeded to consider whether the government acted with the purpose and effect of infringing Charter rights. "[I]t must next be determined whether the purpose or effect of the impugned government regulation was to control attempts to convey meaning through that activity."[59] The purpose inquiry considers whether "the government has aimed to control attempts to convey a meaning either by directly restricting the content of expression or by restricting a form of expression tied to content."[60] Regulation of only harmful physical effects does not usually meet the intent requirement, whereas regulation of the conduct because of its perceived meaning would fail this prong of the inquiry.

Independent of the government's purpose, the effects of a regulation must also be consistent with Charter rights. In considering the effect of a challenged regulation, reviewing courts should take care to consider the importance of free speech as a social value:

> We have already discussed the nature of the principles and values under-lying the vigilant protection of free expression in a society such as ours. They were also discussed by the Court in *Ford* . . . and can be summarized as follows: (1) seeking and attaining the truth is an inherently good activ-ity; (2) participation in social and political decision-making is to be fos-tered and encouraged; and (3) the diversity in forms of individual self-fulfillment and human flourishing ought to be cultivated in an essentially tolerant, indeed welcoming environment not only for the sake of those who convey a meaning, but also for the sake of those to whom it is con-veyed. In showing that the effect of the government's action was to restrict her free expression, a plaintiff must demonstrate that her activity pro-motes at least one of these principles.[61]

Thus, in order for a litigant to prevail in establishing a colorable free speech claim, she "must at least identify the meaning being conveyed and how it relates to the pursuit of truth, participation in the community, or individual self-fulfillment and human flourishing."[62]

The Court ultimately concluded that "[t]here is no question but that purpose of ss. 248 and 249 of the *Consumer Protection Act* was to restrict both a particular range of content and certain forms of expression in the name of protecting children."[63] The precise reason for this conclusion was somewhat fuzzy; the majority never really explains how commercial speech—and especially commercial speech of the sort at issue—advances the public goods that Section 2(b) exists to protect. One could argue that if speech activity does not have the effect of advancing the values that the free speech guarantee exists to advance—"the pursuit of truth," "partici-pation in the community," or "individual self-fulfillment"[64]—the restric-tion simply does not implicate Section 2(b) rights at all. For Section 2 pro-tection to arise, advertising in general, or ads aimed at children in particu-lar, must somehow advance these public goods. Alternatively, one could embrace a market metaphor for the scope of Section 2(b) rights. This ana-lytical move would moot the need to consider whether particular speech activity advances any social interests beyond those of the speaker.

To be clear, I am not suggesting that the Supreme Court has failed to identify relevant considerations in deciding whether a Section 2 claim exists. On the contrary, the Supreme Court's theoretical concerns firmly ground the right to freedom of speech in the Meiklejohnian tradition: free speech enjoys protection because it facilitates democratic self-government. In addition to the project of democratic self-government, the Court endorses "the pursuit of truth" and "self-fulfillment and human flourishing" as relevant social values, thereby avoiding the problem of leaving speech associated with art, literature, and science unprotected (as might be the case under a strict interpretation of the Meiklejohn theory). The Court's actual application of the test, however, seems to reflect more of a marketplace of ideas approach.

That is to say, the Supreme Court's observations about the theoretical underpinnings of the freedom of speech do not seem to constrain the scope of Section 2 rights very much in practice. As in *Irwin Toy* itself, the Justices find that virtually all claimants have properly invoked Section 2 and that the government regulation being challenged abridges Section 2 rights. This liberal application of the *Irwin Toy* factors seldom matters, however, because the Court usually will go on to find that Section 1 saves the enactment from invalidation. If the Justices really believe that Section 2 exists to advance a discrete set of social values, and to protect speech annexed to those values, they should probably decline to find Section 2 claims in cases involving so-called low value speech, rather than rely on Section 1 and *Oakes* balancing to render dubious Section 2 violations irrelevant.[65]

Once a plaintiff establishes a breach of Section 2, a reviewing court must engage in *Oakes* balancing[66] to determine if the offending statute is saved by operation of Section 1. The *Irwin Toy* Court had little difficulty concluding that sections 248 and 249 of the Consumer Protection Act were limitations "prescribed by law"[67] and that the provisions advanced a "pressing and substantial government objective."[68] As the Court observed, "[t]he concern is for the protection of a group which is particularly vulnerable to the techniques of seduction and manipulation abundant in advertising."[69] Moreover, the Justices concluded that the means used were rational, that they impaired the right to freedom of expression only as much as was required to achieve the government's "pressing and important objective," and that the burden on speech was reasonably proportionate to the advancement of the government's legitimate objectives.[70]

Irwin Toy was not a unanimous decision. It was decided by a vote of three to two, with two Justices not participating. Justice McIntyre would have held that Section 1 did not save sections 248 and 249.[71] He agreed that the objective of child protection constituted a "pressing and substantial" government objective.[72] He found, however, that a complete ban could not be deemed "proportional" to the risk of harm such speech presented to children.[73] His assumption was that Section 2 establishes a marketplace of ideas that is not generally subject to government censorship. "Freedom of expression, whether political, religious, artistic or commercial, should not be suppressed except in cases where urgent and compelling reasons exist and then only to the extent and for the time necessary for the protection of the community."[74]

Justice McIntyre solved the problem of defining "the freedom of speech" by assuming that all speech enjoys protection. Government efforts at censorship are presumptively void, absent the most compelling circumstances. McIntyre articulated a theory of free speech that looks remarkably like the strong marketplace paradigm enunciated by Justice Holmes in cases like *Abrams* and *Gitlow*. Moreover, this approach is fully consistent with giving a virtually unlimited scope to Section 2. Finally, applying Section 1 less generously does not mean that judges displace democratically elected legislators as the primary architects of social policy. Instead, it simply forces legislators to invoke Section 33's "notwithstanding" clause and, in so doing, to take full political responsibility for limiting or abrogating free speech rights.

Because the Supreme Court has so broadly defined the scope of protected expression, it has made it correspondingly easier for the government to regulate speech activity under Section 1. Courts are never insensitive to the social costs of rights.[75] As the social costs of a right increase, the willingness of judges strictly to enforce that right decreases.

Given the existence of Section 33, however, outraged politicians need not resort to court-packing schemes to undo an unpopular judicial decision premised on Section 2 rights. Instead, by simple majority votes, legislators could reenact invalid legislation notwithstanding the fact that it trenches on Section 2 rights. There might be some risks associated with creating circumstances that could lead to more aggressive use of the Section 33 override power, but the framers of the Charter plainly envisioned that this device would safeguard the principles of parliamentary sovereignty and democratic self-government. In Canada, no countermajoritarian difficulty exists (at least as to Section 2 rights) because democratically accountable officials may override, at will, unpopular decisions of the Canadian Supreme Court. The practical availability of the "notwithstanding" power, however, seriously undermines this analysis.

An almost complete historical absence of legislative recourse to Section 33 rights exists. At the federal level, Parliament has *never* exercised the "notwithstanding" power.[76] Moreover, only two provincial legislatures have used the power: Quebec, in a generic fashion at the time that the Charter came into force; and Saskatchewan in a more targeted way in 1986 (also at the dawn of the Charter era). Section 33 has never enjoyed broad popular support and "began as and remains a controversial part of the Charter."[77] Section 33 "was a compromise clause that bridged the political gap between those Premiers who objected to the entrenchment of constitutional rights and those Premiers, and the Prime Minister, who supported the Charter's adoption."[78]

Professor Hiebert explains that "[t]he legislative override continues to be characterized as being incompatible with entrenched rights" and, although "many predicted that the popularity of the Charter and public sentiment would ensure that it would be difficult for legislatures to use the override, the language of rights has so captivated our public discourse that section 33 has now, except for the francophone majority in Quebec, generally assumed the mantle of being constitutionally illegitimate."[79] Thus, neither national nor provincial politicians seem anxious to challenge judicial primacy in interpreting and enforcing Charter rights.

Thus, although legislative override of Charter rights remains a theoretical possibility, "the perceived lack of legitimacy for the clause, particularly outside Quebec, has meant that political leaders are reticent to invoke it."[80] Hiebert suggests that "[i]n light of the legitimacy problems associated with Section 33, the more systematic way that provincial legislatures will likely promote community or collective preferences that conflict with protected rights is to argue that the policy is justified under section 1."[81]

In practical terms, then, the judiciary enjoys the final word in deciding whether legislation survives Charter review. Because Section 33 represents a merely symbolic safeguard, rather than a meaningful tool establishing a coequal role for the legislative branch in defining and applying Charter rights, the Supreme Court's Section 1 analyses become definitive (as opposed to tentative) accommodations of competing social interests.

B. Textual Limits on the Freedom of Expression in the Charter
   and Their Application in Free Speech Cases

Although Section 2 is not limited on its face or, for the most part, as applied, two other provisions of the Charter expressly permit both the federal and provincial governments to abridge Section 2 rights. At least in theory, Section 33 presents the biggest limitation on the scope of Section 2 rights. Section 1, operating independently of Section 33, requires the judiciary to enforce limits on Charter rights, if the limits are prescribed by law and demonstrably justified in a democratic society. Even if a law fails to survive judicial review under Section 1 analysis, it may, at least in theory, be enacted and enforced pursuant to the notwithstanding power.

Section 33(1) of the Charter permits both the federal and provincial legislatures to enact laws that abridge Section 2 rights:

> Parliament or the legislature of a province may expressly declare in an Act of Parliament or of the legislature, as the case may be, that the Act or a provision thereof shall operate notwithstanding a provision included in section 2 or sections 7 to 15 of this Charter.[82]

Such "notwithstanding" declarations cease to be effective after five years,[83] unless the federal Parliament or the provincial legislature reenacts the notwithstanding declaration.[84] Provided that the legislature reenacts the notwithstanding declaration at least once every five years, the legislation retains its immunity from a Charter-based challenge.[85]

Thus, Section 33 gives both the federal Parliament and the provincial legislatures the ability to immunize legislation from all Charter-based judicial review, at least for rights set forth in Section 2 or Sections 7–15. Neither the federal Congress nor the state legislatures possess any comparable authority in the United States.[86]

As noted earlier, both in theory and in practice, political realities limit the ability of legislators to use Section 33 authority in a fashion that defeats the Charter's principal objectives. "Outside of Quebec, the override has been used only once."[87] Moreover, that single use of the power took place in 1986 and involved an effort by the provincial government of Saskatchewan "to override freedom of association and end a strike by the public service there."[88]

Quebec has made greater use of the override power, but even there its use has been on the wane. Quebec's most famous recourse to the "notwithstanding" power occurred immediately after the Charter became effective: the province reenacted its provincial laws, writing a "notwithstanding" declaration into every provision of its provincial statutes.[89] This action provoked judicial challenges, in which the plaintiffs argued that a generic notwithstanding declaration did not satisfy the substance of Section 33(1).

In *Ford v. Quebec (Attorney General)*, the Supreme Court of Canada squarely rejected these arguments, holding that generic notwithstanding declarations satisfied the requirements of Section 33(1).[90] "With great respect for the contrary view, this Court is of the opinion that a s. 33 declaration is sufficiently express if it refers to the number of the section, subsection, or paragraph of the Charter which contains the provision or provisions to be overridden."[91] Of course, this reading of Section 33 permits a legislative body largely to escape responsibility for overriding particular Charter rights—a legislator, if questioned about the effect of an override, could plead ignorance regarding its effect. The use of generic language effectively hides the sum total effects of an override provision from the general public.

The Supreme Court of Canada, however, believes that Section 33 overrides need not elaborate with specificity their intended effects vis-à-vis specific Charter rights. The *Ford* Court observed that "[t]here is no reason why more should be required under s. 33" and held that "a reference to the number of the section, subsection, or paragraph containing the provision or provisions to be overridden is a sufficient indication to those concerned of the relative seriousness of what is proposed."[92] Specific reference to the Charter provision rights being suspended is not a mandatory part of an override, even though the Charter requires overrides to be "express."

Again, one must keep in mind that the federal Parliament has never exercised the "notwithstanding" power and that, for the most part, provincial legislative authorities have not invoked Section 33 either. The fact remains, however, that any decision of the Supreme Court of Canada arising under Section 2 or Sections 7–15 of the Charter could be repealed legislatively by a simple majority vote in the relevant legislative body. Thus, at a formal level of analysis, the "countermajoritarian problem" identified by Professor Bickel in the U.S. system of judicial review[93] has no salience in Canada. Popular legislative majorities may work their will free and clear of the Charter via recourse to Section 33(1). The "notwithstanding clause" in Section 33 upholds the system of parliamentary sovereignty characteristic of the British constitution by permitting direct legislative overrides of the rights set forth in Section 2 and Sections 7–15.[94]

In practice, the Supreme Court of Canada enjoys broad public support and politicians have proven very reticent to challenge the interpretive primacy of the Supreme Court by exercising their Section 33 powers.[95] One Canadian legal academic explains that "[p]oll after poll shows Canadians trust the Court more than politicians, and no politician is strong enough to take on the Court."[96] Moreover, the Supreme Court itself sometimes avoids taking steps that would likely provoke a legislative response. A combination of legislative deference and judicial self-restraint has greatly limited the constitutional significance of Section 33.

Another reason that Section 33 declarations have been relatively rare has to do with Section 1 of the Charter. Section 1 directly invites judicial balancing of rights against other social interests, which often leads to the conclusion that a statute offending a Charter right is nevertheless saved from judicial invalidation. Given the lack of popular support for Section 33 overrides of Charter rights, Professor Hiebert predicts that legislators "will likely promote community or collective preferences that conflict with protected rights [by arguing] that the policy is justified under section 1."[97]

Section 1 of the Charter states:

> The *Canadian Charter of Rights and Freedoms* guarantees the rights and freedoms set out in it subject only to such reasonable limits prescribed by law as can be demonstrably justified in a free and democratic society.[98]

By way of contrast, the Free Speech Clause of the First Amendment makes no provision for direct rights balancing.[99] As noted in Chapter 2, however, the United States Supreme Court engages in a process of categorization that, in effect, balances free speech claims against other social interests. Such balancing also is implicit in the tests that the U.S. Supreme Court has created and employed in its free speech decisions.

C. The Section 1 Standard and Judicial Protection of Charter Rights against Legislative Infringement

Section 1 of the Charter requires the judiciary to enforce limits on certain Charter rights, provided that the limits are "prescribed by law" and "demonstrably justified in a free and democratic society." In the landmark *Oakes* case, the Supreme Court provided a definitive interpretation of this provision that continues to govern Section 1 analysis.

Under Section 1, the burden of justifying the breach "rests on the party seeking to uphold the limitation."[100] The *Oakes* Court emphasized that "[i]t is clear from the text of s. 1 that limits on the rights and freedoms enumerated in the *Charter* are exceptions to their general guarantee."[101] The claimant of a Charter right should prevail in the Section 1 analysis "unless the party invoking s. 1 can bring itself within the exceptional criteria which justify their being limited."[102] Thus, "the onus of justification is on the party seeking to limit."[103]

In evidentiary terms, this means that the party seeking to justify the breach must show "proof by a preponderance of probability" that the limitation is demonstrably justified in a free and democratic society.[104] The evidence offered to meet this standard "should be cogent and persuasive and make clear to the Court the consequences of imposing or not imposing the limit."[105]

In approaching Section 1 balancing, the government must establish that two criteria have been met. "First, the objective, which the measures responsible for a limit on a *Charter* right or freedom are designed to serve, must be of sufficient importance to warrant overriding a constitutionally protected right or freedom."[106] The government must demonstrate that the restriction on Charter freedoms relates "to concerns which are pressing and substantial in a free and democratic society before it can be characterized as sufficiently important."[107]

The second prong of the test requires the government to show that the means used to achieve the "pressing and substantial" ends are themselves "reasonable and demonstrably justified."[108] The Supreme Court has described this part of the Section 1 inquiry as a kind of "proportionality" test. *Oakes* sets forth a separate three-part test for conducting the proportionality inquiry:

> There are, in my view, three important components of a proportionality test. First, the measures adopted must be carefully designed to achieve the objective in question. They must not be arbitrary, unfair, or based on irrational considerations. In short, they must be rationally connected to the objective. Second, the means, even if rationally connected to the objective in this first sense, should impair "as little as possible" the right or freedom in question.... Third, there must be a proportionality between the *effects* of the measures which are responsible for limiting the *Charter* right or freedom, and the objective which has been identified as of "sufficient importance."[109]

The *Oakes* Court emphasized that "[t]he more severe the deleterious effects of a measure, the more important the objective must be if the measure is to be reasonable and demonstrably justified in a free and democratic society."[110]

The test, as articulated, sounds quite demanding. As Professor Hiebert has observed, "[o]n the surface the *Oakes* test appears to make it quite difficult to justify limits on protected rights."[111] A reasonable observer might assume that few laws trenching on Charter rights would survive *Oakes* balancing. And, in the context of *some* Charter rights, the Supreme Court has applied the *Oakes* test in a demanding fashion. "These decisions [applying *Oakes*] reflect different normative conceptions of which values are essential in a free and democratic society and varying assumptions of the appropriate bounds of judicial authority in a parliamentary democracy."[112] In the area of Section 2 rights, however, the Supreme Court has applied the *Oakes* test quite deferentially.

In case after case, the Supreme Court of Canada has found that laws violating Section 2 are nevertheless saved by operation of Section 1. In practice, the *Oakes* test lacks much real bite, requiring only a generalized analysis of whether the government has a plausible reason for regulating speech activity and whether the regulation enacted bears a rational relationship to the objective.[113] As Professor Hiebert has noted, "[a]lmost immediately after outlining the criteria for conducting a section 1 inquiry a majority of the Court began relaxing the requirements governments must meet to demonstrate the justification of a limit."[114] Moreover, the Justices often seem to credit fairly unrigorous social science data proffered by the government in support of regulations that transgress Charter rights (including free expression rights under Section 2).

Indeed, the Justices almost never invalidate legislation regulating free speech on Section 2 grounds. Only a few examples exist at the Supreme Court level. The Supreme Court of Canada invalidated a complete ban on tobacco advertising, finding that the means used to effect the ban were not reasonably proportionate to the burden imposed on the exercise of Section 2 rights.[115] This decision closely tracked the reasoning and result of an earlier case that invalidated a ban on advertising by dentists.[116] And, both cases reflect the precedential weight of *Ford,* which struck down a Quebec provincial law that prohibited any commercial signage in English.[117] All three of these cases involve complete bans on protected commercial speech and the Supreme Court of Canada has made clear that total bans on expression require more justification than less drastic speech regulations.

But these cases are exceptions that prove the general rule. For the most part, the Supreme Court of Canada defers to legislative judgments about both the need for speech restrictions and the reasonableness of the fit between the burden placed on expressive activity and the advancement of the government's interest. In cases like *Butler*[118] and *Keegstra,*[119] the Court signaled that it would credit reasonable legislative judgments about the need for regulation, the reasonableness of the burden imposed on speech activities, and the lack of less restrictive alternative means of achieving the government's objective.

The Supreme Court's approach to *Oakes* balancing in *R. v. Butler* is highly instructive on this point.[120] *Butler* involved a challenge to section 163 of the Criminal Code, which prohibited the commercial sale, distribution, or display of materials that contain "an undue exploitation of sex, or of sex and any one or more of the following subjects, namely, crime, horror, cruelty and violence."[121] The case raised the issue of whether erotica enjoyed protection under Section 2 of the Charter and, assuming that such material enjoys Section 2 protection, whether the obscenity statute could be saved by Section 1 as demonstrably justified in a free and democratic society.

In a unanimous opinion, the Supreme Court limited the scope of the statute to violent or degrading pornography and also found that the remaining subclass of erotica—even hard-core erotica featuring violence or human degradation—enjoys protection under Section 2(b).[122] The only remaining question was whether Section 1 saved section 163 from invalidation under the Charter.

Justice Sopinka acknowledged that the government had failed to establish any conclusive link between hard-core erotica and harm, whether to women as a class or to society in general. Nevertheless, "[w]hile a direct link between obscenity and harm to society may be difficult, if not impossible to establish, it is reasonable to presume that exposure to images bears a causal relationship to changes in attitudes and beliefs."[123] The government, however, did not have a duty to prove that speech causes harm—it needed only to establish that a "reasonable basis" existed for supposing that such speech activity causes harm.[124] Once one accepts that a certain type of speech is per se harmful, the minimal impairment and balancing prongs of *Oakes* become very easy to meet.

Obviously, if a particular category of speech causes harm by its very existence, nothing short of a complete ban would entirely suppress the harm. Similarly, the ban's effectiveness is entirely coextensive with its scope. A regulation advances the government's "reasonable" objective of suppression in exactly the same proportion as it effectively suppresses the speech in question. In practice, then, the *Oakes* test is remarkably easy to satisfy when the Justices accept the proposition that the speech at issue itself constitutes a social harm.[125] So, it is not surprising to find that the

Supreme Court of Canada has sustained bans on advertising aimed at children[126] and on hate propaganda,[127] largely on the theory that these categories of speech are intrinsically socially harmful and, therefore, subject to complete legislative proscription.

Thus, although the *Oakes* test seems quite demanding at first blush, in reality it does not screen out many speech restrictions. When applying *Oakes,* the Justices are remarkably deferential to democratically elected legislative bodies in Section 1 analyses, at least in free speech cases.[128] The Court openly acknowledged this practice in *Irwin Toy*:

> When striking a balance between the claims of competing groups, the choice of means, like the choice of ends, frequently will require an assessment of conflicting scientific evidence and differing justified demands on scarce resources. Democratic institutions are meant to let us all share in the responsibility for these difficult choices. Thus, as courts review the results of the legislature's deliberations, particularly with respect to the protection of vulnerable groups, they must be mindful of the legislature's representative function.[129]

In sustaining Quebec's provincial ban on advertising aimed at children, the Justices emphasized that "[t]his Court will not, in the name of minimal impairment, take a restrictive approach to social science evidence and require legislatures to choose the least ambitious means to protect vulnerable groups."[130]

This approach to legislative deference arguably underprotects rights that, by their very nature, are meant to be countermajoritarian. In the United States, the whole point of a written Bill of Rights is to entrench certain rights against democratic limitation or abrogation. The fact that a legislative body believes that a particular limitation on free speech is necessary should not excuse the judiciary from making an independent examination of the facts that serve as the legislature's predicate for the decision to regulate.

Perhaps the lesson of Section 1, both as written and as applied, is that Charter rights were not designed to be immune from communitarian considerations in shaping and limiting them. To be sure, the Charter protects individual rights, but it also protects the ability of the community to advance its vision of the good by limiting individual autonomy to exercise Charter rights. Thus, the Canadian conception of human rights is perhaps more limited in scope than the standard U.S. understanding. Section 1 presupposes the legitimacy of democratically imposed limits on fundamental rights, and Section 33 ensures the possibility of democratic control over the exercise of most Charter rights.

Even if Charter rights are not absolute, the question remains whether the Supreme Court's application of Section 1 and *Oakes* in the context of Section 2 cases adequately protects free expression. Moreover, the Charter's framers expressly provided a mechanism for legislative override of certain Charter rights—Section 33 permits the enactment of both federal and provincial laws "notwithstanding" a conflict with many of the Charter's human rights (including all of the rights set forth in Section 2). By coloring Section 1 analysis with a high margin of appreciation for legislative work product, the Supreme Court has rendered legislative recourse to Section 33 unnecessary (even if, in practical political terms, such recourse is highly unlikely in any event).

If reasonable minds might disagree about whether a particular burden on free speech constitutes a reasonable limit "demonstrably justified in a free and democratic society," then the Justices should conclude that Section 1 does not save the provision. If Parliament or a provincial legislature views the matter differently, it should reenact the provision and invoke its Section 33 power to override the Charter. The *Irwin Toy/Butler/Keegstra* approach to Section 1 analysis undermines the Charter by inviting considerations of democratic legitimacy at a point when the assumption should be that laws that transgress Charter rights are void, absent invocation of the "notwithstanding" clause power.

Such an approach would not render Section 1 a nullity. Many laws that transgress Section 2 are obviously "demonstrably justified in a free and democratic society." Laws against commercial fraud provide an easy example. Laws prohibiting threats are another. Such laws could be saved under Section 1 without granting Parliament or the provincial legislatures reflexive deference.

On the other hand, if reasonable doubts exist about whether Section 1 saves a law that plainly violates a Charter right, then the judiciary should simply invalidate the law and leave it to legislative authorities to either accept their decision or to reenact the law under Section 33. This approach has an additional benefit: it forces contemporary legislators to revisit the need for laws burdening Charter rights every five years.

When the Supreme Court holds that Section 1 saves a particular statute from invalidation, the statute is valid now and for evermore. Legislators need do nothing to keep the law in force, regardless of changes in social conditions that might render the law more burdensome than necessary. Because legislation passed pursuant to Section 33 must be reenacted every five years, legislators must continually accept political responsibility for violating Charter rights. The requirement of reenactment (or sunset) forces legislators to take political responsibility for limitations on Charter rights. The process also might facilitate broader social debate about the wisdom or fairness of particular burdens on Charter rights. If, after debate, a legislature enacts or reenacts a law that violates a Charter right, the democratic legitimacy of the action could not be greater.

Of course, given the lack of popular support for the use of Section 33, this model represents more of a theoretical, rather than practical, suggestion. If use of the override power is highly unlikely to occur, then the Supreme Court's application of Section 1 represents the last clear chance to validate the community interest advanced by the legislative restriction on a Charter right.

Finally, it bears noting that the Supreme Court's approach to Section 1 has an uncanny relationship to Justice Frankfurter's model of fundamental rights analysis. Although the First Amendment does not contain a provision saving laws that are "demonstrably justified in a free and democratic society," Justice Frankfurter argued that federal judges should be very reticent to invalidate laws enacted by democratically accountable legislatures.

In the famous case of *West Virginia Board of Education v. Barnette*,[131] the U.S. Supreme Court invalidated a statute that mandated a daily flag salute ceremony in the West Virginia public schools. The majority reasoned that "[i]f there is any fixed star in our constitutional constellation, it is that no official, high or petty, can prescribe what shall be orthodox in politics, nationalism, religion or other matters of opinion or force citizens to confess by word or act their faith therein."[132] Accordingly, the Supreme Court invalidated the West Virginia statute on First Amendment grounds.[133]

Justice Felix Frankfurter strongly dissented from this ruling and the reasons offered in support of it. In his view, the majority overstepped the limits of its institutional duty. "As a member of this Court I am not justified in writing my private notions of policy into the Constitution, no matter how deeply I may cherish them or how mischievous I may deem their disregard."[134] The judicial duty "is not that of an ordinary person" and "[i]t can never be emphasized too much that one's own opinion about the wisdom or evil of a law should be excluded altogether when one is doing one's duty on the bench."[135]

According to Justice Frankfurter, the only legitimate judicial inquiry is "whether legislators could in reason have enacted such a law."[136] The majority's approach, which applied strict scrutiny to the West Virginia statute, required the Court "to assume, however unwittingly, a legislative responsibility that does not belong to it."[137] Even if the Justices believe the law to be misguided or foolish, "the point is that this Court is not the organ of government to resolve doubts as to whether it will fulfill its purpose."[138] "Only if there be no doubt that any reasonable mind could entertain can we deny to the states the right to resolve doubts their way and not ours."[139]

Thus, Justice Frankfurter advocated extreme deference to legislative judgments that adjusted legitimate government policies against the right to freedom of expression. Only if a legislature strikes a patently absurd balance should the Supreme Court invalidate it. This largely tracks the Supreme Court of Canada's application of the *Oakes* balancing test in free speech cases: the federal and provincial legislatures enjoy very broad discretion in deciding how far to restrict speech rights in order to advance a "pressing and substantial" government interest.[140]

Of course, some balancing of the government's interest in regulating speech activity against the burden on free speech is probably unavoidable. In the United States, the federal Supreme Court often evaluates restrictions on free expression using tests that feature overt balancing of interests. Landmark cases involving expressive conduct,[141] commercial speech,[142] speech by public employees in the workplace,[143] and even speech in a classic public forum[144] all rely on balancing devices to resolve the conflict between a would-be speaker and the government. The objection to *Oakes* balancing, then, is not to the use of a balancing device itself. Rather, the objection relates to the relatively modest burden that, in practice, rests on the government to justify significant burdens (indeed, in some cases, complete bans) on ostensibly protected speech activity.

D. Collective Rights, Equality, and the Section 1 Savings Clause

The most salient characteristics of the Canadian approach to freedom of expression are a reliance on balancing tests and a strong commitment to advancing values associated with cultural pluralism and equality. Section 1 of the Charter directly mandates rights balancing—even if a government action breaches a Charter right, the government still prevails if the breach results from a "reasonable limit" on the right that is "prescribed by law" and "can be demonstrably justified in a free and democratic society."[145] As one commentator describes the situation, "[o]ne might say that Canada has clearly rejected the idea of absolute principles."[146] Alternatively, "[o]ne might say that Canada has adopted the idea of balancing itself as a principle, or at least a method that can be described as principled."[147] Accordingly, the Supreme Court of Canada has found it necessary to operationalize the generic saving provision set forth in Section 1 when analyzing claims arising under the various substantive provisions of the Charter.

In framing the Section 1 inquiry, the Supreme Court has emphasized:

> It is important to observe at the outset that s. 1 has two functions: first, it constitutionally guarantees the rights and freedoms set out in the provisions which follow; and, second, it states explicitly the exclusive justificatory criteria (outside of s. 33 of the Constitution Act, 1982) against which limitations on those rights and freedoms must be measured.[148]

The Court will apply section 1 only after determining that a breach of a Charter right existed as a consequence of the government action at issue: "[A]ny s. 1 inquiry must be premised on an understanding that the impugned limit violates constitutional rights and freedoms—rights and freedoms which are part of the supreme law of Canada."[149]

The "free and democratic society" requirement calls for judicial evaluation of the government objectives and their consistency with the traditions of Canadian society. These considerations include, for example, "respect for the inherent dignity of the human person, commitment to social justice and equality, accommodation of a wide variety of beliefs, respect for cultural and group identity, and faith in social and political institutions which enhance the participation of individuals and groups in society."[150] These considerations define a "free and democratic society" and therefore serve "as the ultimate standard against which a limit on a right or freedom must be shown, despite its effect, to be reasonable and demonstrably justified."[151]

To the eyes of a U.S. constitutional lawyer, the list is surprising in several ways. First, and most obviously, the Supreme Court of Canada is placing a great deal of value on equality concerns. This is, in itself, not surprising, but the cast of the equality project is overtly *group* based, rather than focused on the *individual* citizen. In Canada, constitutional rights do not simply belong to individual citizens, acting as free agents, but also appear to have a very strong communitarian component. To be sure, rights belong to individuals—but rights also belong to groups. Individual empowerment is important, but so too is "cultural and group identity."

By way of contrast, the United States Supreme Court invokes the rhetoric of equality not in the service of group or cultural identity but as a means of protecting the individual from being treated merely as a member of a group.[152] The contemporary Supreme Court has left very little room for government to create and enforce rights that protect individuals collectively, based on membership in a cultural or ethnic group. Instead, as a general rule, government must act indifferently to group membership when deciding whether to grant a benefit or impose a burden. The idea that government has a cognizable interest in facilitating group identity—via membership in a cultural or ethnic group—is largely foreign to contemporary U.S. constitutional law.

The second material departure from the U.S. conception of rights relates to the role of government. In the United States, judges almost inevitably view government as the enemy of rights and tend to ignore private ordering arrangements that affect the exercise of constitutional rights. The idea that "faith in social and political institutions which enhance the participation of individuals and groups in society" should play a significant role in constitutional adjudication finds very little support in the pages of *U.S. Reports*. On the contrary, the contemporary United States Supreme Court usually has been overtly hostile to efforts by Congress to enact laws protecting individuals and groups from both governmental and private-sector bias. In cases like *United States v. Morrison*[153] and *Board of Trustees v. Garrett*,[154] the Supreme Court has invalidated legislation Congress adopted to enhance the quality of life enjoyed by women and persons with disabilities. Indeed, the frequency with which the Supreme Court invalidates such enactments has led some scholars to suggest that the Supreme Court is bent on "dissing" Congress.[155]

Rather than "faith" in political institutions to enhance a pluralist vision for the nation, the contemporary U.S. Supreme Court has exhibited a deep and abiding skepticism about such arrangements. Using doctrines of federalism and judicial primacy in defining the scope of constitutional powers, the Rehnquist Court has fought a (successful) rearguard action against laws aimed at advancing a pluralist vision for the country. The idea that it owes some measure of "faith" in the work product of the Congress has virtually no salience whatsoever when Congress attempts to advance group-based rights through legislation.

To be clear, the Supreme Court's efforts are hardly lawless or without any basis in constitutional text or precedent. Rather, the Rehnquist Court takes seriously its obligation to enforce limits on federal power and, moreover, defines the equality project exclusively in individual terms. When Congress attempts to construe its legislative powers broadly to advance group-based rights, the efforts run against both of these Rehnquist Court jurisprudential projects.

The Supreme Court of Canada, by way of contrast, does not see rights solely in terms of the individual but, rather, as advancing both individual and collective, or group, interests. It necessarily follows that, at least in some instances, legislation aimed at enhancing the circumstances of particular marginalized groups in Canadian society might take precedence over individual claims to Charter rights. The interests of groups count in Canadian constitutional jurisprudence in a way that the United States Supreme Court has not embraced since *Beauharnais*.[156]

So, when deciding whether a legislative measure is demonstrably justified in a free and democratic society, equality concerns and a respect for cultural pluralism will play a significant role in the Supreme Court of Canada's decisional matrix. One would anticipate that the Canadian Supreme Court would probably sustain laws aimed at advancing the equality project, even if the laws transgress Charter rights. As will be demonstrated below, subsequent cases bear out this prediction. The Canadian Supreme Court almost never fails to sustain a equality-enhancing law, even if it has the effect of silencing individual speech activity. This is not because the laws do not violate Section 2—the Supreme Court has held that these enactments most certainly transgress the Charter. Rather, Section 1's savings clause justifies the breach because such limits on speech are demonstrably justified in a free and democratic society dedicated to equality, group rights, and cultural pluralism.[157]

III. Accommodating Community, Equality, and the Freedom of Expression: Free Speech as a Dispreferred Freedom

The Supreme Court of Canada has failed to protect free speech when it transgresses the community's commitment to equality, tolerance, and inclusion. Moreover, it has done so repeatedly and in at least two different areas. In cases involving political speech of a racist cast, the Canadian Supreme Court has upheld laws criminalizing such utterances. This represents a radical break with the approach taken in the United States, where such utterances are unprotected only if they present a "clear and present danger of imminent lawlessness"[158] or constitute a "true threat."[159]

The Supreme Court of Canada also has found that the government's interest in suppressing certain forms of pornography transcends the individual's interest in possessing or using such materials. Professor Mahoney's observations about hate speech seem to encapsulate the understanding that governs the Supreme Court's approach: "In the case of highly emotive hate speech directed against minorities and women, where the speech seeks to subvert the truth-seeking process itself, a forceful argument can be made that the interests of seeking truth work against, rather than in favor of, speech."[160] The question turns not on whether the materials at issue are graphic or explicit but, rather, on whether they are "violent" or "degrading and dehumanizing."[161] Thus, the Supreme Court of Canada has embraced a viewpoint-based test to determine whether pornography may be criminalized.

Both of these lines of cases will be discussed below. Taken together, they demonstrate the radically different approach to free speech that prevails in Canada. The Canadian approach elevates civil tranquility and domestic peace over the free speech project. It also reposes tremendous faith in the government to exercise its censorial powers in a fair and evenhanded fashion. This suggests a much greater degree of trust in government than most U.S. citizens (and judges) currently possess.

A. The Supreme Court of Canada and Content-Based Restrictions on Freedom of Expression That Promote Cultural Pluralism

In a series of cases in the early 1990s, the Supreme Court of Canada confronted the problem of hate speech. To what extent does such speech enjoy Section 2 protection? And, even if protected under Section 2, may legislatures nevertheless enact burdens on such speech to advance the equality project? These cases represent a very marked departure from contemporary free speech doctrine in the United States.

1. *R. v. Keegstra*[162] and Racist Propaganda

In *Keegstra*, the Supreme Court of Canada faced a challenge to section 319(2) of the Criminal Code, a federal statute that criminalized "promoting hatred against an identifiable group."[163] James Keegstra worked as a high-school teacher in Eckville, Alberta. His curriculum included a healthy dose of anti-Semitism:

> Mr. Keegstra's teachings attributed various evil qualities to Jews. He thus described Jews to his pupils as "treacherous," "subversive," "sadistic," "money-loving," "power hungry," and "child killers." He taught his class that Jewish people seek to destroy Christianity and are responsible for depressions, anarchy, chaos, wars, and revolution. According to Mr. Keegstra, Jews "created the Holocaust to gain sympathy," and, in contrast to the open and honest Christians, were said to be deceptive, secretive and inherently evil.[164]

Significantly, "Mr. Keegstra expected his students to reproduce his teachings in class and on exams."[165] "If they failed to do so, their marks suffered."[166] In addition to serving as a school teacher, Keegstra also served as mayor of Eckville.[167]

The school district fired Keegstra in 1982. "Officially, he was fired for failing to follow the education department's social studies curriculum."[168] However, Keegstra's dismissal from employment as a high-school history teacher was not at issue in the Supreme Court case. In addition to discharge, local authorities charged him with violating section 319 of the Criminal Code, a criminal charge carrying the possibility of imprisonment.

In relevant part, section 319 provides that "[e]very one who, by communicating statements, other than in private conversation, wilfully promotes hatred against any identifiable group is guilty of . . . an indictable offense and is liable to imprisonment for a term not exceeding two years; or . . . an offence punishable on summary conviction."[169] Section 319(3) prohibits conviction of a 319(2) charge if the defendant establishes the truth of the statements, shows that the statements related to an argument on a religious subject, related to the public interest and the defendant had a good faith belief in their truth, or if the defendant was trying to call attention to the hate speech of others.[170] Finally, at the time, only the government could initiate section 319 charges; a private party could not independently prosecute a section 319 charge.[171]

Following trial, a local jury convicted Keegstra of "unlawfully promoting hatred against an identifiable group by communicating anti-semitic statements to his students."[172] On appeal, however, the Alberta Court of

Appeals reversed the conviction and struck down section 319(2) on free speech grounds.[173] The Supreme Court of Canada then agreed to review the provincial appellate court's decision.

Writing for the majority, Chief Justice Dickson found that racist propaganda enjoys protection under Section 2(b) of the Charter. "Apart from rare cases where expression is communicated in a physically violent form . . . freedom of expression [ensures] that 'if the activity conveys or attempts to convey a meaning, it has expressive content and *prima facie* falls within the scope of the guarantee.' "[174] The government argued that hate propaganda is "analogous to violence, and through this route" should be excluded altogether from Section 2(b) protection.[175] The Justices rejected this contention unanimously. Because hate propaganda expresses an idea and the government sought to suppress such speech because of its communicative value, "hate propaganda is to be categorized as expression so as to bring it within the coverage of s.2(b)."[176]

Whether hate propaganda could be proscribed as a "threat of violence" remained to be determined. *Irwin Toy* held that both violence and threats of violence fall outside Section 2's protections.[177] *Keegstra* appears to overrule *Irwin Toy* on this point, extending Section 2 protection to threats of violence:

> While the line between form and content is not always easily drawn, in my opinion threats of violence can only be so classified by reference to the content of their meaning. As such, they do not fall within the exception spoken of in *Irwin Toy,* and their suppression must be justified under s. 1.[178]

Accordingly, it was not necessary for the Justices "to determine whether the threatening aspects of hate propaganda can be seen as threats of violence, or analogous to such threats, so as to deny it protection under s.2(b)."[179]

Having found that section 319(2) violated Section 2(b) of the Charter, the majority proceeded to engage in Section 1 balancing to determine if section 319(2) was, nevertheless, a valid enactment. As usual, *Oakes* balancing framed this inquiry. And, as is so often the case, the government met its burden under *Oakes*. Section 319(2) related to a pressing and substantial government concern, was prescribed by law, was rational, constituted a minimal impairment of free speech, and did not impose a disproportionate burden on free expression.[180]

Despite repeated invocations of concerns about pluralism and multi-culturalism,[181] neither the Court nor the government could produce any concrete evidence showing that hate speech caused harm to the targeted groups—the government's rationale for adopting and enforcing section 319(2) was entirely conjectural.[182] Chief Justice Dickson explained that "in my view, the international commitment to eradicate hate propaganda and, most importantly, the special role given equality and multiculturalism in the Canadian Constitution necessitate a departure from the view, reasonably prevalent in America at present, that the suppression of hate propaganda is incompatible with the guarantee of free expression."[183]

In other words, hate speech presumptively humiliates and degrades its victims,[184] making it an appropriate target for legislative proscription. As Professor Mahoney explains, "[h]ate propaganda is not legitimate speech."[185] Rather, "[i]t is a form of harassment and discrimination that should be deterred and punished just like any other behavior that harms people."[186] Chief Justice Dickson's majority opinion in *Keegstra* seems to track this approach very nicely. But, as Professor Heinrichs has aptly observed, "[a]bsent any hard evidence demonstrating a causal connection between hate speech and anti-social conduct, we are forced to conclude that *it is the message alone* that offends the Court's sensibilities."[187]

Of course, religiously motivated bigotry enjoys statutory protection under section 319(3), so the eradication of hate speech is far from total, Canada's commitment to multiculturalism notwithstanding. Moreover, private statements, of whatever nature, are never subject to punishment under section 319(2). One also should note that section 319 does not ban the expression of racist, sexist, or homophobic ideas per se but, rather, the expression of epithets that "promote racial hatred." Finally, public use of racial epithets counts only if the government decides that it counts—something that appears to have a strong political cast, given the failure of the Canadian government to bring charges against Quebec separatist leaders who repeatedly uttered racist and xenophobic remarks on national television and radio.[188]

Given the uncertainties associated with the enforcement of proscriptions against hate speech, Canada's commitment to protecting cultural minorities, at least in some cases, is not unwavering. Perhaps minorities are comforted by the mere existence of section 319(2) on the theory that it serves an important expressive value independent of the regularity with which provincial authorities enforce it. But if progressives outside Canada look at the operationalization of section 319(2), they may not like what they see.

In fairness to the federal Canadian government, both the Charter and Canadian constitutional thought incorporate pluralism and multicultural-ism as important public values. Moreover, these values enjoy broad sup-port not only in the legislature but also in the federal courts. The *Keegstra* Court observed that hate speech sends the message "that members of identifiable groups are not to be given equal standing in society, and are not human beings equally deserving of concern, respect and considera-tion."[189] "The harms caused by this message run directly counter to the values central to a free and democratic society, and in restricting the pro-motion of hatred Parliament is therefore seeking to bolster the notion of mutual respect necessary in a nation which venerates the equality of all persons."[190]

This is very strong language: "a nation which *venerates* the equality of all persons." Chief Justice Dickson's language uses nomenclature that con-notes a religious faith, rather than a secular value. "Veneration" implies faith, reverence, and worship, not a crass accommodation of competing political values. And, one cannot help but notice that the idea of equality receives much greater solicitude in the decisions of the Supreme Court of Canada than in comparable decisions of the United States Supreme Court. In Canada, government has an obligation to create and maintain condi-tions that actively promote equality and civility, not that merely might support them if they come to exist by operation of private, market forces —or at least this is how the Supreme Court of Canada seems to view things. Accordingly, when government legislates to advance the equality project, reviewing courts tend to review such legislative efforts quite sym-pathetically. As Professor Mahoney puts the matter, "Free speech cannot be degraded to the extent that it becomes a license to harm" those it targets.[191]

In the United States, by way of contrast, efforts to equalize citizens tend to get short shrift. The Violence Against Women Act, a measure aimed at creating gender equality, fails on the theory that securing gender equality (as it affects the national economy) goes beyond the legitimate powers of the federal government.[192] Laws aimed at limiting influence in federal elections to reduce the effects of wealth disparities fail on free speech grounds.[193] And, of course, laws aimed at protecting minorities from racial vilification fail because they inhibit the speech rights of racists.[194]

The Canadian Supreme Court clearly has abandoned both Holmes's *and* Meiklejohn's conception of the free speech project. Most obviously,

Holmes would not endorse any content- or viewpoint-based restrictions on free speech, absent the most exigent of circumstances. The potential harms identified by the Canadian Justices—feelings of alienation from the community, low self-worth, voluntary withdrawal from public life, general anxiety over issues of personal safety and security—all fall far short of the mark Holmes identified as the predicate for proscribing speech. Similarly, Meiklejohn imagines the possibility of enhancing some voices, perhaps through government subsidies or other programs that encourage the dissemination of particular points of view, but he does not endorse content- or viewpoint-based suppression of ideas because they are hateful or controversial within the community.

The Canadian approach elevates concerns about equality over free expression values, at least in a limited way. Once again, it bears noting that Canada does not ban the expression of any particular idea (other than advocacy of race hate itself), it merely limits the means of expression that can be used to deliver a message.[195]

Of course, a restriction on the means of expression obviously constitutes a burden on the ability to express at least some ideas. The commitment to equality does not mean that certain ideas cannot be proposed or discussed, but it does impose limits on the precise means used to do so. Because hate speech "undermine[s] our [Canada's] commitment to democracy where employed to propagate ideas anathemic to democratic values," it is "wholly inimical to the democratic aspirations of the free expression guarantee."[196] When "individuals are denied respect and dignity simply because of racial or religious characteristics," the democratic process suffers because it discourages minorities from full and equal participation in the political process.[197] In balancing the social value of free and open political debate against the possibility that some citizens will exit the system if the debate includes vitriolics against them for merely existing, Parliament may regulate the marketplace of ideas to make it more accommodating to racial, cultural, and religious minorities.[198]

In the Court's view, this approach reflects and incorporates the political values of pluralism and multiculturalism. The Court explains that "[t]he many, many Canadians who belong to identifiable groups surely gain a great deal of comfort from the knowledge that the hate-monger is criminally prosecuted and his or her ideas rejected."[199] In addition, section 319(2) reminds the community as a whole of "the importance of diversity and multiculturalism in Canada, the value of equality and the worth and dignity of each human person."[200]

The problem of enforcement, of course, remains to be resolved. A theoretical commitment to equality, pluralism, and multiculturalism does not mean that government officials are capable of operationalizing the commitment in an evenhanded way. Indeed, civil liberties advocates brought a number of disturbing incidents to the Supreme Court's attention. People distributing anti-American pamphlets have been arrested and charged with section 319 offenses. Canadian authorities prohibited the importation of a movie about Nelson Mandela based on customs regulations that track section 319 principles. Even Salman Rushdie's novel *The Satanic Verses* ran into trouble as "hate speech."[201]

Such excesses, Chief Justice Dickson opined, are "surely worrying," but section 319(2) still has a place in Canadian law. Because "only the most extreme forms of expression will find a place within s. 319(2)," the risk of overzealous enforcement is not significant, especially when weighed against the social benefits section 319(2) provides.[202]

These reassurances notwithstanding, one might still worry about the ability of government, even attempting to act in good faith, to operationalize section 319(2) in a way that advances, rather than impedes, the position of racial, ethnic, and cultural minorities.

Professor Mahoney uses a very stark hypothetical to explain why hate speech laws are essential to achieving social equality for all citizens:

> A dozen heterosexual males pursuing one gay male screaming epithets at him, an anonymous death threat slipped under a door, burning a cross on another's lawn, or a dead dog left in a lesbian's mailbox do not constitute situations where "talking back" is a viable option. Either the hate monger has slipped away in the night or has created such an intimidating situation through ganging up or bullying that vigorous debate or "more speech" is not a reasonable response. Speech in these examples is nothing more than a weapon, used to silence and terrorize victims and deepen their inequality.[203]

Notwithstanding the rhetorical power of Professor Mahoney's examples, the real-world effects of hate speech laws are not exactly as she has envisioned them.

Butler's standard for obscenity, meant to protect women from objectification, served as a basis for a sustained and active campaign to suppress the speech rights of gays and lesbians in Canada, with remarkable success.[204] Similarly, hate speech laws seem to be invoked as often against minorities as in their defense— as a First Nations leader recently learned.[205] Mahoney's approach could work only in a community that has angels as civil servants. As will be shown in the materials that follow, such conditions do not currently exist in Canada.

Moreover, the examples the Court acknowledges (anti-American propaganda, a pro–African National Congress film, and a Salmon Rushdie book) all involve dissenting speech. In the case of the African National Congress, the speech is by and about a group that has been historically oppressed in extraordinary and horrifying ways.

Hate speech codes such as section 319(2) that protect both dominant and oppressed groups are as likely as not to be deployed to enhance the position of elites, as to protect the position of the oppressed. This is true in the United States, and it is also true in Canada. Indeed, in deciding what kinds of pornography are "degrading" and "dehumanizing," Canadian customs officials routinely targeted gay and lesbian pornography. Why? Because in constructing and applying standards of decency, the average, 42-year-old, white, heterosexual customs agent does not see dehumanization or degradation in *Penthouse, Hustler,* or *Oui.* Such materials represent a familiar, and not entirely unwelcome, view of human sexuality. When gay or lesbian erotica appears at the border, however, the agent recoils in horror from the manifestation of "The Other."

The Supreme Court of Canada exhibits an extraordinary amount of optimism about the ability of a democratic society to write and enforce rules that will enhance the position of the minority at the expense of the majority. The lessons of history suggest that democratically accountable elected officials will use government power to enhance their prospects for reelection. This being so, discretionary government power will almost always be deployed to enhance, not degrade, the relative position of dominant groups. As Professor Heinrichs notes, "even granting that individuals are often mistaken in their sortings, why should government be thought any more capable?"[206] Accordingly, hate speech codes are as likely to marginalize, as empower, minorities within the community.[207]

Before moving on, one should take care to note that *Keegstra* was not a unanimous decision. The Supreme Court divided 4-3 on the question whether Section 1 saved the statute from invalidation. Then-Justice McLachlin (who now serves as Chief Justice) authored a powerful dissent that argued that free speech protects not only speech that people find tasteful and persuasive but also speech that offends, wounds, and angers.[208] "[R]estrictions which touch the critical core of social and political debate require particularly close attention because of the dangers inherent in state censorship of such debate."[209] Section 319 creates a risk to important works of art and literature, and it has a chilling effect on all forms of expression.[210] In light of the scope of section 319(2) and the punishments it creates, Justice McLachlin concluded that "criminalization of hate statements does not impair free speech to the minimum extent permitted by its objectives."[211]

The Chief Justice was an optimist and saw section 319(2) as a reasonable means of promoting the equality project by restricting a limited class of expression. Associate Justice McLachlin, something of a pessimist, concluded that the statute swept too broadly and created too much of a chilling effect on core political speech. One's confidence in the ability of government to enforce section 319 fairly, rationally, and evenhandedly would undoubtedly color one's perception of the burden it places on the free speech project.

2. *Taylor v. Canadian Human Rights Commission*[212]

Taylor was a companion case to *Keegstra* that presented a challenge to the Canadian Human Rights Act, a civil law that prohibits incitement to racial hatred. John Ross Taylor was a member of the Western Guard Party, a racist and anti-Semitic organization promoting the doctrine of white racial supremacy. Taylor established an anti-Semitic telephone message service operating in Toronto, Ontario. Taylor and his associates would clandestinely distribute cards emblazoned with the slogan "White Power Message" and the telephone number; callers would then dial the number and receive the organization's anti-Semitic or racist message du jour.[213]

Section 13 of the Canadian Human Rights Act prohibits the use of telecommunications facilities to disseminate "any matter that is likely to expose a person or persons to hatred or contempt by reason of the fact that the person or those persons are identifiable on the basis of a prohibited ground of discrimination."[214] In turn, section 2 of the act identifies "race, national or ethnic origin, colour, religion, age, sex, marital status, family status, disability, or conviction for an offence for which a pardon has been granted" as prohibited grounds of discrimination.[215] The Canadian Human Rights Commission (the "Commission") enforces the Act through civil administrative proceedings.[216]

After learning about the racist telephone message service, the Commission initiated proceedings against Taylor and, after a hearing, found that his activities violated section 13 of the Human Rights Act. The Commission issued an order directing Taylor and the Western Guard Party to "cease their discriminatory practice of using the telephone to communicate repeatedly the subject matter which has formed the contents of the tape-recorded messages referred to in the complaints."[217]

Taylor and the party disregarded this order. After a court hearing, a federal trial court found Taylor and the party in contempt of the Commission's lawful order and fined the party $5,000 and sentenced Taylor to a year in jail. Both the fine and the prison term were suspended, on condition that Taylor and the Western Guard Party comply with the Commission's cease and desist order.[218] Alas, neither Taylor nor the party complied with the order; accordingly, the party paid the fine and Taylor served his time.

Immediately upon his release from jail in 1983, Taylor once again resumed his anti-Semitic recorded telephone message service. The Commission brought charges, once again seeking an order requiring compliance with the cease and desist order or sanctions for its continued violation. At this point, however, the Canadian Charter had come into force and effect; Taylor defended against the Commission's action by invoking his Section 2(b) rights under the Charter. Both the trial court and the Federal Court of Appeal rejected Taylor's Charter claims. Both found that section 13(1) of the Human Rights Act violated Section 2(b), but both also found that Section 1 saved the statute from judicial invalidation.[219]

As in *Keegstra*, the Supreme Court of Canada found that Taylor's racist phone recordings enjoyed protection under Section 2(b).[220] Any communicative act, save "physical forms of violence" comes within the scope of Section 2(b)—the *Irwin Toy* exception "extends neither to analogous types of expression nor to mere threats of violence."[221] One might question why a true threat should enjoy any constitutional protection. For better or worse, the majority's approach casts a remarkably wide net in setting the metes and bounds of Section 2(b).

And, again as in *Keegstra*, a majority of the Court found that Section 1 saved section 13(1) from judicial invalidation on Charter grounds. Applying *Oakes*, the majority concluded that eradicating racism and anti-Semitism constituted a "pressing and substantial" government objective and found that the means used were reasonable, proportionate, and constituted a minimal impairment of the freedom of speech.[222] This outcome represented a logical extension of the Supreme Court's very similar analysis in *Keegstra*.

One of the most questionable aspects of the majority's *Oakes* analysis was its reflexive deference to legislative reports finding that hate speech represents a serious problem in Canada. Citing Parliamentary studies undertaken in 1966, 1981, and 1984, the Court accepted both the proposition that hate speech is a growing problem in Canada and that it has terrible effects on its victims. Both propositions might well be true, but the studies cited by the majority make no effort to conduct any empirical examination of the issues; instead, the reports present an entirely normative analysis that presumes such activity is a growing problem and treats as self-evident its adverse effects on targeted individuals and groups.[223]

The *Taylor* majority accepted uncritically, without any discussion of methodology, social science validity, or reliability, every supportive assertion in the government reports. Based on a report prepared by politicians, the Court found that "[i]t can thus be concluded that messages of hate propaganda undermine the dignity and self-worth of target group members and, more generally, contribute to disharmonious relations among various racial, cultural and religious groups, as a result eroding the tolerance and open-mindedness that must flourish in a multicultural society which is committed to the idea of equality."[224] This is all well and good as political theory. On the other hand, if *Oakes* requires real empirical evidence, as opposed to conjecture, supposition, and intuition, the majority's conclusion that section 13(1) addressed a "pressing and substantial" problem in a "reasonable and proportionate" fashion is not very persuasive.

Yet, the requirement of empirical proof appeared to rest not on the government to defend the Human Rights Act but, rather, on Taylor to prove that a serious breach of free speech resulted from the Commission's application of section 13(1). "It is not enough to simply balance or reconcile those interests promoted by a government objective with abstract panegyrics to the value of open expression," instead "a contextual approach to s.1 demands an appreciation of the extent to which a restriction of the activity at issue on the facts of the particular case debilitates or compromises the principles underlying the broad guarantee of freedom of expression."[225] In other words, if a litigant's speech is of low value in the Supreme Court's view, the Justices will place a thumb on the scale in favor of the government when engaging in *Oakes* balancing. This effectively shifts the burden from the government, to defend the measure, to the defendant, to prove that his speech has social value. Because "suppression of hate propaganda does not severely abridge free expression values," the balancing test should generally favor a result sustaining the restriction.[226]

Taylor epitomizes the Supreme Court of Canada's two-step approach to free speech claims: at step one, virtually everything counts as free speech, but, at step two, virtually no government restriction fails to prove demonstrably necessary in a free and democratic society.[227] A litigant's initial victory at step one means very little because the government's burden under Section 1 is so easy to meet (at least in the context of free speech claims). One wonders why the Justices, rather than degrading the *Oakes* balancing process, are not more demanding in defining the scope of Section 2 rights. If speech has little or no social value, and in light of Section 27's admonition to advance multiculturalism, why not simply exclude hate speech from constitutional protection at step one?

Like *Keegstra*, the Supreme Court of Canada divided 4 to 3 in *Taylor*. Once again, Justice McLachlin authored the principal dissenting opinion. She agreed with the majority that section 13(1), as applied to Taylor and the Western Guard Party, violated Section 2(b) of the Charter.[228] Unlike the majority, however, Justice McLachlin would exclude not only violence but also true threats of violence from Section 2 protection. "The guarantee of free expression protects all content of expression but may not protect some forms of expression, for example, violence and threats of violence."[229]

Turning to the Section 1 analysis, the dissenters found that section 13(1) related to a pressing and substantial government objective.[230] The harder question, according to Justice McLachlin, was whether the law was proportionate and a minimal impairment of free speech rights. She concluded that section 13(1) did not pass muster under these factors of the *Oakes* balancing test.

First, the absence of any intent requirement made the application of the law turn on the sensitivity of the audience, rather than the mens rea of the speaker. As such, "the section is capable of catching conduct which clearly goes beyond the scope of its objects."[231] In addition, the statute vested the Commission with broad discretion to define and punish offenses based on its own subjective criteria. "Rights and freedoms guaranteed by the Charter cannot be left to the administrative discretion of those employed by or retained by the state."[232]

For Justice McLachlin, the Human Rights Act directly regulated the marketplace of ideas by attempting to ban certain ideas from the public sphere.[233] "The significance of the infringement of the right at issue in this case is most serious" because it "touches expression which may be relevant to social and political issues."[234] "Free expression on such matters has long been regarded as fundamental to the working of a free democracy and to the maintenance and preservation of our most fundamental freedoms."[235] Thus, Justice McLachlin embraced the Meiklejohn theory of the freedom of speech and found that section 13(1) unduly limited the scope of political speech—"I conclude that the benefits to be secured by s. 13(1) of the Canadian Human Rights Act fall short of outweighing the seriousness of the infringement which the section effects on freedom of expression."[236] Justice McLachlin's analysis, although highly persuasive from a U.S. perspective, failed to win the endorsement of a majority of her colleagues.

Accordingly, *Taylor* stands with *Keegstra* as an endorsement of legislative efforts to promote equality, even at the cost of silencing core political speech. In Canada, attempts to promote pluralism and multiculturalism can trump the individual's interest in free expression, whether or not one grounds that interest in the project of democratic self-government, self-fulfillment, or the pursuit of truth.

3. *Zundel v. R.*[237]

Free speech litigants have not always failed to win their cases before the Supreme Court of Canada. *Keegstra* and *Taylor* involve proscription of the particular *means* used to express an idea, not necessarily the proscription of an *idea* itself. If it is possible to advance an idea without the use of racial, ethnic, religious, or gender-based epithets, the statements might not be subject to regulation under Section 1 of the Charter.

In *Zundel*, the Supreme Court faced the issue of "false speech"—namely, may the government proscribe the propagation of ideas or factual propositions that it believes to be without a factual foundation? Section 181 of the Criminal Code provides that "[e]very one who wilfully publishes a statement, tale or news that he knows is false and that causes or is likely to cause injury or mischief to a public interest is guilty of an indictable offense and liable to imprisonment for a term not exceeding two years."[238]

Ernst Zundel, the defendant, circulated materials denying the historical fact of the Holocaust. His publication, a thirty-two-page booklet entitled "Did Six Million Really Die?" argued "that it has not been established that six million Jewish people were killed before and during World War II and that the Holocaust is a myth perpetrated by a worldwide Jewish conspiracy."[239] Zundel was charged and convicted of violating section 181. The Ontario Court of Appeal reversed his conviction but rejected Zundel's claim that distribution of his booklet enjoyed Charter protection under Section 2.

Justice McLachlin wrote a majority opinion that strongly defends the right of all Canadians to speak their mind—so long as they do so without resorting to racial epithets. "To permit the imprisonment of people, or even the threat of imprisonment, on the ground that they have made a statement which 12 of their co-citizens deem to be false and mischievous to some undefined public interest, is to stifle a whole range of speech, some of which has long been regarded as legitimate and even beneficial to our society."[240] Although Parliament is free "to criminalize the dissemination of racial slurs and hate propaganda," such laws "must be drafted with sufficient particularity to offer assurance that they cannot be abused so as to stifle a broad range of legitimate and valuable speech."[241]

All seven members of the Supreme Court found that Zundel's booklet enjoyed protection under Section 2(b).[242] The Justices divided four to three, however, when applying the Section 1 *Oakes* analysis. Justice McLachlin, writing for the majority, held that Section 1 did not save section 181 from invalidation. She rejected the idea that Parliament intended section 181 to prohibit hate speech, noting that "[t]o suggest that the objective of s. 181 is to combat hate propaganda or racism is to go beyond its history and wording and to adopt the 'shifting purpose' analysis that the Court has rejected."[243] Moreover, section 319 (the statute at issue in *Keegstra*) regulates hate speech directly and comprehensively.[244] Section 181's purpose was to "protect the mighty and powerful from discord or slander; there is nothing to suggest any legislative intention to transform s. 181 from a mechanism for the maintenance of the status quo into a device for the protection of 'vulnerable social groups.' "[245]

Given the ambiguity of precisely what section 181 proscribes, its potential chilling effect on core political speech, and its redundancy with section 319, the provision flunked virtually all aspects of the *Oakes* balancing test —it did not address a pressing and substantial problem, given the existence of section 319; it was not rational, given its unlimited scope; and the statute represented neither a proportional approach nor a minimal impairment of Section 2(b) rights.[246] Accordingly, "the restriction of expression effected by s. 181 of the Criminal Code, unlike that imposed by the hate propaganda provision at issue in *Keegstra,* cannot be justified under s. 1 of the Charter as a 'reasonable limit prescribed by law as can be demonstrably justified in a free and democratic society.' "[247]

The three dissenting Justices, led in a joint opinion by Justices Cory and Iacobucci, attempted to save section 181 by rewriting it to limit its scope and effect, making it essentially an analogue to section 319. They agreed with Justice McLachlin that the statute, as originally intended, probably failed Section 1 analysis. However, the purpose of the statute had changed, over time, into one of advancing pluralism and multiculturalism.[248]

The dissenters argued that "[a] democratic society capable of giving effect to the Charter's guarantees is one which strives toward creating a community committed to equality, liberty and human dignity."[249] Any law that materially advances these objectives promotes the public interest. Citing and quoting Professor Mari Matsuda's work, the dissenters argued that "[t]he government's denial of personhood by denying legal recourse may be even more painful than the initial act of hatred."[250]

Arguing the position articulated by the majority in *Keegstra,* the dissenters found that "it would be impossible to deny the harm caused by the wilful publication of deliberate lies which are likely to injure the public interest."[251] One should note that, as in *Taylor,* no empirical evidence supported this proposition. Normative arguments and narrative, along with basic human intuition, were sufficient, in the dissenting Justices' view, to prove the harmful nature of the proscribed speech.

Once again, speech restrictions should be seen as enhancing, rather than debasing, democratic discourse: "The salutary nature of this section should be emphasized. It can play a useful and important role in encouraging racial and social tolerance which is so essential to the successful functioning of a democratic and multicultural society."[252] Advancing these goals constitutes, for the dissenters, a "pressing and substantial objective" that justifies the abridgment of free speech rights.[253]

Applying the rational connection, proportionality, and minimal impairment tests, the dissenters argued that the low value of the speech made the impairment caused by section 181 relatively unimportant. In fact, they asserted that "[a] careful examination of the philosophical underpinnings of our commitment to free speech reveals that prohibiting deliberate lies which foment racism is mandated by a principled commitment to fostering free speech values."[254] Censorship, contrary to the view commonly held in the United States, actually enhances the quality of free speech. Given the potential harm of false speech causing racial unrest, arguments against censorship by the state "fade into oblivion."[255] "To protect only the abstract right of minorities to speak without addressing the majoritarian background noise which makes it impossible for them to be heard is to engage in a partial analysis."[256]

Zundel alters the free speech landscape significantly. It seems to protect speech dismissive of positions held dear by racial, cultural, and religious minorities, provided that such speech does not directly incite racial hatred or involve the use of epithets. Thus, calls for an end to African and Asian immigration to Canada because of the dangers of minority culture overwhelming traditional Canadian values, even if advanced because of a subjective racist attitude toward persons of color, would likely constitute protected speech so long as the speaker did not attempt to vilify or dehumanize minority immigrants on the basis of race, and a law attempting to banish the public dissemination of this view would have to be enacted under the "notwithstanding" clause of Section 33. In Germany, by way of contrast, advocacy of false ideas can lead to both criminal and civil penalties.[257]

Canada's approach to hate speech certainly reflects a greater concern for multiculturalism and pluralism than prevailing free speech doctrine in the United States. But, given *Zundel*, it fails to elevate equality and dignity rights above the freedom of expression routinely or as a matter of course. Canada's jurisprudence thus represents a kind of middle course between the free speech orthodoxy practiced in the United States and the ascendancy of dignity and equality reflected in the German Constitutional Court's decisions.

In many respects, Canada's approach to hate speech seems to represent a kind of mirror image of *Cohen v. California*.[258] In *Cohen*, the United States Supreme Court overturned a state criminal conviction based on the use of offensive language in a public place. Cohen wore a jacket emblazoned with the phrase "Fuck the Draft" in a Los Angeles County Courthouse and was charged and convicted of "maliciously and willfully disturbing the peace."[259] Justice Harlan's majority opinion squarely rejects the idea that government has the power to "excise, as offensive conduct, one particular scurrilous epithet" from the marketplace of ideas.[260]

Justice Harlan's argument recognizes that permitting offensive speech will have social costs. Even so, "[t]he constitutional right of free expression is powerful medicine in a society as diverse and populous as ours."[261] Individual citizens, not the government, have the "decision as to what views shall be voiced . . . largely in the hope that use of such freedom will ultimately produce a more capable citizenry and more perfect polity and in the belief that no other approach would comport with the premise of individual dignity and choice upon which our political system rests."[262]

Some observers might perceive the resulting free-for-all as "only verbal tumult, discord, and even offensive utterance." However, "these are . . . in truth necessary side effects of the broader enduring values which the process of open debate permits us to achieve."[263] Government cannot censor the means of expressing an idea without "running a substantial risk of suppressing ideas in the process."[264] Accordingly, Harlan held that government could not proscribe the public use of the word "fuck": "That the air may at times seem filled with verbal cacophony is, in this sense, not a sign of weakness, but of strength."[265]

Justice Blackmun, joined by Chief Justice Burger and Justice Black, wrote a very brief, two-paragraph dissent that argued that "Cohen's absurd and immature antic . . . was mainly conduct and little speech" and, even if speech, constituted unprotected "fighting words."[266] The dissent utterly failed to engage whether or not a society dedicated to free speech and democratic self-governance could impose regulations designed to require a minimum of civility in public debate without betraying its commitment to free speech. As I have noted previously, "[t]here was probably a good dissent to be written in *Cohen*; in some respects, it is a shame that the dissenters deemed the case too picayune to warrant more consideration than two paragraphs."[267]

One could view *Keegstra, Taylor,* and *Zundel* as an extended argument in favor of minimum rules of civility in public debate. Speech aimed not at moving public policy in one direction or another but, rather, designed to humiliate and dehumanize one's fellow citizens does nothing but detract from the process of democratic deliberation; even if government should not establish viewpoint-based limits on the scope of political speech—there is no such thing as a false idea—the expression of ideas must respect the basic personhood of one's fellow citizens. Even if "[o]ne man's vulgarity is another's lyric,"[268] some lyrics are simply too offensive, and contribute too little to the debate, to warrant constitutional protection.

At the end of the day, I do not find myself in agreement with the balance that the Supreme Court of Canada has struck; the risk of a censorial government acting to advance its own interests strikes me as a greater threat to democratic self-government than racist, sexist, or homophobic diatribes. As Justice Harlan noted, government cannot ban the use of particular words without "running a substantial risk of suppressing ideas in the process."[269]

The Supreme Court of Canada has taken a different approach, one that reflects greater concern for maintaining the dignity and well-being of all its citizens. Moreover, the Canadian approach reflects and incorporates a commitment to honor certain international treaty obligations that require signatories to eradicate hate propaganda.[270] The Court has observed "that the prohibition of hate-promoting expression is considered to be not only compatible with a signatory nation's guarantee of human rights, but is as well an obligatory aspcct of this guarantee."[271] In sum, Canada has decided that a meaningful commitment to free expression does not imply an utter inability to create and enforce norms of civility. Whether or not one agrees or disagrees with this approach, it represents a thoughtful and considered response to Justice Harlan's "Wild West" paradigm for free speech.

B. Balancing Gender Equality and the Freedom of Speech:
The Supreme Court of Canada and Erotica

As in the case of hate speech, the Supreme Court of Canada has faced free speech challenges to laws regulating and, in some cases, proscribing sexually explicit materials. Consistent with its approach to hate speech, the Supreme Court generally has sustained these enactments. Significantly, however, the Justices have done so not on a public morality rationale but, rather, as an incident of the equality project.

1. *R. v. Butler*[272]

In *Butler*, the Supreme Court of Canada faced a challenge to the national statute proscribing the distribution, sale, and possession of "obscenity." Donald Butler owned and operated the Avenue Video Boutique in Winnipeg, Manitoba. His shop sold a variety of "adult" products, including sex toys, magazines, and videotapes. Butler warned potential patrons of the nature of his store with large signs, and limited admission to persons at least 18 years of age.[273]

On August 21, 1987, Winnipeg police officers raided the Avenue Video Boutique, seizing the entire inventory and charging Butler with multiple charges of selling and possessing obscene materials. He subsequently reopened the store, which the police raided again on October 29, 1987. Police arrested and charged his employee, Norma McCord, incident to this second raid.

The government obtained a joint indictment against Butler and Mc-Cord, which alleged more than 150 separate violations of the obscenity provisions of the federal criminal code. A trial judge convicted Butler of eight counts and fined him $1,000 per offense.[274] On appeal, the provincial appellate court reversed the trial court's verdict of acquittal on the remaining counts and found Butler guilty of all the charges alleged in the indictment.[275]

Section 163 of the Criminal Code prohibits the making, printing, publishing, distribution, circulation, or possession of "any obscene written matter," in whatever fixed form.[276] Displaying or advertising such materials also constitutes an offense.[277] The statute defines obscenity as "any publication a dominant characteristic of which is the undue exploitation of sex, or of sex and any one or more of the following subjects, namely, crime, horror, cruelty and violence."[278] Ignorance of the obscene nature of the materials provides no defense,[279] but if the defendant's actions "serve the public good," they cannot serve as the basis of a conviction.[280] Thus, in order to convict Butler, the prosecution had to establish that the erotica at issue constituted "an undue exploitation of sex" by demonstrating a tangible nexus to "crime, horror, cruelty, or violence."

At trial and on appeal, Butler took the position that the Charter protected his wares from criminal proscription. The provincial trial and appellate courts rejected these arguments squarely, and Butler took an appeal to the Supreme Court of Canada.[281]

In a unanimous opinion, the Supreme Court found that section 163 violated Section 2(b) of the Charter, but also found that Section 1 saved the provision from judicial invalidation. Along the way, the Justices offered a limiting construction that substantially reduced the scope of the obscenity statute.

Before applying Charter standards to section 163, the Justices felt it necessary first to render an authoritative interpretation of the statute. Doing so was necessary to determine, in the first instance, whether Butler's materials came within the scope of the statute.

In defining the "undue exploitation of sex" standard, the Court held that it requires a prosecutor to establish that the materials at issue violate prevailing community standards of decency. A primary means of doing this would be to show that the material presents "degrading" or "dehumanizing" sex acts.[282] The Court explained that "[t]here has been a growing recognition in recent cases that material which may be said to exploit sex in a 'degrading or dehumanizing' manner will necessarily fail the community standards test."[283] Such material may be proscribed not because it is dirty or immoral but, rather, "because it is perceived by public opinion to be harmful to society, particularly to women."[284] Although "the accuracy of this perception is not susceptible of exact proof," it "would be reasonable to conclude that there is an appreciable risk of harm to society in the portrayal of such material."[285]

The Court divided the world of erotica into three distinct types: "(1) explicit sex with violence, (2) explicit sex without violence but which subjects people to treatment that is degrading or dehumanizing, and (3) explicit sex without violence."[286] The third category falls completely outside the ambit of section 163 and is presumptively legal (unless "it employs children in its production").[287] Materials that come within the first and second categories, however, usually will constitute the "undue exploitation of sex."[288] The Justices explained that "the portrayal of sex with violence will almost always constitute the undue exploitation of sex," whereas "[e]xplicit sex which is degrading or dehumanizing may be undue if the risk of harm is substantial."[289] Works of art or literature that feature explicit sexual themes of a violent, degrading, or dehumanizing nature also fall outside the ambit of section 163, provided that "the dominant theme of the work as a whole" is not the undue exploitation of sex.[290]

Having rendered an authoritative construction of the statute, the Supreme Court proceeded with its Charter analysis. Not surprisingly, the Court found that violent and degrading erotica comes within the scope of Section 2(b). Such materials "convey meaning" and therefore enjoy protection under the rule enunciated in *Irwin Toy*.[291] The lower appellate courts erred in holding otherwise.

Turning to Section 1 and *Oakes* balancing, the Court found that section 163 was demonstrably justified in a free and democratic society. Avoiding the social harms that might be caused by violent, degrading, or dehumanizing pornography constitutes a pressing and substantial government objective;[292] a rational connection betweens ends and means exists;[293] the impairment of Section 2(b) rights is both minimal[294] and reasonably proportional in its scope.[295]

In sum, the objectives section 163 advances are "of fundamental importance in a free and democratic society."[296] The law "is aimed at avoiding harm, which Parliament reasonably concluded will be caused directly or indirectly, to individuals, groups such as women and children, and consequently to society as a whole, by the distribution of these materials."[297] The law's benign purpose is merely to "seek[ ] to enhance respect for all members of society, and non-violence and equality in their relations with each other."[298] Because both the trial court and appellate court applied a definition of obscenity at variance with the Supreme Court's test, the Justices remanded the case for a new trial.[299]

Butler, like *Keegstra*, shows the willingness of the Supreme Court of Canada to permit content-based restrictions on speech activity to enhance the sense of inclusion among some members of the community. Harmonious community relations are more important than whatever autonomy values might be advanced by permitting violent or degrading forms of

erotica. This does not mean that Canada is committed to eradicating smut
—far from it. A great deal of erotica falls completely outside the scope of
section 163 and, under the holding of *Butler,* enjoys protection under Section 2(b). One must exercise care, however, not to offend too deeply when
creating erotic works.

The problem with the test articulated in *Butler* is that "degrading" and
"dehumanizing" erotica is largely in the eye of the beholder. And, if that
beholder is a heterosexual, white man, some forms of traditional erotica
might seem quite familiar, natural, and wholesome, whereas other forms
of erotica—say, gay and lesbian erotica—might well epitomize "degrading" or "dehumanizing" sexual acts. The *Butler* holding, hailed by progressives in Canada and elsewhere, quickly showed the problems inherent in
delegating censorial powers to civil servants drawn from the dominant
cultural groups.

2. *Little Sisters Book and Art Emporium v. Minister of Justice*[300]

Little Sisters brought home the dangers of vesting substantial discretion
in low-level bureaucrats to censor speech. The Little Sisters Book and Art
Emporium, located in Vancouver, British Columbia, caters to the local gay
and lesbian community.[301] "It was not in the nature of a 'XXX Adult'
store" and, moreover, "was considered something of a 'community center'
for Vancouver's gay and lesbian population."[302] Little Sisters imported
many of the books, magazines, and other wares that it offered for sale
from wholesale suppliers in the United States. This, in turn, required the
materials to pass through Canadian Customs.

Canadian Customs, consistent with section 163 and the Supreme
Court's ruling in *Butler,* established regulations that prohibited the importation of violent, degrading, or dehumanizing erotica and told Customs
inspectors to prevent such materials from entering Canada. Accordingly,
Canadian Customs Tariff 9956(a) prohibits the importation of obscene
materials, as defined by section 163(8) of the Criminal Code, into
Canada.[303] Perhaps not surprisingly, erotica aimed at the gay and lesbian
community struck many Customs inspectors as facially "degrading" and
"dehumanizing." Shipments to the bookstore routinely encountered significant delays at the border.[304] Moreover, most of Little Sisters's wholesale
suppliers required immediate payment upon shipment—thus, Little Sisters found itself with significant capital trapped in the Customs process, as
goods bought and paid for languished at the border.

The Customs process was a rather ad hoc affair. The trial judge considering Little Sisters's constitutional complaint against the Customs Service found that "[m]any publications, particularly books, are ruled obscene without adequate evidence."[305] The officers enforcing the ban on importation of obscene materials were "neither adequately trained to make decisions on obscenity nor [were] they routinely provided with the time and the evidence necessary to make such decisions."[306]

Customs officials made no effort to consider artistic or literary merit when making their determinations, nor could importers seek to place such evidence before them. Moreover, small and specialized bookstores faced much greater scrutiny than larger, more generic booksellers.[307] Large-scale booksellers could import titles that Little Sisters could not, and simply did not face the same sorts of highly targeted obscenity inquiries. Over a ten-year period, Little Sisters had difficulty importing more than two hundred items, many of which were available at other commercial bookstores or at the Vancouver public library.[308]

The trial court, after making extensive factual findings regarding the Customs Service's discriminatory enforcement of Tariff 9956, held in favor of Little Sisters.[309] The trial court did not, however, void Tariff 9956 but, rather, instructed the Customs Service to cease its discriminatory enforcement efforts.

The Customs Service appealed the trial court's ruling. On appeal, the Court of Appeal for British Columbia reversed, finding no violation of either Little Sisters's free speech rights (under Section 2(b) of the Charter) or its equal protection rights (under Section 15(1) of the Charter).[310] One member of the three-judge panel, Judge Finch, dissented from this ruling. He would have found a violation of both Sections 2 and 15 of the Charter, and would have suspended enforcement of Tariff 9956. After suffering this setback, Little Sisters sought and obtained review of its case before the Supreme Court of Canada.

The Supreme Court unanimously reversed, but divided as to the proper remedy. Writing for the majority, Justice Binnie held that although Tariff 9956 was lawful, "[t]he administration of the Act, however, was characterized by conduct of Customs officials that was oppressive and dismissive of the appellants' freedom of expression."[311]

The majority steadfastly defended the *Butler* standard, suggesting that poor administration, rather than a misappreciation of the real-world effects *Butler* would have on sexual minorities, lay at the core of the problem. "*Butler* analysis does not discriminate against the gay and lesbian community" and instead "is directed to the prevention of harm, and is indifferent to whether such harm arises in the context of heterosexuality or homosexuality."[312]

The Supreme Court failed to understand the gravamen of Little Sisters's constitutional argument: a standard for obscenity that depends on erotica's causing offense because of "degrading" or "dehumanizing" aspects cannot help but target the erotic expression of sexual minorities. A committed heterosexual man seeing a photo of two men engaged in fellatio or analingus has a higher propensity to perceive such material to be both "degrading" and "dehumanizing." Moreover, asking the Customs official to pretend to view the material from the perspective of its intended audience asks him to perform an impossible feat. A heterosexual cannot assume the aesthetic of a gay man or lesbian. And, members of dominant cultural groups will inevitably view the artistic expression of sexual minorities as, at best, undesirable manifestations of "The Other." In this way, *Butler* greatly disserves the equality project by facilitating targeted enforcement efforts against sexual minorities.

Perhaps if the Justices of the Supreme Court are prepared personally to assume responsibility for Customs inspections, or to require gay and lesbian erotica to be reviewed only by gay and lesbian Customs inspectors, the result might be different. So long as Customs inspectors are members of the dominant sexual community, *Butler*'s standard represents a potential license to discriminate that probably will not go unused.

The majority claims that "[t]his line of criticism underestimates *Butler*."[313] With all due respect, this observation fails to credit adequately the empirical data provided by the Customs inspectors' repeated seizures of Little Sisters's materials. Standards like "dehumanizing" and "degrading" are entirely culturally situated; those applying the standard cannot replace their own aesthetic standards with those of a sexual minority. Indeed, the majority did not even require a trier of fact to attempt to apply standards that are community specific:

> The appellants have in mind a special standard related to their lesbian and gay target audience. The fact is, however, that they operate a bookstore in a very public place open to anyone who happens by, including potentially outraged individuals of the local community who might wish to have the bookstore closed down altogether.[314]

The Court's rejection of a standard geared to the sensibilities of sexual minorities probably does not matter, given the impossibility of application discussed earlier. But the irony of a Court ostensibly committed to pluralism and respect for minority cultures endorsing a standard for regulation that facilitates majoritarian oppression of a discrete and insular minority group demonstrates the structural flaws that inhere in operationalizing the *Butler* standards.

The majority also dismissed the appellant's challenge to the haphazard nature of the review process itself, at least insofar as it related to the validity of the Customs statutes and regulations themselves. "While these complaints have some substance, they address the statutory scheme as operated by officials rather than the statutory scheme itself."[315] The majority's analysis of the discriminatory enforcement scheme boils down to the argument that the regulations and statutes could, at least in theory, be enforced in an evenhanded way, and therefore are valid, even if, in point of fact, the Customs Service had, as a matter of historical fact, often deployed them in a discriminatory way.[316]

Justice Binnie ultimately found that "Parliament has struck an appropriate balance between the limiting effects of the Customs legislation and the legislative objective of prohibiting the entry of socially harmful material."[317] This is so "because the benefits sought by the criminalization of obscenity are the avoidance of harm and the enhancement of respect for all members of society, and the promotion of non-violence and equality in their relations with each other."[318] "Properly administered," the Customs legislation should not raise any serious constitutional problems. Of course, this fails to address directly the fact that the program had not been properly administered, or the fact that the *Butler* standards both invite and permit discriminatory enforcement, which occurred, literally for more than a *decade*.

In addition, the majority also admonished the Customs Service that the burden of establishing that expressive materials are not importable always rests on the government—an importer does not bear the burden of establishing that the materials are nonobscene.[319] This holding represents the majority's only significant relief to Little Sisters.

One also should take care to note that *Butler* has done very little to stem the tide of pornography in most of Canada. Visitors to Yonge Street, one of downtown Toronto's main commercial venues, are met with a potpourri of porn shops, catering to both heterosexual and homosexual tastes, usually with materials imported from the United States (and California in particular). The same conditions obtain in Vancouver and other major cities in Canada. Thus, in practice, *Butler* does not impede the dissemination of pornography, even though it empowers Customs agents to engage in selective prosecution of homosexual erotica and literature, if they are inclined to do so, on the theory that such material, even if not violent, is "degrading" or "dehumanizing."

In the end, Little Sisters convinced the Supreme Court to reinstate the trial court's remedial decree, which required the Customs Service to cease enforcing Tariff 9956 in a discriminatory fashion against gay and lesbian erotica.[320] In so doing, the majority substantially weakened Canada's commitment to meaningful pluralism and multiculturalism, its rhetoric in *Butler* and *Keegstra* notwithstanding. By refusing to require a community-sensitive standard to govern section 163 determinations, the speech rights of cultural minorities were left entirely to the tender mercies of the dominant cultural group, which has the power to censor "degrading" and "dehumanizing" materials that, although not intended for it or even displayed publicly, it *might* be accidentally exposed to.

Before moving on, fairness requires some consideration of Justice Iacobucci's thoughtful dissent in *Little Sisters*. "While I agree with [Justice Binnie's] conclusion that the Customs legislation, as applied to books, magazines, and other expressive materials, violates appellants' rights under s. 2(b) of the Charter, it is my opinion that the legislation itself violates s. 2(b) and is not demonstrably justified in a free and democratic society."[321] Unlike the majority, Justice Iacobucci would have invalidated Canada's Customs regulations, at least insofar as they apply to expressive materials geared toward the gay and lesbian community. He was joined by Justices Arbour and LeBel in reaching this conclusion.

Justice Iacobucci noted that Customs agents receive virtually no training in art or literature, and enjoy virtually unfettered discretion to prevent the importation of expressive materials.[322] The guidelines used to guide the exercise of this discretion plainly contained standards geared toward the exclusion of gay and lesbian erotica. "Until September 29, 1994—mere days before commencement of the trial in this case—Memorandum D9-1-1 prohibited all depictions of anal penetration." The agency maintained this policy even after the Canadian Department of Justice advised it that "there is no jurisprudence supporting the proposition that all depictions or descriptions of anal penetration are obscene in and of themselves on the basis that anal penetration is inherently degrading or dehumanizing."[323] Moreover, whatever substantive standards applied to Customs review for obscenity were applied in a hopelessly subjective and haphazard fashion.[324]

Justice Iacobucci expressed exasperation with the Customs Service and asked: "If Customs officers have no literary training; if they receive no arguments or submissions from importers; if they do not take artistic merit into account; if they do not attempt to investigate the literary reputation of the author; if they know nothing about the culture for which various books are written; one perhaps should not be surprised that mistakes will often be made."[325] He plainly understood the dimensions of the problem in a way that the majority chose largely to ignore. Moreover, given the history of censorship and repression at the agency over a prolonged period of time, he found it impossible to simply go forward with a weak admonition to the agency to "quit it."[326] The picture he paints is not one of an isolated problem but, rather, one of an agency either incapable of, or unwilling to, apply the obscenity standards in an evenhanded fashion.

Although Justice Iacobucci agreed with the majority that a single, national standard should govern *Butler* obscenity analyses,[327] he rejected the majority's view that the Customs statutes and regulations, as currently written, could and would be applied in a constitutional fashion. "This Court's precedents demand sufficient safeguards in the legislative scheme itself to ensure that government action will not infringe constitutional rights."[328] On the facts presented, which demonstrated "an extensive record of unconstitutional application," "it is not enough merely to provide a structure that could be applied in a constitutional manner."[329]

Justice Iacobucci, invoking the general rule that prior restraints are disfavored in communities committed to the freedom of speech, concluded that the Customs Service's obscenity program was not a minimal impairment of Section 2(b) rights.[330] "The flaws in the Customs regime are not the product of simple bad faith or maladministration, but rather flow from the very nature of prior restraint itself."[331] To be minimally intrusive, a regulatory scheme "would ensure that those enforcing the law actually obey its dictates."[332] In point of fact, under the existing Customs program, "[a]bsolute discretion rests in a bureaucratic decision-maker, who is charged with making a decision without any evidence or submissions, without any requirement to render reasons for decision, and without any guarantee that the decision-maker is aware of or understands the legal test he or she is applying."[333] This sort of system "cannot be minimally intrusive."[334]

The Customs program also failed the proportionality of effects test, given its very high error rate.[335] Justice Iacobucci noted that "ordinary Canadians have been denied important pieces of literature," producing an effect that is "particularly significant for homosexuals."[336] He went on to explain:

> That homosexuals are a disadvantaged group in Canadian society cannot be disputed. . . . Homosexual literature is an important means of self-discovery and affirmation for gay, lesbian, and bi-sexual individuals. In a society which marginalizes sexual difference, literature has the potential to show individuals that they are not alone and that others share their experience. To ban books carrying these messages can only reinforce the existing perceptions gay, lesbian, and bi-sexual individuals have of their marginalization in society.[337]

Thus, he recognized that a meaningful commitment to multiculturalism and pluralism requires a modicum of respect for the aesthetics of sexual minorities. Although he would not condition the application of *Butler* on a standard devised for particular cultures or subcultures within the larger national community, he would require the test to be applied in a fashion that gives some consideration to cultural difference when separating the "obscene" from other protected forms of expression (including artistic and literary forms of expression). "Freedom of speech means not just the right to question the dominant political structure, but to question the dominant society and culture."[338]

Given the serious and ongoing Charter violations, the dissenters found mere declaratory relief grossly insufficient. "As a matter of logic, reason, and constitutional precedent, the appellants are entitled to more."[339] "[B]oth constitutional precedent and common sense suggest that when a government agency has systematically violated constitutional rights, structural reforms are necessary."[340]

Little Sisters shows how thin the commitment to meaningful pluralism and multiculturalism can be when actual minorities engage in speech activity that offends the dominant culture. It also demonstrates that Canadian government officers can be just as prone to abuse censorial discretion as are their U.S. counterparts. At a minimum, the facts that gave rise to it and the Supreme Court's rather minimalist response to them should give progressives who endorse Canada's approach to the freedom of speech great pause. A system that celebrates difference only in the abstract, while turning a blind eye on official censorship of minority viewpoints, does not represent a material improvement on the laissez-faire market-based approach that predominates in the United States.

3. *R. v. Sharpe*[341]

In *Sharpe,* the Supreme Court of Canada considered a challenge to a federal statute that prohibited the possession or distribution of child pornography. John Sharpe attempted to import various child pornography materials into Canada. Following the seizure of these materials, police raided Sharpe's home in British Columbia and found additional erotica featuring young boys, including "books, manuscripts, stories, and photographs."[342] The government charged Sharpe with four counts of violating section 163.1 of the Criminal Code, which prohibits the possession of child pornography.[343]

In relevant part, section 163.1 provides that "[e]very person who possesses child pornography is guilty of an indictable offense and liable for imprisonment for a term not exceeding five years."[344] The statute defines "child pornography" as "a photographic, film, video, or other visual representation, whether or not it was made by electronic or mechanical means," that shows or depicts a person under 18 years of age engaged in sexual activity or "the dominant characteristic of which is the depiction, for a sexual purpose, of a sexual organ or the anal region of a person under the age of eighteen years."[345] It also includes "any written material or visual representation that advocates or counsels sexual activity with a person under the age of eighteen years" that would be illegal.[346]

The trial court invalidated section 163.1 on Charter grounds, finding that it violated Section 2(b) without sufficient justification to be saved by Section 1.[347] The trial judge concluded that there was "little scientific evidence linking the possession of child pornography" to harm to actual children and that section 163.1 had a "profound" deleterious effect on free speech rights.[348] The British Columbia Court of Appeal affirmed this judgment,[349] and the government appealed to the Supreme Court.

Although the government did not attempt to contest the applicability of Section 2(b) to child pornography,[350] Chief Justice McLachlin, writing for the majority, squarely addressed this preliminary question on the merits. The protection of free expression extends not only to political matters or the search for truth but also to personal fulfillment. Accordingly, "the possession of expressive materials falls within the continuum of rights protected by s. 2(b) of the Charter."[351] Although "the prurient nature of most of the materials defined as 'child pornography' may attenuate its constitutional worth, it does not negate it, since the guarantee of free expression extends even to offensive speech."[352]

This holding actually expands the universe of free speech rights as explicated in *Butler*—*Butler* found that erotica featuring adult subjects came within the ambit of Section 2(b), but also found that explicit materials featuring children would constitute the "undue exploitation of sex" for purposes of Canada's antiobscenity statute, suggesting that, whether or not Section 2(b) protects such materials, a statutory proscription against them would be constitutional.[353] It reaffirms the trend, starting with *Dolphin Delivery* and *Irwin Toy*, to interpret Section 2(b) as protecting any communicative effort, other than acts of violence. This approach also conflicts with constitutional rulings in the United States, which squarely hold that child pornography featuring real children lies entirely outside the protection of the First Amendment.[354]

But, as in all other cases arising under the Charter, finding a violation only begins the constitutional analysis. Applying Section 1 to the statute, Chief Justice McLachlin found section 163.1 to be constitutionally permissible, with two exceptions. First, the law cannot be applied to "self-created, privately held expressive materials."[355] "Private journals, diaries, writings, drawings and other works of the imagination, created by oneself exclusively for oneself, may all trigger the s. 163.1(4) offense," a result that would limit free speech rights too deeply to survive Charter scrutiny.[356] To avoid constitutional difficulties, the Court "read into the law an exclusion of the problematic applications of s. 163.1" that protects "[s]elf-created expressive material," including "any written material or visual representation created by the accused alone, and held by the accused alone, exclusively for his or her own personal use."[357]

In addition, the Court created a statutory exemption for "[p]rivate recordings of lawful sexual activity," including "any visual recording, created or depicting the accused, provided it does not depict unlawful sexual activity and is held exclusively for private use."[358] This exemption protects young persons who, under Canadian law, have reached the age of consent but who, under the statute, would be liable for possession of child pornography if they were to memorialize in some way their tryst.

Chief Justice McLachlin extended the exemptions beyond possession to include creation as well. She explained that "otherwise, an individual, although immune from prosecution for the possession of such materials, would remain vulnerable to prosecution for their creation."[359]

In addition, the majority construed section 163.1 very, very narrowly. First, Chief Justice McLachlin read the prohibition to reach only "acts which viewed objectively fall at the extreme end of the spectrum of sexual activity—acts involving nudity or intimate sexual activity, represented in a graphic and unambiguous fashion, with persons under or depicted as under 18 years of age."[360] This narrowing construction removes from the statute's operation cinematic representations of teen sexuality, such as Franco Zefferelli's film version of *Romeo and Juliet,* or movies like *American Beauty* and *Europa Europa.* All of these films feature nudity on the part of actors depicted as being younger than 18 years of age, but none of them feature sexual activity "at the extreme end of the spectrum." In addition, the "dominant purpose" requirement will save most serious works of art and family photographs—"[t]o secure a conviction the Crown must prove beyond a reasonable doubt that the 'dominant characteristic' of the picture is a depiction of the sexual organ or anal region 'for a sexual purpose.' "[361]

Finally, the "artistic merit" defense provides a great deal of leeway to present teen nudity. Section 163.1(6) excludes from the statute's application works having "artistic merit." The question, of course, is: How much merit? The majority holds that "art of any kind is protected, however crude or immature the result of the effort in the eyes of the objective beholder."[362] The exemption applies to "any expression that may reasonably be viewed as art" and "[a]ny objectively established artistic value, however small, suffices to support the defence."[363] Chief Justice McLachlin emphasized that "artists, so long as they are producing art, should not fear prosecution under s. 163.1(4)."[364] Later, for emphasis, she added that "[w]orks of art, even of dubious artistic value, are not caught at all."[365]

Additional defenses for "educational, scientific, or medical purpose" and "the public good" further restrict the scope of section 163.1. Courts are to interpret both defenses "liberally."[366]

Although the Supreme Court, as a formal matter, sustains the constitutionality of section 163.1, its broad interpretation of the defenses, its narrow interpretation of the materials covered by the statute, and its judicially engrafted exemptions for self-created materials all work to create a result that does not differ very much from judicial invalidation of the scheme. Very little material will come within the scope of the statute, and a dedicated pedophile should have little trouble finding materials that possess the mere modicum of artistic, literary, or scientific value that Chief Justice McLachlin says will save a possessor of such material from prosecution.

Of course, section 163 remains in effect and would permit an obscenity prosecution independent of section 163.1, so one should be careful not to overstate the effect of the *Sharpe* ruling. Moreover, Chief Justice McLachlin noted that the artistic defense scheme under section 163.1 does not operate in exactly the same fashion as the judicially created scheme that protects art from prosecution under section 163.[367]

Nevertheless, *Sharpe* is a remarkably free speech–friendly decision in an area where judges often strive to sustain speech restrictions. After all, being perceived as the friend and defender of child pornographers and pedophiles is not a role that most judges relish. And, in the United States, the Supreme Court has largely abdicated any role for the federal courts in protecting graphic materials featuring live children,[368] although it has been somewhat braver in a recent case involving "virtual" or faux child pornography.[369] *Sharpe* strongly suggests that free speech values do have a real currency in Canada and among the Justices of the Supreme Court of Canada. It also suggests that in cases where the equality project is not threatened, the Supreme Court can and does act as a strong defender of speech rights, even for radically unpopular speakers.

C. Considering the Costs and Benefits of Canada's Efforts to Promote Equality through Speech Regulations

In cases where the social goals of promoting equality, pluralism, and multiculturalism run up against free expression claims (such as *Keegstra, Taylor,* and *Butler*), the Supreme Court of Canada appears quite willing to sustain legislation aimed at controlling the means used to express an idea —but not necessarily restrictions on ideas themselves (see, e.g., *Zundel*). The burden on the precise means of expressing an idea is offset by the benefit of encouraging broad-based participation in the marketplace of ideas —certain forms of expression have the effect of alienating racial, cultural, and ethnic minorities, as well as women, from public discourse. Accordingly, the rules arguably enhance free speech as much as they restrict it, by creating conditions conducive to broader participation in public discourse by minorities and women.

All of this is fine in theory, but operationalizing the principles permitting restrictions on the means of communication presents real problems. Notwithstanding the Canadian government's commitment to cultural pluralism and multiculturalism, one finds that the government's willingness to enforce speech restrictions against racist or sexist speech is not consistent.

For example, a Native American leader who made positive remarks about Hitler, coupled with anti-Semitic comments, finds himself facing formal legal proceedings for engaging in hate speech.[370] Of course, Native Americans (or, as the Canadian nomenclature would have it, members of the "First Nations") are a disempowered minority group who have suffered a history of oppression and mistreatment. It is odd, therefore, to punish speech by a member of one disempowered minority in an attempt to enhance the status of another. Thus, the assumption that hate speech rules will reflexively benefit, rather than burden, ethnic and cultural minorities may not always hold true.

By way of contrast, Canadian officials have permitted leaders of the Quebec independence movement to deploy racist rhetoric in their campaigns and to scapegoat ethnic minorities after losing a plebiscite on Quebec independence. Quebec Provincial Premier Jacques Parizeau, after losing the 1995 Quebec sovereignty vote, blamed his defeat on the racial and ethnic minorities living in Quebec.[371] He said: "It's true that we were beaten, but by whom? Money and the ethnic vote."[372] Parizeau vowed that "[w]e want a country and we will have it."[373] He also emphasized that "[w]e will reap our revenge."[374] And, in great measure, the defeated pro-sovereignty forces made good on Parizeau's threat: "[A] crowd of about a thousand disappointed separatists marched through the streets of Montreal, breaking store windows and threatening to upset the victory party of the federalists."[375]

Although widely criticized for these remarks, "Parizeau declined to apologize." He later resigned from his leadership post and admitted that his words were perhaps "too harsh."[376] Parizeau also "confessed to 'not the best choice of words,' but clung to 'the reality' of what he had said"[377] because his words "underline a reality that exists."[378] If there was any doubt about Parizeau's true feelings about the immigrant community in Quebec, he helpfully added that "[i]t is not healthy in a society such as ours that groups, particularly when they come from cultural communities, vote 95 percent in the same direction" (i.e., against separation from the Canadian federation).[379]

Nor were Parizeau's comments an isolated example of xenophobia. Lucien Bouchard, another principal leader of the Quebec sovereignty movement, exhorted (white) francophones to have more children with greater gusto. He asked, rhetorically, "Do you think it makes sense that we have so few children in Quebec? We're one of the white races that has the least children. That doesn't make sense."[380] He said that the low birthrate "means we haven't resolved our family problems."[381] Thus, Bouchard would like white Canadians to have more babies, in order to ensure that francophones will retain control over the political future of Quebec. To encourage greater procreation, Quebec maintains a "bebe-bonus program akin to many in European countries" that "offers mothers $375 for the first baby, $750 for the second, and $6,000 for the third and any more."[382]

After being roundly criticized for his comments, Bouchard refused to apologize. "I am not apologizing, I do not apologize," he said at a public news conference.[383] Bouchard, incidentally, succeeded Parizeau after Parizeau resigned as Premier of Quebec.

Yet another Quebec Nationalist leader, Bernard Landry, Parizeau's deputy premier (and now premier), said that "it is not healthy that democracy in Montreal is at the complete mercy of the vote in ethnic communities."[384] Landry was embroiled in further controversy after the 1995 secession vote failed to garner a majority: "Landry railed at a Latina desk clerk as he checked into a Montreal hotel following the vote count, accusing her and fellow immigrants of tipping the vote against separation."[385]

In a similar vein, the head of the St. Jean Baptiste Society, "a separatist stronghold, said the hajib, seen by some Muslims as a sign of piety, 'defies the values of the equality of men and women that we have here in Quebec.'" In addition, he "compared the ban to prohibitions against neo-Nazi skinhead symbols in the classroom."[386]

And, consistent with the concerns about the place of minorities in the community, Quebec society seems to have a problem accepting immigrants who do not assimilate quickly into the dominant French culture. "French Quebecers call it pure laine—literally pure wool, or true Quebecers, those descended from French stock, whose ancestors were here when Gen. James Wolfe defeated the Marquis de Montcalm on the Plains of Abraham near Quebec City in 1759 and established British dominion over what was to become Canada."[387] Old-line Quebecers say of immigrants that "we can't feel what they feel: pride in country, pride in sovereignty."[388]

Notwithstanding such harsh, racially tinged political rhetoric, local prosecutors made no effort to punish Parizeau, Bouchard, or Landry under the applicable hate speech laws. Why? Probably because the political objective of keeping Quebec in the federation outweighed the government's commitment to enforcing the hate speech laws.

The federal government, as opposed to the provincial government, did respond—but not with either formal legal proceedings (which would have been under the control of Quebec's provincial government anyway) or an administrative complaint before the Human Rights Commission. Following Bouchard's racist remarks, Federal Prime Minister Jean Chretien wryly suggested that "[i]n order to be a good Quebecer you have to be white rather than colored, you certainly have to speak French rather than English, and you definitely have to be a separatist."[389] Similarly, federal Intergovernmental Affairs Minister Marcel Masse said that separatist leaders like Bouchard "should be ashamed to be racists."[390]

I am not suggesting that criminal or civil charges would have been preferable. On the contrary, counterspeech was far more effective at blunting the racist rhetoric deployed by the Quebec separatist leaders. Bringing them up on hate speech charges would only have made political martyrs of them, something that federal authorities wisely seemed to recognize. But this begs the question of why, after firing Mr. Keegstra from his job as a public-school teacher and denouncing him as a racist and anti-Semite, the government also felt compelled to put him in jail for his views. If counterspeech is a sufficient response to racist politicians, it should also be a sufficient response to racist former schoolteachers.

To be sure, Keegstra effectively hijacked his classroom to foment racism and anti-Semitism. One could reasonably characterize this as a kind of theft or conversion of government property for which some sort of punishment, beyond mere loss of his job, should be imposed. The legal basis for Keegstra's criminal conviction, however, was entirely viewpoint based —he was punished for his ideas, rather than for violating curricular standards and practices.

The double standard that seems to apply is deeply troubling: highly visible public officials may use racist rhetoric with legal impunity, while relatively obscure citizens, like Keegstra and Taylor, may not. If one is trying to measure harm to minority communities, the comments of leaders like Parizeau, Bouchard, and Landry are far more likely to cause significant damage to community relations than the rantings of Keegstra or the bizarre messages of Taylor.

Nevertheless, the full power of the government was brought to bear against both Keegstra and Taylor, while the Quebec leaders enjoyed the ability to proceed with their lives. Most refused to apologize for their re-marks and even repeated them. Yet, unlike Taylor, they did not face pro-ceedings before the federal Human Rights Commission or injunctions against future racist outbursts.

David Ahenakew, a "prominent native leader in Canada," by way of contrast, "said that Hitler 'fried 6 million' Jews to make sure that they did not take over Europe.[391] Ahenakew, after receiving national criticism for his remarks, resigned as chair of the Senate of the Saskatchewan Indian Nations, in addition to various boards and other organizations associated with the rights of First Nations.[392] These actions were not entirely volun-tary, however: "The Saskatchewan attorney general [had] called for a po-lice investigation into whether Ahenakew's comments constitute a hate crime."[393] An official of the Royal Canadian Mounted Police helpfully noted to the press that "anyone making statements that can be 'character-ized as public incitement of hatred against any identifiable group,' leading to a 'breach of the peace,' could be sentenced to two years in prison."[394] In fact, the provincial attorney general did decide to initiate criminal hate speech charges against Mr. Ahenakew and, after trial, Ahenakew was con-victed of these charges on July 8, 2005.[395]

Professor Mahoney urges that "[n]o democracy should be embarrassed or uncomfortable prioritizing the needs of the impoverished, disempow-ered, and disadvantaged over those who are more privileged."[396] This may well be true. But the fact remains that Canada's efforts to censor speech have not reliably or consistently advanced these values. Gays and lesbians are marginalized in Canadian society (or so says the Supreme Court of Canada),[397] yet *Butler*'s framework served as a tool for government cen-sorship, not group empowerment. And Native Canadians, like Ahenakew, are themselves socially, economically, and politically disadvantaged. Nev-ertheless, hate speech laws target angry minorities engaged in hyperbolic speech every bit as much as they target members of dominant groups who use such rhetoric. The laws and precedents that Mahoney celebrates can—and do—serve as instruments of oppression every bit as much as they em-power their intended beneficiaries.

Many supporters of hate speech regulations seem to believe that the regulations work against only members of the dominant group bent on oppressing members of minority groups. Professor Mayo Moran argues that "[a]s decisionmakers occasionally recognize, protecting hate speech does benefit racist and sexist speakers at the expense of the disadvantaged who are their targets."[398] She also claims that "the losers are members of the very groups whose inequality the legal system has too often been complicit in sanctioning."[399] These statements might be true, if one considered all hate speech, whether in the United States or in Canada, in the abstract. But, this is the wrong denominator. The proper denominator for the analysis is hate speech resulting in government prosecutions. It is not at all clear that, as applied, hate speech codes do more to empower than to silence minorities.

One could, of course, attempt to draw a principled distinction between the remarks based on the specificity and context of Ahenakew's comments relative to those of the Quebec separatist leaders. There are certainly important differences in the form and context of the comments. My point is that the hate speech laws did not seem to either impede or lead to meaningful consequences for the intentional use of code words aimed at vilifying minority voters in Quebec—who overwhelmingly opposed Quebec sovereignty. If multiculturalism and pluralism are to be meaningful, they must encompass the right of minorities to pursue rational self-interest, as they perceive it, without facing a targeted backlash that disparages them as somehow less loyal or patriotic than other citizens.

Anti-American sentiment also seems to enjoy some sort of de facto exemption from the hate speech codes. Provincial officials in Ontario raised a hue and cry when Marshall Mathers, the Detroit-born rapper known professionally as "Eminem," announced a concert in Toronto. "Ontario Attorney-General Jim Flaherty had asked the federal government to prevent the Grammy-winning musician from crossing into Canada, saying his lyrics are misogynist and advocate violence against women."[400] Valerie Smith, an anti-media-violence activist, filed a complaint seeking criminal prosecution of Mathers. However, "Toronto police said they reviewed Eminem's material after receiving Smith's complaint but found it did not meet their criteria to take any action against the singer."[401] At his Toronto show, Mathers, with characteristic restraint, dedicated the song "Kill You," which Smith had identified specifically in her complaint, "to that bitch, Valerie Smith."[402]

But the police failed to act only because "gender" does not constitute a proscribed category of speech under the hate speech laws. Only "race, ethnic origin, religion, and sexual orientation" count for purposes of enforcing the law. "Gender doesn't fall under the legal criteria, so police cannot lay charges based on offensive lyrics attacking either women or men," Detective Rob Cooper, of the Toronto police department's hate crime unit, explained.[403]

Various local officials, including the mayor and chief of police, denounced Mathers and urged citizens to boycott his performance. Mayor Mel Lastman publicly stated that he wanted Mathers "the hell out of Toronto." Although they did not stop his concert from taking place, city leaders did ban Eminem from performing at the city's "New Muzik Festival" in July 2001.[404]

Eminem's racist, sexist, and homophobic lyrics evidently have no place in Ontario (even though Mr. Parizeau's comments, set to the proper beat, could easily make it into an Eminem album). The answer to the seeming paradox is quite obvious: Opposing a U.S. rapper with views at variance from those of the Canadian government presents a great deal more political upside than prosecuting a popular separatist leader.

More recently still, a prominent Liberal MP exclaimed, in remarks rebroadcast on national media, "Damn Americans! I hate those bastards."[405] MP Carolyn Parrish subsequently apologized, stating that "I deeply regret the comments that I made today in the heat of the moment."[406] James Kenney, an opposition party member, said that Parrish's "comments represent part of an inexcusable string of anti-American bigotry coming from the Liberal Party."[407]

There was never any hint that these comments might serve as the basis for a civil or criminal hate speech enforcement action. Moreover, the Canadian press reported that Prime Minister Chretien "never even criticized her, let alone boot her out of the Liberal caucus, as he should have."[408] One commentator suggested that "he condoned her words—as he did later an anti-American attack by one of his cabinet ministers."[409]

Other forms of anti-American hate speech go unpunished in Canada too. Flag burnings in Halifax, Nova Scotia, featured angry crowds spitting on American flags and stamping on them before setting them on fire. The press reported that "there was no report of offended bystanders protesting and trying to rescue the flags, nor of the authorities arresting the perpetrators for desecrating the flags or setting a fire in public"—much less for inciting ethnicity- or nationality-based hatred.[410]

Along similar lines, University of British Columbia feminist scholar Sunera Thobani has described "the American people as 'bloodthirsty, vengeful, and calling for blood'" at the "Women's Resistance Conference," a public meeting sponsored in part by the government and attended by prominent government officials (such as the secretary of state).[411] According to Thobani, "[T]hey [U.S. citizens] don't care whose blood it is, they want blood."[412] She denounced the United States as "'the world's biggest threat" as "[n]early 500 women—including a conspicuously silent Canadian Secretary of State—greeted Thobani's speech . . . with thunderous applause."[413] When questioned about her remarks, Thobani responded that she "didn't regard her comments as controversial."[414] As with MP Parrish, no legal action was brought or even threatened.

If the gravamen of a section 319 violation is inciting racial or ethnic hatred, these comments were deserving of some sort of formal government response, if not outright prosecution. Fomenting hatred of Americans ought to count for purposes of eradicating hate propaganda—yet, neither the provincial nor federal governments took any action against either Parrish or Thobani. This provides yet another example of the very real danger of selective enforcement associated with such laws.

It is easy to understand the distinction between David Ahenakew and Eminem, on the one hand, and Mr. Parizeau, Ms. Parrish, and Dr. Thobani on the other. Government officials, in each case, made a political calculation about the potential popularity of attempting to silence or punish each speaker. In the case of a Native American or a foreign performing artist, the calculus favored enforcement (or attempted enforcement) of the hate speech laws. In the case of Parizeau, the benefits of prosecution were dwarfed by the political costs of making Parizeau appear to be a martyr to his followers. In this regard, one should note that federalists barely prevailed in the 1995 Quebec sovereignty referendum, by a margin of 50.6 percent to 49.4 percent—a margin of only 53,498 votes out of 4,669,554 votes cast, in an election featuring a remarkable a 93.5 percent turnout of eligible voters.[415]

In the cases of Parrish and Thobani, no high-ranking official denounced the comments (which was not the case with Parizeau's comments), and no one, at any level of government, appears to have given any serious thought to punishing these popular leaders for expressing, and perhaps encouraging, hatred of the United States and its citizens. This is not entirely surprising, given the fact that dislike of the United States is relatively widespread in contemporary Canada. But hate speech protections should not shield only popular racial and ethnic groups—indeed, in theory they should be applied most aggressively to defend groups that suffer from widespread prejudice.

IV. Conclusion: Reconciling Civility Norms with a Meaningful Commitment to Freedom of Expression

The Supreme Court of Canada has developed a defensible theory of the freedom of speech. Free speech enjoys protection, but only insofar as it does not prove unduly disruptive to the community as a whole. Racist speech threatens to alienate fellow citizens and is generally associated with civic strife. In the Canadian Supreme Court's view, the government has a sufficient predicate to suppress and punish such utterances.

Even though one can plausibly posit a free speech doctrine that limits expression to advance values associated with equality and civility, serious methodological problems remain with the Supreme Court of Canada's approach. The first difficulty relates to the scope of Section 2(b). It is far from clear that criminal solicitations and anti-Semitic classroom lessons should come within the scope of the free speech guarantee in the first place.

Protecting everything short of violence under the rubric of "free expression" defines protected speech far too broadly and arguably cheapens Section 2(b)'s free speech guarantee. Indeed, given the remarkably broad scope of Section 2(b), the outcome of Section 1 balancing becomes an almost foregone conclusion. A narrower definition of Section 2(b) rights that incorporates and reflects the public values that the Supreme Court of Canada has identified as animating the protection of free expression would make Section 1 analysis much harder because the effect of an infringement would be more serious to the core values that Canada's free speech guarantee exists to advance and protect.

A second potential weakness in the protection of free expression in Canada relates to the Supreme Court's application of the *Oakes* balancing test. In practice, a test that appears quite demanding has proven remarkably easy to meet. Some have suggested that "[f]aced with Charter claims that involve controversial social issues and challenges to judicial orthodoxy, judges have recoiled from all but the formal trappings of the *Oakes* test."[416] This certainly holds true in Section 2(b) cases.

But, even if many routine legislative enactments transgress Section 2(b), that does not justify or excuse an unduly deferential approach to applying the Section 1 savings clause. Very weak government showings have been sufficient to support bans on racist and sexist speech, as well as advertising targeted at children. To say that complete bans on entire classes of speech activity constituted "minimal impairments" of the right to freedom of expression is not persuasive. One also might question whether the bans constitute reasonable measures that burden speech in proportion to the degree they advance the government's objectives. Thus, *Oakes* balancing, in practice, does not seem to restrain many government regulations of speech activity.[417]

Moving beyond doctrinal critiques, the Canadian approach to protecting freedom of expression does not appear to achieve its stated objective of silencing speech hostile to women and members of racial, ethnic, or cultural minorities. At most, the hate speech laws limit the precise articulation of ideas to exclude speech that openly vilifies a particular group or person for membership in a group. But these laws do not seem to limit seriously the ability of citizens to propose particular social or political ideas.

For example, publicly referring to immigrants as "subhumans too stupid to vote who should not be permitted to live" would run a substantial risk of a prosecution under the civil or criminal hate speech laws. Suggesting that "there are too many immigrants in Canada, they take too many social services, immigration has served its useful purposes and, accordingly, all legal immigration to Canada should immediately cease," coupled with advocacy of a constitutional amendment to deny all noncitizens naturalization rights would be outside the scope of the hate speech codes. In other words, a racist, sexist, or homophobe need only choose his words carefully in order to get his larger message out to potential adherents. Exorcising the ugliest racial epithets from the marketplace of ideas does not really advance the project of multiculturalism very far.

If one modifies the hypothetical to exclude any comments about immigrants to encompass just a change in Canada's immigration and naturalization policies, the speech would unquestionably enjoy strong protection under Section 2(b) and, given *Zundel,* a legislative effort to ban the speech would probably not be saved by operation of Section 1. So too would calls for the repeal of the Charter itself, or the creation of a military dictatorship. Whatever the merit of Canada's hate speech laws and limits on erotica to promote gender equality, these rules do not silence or limit direct calls for political change.

When one couples the limits on the scope of the hate speech laws with the government's highly discretionary application of them, these enactments become a great deal less effective at ensuring that the marketplace of ideas is a welcoming place for all comers.[418] It would, of course, be possible to enact and enforce hate speech laws that work at eradicating bad ideas from public life. Canada, however, has not really taken this approach.

On the other hand, Germany, as discussed in the next chapter, has done a very effective job of enacting and enforcing laws designed to protect not only minorities but the personal dignity of all citizens. In Germany, no matter how politely phrased, some *ideas* are not legal—at least if expressed publicly.[419] The Canadian Supreme Court has not held that some ideas are simply wrong and therefore may be banned. *Zundel* makes this point very clearly: there is no such thing as a false idea under Canadian free speech law. If one articulates an idea in terms that include racial vilification or gender subordination, however, the means used to propagate the idea are subject to proscription by appropriate legislation.[420]

Thus, the Supreme Court of Canada largely has rejected the teachings of *Cohen v. California*.[421] Even if "one man's vulgarity is another's lyric,"[422] in Canada, the community's interest in protecting women and racial, ethnic, and cultural minorities from abuse outweighs the autonomy interest of a would-be speaker in using an epithet in public discourse. This reflects a different accommodation of interests than exists at the present in the United States; Canada's conception of free speech has a distinctly more communitarian cast than does contemporary free speech jurisprudence in the United States. Nevertheless, limits on the precise means used to express an idea in order to secure a greater measure of social equality for all citizens might well represent a better balancing of the competing interests —equality and free speech—than the U.S. approach of privileging free speech over most equality concerns.

In sum, Canada both respects and protects the freedom of expression. It would be quite inaccurate to suggest that Canada utterly subordinates free speech in order to advance the equality project; whether Canada's speech restrictions to promote equality and multiculturalism are desirable or effective presents a different question from whether Canada values and respects free speech in the abstract.

4

Free Speech in Germany
Militant Democracy and the Primacy of Dignity as a Preferred Constitutional Value

Following the end of World War II, the portion of Germany under the control of the Western Alliance worked to establish a functioning constitutional democracy. One of the primary bulwarks of this new democratic order was the adoption of the Basic Law.[1] On May 8, 1949, precisely four years to the day after the collapse of the Third Reich, the postwar German government enacted the Basic Law.[2] The drafters intended for it to serve merely as a temporary measure for the western sector until a formal constitution could be written and enacted for a unified Germany. The Basic Law took effect on May 23, 1949, and has remained Germany's foundational legal document ever since.

Notwithstanding hopes for a quick reunification process, Germany remained divided for some forty years. Accordingly, the permanent "Constitution" that the Basic Law's framers envisioned never came into being. In fact, the Basic Law, over time, itself took on the character and function of a constitution. Following the reunification of Germany in 1990, the Basic Law became the basis for a new, democratic government for a united Germany. The Basic Law, drafted and enacted as a temporary measure, finally enjoyed an official status that reflected what for many years had been its de facto status: constitutional blueprint for democratic self-government in Germany.

Although the Basic Law protects the freedom of speech, it does so to a much more limited degree than does the Free Speech Clause of the First Amendment. The reasons for this are many and varied. Perhaps most significant, free speech simply is not the most important constitutional value in the German legal order; instead, pursuant to the first clause of the Basic Law, human dignity holds this position.[3] Article 1 of the Basic Law "is both 'the supreme Constitutional principle' and a fundamental right."[4] Accordingly, when cases present facts in which human dignity and free speech collide, free speech usually must give way.

A second reason for the weaker version of free speech in Germany relates to Germany's status as a "militant democracy." Free speech, including core political speech, has definite limits in Germany: speech that has as its aim the destruction of democratic self-government enjoys absolutely no constitutional protection under the Basic Law. Obviously, the history of National Socialist dictatorship under Hitler colors the German judiciary's view of the relative importance of free speech. Indeed, the Basic Law itself prohibits political parties who wish to disestablish democratic self-government in Germany.[5] Accordingly, an entire category of core political speech activity enjoys no protection whatsoever in the German constitutional system.

Finally, the Basic Law limits the right to free speech directly, by inviting balancing of other social interests against free expression claims.[6] The First Amendment, by way of contrast, makes no provision for rights balancing; on its face, the right to free speech is absolute. As one might predict, the weighing exercise mandated by the text of the Basic Law does not always redound in favor of free speech claimants.

In Germany, then, one finds a nation that is committed to the freedom of speech, but only within carefully circumscribed limits, and only to the extent that the commitment to free speech does not conflict with other constitutional values (including human dignity and the preservation of the democratic order). One would be mistaken, however, to dismiss Germany's approach to freedom of expression as self-evidently misguided or insufficiently sensitive to the value of free speech in a democratic society. Germany has simply weighed the various social costs and benefits very differently than has the United States. Whether Germany has struck an appropriate balance remains to be seen, but a careful student of the field should not automatically assume that labeling the German system "different" is simply a polite way of labeling it "wrong."

I. The Basic Law and Freedom of Expression

The Basic Law contains several provisions that protect speech activity. Although Article 5 is probably the most important of these provisions, it is worth noting that the Basic Law expressly protects speech activity in a variety of forms and contexts. For example, academic freedom enjoys textual protection and, accordingly, the Federal Constitutional Court does not have to infer its existence within a more generic free speech guarantee.[7]

Another major difference between the Basic Law and the First Amendment is the Basic Law's textual inclusion of express limits on the scope of free speech rights. The United States Supreme Court has found that the First Amendment's free speech guarantee is not, in any meaningful sense of the word, absolute. It has, accordingly, examined the government's claim for a need to regulate speech on a case-by-case basis and weighed the government's asserted interests against the values advanced by the free speech guarantee. This balancing exercise has taken place despite the seemingly unqualified language of the First Amendment itself. In Germany, by way of contrast, the Federal Constitutional Court has a textual mandate to balance some interests against the free speech guarantee.

As a formal matter, the Federal Constitutional Court attempts to enforce equally all of the rights and liberties enshrined in the Basic Law. As Dieter Grimm, a German legal academic and a former member of the Constitutional Court, has explained, "the effective protection of fundamental rights is an essential and inalienable feature of the Basic Law."[8]

All constitutional rights, however, are not equal in Germany. The Basic Law establishes an "objective order of values" that the Federal Constitutional Court declares and enforces.[9] As Professor Edward Eberle has observed, "the Basic Law is a value-oriented constitution that obligates the state to realize a set of objectively ordered principles, rooted in justice and equality, that are designed to restore the centrality of humanity to the social order and thereby secure a stable democratic society on this basis."[10] Thus, even if one successfully invokes one provision of the Basic Law, this may prove to be an insufficient condition to avoid liability for speech activity when another constitutional value is also in play. In particular, free speech claims under Article 5 do not seem to do particularly well when balanced against human dignity claims premised on Article 1.

Professor Grimm emphasizes that "[t]he value- or principle-orientation means that the value embodied in a constitutional provision, particularly in a human right, has to be maximized as much as possible."[11] Accordingly, "if a collision between two or more constitutionally guaranteed values occurs, the question is not to determine which one prevails but to find a solution which leaves the greatest possible effect to both of them (*praktische Konkordanz*)."[12] In practice, this approach means that some "unconditionally guaranteed" rights must "allow some limitations if their exercise threatens other constitutionally acknowledged values."[13]

In some cases, it is simply not possible to honor both rights fully. For example, if a political cartoon dehumanizes an incumbent politician, the Federal Constitutional Court cannot both allow and disallow publication. The conflicting rights presented—dignity and free expression—could be said to be mutually accommodated only in a highly formal, theoretical sense. Even though the specific cartoon might be proscribed in order to safeguard the politician's dignity, a less offensive cartoon critical of the politician would enjoy constitutional protection, even if the less offensive cartoon also bruised the politician's feelings. Thus, the accommodation of rights can and does still result in win/lose situations for particular litigants raising conflicting constitutional claims.

The Basic Law attempts to enshrine permanently the balance struck favoring dignity over the freedom of speech, and favoring the preservation of democracy over the exercise of free speech. In relevant part, Article 79(3) provides that "Amendments of this Basic Law affecting . . . the basic principles laid down in Articles 1 and 20, shall be inadmissible."[14] Article 1 establishes the primacy of human dignity as a constitutional value, and Article 20, which declares Germany to be a "democratic and social federal state," charges all citizens to resist efforts to "abolish that constitutional order." Just as Article V of the United States Constitution attempts to preclude certain constitutional changes,[15] Article 79(3) reflects an effort by the framers of the Basic Law to maintain in perpetuity the existing constitutional order.

A. Article 5's Protection of Speech Activity

Article 5(1) of the Basic Law expressly protects the freedom of expression. It provides that

> [e]veryone has the right to freely express and disseminate his opinion in speech, writing, and pictures and freely to inform himself from generally accessible sources. Freedom of the press and freedom of reporting by means of broadcasts and films are guaranteed. There shall be no censorship.[16]

Article 5 also protects academic freedom, stating that "art and science, research, and teaching shall be free."[17] Thus, the Basic Law enshrines the freedom of speech as a constitutionally protected right in the Federal Republic of Germany.

Article 5's guarantees are, however, subject to some significant textual constraints. Perhaps most importantly, Article 5 limits the scope of freedom of speech by inviting judicial balancing of the right against other governmental objectives: "These rights find their limits in the provisions of the general statutes, in statutory provisions for the protection of youth, and in the right to respect for personal honor."[18] Moreover, the right to academic freedom does not extend to advocacy of violent overthrow of the government: "Freedom of teaching shall not release anyone from his allegiance to the Constitution."[19]

Separate provisions of the Basic Law protect the freedom of assembly and the freedom of association. Article 8 states that "[a]ll Germans have the right to assemble peaceably and unarmed without prior notification or permission."[20] The right to assembly in open air meetings "may be restricted by or pursuant to statute."[21] Article 9 provides that "[a]ll Germans shall have the right to form associations and corporations."[22] As with Articles 5 and 8, however, this protection does not extend to groups that seek the overthrow of the democratic constitutional order: "Associations whose purposes or activities conflict with criminal statutes or that are directed against the constitutional order or the concept of international understanding are prohibited."[23] Finally, Article 17 provides that "[e]veryone has the right individually or jointly with others to address written requests or complaints to the competent agencies and to parliaments."[24]

With respect to the creation and operation of political parties, the Basic Law declares that "[t]he political parties shall participate in the formation of the political will of the people" and "may be freely established."[25] German political parties, however, must maintain organizational structures that "conform to democratic principles."[26] Finally, "[p]arties that, by reason of their aims or the behavior of their adherents, seek to impair or abolish the free democratic basic order or to endanger the existence of the Federal Republic of Germany are unconstitutional."[27] When questions arise regarding the consistency of a party's platform with these requirements, "[t]he Federal Constitutional Court shall decide on the question of constitutionality."[28]

The Basic Law contains redundancies that emphasize the importance of protecting the "democratic basic order." Even though the articles conferring specific speech rights on the citizenry expressly exclude speech aimed at overthrowing the government, several independent clauses repeat the rule that the exercise of rights enshrined in the Basic Law does not extend to efforts to abolish democratic self-government in Germany.

Article 18, for example, provides for forfeiture of basic rights, including the rights set forth in Articles 5, 8, and 9, if a citizen exercises those rights "in order to combat the free democratic basic order."[29] "Such forfeiture and the extent thereof shall be determined by the Federal Constitutional Court."[30] Similarly, Article 20 provides that "[t]he Federal Republic of Germany is a democratic and social federal state,"[31] and invites citizens to "resist any person or persons seeking to abolish the constitutional order, should no other remedy be possible."[32]

Thus, one need not even turn to the case law of the Federal Constitutional Court to see the overtly limited scope of free speech in Germany. Certain kinds of political speech are simply beyond the pale—even "core" political speech. A person or group advocating the violent overthrow of the government does not enjoy any right to advocate such action without facing both criminal and civil penalties.[33] This represents a marked break with the tradition in the United States, as represented by such cases as *Brandenburg v. Ohio*[34] and *NAACP v. Claiborne Hardware Company.*[35]

But Article 5's textual limitations are not restricted just to speech critical of the existing democratic constitutional order—Article 5 itself invites regulations that protect the youth, protect personal honor, or find expression in the general statutes. Depending on the exact meaning of these express restrictions on the freedom of speech, the scope of permissible comment could shrink even more. We come to this point without engaging in the balancing exercise that applies when values enshrined in the Basic Law collide—as often happens, for example, when a free speech exercise arguably offends the protection of dignity set forth in Article 1.

Thus, without even getting beyond the text of the Basic Law, it becomes very clear that the German conception of free speech is at great variance with the conception that prevails in the United States.[36] Again, this is not necessarily a bad thing. Perhaps the United States fails to value adequately the dangers that speech advocating violent overthrow of the government represents. Perhaps the U.S. Supreme Court also has failed to recognize sufficiently the relative importance of personal honor or protection of youth. It is far too early in the analysis to draw any firm conclusions. That said, a very preliminary consideration of the issue establishes quickly that the German conception of free speech radically departs from baseline notions in the United States.

Another important distinction between the United States and Germany involves the potential scope of constitutional rights. In the United States, the Bill of Rights and the Fourteenth Amendment secure rights against only the government.[37] No matter how egregious, a private party's actions do not constitute a constitutional violation in the absence of some nexus with the government. Accordingly, one would not normally expect the Free Speech Clause to be invoked in an antitrust case between two private corporations or in an employment dispute involving a private employer's decision to discharge an employee because of the employee's speech activities.[38]

Some legal academics in the United States have argued that rather than engage in state action analysis, the federal courts should simply engage in overt rights balancing when conflicting constitutional claims appear at bar.[39] For example, if a group of nuns complained that the local bishop denied them equal protection of the law on the basis of gender, by refusing to employ them as priests, the district court judge hearing the case would be required to weigh the nuns' interest in being free of gender discrimination against the bishop's interest in enforcing the doctrines of the Roman Catholic Church regarding the sacrament of Holy Orders. Under this approach, the fact that the bishop is not a "state actor" would not preclude consideration of the nuns' equal protection claim on the merits.

Professor Chemerinsky describes the state action doctrine as "incoherent" and suggests that the federal courts apply the state action doctrine strategically, by peeking at the merits, deciding whether the federal courts wish to recognize the plaintiffs' claims, and ruling accordingly on the question of state action.[40] In his view, it would be more intellectually honest to balance the competing claims (assuming that the defendant can assert some sort of constitutional privilege to engage in the behavior that serves as the basis of the plaintiff's complaint). In the hypothetical, the bishop could probably assert a free exercise and free association claim that trumps the nuns' claim to be free of gender discrimination. The state actor status of the bishop would be entirely irrelevant to the proper analysis of the merits.

In Germany, by way of contrast, there is no state action requirement. Professor Grimm explains that "[i]n their capacity as objectives, human rights penetrate the whole social and legal order."[41] "In the Court's view, fundamental rights are at the same time objective principles (or 'values,' in the earlier terminology) permeating the whole legal order and guiding lawmaking as well as the application of the law."[42]

Thus, the Basic Law permeates all social relations, and the state actor status of a defendant does not prefigure the outcome of cases.[43] Professor Grimm suggests that "[t]he most important consequence of the value-oriented interpretation of fundamental rights is the acknowledgment of a duty of the government, and in particular of the legislature, to protect constitutionally guaranteed liberties when they are threatened, not by government, but by third parties or societal forces."[44] Accordingly, "fundamental rights are not only subjective rights protecting the individual against direct intrusions by the state, but also the most sacred principles for the organization of society as a whole."[45]

In the specific context of freedom of expression, Professor Eberle notes that the lack of a state action requirement probably "reflects the belief that the real threats to expression in German society come from private actors and social forces, and not from the state."[46] Thus, in the *Lüth* case (discussed below), the German Constitutional Court balanced a film producer's Article 5 right to free expression against the free speech claims of the organizer of a boycott against the film.

The state had made no effort to suppress the film in question—the case presented a free speech claim raised as a defense to an anti-boycott claim (which also invoked the free speech principle). Professor Grimm observes that "[t]his decision, which was handed down in 1958, constituted a fundamental break with the tradition."[47]

In deciding to apply the Basic Law's provisions to a dispute between two private parties, the German Constitutional Court articulated a doctrine of secondary effects: the Basic Law not only works to disallow civil law provisions that transgress its guarantees but also informs the substantive meaning of the civil code itself.[48] This is especially true with respect to the so-called general provisions of the German civil code, which are intended to advance sound public policies. As Professor Peter Quint has observed, "[b]ecause the basic rights establish 'objective' values, then, those rights must apply not only against the state exercising its authority under public law; according to the Constitutional Court, basic rights must also have an effect on the rules of private law which regulate relations among individuals."[49]

It is certainly reasonable to suppose that the content of a given law should be measured against the provisions of the Basic Law. The United States Supreme Court, in *New York Times Company v. Sullivan*,[50] did exactly this. Justice Brennan explained:

> Although this is a civil lawsuit between private parties, the Alabama courts have applied a state rule of law which petitioners claim to impose

invalid restrictions on their constitutional freedoms of speech and press. It matters not that law has been applied in a civil action and that it is common law only, though supplemented by statute. The test is not the form in which state power has been applied but, whatever the form, whether such power has in fact been exercised.[51]

Thus, because the validity of a state law was directly at issue, state action was present. Alabama exercised its authority by establishing a common law rule that permitted a state officer to recover for libel on a showing of less than actual malice. The fact that the Alabama Supreme Court fashioned this common law rule—rather than the state legislature via statute —did not affect the rule's status as the product of state action.

Thus, the *New York Times Company* Court did not purport to do anything more than ascertain whether the Alabama common law of libel satisfied the requirements of the Free Speech Clause; it did not purport to apply general free speech principles to the merits of the litigation itself. Had the law itself been consistent with the Free Speech Clause (it was not), Alabama would have been free to apply it without any further consideration of the First Amendment. The analysis in Germany would be quite different.

Under the doctrine of secondary effect, the defendant in an action for libel would remain free to argue that an award of damages would violate the Basic Law, even if the statute that gives rise to the action is itself unquestionably constitutional. The secondary effects doctrine treats the application of civil law between private parties as state action triggering the Basic Law. Accordingly, the Basic Law enjoys a far more expansive scope of application than does the Bill of Rights or Fourteenth Amendment. As Professor Eberle helpfully observes, "from the standpoint of law in the 1990s, there is effectively no difference in the standard of review applied by the Constitutional Court to purely private or public law disputes."[52]

Professor Grimm adds that because of "the objective character of human rights," the Constitutional Court has held that the government has a duty "to protect human rights against threats from private individuals or groups."[53] As a general matter, no similar obligation exists under the U.S. Constitution; purely private actions that discourage or burden the exercise of a fundamental right do not raise serious constitutional problems. The German approach, in which "human rights are not only individual rights but objective principles as well," carries with it not only a duty for "government to refrain from certain actions" but also an obligation to "take action to secure or effectuate individual liberties against societal risks or dangers."[54]

Professor Grimm suggests that "[t]his duty can be called the second side of the coin of human rights; the first one being the defense against state actions."[55] He posits that it "seems appropriate to subsume all these effects under the notion of a protective duty (Schutzpflicht)."[56] According to Grimm, "[n]onaction is a violation of this duty."[57]

One also should note that challenges to the application of private law provisions premised on the Basic Law are not limited to any particular provisions. For example, a defendant in a libel action could invoke Article 1's dignity clause rather than Article 5's free speech clause if an argument premised on the dignity guarantee would be plausible. This would be a sound strategic move because the dignity clause guarantee generally takes precedence over other constitutional rights.

In sum, "the German and American doctrines appear to reflect fundamentally different views about the nature of the distinction between the public and private realms."[58] The Federal Constitutional Court has, to a very large degree, collapsed the public/private distinction when enforcing the provisions of the Basic Law.

B. Article 1 and the Countervailing Constitutional Value of Human Dignity

The Federal Constitutional Court has declared that the Basic Law establishes "an objective order of values" with some constitutional interests being more important than others.[59] In this objective order of values, freedom of speech, press, assembly, and association are decidedly inferior to the government's interest in securing and protecting human dignity.[60]

The primacy of dignity leads the German Constitutional Court to reach results that appear odd to a student of the First Amendment. "In part, this reflects the value-ordering function basic rights perform in Germany, including communication rights."[61] For example, the German Constitutional Court has found that preserving the dignity of a dead man outweighed the free expression rights of a living novelist (who died before the final resolution of the case in the Federal Constitutional Court);[62] it has prohibited the publication of a fictional interview involving the wife of the Shah of Iran;[63] enjoined distribution of a docudrama about a gay robber,[64] and refused to protect political satire that presented a politician as a rutting pig.[65] These cases are discussed in greater detail below; together they demonstrate the German Constitutional Court's firm decision to weigh the constitutional value of dignity, which encompasses the interest in personal reputation, above the freedom of speech.

At the outset, one should note the full implications of these holdings: speech routinely protected in the United States might well be unprotected in Germany. For example, it is uncertain that the faux Campari advertisement at issue in *Hustler Magazine, Inc. v. Falwell*[66] would enjoy constitutional protection under Article 5. The differences go even deeper. Orson Welles's masterpiece, *Citizen Kane,* constitutes a thinly veiled commentary —perhaps "personal attack" would be a more apt description—on William Randolph Hearst. Mr. Hearst was very much alive at the time of its theatrical release (he worked strenuously to block the film's distribution) and, given the *Mephisto* decision, his status among the living at the time the film premiered probably would not matter anyway.

As Professor David Currie has aptly noted, "[e]xamination of the German law of free expression reminds one once again how easily two well-intentioned societies, starting from substantially identical premises, can arrive at significantly different results."[67] But Professor Currie, at least to some extent, understates the significant and material differences that exist in the respective treatment of free speech:

> Expression is a cardinal value both in Germany and in the United States, both as an end in itself and as an indispensable tool of democracy. In both countries it must yield on occasion to competing values, and there is room for honest disagreement as to where to draw the line.[68]

In the United States, the freedom of speech is a "preferred" freedom that generally outweighs other constitutional values, such as community or equality. The federal courts disfavor government regulation of speech based on content; the federal courts virtually disallow any regulation of speech based on its viewpoint. Even in areas of "unprotected" expression, such as "fighting words," government may not adopt viewpoint-based regulations.[69] None of these propositions holds true in Germany.[70]

With respect to the freedom of speech, the German approach represents a fundamental and radical break with the marketplace of ideas metaphor. Indeed, the ability of government to suppress speech not only far outstrips the Holmesian ideal of a "marketplace of ideas" but goes far beyond even Alexander Meiklejohn's town hall metaphor. In Germany, "[s]peech is valued according to its utility in promoting desirable social ends."[71] This approach is largely, if not completely, foreign to the post-*Brandenburg* free speech tradition in the United States.

Although Meiklejohn endorsed government regulations that would promote a meaningful debate about the means and ends of democratic self-government, he never suggested that the government's power should extend to banning ideas or points of view that the government thought to be socially harmful. Professor Stanley Fish is undoubtedly correct to posit that speech is never free,[72] but in Germany the realm of "free speech" is significantly narrower than in the contemporary United States. That said, whether this represents a better adjustment of competing constitutional values is a question over which reasonable minds may differ.[73]

Finally, one should take care not to understate the degree or scope of freedom of expression in contemporary Germany. People are quite free to speak their minds on important topics and to question government both publicly and harshly. Political speech is free, as are other kinds of speech (including artistic, scientific, and literary speech). The dignitarian concerns come into the picture only in highly specific contexts in which the purpose or effect of the particular speech is to dehumanize, or insult, or degrade, or to limit or destroy another person's place within the community. Although this chapter will focus on these exceptions to the general rule, it is important to keep in mind that the overall scope of protected free expression in Germany is really quite broad.

II. Balancing Dignity and Free Speech

In a series of landmark opinions, the German Constitutional Court has firmly embraced dignity as a preferred constitutional value over the freedom of speech. Strangely enough, dignity claims even survive the grave— a dead actor's dignity has greater constitutional importance than a living author's interest in publishing his book.

A. *Mephisto*: Bringing Out the Dead

In the famous *Mephisto*[74] case, the German Constitutional Court considered whether an author's interest in free speech justified burdening the dignity interests of a dead actor. The author, Klaus Mann, published *Mephisto*, a novel about an actor who collaborates with the Nazi government during the 1930s and 1940s. The fictional actor, Hendrik Höfgen, was loosely based on Mann's brother-in-law, the German actor Gustaf Gründgens. "The novel describes the rise of the highly gifted actor Hendrik Höfgen, who disowns his political conviction and strips off all human and ethical ties in order to make an artistic career in a pact with the masters of Nationalist Socialist Germany."[75] In another work, *The Turning Point*, Klaus Mann publicly identified Gründgens as the model for the fictional actor Hendrik Höfgen.[76]

Gründgens's adopted son initiated a lawsuit in state court to block the distribution of the novel because it dishonored his dead father's memory.[77] The trial court dismissed the action, but the Regional Appellate Court reversed. It found that "[t]he novel injured Gründgens in his honour, his reputation and his social position, and grossly defamed his memory." Accordingly, the author "could not appeal to Article 5(3) GG" because his novel "constituted insult, disparagement and defamation of Gründgens."[78] The Regional Appellate Court concluded that the deceased Gründgens's Article 1 dignity right and Article 2 personality right, at least on the facts presented, outweighed Mann's Article 5(3) interest in free expression and, accordingly, prohibited distribution of the book in Germany. The Federal High Court of Justice affirmed this decision. Thereafter, the publisher sought review of the decision in the Federal Constitutional Court, on the basis that the injunction violated Article 5(1) and 5(3) of the Basic Law.[79]

The Federal Constitutional Court began its analysis of the case by framing the dispute as involving a conflict of constitutional claims: Mann's publisher and estate claimed rights protected by Article 5(1) and 5(3); Gründgens son and estate sought to protect values enshrined in Articles 1 and 2.[80] The Justices found that Mann's novel constituted "art" for purposes of applying Article 5(3) and that the distribution of art enjoyed constitutional protection:

> Article 5(3) . . . guarantees freedom of operation in the artistic sphere comprehensively. Accordingly, where, to create the relationships between artist and public, means of publication are needed, persons engaged in such mediatory activity are also protected by the guarantee of artistic freedom.[81]

Moreover, the Basic Law protects artistic freedom "without reservations."[82] This conclusion did not answer the ultimate question, however, because

Article 5 claims are subordinate to claims arising under the dignity clause in Article 1. The court explained that "the dignity of man guaranteed in Article 1" may take precedence over an otherwise valid Article 5 claim because dignity is "the supreme value [that] dominates the whole value system of the fundamental rights."[83] Resolving the conflict required "weighing up all of the circumstances of the individual case."[84]

After examining the facts found by the lower courts, notably including the fact that "Gründgens concerned a person of contemporary history and that public memory of him is still alive," the Federal Constitutional Court, by a 3-3 vote, found that the balance favored vindication of Gründgens's Article 1 dignity interests over Mann's Article 5(3) right to freedom of artistic expression. In so holding, it rejected the proposition that "the publication ban was out of proportion to the expected curtailment of the right to respect of the late Gustaf Gründgens."[85] Accordingly, the Justices sustained the publication ban, noting that "[t]he considerations underlying this ban are not inappropriate to the case."[86] As Professor Quint has explained, "[i]t was this countervailing constitutional guarantee of personality, therefore, that could have the effect of limiting artistic expression."[87]

The Constitutional Court divided evenly, 3-3, with the result being an affirmance of the lower court because an absolute majority was necessary for a reversal. Three Justices voted to reverse, arguing that their colleagues failed to examine adequately the balancing of interests undertaken by the lower courts. Justice Stein argued:

> If in cases like the present one . . . the Federal Constitutional Court's reviewing power were to be confined to a narrowly limited check, namely whether the courts had at all seen the application of the fundamental rights, taken it into account and not contravened the general prohibition on arbitrariness . . . then the Federal Constitutional Court would not be properly doing its job of being a guardian of the fundamental rights in all areas of law.[88]

The Justices favoring reversal suggested that the lower courts had emphasized the interest in social reputation too much, and valued the social good of artistic expression too little, in finding for Gründgens. "A free art must in principle be allowed to take off from personal information from reality and give it generalized significance through symbolic value."[89] This is especially true, they argued, when a public official or public figure serves as the artistic inspiration. In necessarily follows that "[t]he guarantee of artistic freedom in principle allows neither the restriction of the range of artistic topics nor the exclusion of means and methods of expression from the process of artistic transformation."[90]

The dissent also argued that the novel did not infringe Gustaf Gründgens's Article 1 dignity rights. The subject was already deceased, his public reputation was largely committed to history rather than current events, and the book was plainly a work of fiction and featured a foreword stating this directly. "For these reasons, no grave detriment to the personality sphere of the late Gustaf Gründgens can be found" and "[c]onsequently, there is no clear infringement of Article 1(1)."[91]

A second dissent, by Justice Rupp-von Brünneck, emphasized that the Federal Constitutional Court had an obligation to engage in a de novo balancing of the relevant interests: "[t]he dismissal of the constitutional complaint is based on a restrictive interpretation of the Federal Constitutional Court's competence for review, which marks a break with existing case law and can lead to very dubious consequences."[92] Absent stronger evidence of an intent by Mann to defame Gründgens, the Basic Law's protection of artistic freedom should prevail. The dissent also invoked the case law of the United States Supreme Court, noting that "in regard to persons and objects of contemporary affairs [it] in principle always rates the general interest in free public debate above the personal interests that may be affected by false information or polemic description, as long as no 'actual malice' is present."[93] On the facts presented, Mann's novel plainly implicated a higher constitutional value than Gründgens's postmortem dignity interest.

B. *Princess Soraya*: Telling Tales out of School

Two years later, in the *Princess Soraya* case, the Federal Constitutional Court sustained an award of damages based on the publication of a fictional interview with the former wife of the then-Shah of Iran. The periodical *Die Welt* published the story, which discussed "intimate details of her private life."[94] Soraya commenced a civil suit seeking money damages. On review from the Federal High Court of Justice, the Federal Constitutional Court had to decide whether Article 5 provided a defense against the action for damages.

The Federal Constitutional Court held in favor of Soraya and rejected *Die Welt*'s Article 5 defense, explaining that "[a]n *imaginary* interview adds nothing to the formation of real public opinion."[95] The Basic Law's protection of dignity, which encompasses personal reputation, required that "[t]he degree of care that must be expended to avoid dissemination of an *imaginary* interview is never too much to expect."[96] Accordingly, in such circumstances, "[a]s against press utterances of this sort, the protection of privacy takes unconditional priority."[97]

In justifying this outcome, the Justices explained that "[t]he personality and dignity of an individual, to be freely enjoyed and developed within a societal and communal framework, stand at the very center of the value order reflected in the fundamental rights protected by the Constitution."[98] Thus, "[a]ll organs of the state" have a responsibility to protect "an individual's interest in his personality and dignity." Whatever free speech value the faux interview possessed paled, at least in the Federal Constitutional Court's view, in comparison to Soraya's interest in avoiding the false presentation about her private life.

C. *Lebach*: Truth Is No Defense

In the same year that it decided *Princess Soraya*, the Federal Constitutional Court also held that interests protected under the dignity clause outweighed any free speech value in a television movie presenting the true story of a gay robber.[99] Lebach, the gay robber, had already completed his prison term at the time the movie was to be televised. As Professor Currie notes, "the Court held the constitution *required* a remedy—this time to protect the right to free development of personality guaranteed by Article 2(1) in conjunction with the right to human dignity, which under Article 1(1) the state has an explicit obligation to protect."[100] As in the *Mephisto* case, the plaintiff sought and obtained injunctive relief against the distribution of the film—essentially, a very strong form of prior restraint.

The Federal Constitutional Court explained that the case presented a conflict of values that required the Court to "balance" or "adjust" the conflicting constitutional rights:

> In case of conflict, [the court] must adjust both constitutional values, if possible; if this cannot be achieved, [the court] must determine which interest will defer to the other in light of the nature of the case and its special circumstances. In so doing, [the court] must consider both constitutional values in their relation to human dignity as the nucleus of the Constitution's value system.[101]

The Justices went on to conclude that the media have a justifiable interest in reporting crimes when they occur, as part of the natural news cycle, but that this interest in reporting on such matters declines rather quickly with time. Thus, "[t]he radiating effect of the constitutional guarantee of the right of personality does not, however, permit the media, over and above reporting on contemporary events, to intrude indefinitely upon the person and private sphere of the criminal."[102]

In the case of a convicted defendant who has completed his prison sentence and been released, the residual news value does not outweigh the felon's interest in dignity and free development of his personality. "Once a criminal court has prosecuted and convicted a defendant for an act that has attracted public attention, and he has experienced the just reaction of the community, any further or repeated invasion of the criminal's personal sphere cannot normally be justified."[103] A television station may not rebroadcast a story about a past crime if doing so "endangers the social rehabilitation of the criminal."[104] This is so because "[t]he criminal's vital interest in being reintegrated into society and the interest of the community in restoring him to his social position must generally have precedence over the public's interest in further discussion of the crime."[105] The Constitutional Court reversed the lower appellate court with instructions that the television network should be enjoined from broadcasting the program about Lebach.

The result in *Lebach* provides virtually no protection to truthful speech about a matter of public concern in order to advance concerns rooted in the dignity and personality clauses. Thus, "the limiting effect of the constitutional right of personality on expression can be substantial."[106] Lebach, unlike Soraya, made no claim that the speech about him was factually false —he merely asserted that it violated his dignity and personality rights and would impede his reintegration into society.

Professor James Q. Whitman observes that "[t]he *Lebach* doctrine has now been altered somewhat by the so-called *Lebach II* decision."[107] In 1999, the Federal Constitutional Court decided a second case involving a docudrama about the Lebach robbery.[108] "In *Lebach II*, another participant in the same crime had tried to enjoin the German TV station SAT 1 from broadcasting a feature film on the crime."[109] Professor Gebhard Rehm explains that, in this case, however, the Federal Constitutional Court "decided in favor of SAT 1's freedom of broadcasting because this second film did neither display photos nor mention the name of the complainant nor identify him in any other way."[110]

Based on *Lebach II*, Professor Rehm argue., that "the revelation of the complainant's identity [in *Lebach I*] was decisive for the outcome of the case."[111] This appears to be a plausible explanation for the differing results and suggests that the Constitutional Court's approach in *Lebach I* and *Mephisto* might be softening. Even if this is true, however, the rule prohibiting truthful speech that plainly identifies a specific person remains in place.

Professor Eberle describes the cases like *Lebach* and *Mephisto* as creating a right to "informational self-determination," which "endows the individuals with the right to control the portrayal of the facts and details of their lives."[112] This right encompasses the ability to "shield hurtful truths from public scrutiny in order to safeguard reputation or other personality interests," as well as "protection of personal honor as an outgrowth of personality."[113] The protection of these interests "can be extended to eclipse other basic rights," notably including "Article 5 expression guarantees."[114]

Thus, Article 1, as construed in both *Lebach* and *Lebach II*, displaces truthful speech about an undoubted matter of public concern, if the speech identifies a specific person and materially burdens that person's interest in dignity and the free development of his personality. This is a very substantial incursion on the freedom of speech (at least to a U.S. constitutional lawyer's eyes) and demonstrates the relatively lower level of importance accorded free speech in the Federal Constitutional Court's objective order of constitutional values.[115]

D. *Böll*: Protecting Public Figures

Some might argue that the Constitutional Court's decisions in the early 1970s reflect a concern for reputation that no longer holds true. Professor David Currie posits that "[t]he overall trend . . . has been toward greater protection of speech, especially in matters of public concern."[116] He suggests that "[d]espite earlier decisions that appeared to embrace a more restrictive philosophy, it thus seems fair to say that, while the Constitutional Court continues to give the constitutionally protected interest in personal honor more weight than do analogous decisions of the Supreme Court, the gap has narrowed considerably."[117] Although *Lebach II* would support this conclusion, other cases suggest that this optimism toward greater protection for the freedom of speech might be somewhat overstated.

It may well be true that "[i]n most cases, the German court seems inclined today to afford political and artistic expression a degree of protection comparable to that afforded by the [United States] Supreme Court."[118] But the Federal Constitutional Court has upheld free speech claims only when the personal insult was not targeted at any particular identifiable individual. In cases involving targeted insults, the Federal Constitutional Court has continued down the path outlined in *Mephisto, Soraya,* and *Lebach.*

In 1980, for example the German Constitutional Court rejected a free press claim in favor of protecting the dignity and reputation of a public figure. In *Böll,* the Federal Constitutional Court had to decide whether the freedom of the press extended to false statements attributed to Heinrich Böll, a famous writer.[119] A local television station ran a commentary that attributed certain statements to Böll—specifically, the newscaster said that Böll had called the contemporary German state a "dungheap," featuring "residues of rotting power, defended with ratlike rage." Finally, Böll was quoted as criticizing the government for pursuing the terrorists who killed the presiding judge of the Berlin Court of Appeal "in a merciless hunt."[120] The Federal High Court of Justice reversed a favorable lower court decision because "[t]he criticism . . . both in content and form and in means employed, [was] within the sphere of freedom guaranteed to expression of one's own opinion in a television commentary by Article 5(1) of the Basic Law."[121]

The German Constitutional Court reversed the Federal High Court of Justice, ruling that the commentary featured false quotes and that these quotes damaged Böll's dignity and personality rights, guaranteed by Article 1 and Article 2 of the Basic Law. "The attacks directed against the complainant in the commentary were of such a nature as to infringe the complainant's constitutionally guaranteed general personality right."[122] The Constitutional Court flatly ruled that "[m]isquotations are not protected by Article 5(1)" and opined that "[i]t cannot be seen that the constitutionally guaranteed freedom of opinion requires such protection."[123] Not only had the lower court overstated the media's Article 5 rights, it also had seriously undervalued the plaintiff's interest in the protection of his dignity and personality, safeguarded under Articles 1 and 2.[124]

Professor Quint has noted that "the *Böll* case . . . affirms a requirement of vigorous judicial review under some circumstances to vindicate the right of personality against the countervailing interests in speech."[125] In other words, appellate courts reviewing a decision in favor of the free speech claim have an obligation to scrutinize closely the facts to ensure that the defendant did not escape liability for causing harm to the dignity interests of the plaintiff. In the United States, by way of contrast, searching review of trial results also applies in defamation cases involving public figures, public officials, or matters of public concern—but this searching review applies only when the *plaintiff* prevails.[126] Thus, in the United States, the presumption runs in precisely the opposite direction: a verdict imposing liability on a press entity receives careful appellate review, including independent review of all matters of constitutional fact.

E. *Strauss Caricature* Case: Protecting Politicians from Harsh Parody

Other, even more recent, cases also seem to contradict Professor Currie's suggestion.[127] For example, in *Strauss*[128] the Constitutional Court had to decide whether a particularly harsh political cartoon merited protection under Article 5 of the Basic Law or, instead, whether the cartoon went "too far" and therefore constituted a violation of Article 1's guarantee of personal dignity. A magazine called *Konkret* published a series of disparaging cartoons featuring Bavarian Prime Minister Franz Josef Strauss as a pig. The Constitutional Court explained that

> [i]n the first of these drawings the pig is copulating with a pig dressed in judicial costume. A further caricature shows both figures of pigs—partly in pairs, partly separately—engaged in a variety of sexual activity. A third drawing shows four pigs, three of them mounting the pig in front. Here too, two of the figures of pigs bear the facial features of the Bavarian Minister-President and two are dressed in judicial robes and toque. The caption to the first drawing is "Satire may do anything: can Rainer Hachfeld too?." The second drawing has the caption: "Which drawing is the right one fairly, Mr. Prosecutor?." The third caricature was preceded by a cut version of a letter from the complainant to the editors of "Konkret," complaining that he kept on having to draw more pictures of little pigs because the Bavarian Minister-President would not give him any rest.[129]

Needless to say, being portrayed as a rutting pig did not sit well with Prime Minister Strauss. He initiated an action for defamation against *Konkret,* seeking money damages. The local trial court found for Strauss, but the Regional Court reversed.[130] At the next level of appeals, however, Strauss prevailed. The Regional Appellate Court reinstated the local court's verdict, finding that the presentation of Strauss as a swine went beyond the limits of fair comment.

The Federal Constitutional Court easily found that "[t]he caricatures at issue are the formed outcome of free creative action" and therefore "meet the requirements" for protection under Article 5(3).[131] The Court went on to find that the Regional Appellate Court had properly balanced the magazine's interest in artistic freedom (and political commentary) against Strauss's interest in personal honor and dignity.[132] It explained that "[t]he necessary balancing of conflicting constitutionally protected interests necessary because of the tension between artistic freedom and the general right to personality of third parties had inevitably in the present case to lead to the result it found."[133]

Although satire and parody enjoy protection under Article 5(1) and 5(3), this protection must give way to the paramount importance of personal dignity. On the facts presented, *Konkret* had gone beyond "usual portrayals" such as "characterizing or exaggerating particular traits or the physiognomy of a person by choosing the form of an animal."[134] Instead, "what plainly was intended was an attack on the personal dignity of the person caricatured."[135]

The Court took some pains to explain:

> It [was] not his human features, his personal peculiarities, that are to be brought home to the observer through the alienation chosen. Instead, the intention is to show that he has marked *bestial* characteristics and behaves accordingly. Particularly the portrayal of sexual conduct, which in man still today forms part of the core of intimate life deserving of protection, is intended to devalue the person concerned as a person, to deprive him of his dignity as a human being. The complainant is thereby condemning him in a way that a legal system that takes the dignity of man as the highest value must disapprove of.[136]

Utterly absent from the Constitutional Court's analysis is any discounting of the politician's interest in dignity as an essential accommodation to the democratic process. Under the Basic Law, a politician enjoys the same claim to personal honor and dignity as a private citizen.[137]

Of course, there is nothing fundamentally inconsistent with maintaining both a commitment to democratic self-governance and, at the same time, a strong commitment to protecting personal dignity. Professor Frederick Schauer, for example, has argued that "[a]lthough there are moral arguments on one side of the private-lives-of-public-figures debate, including moral arguments from the right to vote that are often not recognized, there are moral values on the other side as well."[138] He suggests that "[c]hief among these is the argument that control over information about one's life is itself a central part of what is sometimes referred to as person-hood or personal autonomy, and that there is no good reason why a person should be required to relinquish this right of personal autonomy simply to enter the public domain."[139]

Thus, it is hardly unthinkable that another legal system might decide to protect the dignitarian interests of public officials and public figures more robustly than does the United States. That said, however, history teaches that thin-skinned politicians are often willing to use the power of the state to suppress dissent—and this is certainly true of Germany's history. What reason is there to think that politicians empowered with the credible threat of prosecution would not use this power to silence, or at least chill, dissent?

The balance, then, presents two competing and largely irreconcilable principles. On the one hand, the idea that free and open political debate should not face the chilling effect of sedition or libel law; on the other, whether the price of public service should encompass the complete loss of any serious protection of personhood, honor, dignity, and reputation. To serve one interest, one must compromise the other. Germany has parted company with the United States and decided that public service does not necessarily entail the surrender of personal reputation, honor, and dignity.

F. Dignity as the "Preferred" Freedom

At one time, it was commonplace in the United States to see the First Amendment, and particularly the Free Speech Clause, referred to as a "preferred freedom" or in a "preferred position."[140] Under the preferred position doctrine, First Amendment freedoms should be given priority over other guarantees in the Bill of Rights, and the federal judiciary should exercise a special vigilance when government encroaches on the exercise of these rights.[141] In the mid-twentieth century, the Supreme Court explained the doctrine as follows:

> The case confronts us again with the duty our system places on this Court to say where the individual's freedom ends and the State's power begins. Choice on that border, now as always delicate, is perhaps more so where the usual presumption supporting legislation is balanced by the preferred place given in our scheme to the great, the indispensable democratic freedoms secured by the First Amendment. That priority gives these liberties

a sanctity and a sanction not permitting dubious intrusions. And it is the character of the right, not of the limitation, which determines what standard governs the choice.[142]

By the late 1950s, the Supreme Court's invocation of the "preferred position" of the First Amendment had declined in favor of more open-ended balancing tests.[143] Even so, the Supreme Court's vindication of speech claims against important countervailing interests (such as reputation) continues to reflect the First Amendment's de facto "preferred position" in constitutional adjudication.

Although not every plaintiff with a free speech claim prevails, the U.S. federal courts are remarkably solicitous of such claims, even when the speech at issue does not implicate core concerns of the First Amendment.[144] Indeed, it would be no overstatement to say that free speech stands in more or less the same position in the U.S. constitutional scheme as does dignity under the German Basic Law.

What we find, then, is an inversion of values. The United States Supreme Court routinely subordinates values associated with personal dignity, honor, and reputation in favor of vindicating free speech claims. Cases like *Hustler Magazine v. Falwell*[145] do not have any German counterparts. Nor is this an accident. Simply put, the German constitutional scheme elevates dignity as the "preferred freedom" and does so quite overtly at the expense of the freedom of speech.

If one views this state of affairs critically (as one well might), the question arises as to where the blame should lie. To be clear, one should hesitate before placing principal responsibility on the Federal Constitutional Court. After all, the Basic Law *itself* strictly limits the protection of free speech by conditioning the scope of this freedom on other interests, notably including "the right to respect for personal honor."[146] Thus, the Basic Law itself elevates personal honor as a co-equal interest with the freedom of speech—and does so entirely independently of the effect of Article 1.

When one then turns to Article 1, one finds that the very first constitutional value that the Basic Law articulates is the protection of human dignity. By way of contrast, the Bill of Rights makes the freedom of speech, press, and assembly (along with the Religion Clauses) its first concern. The structural contrast could not be more striking. Article 79(3) further confirms this textual primacy by rendering Article 1 unamendable; it is a permanent and fixed part of the German constitutional order. No comparable protection exists for Article 5. Finally, Article 2 lends further support to the primacy of dignity by protecting a citizen's interest in "the free development of his personality."[147] The Federal Constitutional Court has found that this provision has a synergistic effect with Article 1 that enhances the relative weight of dignity claims in certain contexts (such as those presented in *Lebach*).

Thus, the Basic Law itself goes a very long way toward placing free speech in a decidedly inferior position to dignity interests in general, and reputational interests in particular. But it would be a mistake simply to rest the explanation on a simplistic textualist argument. Clever judges are quite capable of evading textual mandates that they do not like. It would grossly underestimate the Justices of the Constitutional Court to suggest that text alone explains their comparatively weak commitment to the freedom of speech.

As Professor Whitman has observed, "[t]here is, when you add all this up, a very great difference indeed between the American and Continental European legal traditions."[148] But more important, there are significant *cultural* differences at work too. A culture of honor, or respect, has been an important feature of German social life for quite a long time. Although the roots of this tradition are aristocratic, the expectation of respect has been effectively and thoroughly democratized.[149] Professor Whitman traces the broadest extension of personal insult law to the Nazi period. He notes that "[t]his 'nationalization' of honor nicely paralleled a 'nationalization' of honor that took place during the French Revolution, and it had some of the same revolutionary implications: At least potentially, *every* German was a person of honor."[150]

Whitman suggests that, in the United States, "honor is truly absent from our legal thought-world." But this absence in our legal thought-world is a product of our broader culture. In the United States, we really do not worry very much about securing to every person a "minimum of honor," something that Whitman characterizes as "deeply rooted in [German and French] cultural tradition."[151] Germany and the United States have selected different means of advancing the concept of equal citizenship. "Germany and France have *leveled up*" whereas "the United States has *leveled down*"; Whitman goes so far as to posit that "it is not wrong, in contrasting them with the United States, to describe Germany and France as modern honor cultures."[152]

Professor Whitman also has observed that the German laws protecting personal honor and dignity constitute "a body of law that shows, in many of its doctrines, a numbness to free-speech concerns that will startle any

American."[153] This characterization seems spot on: German law's disregard of the chilling effects of the civil and criminal laws' protection of personal honor is utterly antithetical to the free speech project embodied by the First Amendment. That politicians could enjoy not merely statutory but, in fact, an absolute and unamendable constitutional privilege to be free from sharp or caustic personal attacks designed to humiliate or dehumanize their subject represents a complete departure from baseline assumptions about the freedom of speech as it has been conceptualized in the United States.

Returning to Professor Currie's suggestion that "[t]he overall trend, nevertheless, has been toward greater protection of speech, especially in matters of public concern," one can make the case that the Federal Constitutional Court has protected speech when the countervailing dignity interest was diffuse. For example, the Constitutional Court has held that Article 5 protects art that allegedly casts contempt upon the German national flag[154] and a harsh parody of the German national anthem.[155] Thus, when the dignity of the state is itself at issue, the German Constitutional Court *has* vindicated free speech claims. The same result obtained in the *Tucholsky* case, which involved a legal challenge to the use of the phrase "soldiers are murderers."[156] Because the statement was not directed at any particular soldier, no significant dignity interest existed. Only in the context of anti-Semitic speech has the contemporary German Constitutional Court protected dignity at the expense of free speech in near-absolute terms.

Thus, Professor Currie's assertion withstands scrutiny, at least when judged against the dignity of the German government itself or against abstract interests (although remarks of an anti-Semitic cast constitute a notable exception to this general approach). As the German Constitutional Court has explained, "the norm [the protection of personal honor] cannot be justified from the viewpoint of personal honour, since State institutions neither have 'personal' honour nor are bearers of the general right of personality."[157] It is true that "[w]ithout a minimum of social acceptance, State institutions cannot carry out their functions" and "may therefore in principle be protected against verbal attacks that threaten to undermine these requirements."[158] But the protection of state agencies and institutions via the criminal law "may not however have the effect of protecting State institutions against public criticism, possibly even in sharp forms, something intended to be especially guaranteed by the fundamental right of freedom of opinion."[159]

When the dignity interest involves a specific individual, however, the Federal Constitutional Court usually finds that reputation (even of a dead person) trumps the Article 5 interest in freedom of expression. As the Court put the matter in the *Tucholsky* case, "[F]reedom of opinion must always take second place where the statement affects another's human dignity."[160] As late as 1995, the Court emphasized that "human dignity as the root of all fundamental rights cannot be weighed against any individual fundamental right"—including those rights protected under Article 5.[161] The Constitutional Court made very clear that, had the *Tucholsky* defendants plainly called specific soldiers "murderers," a different result would obtain.[162]

This analysis of the phrase "soldiers are murderers" or "soldiers are potential murderers" drew a sharp dissent from Justice Haas, who believed that the lower courts had properly applied the civil code provision protecting personal honor. She observed that "[r]efraining from personal defamation in the political opinion-forming process can only promote that process, by raising the culture of political conflict."[163] She further argued that the majority's failure to protect the honor of German soldiers as a class or group risked the Basic Law's popular legitimacy: "It is a simple matter of course that the constitution must not, if it is not to lose credibility, leave unprotected those who follow its commands and are attacked (exclusively) for that very thing."[164]

Thus, the *Tucholsky* case makes clear that the protection for free speech critical of the government runs to critiques of government institutions and offices, and not to the individuals who staff them. The rule set forth in cases like *Lebach, Soraya,* and *Strauss* remains in place. Free speech enjoys protection only to the extent that it does not displace the Basic Law's principal concern: the protection of personal dignity and honor.

III. Balancing Free Speech and Democracy

In another important series of cases, the German Constitutional Court has vigorously enforced the Basic Law's mandate to safeguard democratic processes and institutions. Germany is a "militant democracy"[165] and the freedom of speech does not extend to advocacy of the abolition of the existing constitutional order.

The Federal Constitutional Court certainly acknowledges and embraces the relationship of free speech to democratic self-government:

> As the most immediate manifestation of the human personality in society, the basic right to free expression of opinion is one of the noblest of all

human rights. . . . To a free democratic constitutional order it is absolutely basic for it alone makes possible the continuing intellectual controversy, the contest of opinions that forms the lifeblood of such an order. In a certain sense it is the basis of all freedom whatever, "the matrix, the indispensable condition of nearly every other form of freedom" (Cardozo).[166]

Professor Currie notes that "[i]n light of this focus on the central role of free expression in the functioning of democracy, it is understandable that the German court, like its counterpart in the United States, has emphasized that political speech lies at the heart of the constitutional provisions."[167] Accordingly, no commercial speech doctrine exists in Germany; the Federal Constitutional Court has sustained both legislation limiting advertising by pharmacies and banning advertising by physicians on the theory that commercial advertising does not implicate Article 5 values in a meaningful way.[168]

In practical terms, this means that even if speech does not offend the dignity clause (Article 1), it may still not enjoy substantial protection from either government or private abridgement if the speech lies outside the scope of Article 5. For example, speech that has as its object the overthrow of the existing constitutional order does not enjoy any constitutional protection;[169] neither does anti-Semitic speech.[170] As Professor Whitman has observed, "[i]t is indeed the case that Jews are extensively shielded from 'disrespectful' insults under current German law."[171] Moreover, "[t]he German commitment to protecting Jewish sensibilities is in this regard remarkably far-reaching."[172]

But to be clear: the proscription of speech by the German government is most assuredly one-sided and viewpoint based. Thus, one can inveigh at will against Nazis, Communists, or anti-Semites. Speech hostile to these positions is not only protected under Article 5 but also seems to be entirely consistent with the rather limited dignity interests of Nazis, Communists, and anti-Semites. Or, stated somewhat more directly, the Federal Constitutional Court appears to be generally more protective of speech that advances the favored government position on these issues than it is of other kinds of speech.

Moreover, the legal proscriptions against hate speech are, in practice, not universal in their application. "It is important to recognize, though, that the *broader* German commitment to respectful treatment is somewhat less far-reaching."[173] Thus, while the German government is committed to protecting Jewish citizens and visitors from the psychological harms associated with hate speech, it is not as vigilant with respect to other groups, such as persons of Turkish ancestry.[174] As the cases discussed below will demonstrate, even if the expression does not transgress an individual's or group's interest in dignity, the content and viewpoint of the speech most definitely matter in Germany.

A. The *Lüth* Case:[175] Free Speech Triumphant?

Lüth is an important case for many reasons. Dieter Grimm calls *Lüth* "the most important decision by the Constitutional Court."[176] Similarly, Professor Kommers describes it as "a linchpin of German constitutional law," and rightly so.[177] The case establishes the general principle that the Basic Law applies to all legal disputes, either directly or indirectly.[178] It also "laid down for the first time the doctrine of an objective order of values."[179] Finally, the case serves as the foundation for German free speech doctrine more generally.

Veit Harlan, a film director, worked closely with the Nazi propaganda machine. In this capacity, he produced and directed a number of highly offensive films, most notably including the infamously anti-Semitic film *Jud Süss* ("The Jew Suess"). Notwithstanding his active collaboration with the Nazi government, the Allies never convicted Harlan of any war crimes for his contributions to the Nazis' genocidal programs.

Following the end of World War II, he attempted to reemerge as a mainstream director. In 1950, he wrote and directed the film *Immortal Beloved*, which was released to favorable critical notices both in Germany and abroad.

Erich Lüth, Hamburg's director of information, was incensed at Harlan's reemergence into the world of cinema as a legitimate auteur. Lüth, acting in his private capacity as a citizen, organized a nationwide boycott of Harlan's film. Domnick-Film-Produktion GmbH, the film's producer, and Herzog-Film GmbH, the film's distributor in Germany, then sought an injunction against the boycott under a general provision of the German Civil Code.[180] A local trial court in Hamburg found in favor of the producer and distributor and enjoined Lüth from pursuing the boycott. The injunction prohibited Lüth from "calling on German cinema owners and film distributors not to include the film 'Immortal Beloved' . . . in their programme" and from "calling on the German public not to go see this film."[181]

After this adverse judgment, Lüth filed an appeal with the Regional Court, which he lost. He then filed simultaneous appeals with the Regional Appeals Court and the Federal Constitutional Court, alleging a violation of his rights under Article 5 of the Basic Law.[182]

The German Constitutional Court began its analysis by noting that the Basic Law creates a system of rights that is not "neutral as to values" and that it erects "an objective value system in its section on fundamental rights."[183] Dignity "must be regarded as the basic constitutional decision for all spheres of law," and this commitment to dignity "manifestly influences the civil law: no provision of civil law may be in contradiction with it; each one must be interpreted in its spirit."[184] This effect on private law is particularly appropriate in the context of the "general clauses" of the Civil Code that serve as the "points where the fundamental rights 'break in' to civil law."[185]

Although Article 5(2) limits the freedom of speech when required by the general laws, the general laws themselves must be interpreted consistently with the Basic Law. Thus, there is a kind of symbiotic relationship between the Basic Law and the Civil Code: "[T]he general laws must themselves be interpreted as far as their effect of restricting the fundamental rights goes in the light of the importance of that fundamental right, . . . which in a free democracy must lead to a basic presumption in favour of freedom of speech in all areas but particularly in public life."[186]

The Federal Constitutional Court extols the value and importance of free speech, describing it "as the most direct expression of human personality in society, one of the foremost rights of all."[187] The Court explains that

> [f]or a free democratic State system, it is nothing other than constitutive, for it is only through it that the constant intellectual debate, the clash of opinions, that is its vital element is made possible. . . . It is in a certain sense the basis of every freedom whatever, "the matrix, the indispensable condition of nearly every other form of freedom" (Cardozo).[188]

This language strongly foreshadowed the ultimate result in the case, which was favorable to Lüth.

The Constitutional Court found that the lower courts had failed to consider adequately Lüth's interest in self-expression when applying section 826 of the Civil Code. The trial judge must "in each case . . . weigh the importance of the fundamental right against the value of the legal good protected by the 'general law' for the person allegedly injured by the utterance."[189] The Court emphasized that "[t]he decision can be taken only on the basis of an overall view of the individual case, taking all essential circumstances into account."[190]

The Constitutional Court went on to engage in a balancing of the plaintiffs' interests in being free from economic coercion and lost profits against Lüth's interest in freedom of expression. The Court found that Lüth acted in good faith and on the basis of a sincere political conviction that Veit Harlan should not be permitted to simply resume his professional life, given the appearance this would create to the larger world, i.e., "that nothing has changed in German cultural life by comparison with the National Socialist period" with "Harlan now again, as then, the representative German film director."[191]

The Court noted that the German government benefited from Lüth's speech: "There is therefore a decisive interest in having the world assured that the German people has turned away from this mental attitude and condemns it not merely for reason of political opportunism but from insight into its contemptibility, gained from their own inner conversion."[192] In other words, Lüth's boycott represented a source of good publicity for both the West German government and the German people as a whole.

As for Harlan's interest in reintegration into society, pursuit of his career, and, moreover, his personal dignity and reputation? The Federal Constitutional Court posited counterspeech as an effective remedy for any harm to these interests that Lüth's activity caused: "Anyone who feels injured by a public statement of another can similarly reply before the public."[193] In fact, the Regional Court had applied Article 2, which protects the free development of individual personality, to sustain the trial court's judgment. The Constitutional Court was far less interested in protecting Harlan's Article 2 (or Article 1) rights. If the boycott ended Harlan's career as a film director, "he would still nevertheless have other possibilities of artistic activity . . . so there could be no talk of a total annihilation of his artistic and human existence."[194]

Lüth's remarks against Harlan even contained arguable factual mistakes: "the complainant had made the objectively untrue assertion that Harlan had been only formally acquitted by the Court of Assizes, while the grounds of judgment had been a moral condemnation."[195] Recall that false assertions of fact supposedly have no call, whatsoever, on Article 5. In the context of sham interviews, erroneous quotation marks, and quotes taken out of context, the Constitutional Court flatly denied any protection to the speaker.

Lüth's statements were at best inaccurate and at worst total mischaracterizations. The Federal Constitutional Court found that the war crimes court judgment "goes on to explain in detail that at the time when Harlan was ordered to make the film there had been scarcely any further possibilities for him of avoiding cooperation, sabotaging the film or significantly moderating its anti-semitic content; it is explicitly attested that he had at least attempted the latter."[196] Harlan's activities constituted a "crime against humanity" but were excused because he was simply following orders and would have faced personal danger "to life and limb" if he refused to work for the Nazi government.[197]

Lüth simplified a rather complicated verdict into the statement that "[h]is acquittal in Hamburg was purely a formal one" and "[t]he grounds of judgment were a moral condemnation."[198] This sort of spin fails to pass muster in later cases. Indeed, even an accurate quotation, taken out of context, gives rise to a private action for damages in *Böll*. So why does the German Constitutional Court excuse Lüth from observing the standard of care it demands of others?

The reason is as simple as it is startling: Lüth's speech helped contribute to Germany's reemergence as a legitimate nation-state and therefore deserved protection. Indeed, the Federal Constitutional Court takes pains to note that his speech closely corresponded to a speech in the Bundestag condemning Harlan's reemergence as a film director. The correspondence of views was a felicitous one: "In assessing the conduct of the complainant, the view of the representative body of the German people expressed here cannot be irrelevant."[199] Simply put, speech critical of Nazi collaborators or those who supported them is broadly protected, at least insofar as the government itself agrees with the speaker's characterization of the object of the accusation. The best way to win an Article 5 case before the German Constitutional Court is to attack a known Nazi. But, one should not draw any broad generalizations from the result in *Lüth*. Instead, it merely represents the viewpoint-based jurisprudence of Article 5.

Not only does German law protect those who disparage the Nazis, it also generally *prohibits* political speech that endorses or supports Nationalist Socialist ideologies. The best way to lose a free speech claim is to embrace anti-democratic values or anti-Semitic ideologies. Simply put, certain ideas enjoy virtually no legal protection in German constitutional law. The cases that follow demonstrate the oddity of *Lüth* and the strength of the countervailing censorial tradition.

B. *Socialist Reich Party*[200] and *Communist Party Ban*:[201] The "Militant Democracy" in Action

As noted in the introduction, the Basic Law itself proscribes activities aimed at the overthrow of the democratic constitutional order. Although Article 9 generally protects the freedom of association, Article 9's protection does not extend to associations "whose purposes or activities . . . are directed against the constitutional order."[202] Similarly, Article 18 declares free speech rights null and void for "abuse" if deployed "to combat the free democratic basic order."[203] Finally, Article 21 prohibits the existence of political parties "that, by reason of their aims or the behavior of their adherents, seek to impair or abolish the free democratic basic order or to endanger the existence of the Federal Republic of Germany."[204] These three provisions collectively establish that constitutional freedoms that otherwise enjoy protection under the Basic Law lose such protection if deployed in an effort to disestablish the "free democratic basic order." Article 5 does not itself contain this proviso, but Articles 9, 18, and 21 clearly establish that the freedom of speech does not extend to speech aimed at promoting the overthrow of the government.

In a pair of cases decided in the 1950s, the Federal Constitutional Court enforced bans against the Socialist Reich Party and the Communist Party. Although these decisions appear rather extreme when contrasted with the *Brandenburg* free speech orthodoxy that has prevailed in the United States since 1969, one cannot really fault the Federal Constitutional Court for enforcing the express textual limitations that the Basic Law itself establishes.

In the *Socialist Reich Party* case, the government petitioned the Constitutional Court to ban the SRP under Article 21(2) of the Basic Law. The Court recognized the inherent contradiction of positing full democracy with limitations on electoral speech. It noted that "the principle of democracy" requires freedom for "any political orientation to manifest itself in political parties, including—to be consistent—anti-democratic orientations."[205] The nature of serving as a democratic representative also implies the ability "to be a free representative of the entire people and at the same time be bound by a concrete party program." "Both fundamental ideas lead to the basic conclusion that the establishment and activity of political parties must not be restrained."[206]

Banning anti-democratic political organizations violates both principles —something that the Constitutional Court found deeply problematic. It noted that "[t]he Framers of the German Constitution had to decide whether they could fully implement this conclusion or whether, enlightened by recent experiences, they should instead draw certain limits in this area."[207] Article 21(2) and Article 9 resolve this question in favor of limiting the full freedom of association, whether by political parties or other groups, in order to safeguard the democratic constitutional order. Consistent with Article 21(2), the Constitutional Court may ban a party "if, but only if, they seek to topple supreme fundamental values of the free democratic order which are embodied in the Basic Law."[208]

After examining the membership of the SRP, its objectives and platform, and its internal structure, the Constitutional Court concluded that it represented a de facto proxy for the Nazi Party and, hence, fell within the ban Article 21(2) establishes.[209] Accordingly, it held that "[t]he SRP is thus unconstitutional within the meaning of Article 21(2) of the Basic Law" and "must be dissolved."[210]

Four years later, the Federal Constitutional Court issued a decree banning the Community Party (or KPD). Professor Kommers reports that "[t]he Court found, as a matter of ideology and fact, that the KPD directed all of its operations against the existing constitutional system."[211] It cautioned that the mere abstract advocacy of the overthrow of the government was not a sufficient condition for banning a political party. Instead, the party must have "a fixed purpose constantly and resolutely to combat the free democratic basic order" and must pursue this agenda "in political action according to a fixed plan."[212]

Although the Basic Law establishes a democratic constitutional order, its framers did not intend to tolerate any and all political agendas. The framers, "based on their concrete historical experience" concluded that "the state could no longer afford to maintain an attitude of neutrality toward political parties."[213] The Basic Law thus establishes a " 'militant democracy,' " which the Federal Constitutional Court has an obligation to defend and maintain.[214] In light of its finding that the KPD sought to overthrow the democratic basic order, the Court ordered its dissolution and confiscation of its property.[215]

The Federal Constitutional Court has been less strict in its enforcement of Article 21(2) since the 1970s,[216] but the government retains the power to abolish any party that it deems a sufficient threat to the existing constitutional order. Kommers notes that "the level of tolerance for extremist political speech and activity appears to have risen in the Federal Republic as Germans have gained greater confidence in their democratic institutions and processes."[217]

That said, one should not assume that the contemporary German government maintains a weakened commitment to "militant democracy." In many cases, a band of lunatics with little electoral support probably would benefit more from a government ban than suffer from it. The German government's behavior thus reflects much greater tolerance for extremist parties that show little sign of garnering significant electoral support. But, make no mistake, the toleration reflects pragmatism rather than an absolute commitment to entirely free and open democratic politics.[218] As Professor Currie notes, the government moved to invoke its powers to suppress organizations dedicated to overthrow of the democratic order in the immediate aftermath of German reunification because of "a rash of violent attacks on foreigners" that "reached alarming proportions."[219]

C. The *"Auschwitz Lie" (Holocaust Denial)* Case:[220] The Exclusion of False Ideas from Article 5's Protection

In the United States, "[u]nder the First Amendment there is no such thing as a false idea."[221] As Professor Martin Redish has noted, "the Supreme Court has adopted as its doctrinal baseline the principle that the government may not constitutionally regulate private expression because it disagrees with the viewpoints expressed."[222] Thus, "[h]owever pernicious an opinion may seem, we depend for its correction not on the conscience of judges and juries, but on the competition of other ideas."[223]

Under the Basic Law, Germany takes a somewhat more hands-on approach to demonstrably false speech. The *Auschwitz Lie* case incorporates and reflects the German view that some ideas are both demonstrably false and sufficiently evil to justify an immediate government response to suppress them.

The facts of the case are relatively simple. The National Democratic Party (NDP) planned on staging a rally in Munich, at which David Irving, a self-styled "revisionist historian" and known Holocaust denier, would present the keynote address. The local government threatened the NDP with criminal prosecution unless it promised to take "appropriate measures" to ensure that the fact of the Holocaust would not be denied.[224] The German administrative courts upheld the restrictions on the theory that a law prohibiting the denial of the Holocaust was presumptively constitutional and did not violate Article 5. The NDP appealed these adverse decisions to the Federal Constitutional Court, alleging a breach of Article 5(1).

The Federal Constitutional Court easily concluded that "[t]he contested decisions do not violate Article 5(1)."[225] It explained that Article 5(1) protects the expression of opinions because "[o]pinions are marked by the individual's subjective relationship to his statement's content" and "[t]o this extent, demonstration of their truth or untruth is impossible."[226] On the other hand, "factual assertions are not, strictly speaking, expressions of opinion."[227] Factual assertions feature "an objective relationship between the utterance and reality" that permits an objective observer to ascertain "their truth or falsity."[228]

Factual assertions that "cannot contribute anything to the constitutionally presupposed formation of opinion" do not enjoy any Article 5(1) protection. "Viewed from this angle, incorrect information is not an interest that merits protection."[229] This is particularly true when the false statements cause injury to reputational interests protected by Article 5(2) and dignitary interests safeguarded by Article 1. The Court explained that "[w]here an expression of opinion must be viewed as a formal criminal insult or vilification, protection of personality routinely comes before freedom of expression."[230] It went on to find that the prohibited statements were both factually untrue and caused harm to the reputation and dignity of Holocaust survivors and their families.[231]

The contrast with *Lüth* is startling. Lüth, one should recall, misrepresented facts regarding Veit Harlan's acquittal by the Court of Assizes in his speeches calling for a boycott of *Immortal Beloved*. The Constitutional Court simply glossed over these inaccuracies in sustaining Lüth's Article 5(1) claim. David Irving and the NDP do not receive the same solicitous consideration. Why? Because the German government supported the views and attitudes espoused by Lüth and detests and opposes the views expressed by Mr. Irving and NDP. It is a simple case of state-enforced viewpoint discrimination. Again, however, one should keep in mind that the Basic Law itself strikes this balance—to a large extent, the Federal Constitutional Court is simply enforcing limits that the text of the German Constitution itself establishes.

D. *Nazi Symbols* Case:[232] Viewpoint-Based Protections for Political Speech

To bring matters to a fitting close, one should note that the German government does not proscribe *all* uses or displays of Nazi symbols. It prohibits the display of such symbols only by those who appear to support or sympathize with the Third Reich and its anti-Semitic and racist policies. The *Nazi Symbols* case makes clear that the attitude of the person using Nazi iconography will prefigure the protected or unprotected nature of the speech.

In the *Nazi Symbols* case, the complainants produced satirical T-shirts featuring "Adolph Hitler's body in a uniform jacket with a swastika armband" and "his body appear[ed] sideways in front of a map outline of Europe." Hitler's name appeared over his image, with the dates "1939" and "1945" appearing to either side of the image; in gothic lettering under this picture the phrase "European Tour" appeared, with a series of dates and countries corresponding to the German conquest and occupation of various European nations during World War II. The September 1940 entry for "England" and the August 1942 entry for "Russia" both featured a strike out over the country's name and the notation "Cancelled" in the margin. The copyright lists "Third Reich Promotions" as the tour promoter.[233] A second T-shirt featured Hitler with a yo-yo and the caption "European Yo-Yo Champion, 1939–1945."[234] The complainants sold 156 T-shirts: "153 with the first picture and 3 with the second picture."[235]

The trial court convicted the complainants of using the symbol of an unconstitutional organization, in violation of section 86 of the Criminal Code, and sentenced each of them to pay a fine. The T-shirt company's owners unsuccessfully appealed the conviction to the Regional Court and the Bavarian State Supreme Court.[236] Evidently, the concept of sarcasm was lost on the lower courts. The defendants then filed an appeal with the Federal Constitutional Court, alleging infringement of their rights under Article 5(1) and (3).

The Federal Constitutional Court found that the complainants' argument had merit on Article 5(3) grounds. It noted that "[t]he Regional Court failed to appreciate the artistic content of the pictures."[237] "The assumption that an 'informed observer' could not see any derision or ridicule of Hitler in the pictures and that in the first picture a 'reasonable average citizen' could only recognize a chronological list of the campaigns, the failure of the attacks against England and Russia, as well as Hitler's end, does not do justice to the content of the portrayals."[238] The same conclusion applied with respect to the "yo-yo" Hitler T-shirt. "Contrary to the Regional Court's opinion, both pictures are open to the interpretation that Hitler and his megalomania are intended to be ridiculed by using satire."[239] The T-shirts enjoyed protection, not as political speech or opinion, but as art.

This decision is, at least superficially, free speech friendly. But on a deeper level, it is more disturbing than reassuring. The complainants win their case only because the Constitutional Court accepted their characterization of the T-shirts as disparaging of Hitler. Had the NDP produced T-shirts with a heroic Hitler dressed in classical garb, convictions under section 86 would undoubtedly have stood. Would the T-shirts have been any less "artistic"? Not really. But the T-shirts would have conveyed the wrong message about Hitler—they would have transmitted an officially proscribed viewpoint. As such, the Basic Law would not have stood as an impediment to civil or criminal punishments.

It is certainly true that "free speech" is not truly free anywhere. Every nation maintains some limits on the scope of lawful expression. For example, an attempt to "joke" with an airport security guard will lead to criminal punishment very quickly in the United States. But the scope of permissible speech in Germany seems significantly more narrow than in the contemporary United States. The government has arrogated to itself the power to ban bad ideas and organizations that attempt to disseminate bad ideas. The system reflects scant trust in the good sense of the German people to separate wheat from chaff in the marketplace of ideas.

From an American perspective, speech is not really "free" at all in Germany. The government maintains strict editorial control over core political speech and, for the most part, these restrictions are aggressively enforced. One cannot legally sell copies of *Mein Kampf* either in Germany or to Germans in Germany, and Web sites featuring prohibited political ideas give rise to criminal prosecutions.[240] The German government's efforts to eradicate disfavored political viewpoints have not abated—its campaign against German language neo-Nazi Web sites continues into the present.[241] Although the German government may be somewhat less eager formally to ban parties, it has not slackened in its efforts to suppress publication of pro-Nazi sentiments.

In sum, these efforts are both content- and viewpoint-based censorship and reflect a radical break with the free speech tradition in the United States. Given the continuing problems the German government faces with extreme right-wing parties and politicians, it should perhaps re-examine whether its program of official government censorship is doing more good than harm. Regardless of whether the censorial approach is consistent with democratic self-government, as a practical matter it does not seem to be very effective at suppressing racist and xenophobic viewpoints.[242] As Professor Currie delicately states the matter "[t]hose who believe in constitutional liberties will continue to differ as to whether such measures [as prohibitions on extremist parties and their rhetoric] are appropriate means of protecting them."[243]

IV. An Imperfect Equality: Speech Restrictions as an Imperfect Means of Achieving Equal Citizenship

Professor Dieter Grimm is undoubtedly correct when he suggests that the Federal Constitutional Court "has elaborated a theory of human rights which exceeds the jurisprudence of most other countries with judicial review."[244] And, in the area of freedom of expression, this assertion certainly holds true: the German Federal Constitutional Court has broken important new ground in free speech theory. The Justices have squarely rejected the marketplace metaphor, not merely endorsing but effectively requiring the government to police speech that transgresses the dignity guarantee and to proscribe and punish speech, speakers, and organizations that advocate the overthrow of the democratic social order. The German Constitutional Court's free speech jurisprudence utterly fails to embrace a marketplace of ideas—to the extent that a marketplace of ideas exists in Germany, all ideas are subject to government control not only for their content and viewpoint but, by virtue of the dignity clause, for the manner in which a speaker chooses to express an idea or viewpoint.

If speech is a "preferred" freedom in the United States,[245] it represents a dispreferred freedom in Germany. Constitutional objectives associated with dignity and the survival of contemporary government institutions routinely supersede the Article 5 right to freedom of expression. German constitutional law intentionally subordinates the freedom of expression in order to promote values associated with dignity, community, and support for democratic self-government. As Eberle has noted, "[t]he German vision, set out with reasonable clarity and reflecting the systemization of German legal science, centers around the human person and her dignity."[246]

Although the marketplace approach that generally prevails in the United States is certainly subject to serious criticisms,[247] the German approach seems seriously flawed in several key respects. The Basic Law has criminalized speech advocating the overthrow of the existing constitutional order, yet citizens have continued to join organizations having this objective. More than fifty years of censorship have failed to get the job done. Reports of anti-Semitism and acts of violence against ethnic minorities in Germany continue, particularly in the parts of Germany formerly constituting the GDR.[248] The use of a speech ban as a means of eradicating bad ideas has, as an empirical matter, simply failed to work. Moreover, the aggressive use of criminal law to ban parties and politicians espousing the wrong ideas serves only to lionize racist thugs and, by imbuing the ideology of hate with a strong musk of the taboo, to make such ideologies intrinsically more appealing to Germany's youth.

The failure of the speech ban is not really surprising. Banning speech as a primary means of creating and maintaining an egalitarian society seems an odd approach. Consider, for example, Germany's restrictive citizenship laws. Since World War II, Germany has maintained a very liberal policy on immigration and asylum, while restricting citizenship on the basis of blood. As of 2002, some 7.3 million residents, representing fully 9 percent of Germany's population, were legal foreign residents.[249] Of these non-citizen permanent residents of Germany, 2.5 million are Turks.[250] Until very recently, however, only the natural or adopted children of German citizens were entitled to claim German citizenship; birth on German soil did not (and still, standing alone, does not) automatically convey German citizenship.

The results of these two policies—relatively open immigration coupled with highly restrictive naturalization laws—are not difficult to predict: the establishment of a permanent underclass of non-citizen nationals, people born, educated, and employed in Germany who had no right to participate in civic affairs. Their presence served as an irritant to Germans enjoying citizenship—something that, in a democratic society, politicians are bound to notice. Meanwhile, the non-citizen nationals had no ability themselves to participate in the electoral process by supporting candidates sympathetic to their plight.

As one commentator has observed, "[o]ne possible means of ensuring the protection of foreigners would be to grant foreigners easier access to citizenship and thus to voting rights."[251] The German Constitutional Court, however, has held that it is unconstitutional to grant voting rights to non-citizens in federal, state, and local elections.[252] Accordingly, the extension of voting rights would require liberalization of citizenship rules.

Until the enactment of major naturalization reforms in 1999, which took effect in 2000, German citizenship rested on *jus sanguinis,* or a child's bloodline: "for a child to be born a German citizen, one of his or her parents must be German."[253] Naturalization was highly disfavored and constituted "an exception based on full integration into German society and the public interest."[254] Thus, Germany maintained "a '*Volkisch*' view of nationality based on blood rather than a liberal, republican view of citizenship."[255]

In practice, these restrictive rules could lead to absurd results:

> This law has two important consequences. First, the child of non-naturalized Turkish parents in their third generation in Germany is born a Turkish citizen. Second, the child of [a] Polish couple whose parents and grandparents have never seen Germany and speak no German but are of German descent has the automatic right to German citizenship. Germany, Austria, and Luxembourg are the only three countries in Europe that still determine citizenship by bloodline. . . . Although there might be a rational explanation for basing German citizenship on descent, the message is clear: the color of your blood is what being German is all about, and foreigners' blood is not the right color.[256]

Ironically, then, the German government maintained a citizenship policy that appeared to use troublesome racial stereotypes while at the same time it aggressively attempted to suppress potentially embarrassing displays of Nazi symbols. Thus, the German government sent a highly mixed message by denying full civic participation to third-generation permanently resident non-citizens.

In a bold and somewhat politically risky move,[257] Chancellor Gerhard Schröder successfully advocated the overhaul of Germany's naturalization law, which dated back to 1913.[258] These reforms passed the federal Parliament on July 15, 1999, and took effect on January 1, 2000.[259] Under the reforms, "children born in Germany to foreign parents acquire German citizenship by birth, provided that one parent has been a permanent resident in Germany for at least eight years and has a permanent residence permit."[260] The child's German citizenship is only provisional, however; the child must make an election between German citizenship and her parent's citizenship between the ages of 18 and 23. "German nationality is lost automatically if a dual national reaches the age of twenty-three" without having renounced any other citizenship or claim to citizenship.[261] In addition, the law reduced the naturalization waiting period for adult immigrants from fifteen years to eight years.[262]

Both children born in Germany and foreign nationals seeking to become naturalized citizens must effectively and affirmatively renounce any other citizenship that they hold or to which they may be entitled. Thus, even after the reforms, "there is no automatic path, or 'tenure track,' that leads to German citizenship."[263]

Even though citizenship will now be possible for many of the permanent guest workers and their children, considerable unease remains among some current German citizens. "For adversaries [of the reforms], it is a fundamental change endangering the identity of the German nation."[264] For example, Professor Hailbronner expresses considerable reservations about the possible effects of the naturalization and citizenship reforms:

> The final test will be whether a reform of nationality will contribute to the maintenance of the elements stabilizing the "identity" of the nation. The law would be a fundamental failure if it would lead to the establishment of national ethnic minorities with privileged political and social rights. The reform legislation makes clear that together with the requirement of sufficient German language knowledge and a commitment to the principles of the Basic Law, admission to the political community is dependent on the intention to integrate into German society.[265]

Thus, for Germans citizenship, even after the reforms, has (or should have) as much to do with cultural identity as with simply paying one's taxes and voting.[266]

Such a requirement of full cultural assimilation undoubtedly raises the stakes of naturalization. As Professor Martin notes, "pangs of regret or wonder, emotional ties to the old country, and especially continuing relations with a family still residing there make it impossible to accomplish a full and complete break."[267]

The liberalized rules governing citizenship should lead to greater political participation by ethnic minorities in Germany. This, in turn, should ensure the election of government officials more attuned to the needs, wants, and desires of these communities. This assumes, of course, that the immigration reforms will be implemented effectively. If a complete loss of ethnic identity is a de facto requirement for naturalization, many persons eligible for citizenship might deem the price too dear to pay.[268]

In many ways, the situation prior to the enactment of the immigration reforms was not entirely unlike that in the American South in the pre–

Voting Rights Act era. Prior to 1965, African Americans could not vote. This was not a function of citizenship—any person born on United States soil is a citizen, by virtue of the citizenship clause of the Fourteenth Amendment.[269] But citizenship, by itself, does not establish the right to vote. One must register in order to enjoy suffrage. Thus, if local officials can systematically prevent a class of persons from registering to vote, the fact that they happen to be citizens is quite irrelevant.

State and local officials in the states of the former Confederacy deployed a variety of devices, including poll taxes, literacy tests, and physical violence to prevent African American citizens from voting. In consequence, politicians seeking office in states with 35 percent minority populations ran as open racists. The electorate was entirely white, so a politician seeking public office had no need to address the concerns of the minority community. Indeed, speaking to such issues virtually ensured electoral defeat.

Whatever his faults (and they were legion), President Lyndon B. Johnson instinctively realized that the key to meaningful equality in the South involved reform of the political process. Through sheer willpower and brass-knuckle political tactics, President Johnson forced the Voting Rights Act of 1965 through the Congress. Following passage of the Voting Rights Act, literally millions of African American citizens registered to vote and, in fact, voted. A sea of change swept the Deep South, as incumbent politicians fell over themselves trying to show support for the minority community. Avowed Dixiecrats, such as Senator John C. Stennis of Mississippi and Strom Thurmond of South Carolina, supported the renewal of the Voting Rights Act in 1982. The ultimate race-baiter, Governor George C. Wallace of Alabama, had an epiphany and went to an historically black Baptist Church in Montgomery, Alabama, to seek forgiveness for his past sins—before seeking an unprecedented fourth term as Alabama's governor in 1982.[270]

Thus, the political enfranchisement of minority citizens radically transformed the political scene. More than any judicial effort to enforce the Fourteenth Amendment, the Voting Rights Act of 1965 completed the process of national reconstruction that commenced with the Civil War in 1861.[271] The key to equality was not a speech code that banned the use of racial epithets or prohibited parties that advocated the maintenance of segregation. Instead, the enfranchisement of minority voters led to a transformation of the region's politics. The state and local governments in the states of the former Confederacy, once utterly indifferent to the needs and wants of minority citizens, suddenly exhibited a new solicitousness that continues to this day. As between a prohibition on hate speech and a ballot, the leaders of the American civil rights movement would undoubtedly have preferred the ballot.

Chancellor Gerhard Schröder's immigration reforms present the potential of seriously addressing the structural marginalization of ethnic minorities in Germany. Indeed, over time, the 1999 reforms may come to play the same role for remaking German society that the Voting Rights Act played in remaking the American South. The reforms are a significant and highly important step toward integrating Germany's multigenerational guest workers (or "*gast-arbeiters*") into the political life of the nation.[272]

All that said, however, Germany's hate speech laws are a very poor proxy for enfranchisement of ethnic minorities. But there is good reason for this. The hate speech laws are neither designed nor enforced to empower ethnic minorities. The Basic Law's protection of dignity privileges members of the dominant cultural group much more than the average Turk. Moreover, this is not accidental.

As Professor James Q. Whitman eloquently has explained, German dignity concerns stem from a culture of respect that democratized aristocratic forms of politesse and protected these interests through the civil and criminal law.[273] "Standing behind both German and French attitudes toward the regulation of civility is something else: a commitment to the broad distribution of 'honor' or 'dignity' throughout society."[274] He emphasizes that "[t]hese Continental systems, in short, have human 'dignity' today largely because they had personal 'honor' in the past."[275]

The concept of honor, or dignity, goes to personal affront and not to core concerns with the equality of all persons. Accordingly, posting a sign in a local bar that states "no Turks allowed" does not necessarily give rise to a cause of action under the German civil or criminal code provisions protecting personal honor. Why? Because the total rejection of another person based on his membership in a particular racial or ethnic group is not the same as a targeted personal insult.[276] Professor Whitman explains:

> It is important to recognize, though, that the *broader* German commitment to respectful treatment is somewhat less far-reaching. Members of other groups [besides Jews]—notably Turks, the focus of disproportionate hostility in the German public sphere today—are certainly protected against insults, like all Germans. But allegations of anti-Turkish insults, unlike allegations of anti-Jewish ones, are subjected to the usual juristic

analysis, that is, to a factual inquiry as to whether they display an intentional "lack of respect or disrespect" on the part of the person delivering the insult. This is why bar owners who post signs excluding Turks may not have committed an "insult" under German law. The operative question, under the law of insult, is again whether the individual bar owner has indulged in an open and unambiguous display of "his *own* lack of respect for the victim."[277]

Thus, Germany's insult and hate speech laws are not really designed either to create or maintain comprehensive social equality.

For example, if a Turkish woman driving a car gives "the bird" to a fellow driver after being cut off, the woman, if caught and identified, could be prosecuted civilly for insult.[278] If the other driver, in response, called the woman a "Turkish whore," it is far from certain whether a claim would lie, under either the laws of personal insult or the anti-hate speech laws. In a reported case from 1978, a German trial court found no actionable insult on these facts because the matter was "trivial"—although a state appeals court reversed, finding that also calling the woman a "witch" might be actionable.[279] German law simply "does not aim to guarantee an atmosphere of dignity" or "establish structural ground rules for respectful interracial relations that will operate regardless of the (ever-elusive) subjective intent of the persons involved."[280]

This explanation helps to square the German legal system's historical failure to afford full civil rights, including suffrage, to non-citizen permanent residents. The apparent contradiction is more imagined than real: the goals of the civility laws regulating speech are about protecting personal dignity from direct insult, not about the creation of an inclusive and egalitarian society. And, even this commitment is somewhat shaky when one focuses on unpopular immigrant groups, like the Turks. Understood in this way, the failure (until 2000 in any event) to provide citizenship to literally thousands of permanent residents and their children becomes a great deal less puzzling.

Does Germany protect the freedom of speech? Undeniably, the answer is yes.[281] But the Federal Constitutional Court has broadly and consistently declined to afford the freedom of speech the primacy that it enjoys in the United States. In part, this reflects a constitution that elevates dignity above free speech and specifically and strictly limits free speech itself. But, in a broader sense, Germany's treatment of free speech reflects a larger cultural fact: free speech is less important to Germans than personal honor. In the United States, there simply is no comparable legal protection for personal honor or reputation: "American law has, it must be emphasized, remarkably little to say about norms of hierarchical respect."[282] Thus, "American law is just different."[283]

I would not assert that U.S. free speech law is inherently superior to German law. The legal systems, and indeed, both the legal and broader cultures, achieve different results by design, and not by accident. It would make little sense to criticize the Constitutional Court for failing to advance values that the Justices of that Court self-consciously choose to subordinate in order to advance other values. One also would be hard pressed to make a serious case that Germany does not protect free speech. China does not respect free speech, but Germany certainly is not China. Although Germany protects less speech than the United States, a great deal of speech does enjoy formal constitutional protection.

The German approach deals a serious blow to efforts to establish a universal definition of "the freedom of speech." Indeed, as Professor Currie suggests, "[e]xamination of the German law of free expression reminds one once again how easily two well-intentioned societies, starting from substantially identical premises, can arrive at significantly different results."[284] German constitutional law defines free speech in a plausible way and reflects a sophisticated, and highly nuanced jurisprudence. The Constitutional Court has endorsed neither a "marketplace of ideas" nor a paradigm that absolutely privileges speech annexed to the project of democratic self-governance.

Free speech, of course, has an important role in self-governance, but the German Constitutional Court has made clear that free speech can accomplish this role without reaching hate speech, speech opposing the basic democratic order, or speech that impinges on personal dignity and honor. Although one can finds strains of Holmes and Meiklejohn in the opinions of the Federal Constitutional Court, the melody is radically different. Outside observers also should take care not to overstate the German Constitutional Court's equality project. The limitations on free speech only incidentally advance equality. Their principal purpose and effect is to advance an overarching civility project and the protection of personal reputation represents one piece of this larger project.

V. Conclusion

Consideration of the German example suggests two important problems that proponents of greater regulation of hate speech in the United States must address. First, German hate speech regulations are part and parcel of a larger effort to protect human dignity and personal honor. Indeed, the subordinated position of free speech significantly predates adoption of the Basic Law and reflects cultural values largely absent in the contemporary United States.[285]

Second, hate speech laws are a very poor substitute for formal legal equality. Equal citizenship, now possible thanks to the German government's recent naturalization reforms, will do more to empower racial and ethnic minorities in Germany in the years to come than the hate speech laws have accomplished in several decades. In considering how to create an egalitarian society, rules requiring polite interaction should probably constitute a lesser priority than securing more basic civil rights, such as suffrage. Simply put, hate speech laws should not serve as a substitute for formal rights to participate in the project of democratic deliberation— happily, something that the German government has acknowledged and acted to remedy.

5

Freedom of Speech in Japan

Disentangling Culture, Community, and Freedom of Expression

Article 21 of the Japanese Constitution guarantees the citizens of Japan the freedom of speech and presents an excellent subject for cross-cultural study of the freedom of expression.[1] This is because Japan intentionally and self-consciously (though perhaps not voluntarily)[2] decided to guarantee freedom of speech from government abridgment. Japan did so in the aftermath of the Second World War by adopting the Constitution of 1947, which contains Article 21, a provision that explicitly protects freedom of expression.[3] Prior to the adoption of the Constitution of 1947, Japanese citizens did not enjoy an effective generalized right of freedom of expression.[4] On the contrary, from the Meiji Restoration in 1868 to Emperor Hirohito's surrender on General MacArthur's battleship in Tokyo Bay in 1945, constitutional rights under the Meiji Constitution were subject to legislative abrogation.[5] As a general matter, the relationship of imperial subjects to the emperor and his government revolved around the duties and obligations that the former owed to the latter. The idea of asserting formal legal rights against the Chrysanthemum Throne was a theoretical possibility, but even in the absence of legislative abrogation had little, if any, cultural salience.[6]

Japan also presents a good candidate for a case study because it, like the United States, is an industrialized democracy. Both the United States and Japan have enjoyed a long period of economic prosperity in the latter half of the twentieth century. To the extent that differences exist in legal norms, they are not the products of radically different economic circumstances.

On the other hand, many commentators have argued that Japanese society is radically different from the United States in myriad ways: Japan is much more homogeneous, Japanese are inherently conformists, Japanese place much less reliance on lawyers and formal legal institutions than do Americans, and so forth.[7] Accordingly, one would not expect the Japanese version of the First Amendment to bear much resemblance to its American cousin. As it happens, one would be wrong to harbor such an assumption.

The Japanese Supreme Court seems to share many of the same theoretical insights about the role and importance of free speech that the United States Supreme Court has articulated over the past half century. The Supreme Court of Japan, for example, has framed free speech questions in terms immediately familiar to students of the First Amendment, routinely linking free speech values with the project of democratic self-government.

At the same time, however, one should be careful not to overstate the similarities. For instance, the Japanese Supreme Court largely has failed to strike resounding blows in favor of freedom of speech, principally for reasons related to the Court's view of its proper institutional role within the Japanese constitutional framework and within Japanese society more broadly. In addition, Japan also offers a cautionary note on the potential importance of nongovernmental restrictions on freedom of speech.[8]

In sum, the Japanese experience provides valuable lessons about the potential for successful line-drawing based on the relationship of speech to democratic self-governance. Careful study of the freedom of speech in Japan should lead to a more insightful understanding of our domestic speech rights and a heightened awareness of the implicit costs and benefits associated with maintaining these rights.[9]

I. An Introduction to Japanese Constitutional Law

The Supreme Court of Japan's insistence on a clear linkage between constitutionally protected free speech and the project of democratic self-governance represents the most salient characteristic of Japan's iteration of the right to freedom of expression. The Supreme Court of Japan has firmly and consistently demanded a clear nexus between expressive activity and the project of democratic self-government before affording speech activity constitutional protection under Article 21. Thus, the free speech decisions of the Supreme Court of Japan are much more consistent with Meiklejohn's vision of freedom of expression than comparable decisions of the United States Supreme Court.

The Japanese Supreme Court generally has proven unwilling to interpose—at least directly—the constitutional guarantee of freedom of expression over legislative or executive acts;[10] nevertheless, it has exhibited a strong and abiding appreciation for the importance of free speech in a participatory democracy. Moreover, the Supreme Court consistently has read statutory and administrative restrictions on freedom of expression narrowly in order to minimize their impact.[11] At the same time, government authorities have not attempted to censor speech activities on any widespread basis. Indeed, Japanese political parties offer voters a much broader political spectrum from which to choose than U.S. citizens at present enjoy[12] and Japanese elections are usually highly competitive.[13]

To the extent freedom of speech faces serious threats in Japan, these threats are much more a function of *privately* imposed constraints than of official government repression or censorship.[14] In this regard, the Japanese experience offers a cautionary tale for the United States. It is not always the government that is the enemy of freedom of expression;[15] corporations, churches, and communities can be far more effective at stifling dissent than bureaucrats and misguided police chiefs.[16]

A. The Constitutional Text

As in the United States, freedom of expression in Japan enjoys explicit constitutional protection. Article 21 of the Japanese Constitution guarantees to all citizens "[f]reedom of assembly and association as well as speech, press and all other forms of expression."[17] In addition, it provides that "[n]o censorship shall be maintained, nor shall the secrecy of any means of communication be violated."[18]

Like the Free Speech Clause in the U.S. First Amendment, the right to freedom of expression is unqualified as written; Article 21 does not invite the judiciary to balance the right of freedom of expression against other public interests. The textually unqualified nature of the right notwithstanding, the Supreme Court of Japan routinely has balanced the individual's interest in freedom of expression against other private interests[19] and public interests.[20] The Supreme Court of the United States has, of course, also engaged in similar balancing exercises.[21] Such balancing exercises are, to a large extent, unavoidable. From time to time, rights collide and courts are forced to establish a proper boundary line between competing constitutional interests.[22]

Moreover, the Japanese Constitution invites balancing, although it does not require it. Article 12 provides that "[t]he freedoms and rights guaranteed to the people by this Constitution shall be maintained by the constant endeavor of the people, who shall refrain from any abuse of these freedoms and rights and shall always be responsible for utilizing them for the public welfare."[23] This notion of "abuse of rights" establishes a textual justification for weighing the cost of an individual's or group's exercise of a particular right against the relative cost of such exercise to the community as a whole.[24] As in the United States, however, this balancing of interests does not necessarily redound in favor of the state.[25] Indeed, the mandate to balance has proven far less deadly to the protection of constitutional rights in Japan than in Canada, where textually mandated balancing has led the Canadian Supreme Court to reject speech claims routinely, sometimes in favor of other rights (such as equality) and other times in favor of generalized social interests.[26]

Significantly, the Japanese Constitution, unlike its American counterpart, directly vests the judiciary with the power of judicial review. "The Supreme Court is the court of last resort with power to determine the constitutionality of any law, order, regulation or official act."[27]

Finally, the Supreme Court of Japan, like the United States Supreme Court, has required a showing of state action as a prerequisite to invoking successfully a constitutional right. Thus, a private company's decision to fire three employees who circulated to their fellow employees communist tracts critical of the company and its policies did not implicate Article 21's guarantee of freedom of speech.[28] Government played no role in the decision, and therefore Article 21 simply did not apply; the dispute was purely a private matter.[29]

B. The Japanese Constitutional Style

Although the Japanese Supreme Court enjoys a textual mandate to protect freedom of expression and a textual right to exercise the power of judicial review, it has never struck down a local, prefectural, or national ordinance or law on free speech grounds.[30] It has, however, recently signaled that it will not sustain *every* governmental program abridging academic freedom. A panel of the Supreme Court of Japan has held that the Ministry of Education's program of approving textbooks for use in the public schools violates the academic freedom of an author whose works were rejected on purely ideological grounds.[31] Whether this decision reflects a new trend or simply an additional datum on the preexisting free speech jurisprudential framework remains to be seen. Indeed, given that the Japanese Supreme Court has struck down national legislation only five times in as many decades,[32] something more than a single five-Justice panel decision will be needed to establish the existence of a new, more activist tradition. As the saying goes, one swallow does not a summer make.

In its boldest line of cases to date, the Supreme Court declared the Diet's electoral districts to be so badly malapportioned as to violate the Japanese Constitution's guarantee of equal protection of the laws.[33] Even in this series of decisions, however, the Supreme Court declined to void the election results, preferring instead to allow the (malapportioned) legislative bodies at issue to take corrective action.[34]

Although the Japanese Supreme Court has proven exceedingly reluctant to strike down legislative work product, it has given concrete meaning to the Constitution's various guarantees, most often by describing the contours of a constitutional right and the limits of legislative discretion without holding that a particular law transgresses the line established by the Court.[35] Lower Japanese courts, including both district courts and the high courts (the intermediate courts of appeal), have not proven so reticent: A number of the Supreme Court's free speech decisions reverse lower court decisions that held in favor of the litigants challenging the government behavior at issue.[36]

One could conclude that the Japanese Supreme Court's unwillingness to hold unconstitutional legislative work product or executive branch behavior demonstrates the weakness of Article 21's guarantee of freedom of expression. Although this interpretation is tenable, it is too simplistic and fails to appreciate the effect of the Supreme Court's line-drawing efforts.[37] Moreover, to the extent that it implies a lack of appreciation for the value of freedom of expression on the part of the Japanese Supreme Court, it is also quite inaccurate.

Before the promulgation of the Constitution of 1947, the Japanese courts did not enjoy the power of judicial review over properly promulgated legislative enactments that specifically overrode particular constitutional guarantees.[38] Japan's Meiji Constitution borrowed heavily from the German and French civil law traditions. These traditions largely relegated the judiciary to enforcing the code provisions adopted by the Diet and approved by the emperor;[39] as in the present-day United Kingdom, the courts did not possess the constitutional authority to strike down legislation or executive action.[40]

The Constitution of 1947 modified this scheme. Japan currently maintains a parliamentary system of government with an independent judiciary that enjoys the power of judicial review.[41] To date, however, the judiciary has proven to be extremely deferential to the political branches of government.[42] In a functioning participatory democracy, this deference makes a great deal of sense: the political branches are directly accountable to the people, and their actions therefore deserve a presumption of legitimacy.[43] Thus, that the Japanese Supreme Court has not routinely struck down laws or executive actions that burden the exercise of speech rights reflects less a lack of respect for freedom of expression than a lack of comfort with interposing the judiciary's will over that of elected officials.[44]

This deference is hardly unique to speech rights. Across the board, the Japanese Supreme Court has strained to sustain government actions that appear to conflict with constitutional restrictions.[45] The question naturally arises: Of what value are constitutional rights if the Supreme Court generally refuses to enjoin legislative or executive actions that abridge them?

It is difficult to offer any simple responses. Litigants continue to press constitutionally guaranteed rights before both the Supreme Court and the lower courts; if Japanese citizens viewed these constitutional rights as empty, they would probably not bother to assert them at all.[46] Moreover, the Japanese Supreme Court routinely selects "prominent" cases for translation into English. Even a cursory perusal of these documents reflects the perceived importance of Article 21 cases: Of the twenty-seven cases selected for translation into English from 1947 to 1998, ten involve claims arising under Article 21.[47]

It is unthinkable that the Justices of the Japanese Supreme Court would undertake special efforts to make these decisions more widely available outside Japan if they thought the opinions would reflect badly on the Japanese Supreme Court or the Japanese legal system as a whole.[48] Thus, it seems likely that the Supreme Court's efforts to circulate these decisions in the United States and other English-speaking jurisdictions reflects pride in its work product and an implicit assumption that the decisions will wear well in foreign jurisdictions.

Perhaps most importantly, Japanese citizens continue to press claims premised on Article 21's guarantee of freedom of expression. In Japan, "the threat of a lawsuit or criminal complaint may produce a positive reaction" because of concerns that lawsuits, whether civil or criminal in nature, "damage reputation."[49] According to Professor John Haley, "[t]he social stigma of the disclosure of wrongdoing can function as an equally effective and far more efficient substitute for state coercion."[50] Thus, whether a litigant prevails before the Supreme Court may not be as important as the fact of the lawsuit itself; to the extent that a lawsuit brings a government agency into direct conflict with members of the community, it detracts from the agency's standing within the community. In contemporary Japan, lawsuits constitute a powerful form of political action.[51]

This explanation of the existence and frequency of "hopeless" lawsuits raising constitutional claims also makes sense in a society that prizes social harmony, or *wa,* and consensus-based decision making.[52] In traditional Japanese villages, decision making took place through an informal system of give-and-take aimed at reaching a unanimous decision.[53] Professor Nakane explains that in such villages, "[i]t is most important that a meeting should reach a unanimous conclusion; it should leave no one frustrated or dissatisfied, for this weakens village or group unity and solidarity."[54] Such an ethic empowers dissenters while at the same time imposing a high opportunity cost on persistent dissent—simply put, dissent is both effective and disfavored.

It is difficult to overstate the importance of consensus. For example, Professor Benedict has reported that, even during World War II, prominent Japanese leaders recognized the importance of free speech to building consensus and to maintaining group commitment to a particular objective or task.[55]

On balance, it seems that the Supreme Court's reticence to strike down legislative and executive actions burdening speech rights has much less to do with the level of solicitude the Supreme Court grants freedom of expression than with the Supreme Court's own view of its proper constitutional role. Moreover, considered in cultural context, this reticence may prove to be a distinction without a difference: "Protracted litigation calls into question the legitimacy of the political system with consequently greater likelihood—albeit no certainty—of a political response."[56] To the extent that litigation demonstrates the absence of social consensus, it undercuts the legitimacy of the government's objectives and impedes the government's ability to implement contested policy objectives.

II. Freedom of Speech in Japan: Rhetoric, Revision, and Meiklejohn's Theory of Freedom of Speech

The Japanese Supreme Court has recognized and broadly endorsed the proposition that freedom of speech is a necessary condition for democratic self-government. As Justice Ito Masami of the Supreme Court of Japan has explained, "[c]onstitutionally guaranteed freedom of expression forms the central pillar of a state based on liberalism, and the United States and Japan have constitutional systems that provide the strongest guarantees of this freedom in the world."[57] Because of the notable lack of success enjoyed by plaintiffs, one might reasonably question whether the decisions of the Japanese Supreme Court entirely support Justice Masami's assertion that freedom of speech is a "central pillar" of Japanese constitutional law.

A. Canvassing the Voters

Consider, for example, the severe restrictions that limit political speech incident to elections.[58] Japan maintains a pervasive system of restraints that restrict the time, place, and manner of canvassing the electorate for support; not only are candidates' activities restricted, but these laws also subject the press to strict limitations on its coverage of candidates and candidate activities.[59] The Supreme Court of Japan has both sustained convictions and overturned acquittals for violations of the Election Law's ban on door-to-door canvassing.[60] These results contrast vividly with the United States Supreme Court's treatment of door-to-door canvassing in cases such as *Cantwell v. Connecticut*[61] and on the First Amendment right of individuals to support or oppose candidates for political office set forth in *Buckley v. Valeo.*[62]

Although a number of American legal academics have advocated public financing of political campaigns, limits on campaign spending, and similar measures to level the playing field and reduce the influence of special interest contributions,[63] all of these proposals pale in comparison to the restrictions imposed by the Election Law, such as prohibitions on door-to-door canvassing by candidates for office and strict limits on candidates' purchase of television and radio time for promotional advertisements.[64] To be sure, Japan conducts meaningful elections, and voters have access to information about candidates for political office from myriad sources. Even so, the Election Law seems to place significant restraints on core political speech.

Professor Curtis has explained that

[t]he result of this system of legal restraints and the institutionalization of modes for circumventing them has been to turn the election law into a kind of obstacle course through and around which candidates move in their search for votes, rather than an accepted and respected framework within which campaigns are conducted.[65]

Thus, the net effects of the Election Law may be somewhat less draconian than one would otherwise expect. Essentially, Curtis is asserting that the Election Law constitutes *tatemae,* or the official line, rather than *honne,* or the actual situation.[66] The problem, as seen through American eyes, is that the theoretical proposition that there can be too much political speech is fundamentally inconsistent with the guarantee of freedom of expression.[67] Nevertheless, neither legislative nor judicial change is in the air. "Although deregulation in other areas of Japanese life has become a major thrust of recent government policy and has been forced on often reluctant bureaucrats, there is no strong constituency advocating the deregulation of election campaigning."[68]

The Election Law reflects a desire to minimize the disruptive impact of elections, even at the cost of squelching speech and limiting the channels through which candidates can reach the voters.[69] This elevates civility over speech and limits deliberation to protect privacy. Simply put, the Japanese have struck a radically different balance between the respective rights of would-be speakers and their potential audience: In Japan, the interests of the audience in being free from unwanted speech in no small measure outweigh the interests of the speaker in being heard.

B. Time, Place, and Manner Regulations

In a series of cases beginning in the 1950s, the Japanese Supreme Court has sustained a variety of time, place, and manner restrictions on speech activities on public property. The United States Supreme Court has, of course, endorsed the creation and enforcement of content-neutral, reasonable time, place, and manner restrictions on the use of public property for speech activities.[70] This basic framework has been supplemented with a "public forum" gloss that permits government to further restrict access to certain public property: nonpublic and limited-purpose public forums.[71] Thus, in the United States, a citizen does not enjoy an unfettered right of access to public spaces for the purpose of engaging in speech activity. That said, unpopular political minorities do have a right to use public spaces under the same terms and conditions as other citizens; moreover, government may not unreasonably withhold its permission or impose less favorable terms and conditions on disfavored groups for the use of public forums for speech activities.[72]

The Japanese Supreme Court has sustained local ordinances that, on their face, confer effectively unfettered discretion on local authorities to grant or withhold permission for the use of public property for speech activity. Cases involving local ordinances from Niigata and Tokyo provided the vehicles for the Supreme Court's review of the issue.

In the *Niigata Ordinance Decision*,[73] a Niigata prefectural ordinance prohibited citizens from engaging in public demonstrations without first obtaining the permission of local police authorities.[74] These officials could refuse permission or place restrictions on the protest activity in order to protect the public safety or welfare.[75] However, if they failed to respond to a request within twenty-four hours of a planned march, the speech activity could proceed as though permission had been granted.[76]

The Japanese Supreme Court sustained the ordinance, reasoning that it really required little more than advance notice of the planned speech activity.[77] The Court emphasized the limited nature of the local authorities' discretion to deny a permit and suggested that permission could be denied only "if it is foreseen that [the activity] may involve a clear and present danger to the public safety."[78] Essentially, the Supreme Court saved the local ordinance by imposing a limiting interpretation on the law enforcement authorities' discretion.[79]

The Court had occasion to revisit its holding in the *Niigata Ordinance Decision* in the *Tokyo Ordinance Decision*.[80] Like the Niigata prefecture, the City of Tokyo adopted an ordinance requiring notification and permission for mass marches and demonstrations.[81] The ordinance required the permission of the local public safety commission before engaging in meetings or mass parades on public property and for mass demonstrations, whether on public or private property.[82] Article 3 of the ordinance required local police officials to grant permission unless the proposed speech activity "is recognized as clearly and directly dangerous to the maintenance of public peace."[83] Unlike the Niigata ordinance, affirmative permission was required prior to any covered speech activity; silence on the part of local officials did not imply consent.

A group of protestors violated the ordinance, engaging in unapproved protest activity. Following their arrest, the Tokyo district court acquitted them of wrongdoing based on Article 21's guarantee of freedom of expression and assembly.[84] The public prosecutor then took a direct appeal (or *jokoku* appeal) to the Supreme Court, based on the constitutional issues presented in the case.

The Supreme Court began its opinion by recognizing the importance of the interest at stake:

> There is no need to dwell upon the fact that the freedom of assembly and association, as well as the freedom of speech, press and all other forms of expression provided for in Article 21 of the Constitution of Japan, belongs to eternal and inviolate rights, the basic human rights and that the absolute guarantee of the above is one of the fundamental rules and characteristics of democratic form[s] of government which distinguishes democracy from totalitarianism.[85]

Nevertheless, Article 21 rights were subject to "abuse," and the Supreme Court viewed its task as "protecting the freedom of expression, preventing its abuse, maintaining harmony with the public welfare, and of drawing a line which would provide a reasonable demarcation between the freedom of the individuals and the welfare of the public with regard to concrete indi[v]idual cases."[86]

Noting the dangers associated with mass protest and movements, the Court observed that "a local entity may be justified in imposing certain restrictions with respect to the freedom of expression, involving group demonstration notwithstanding the clear prohibition of pre-control, the censorship of publications, etc."[87] The majority then went on to adopt a restrictive interpretation of the Tokyo ordinance. Although the text of the ordinance seemed to adopt a permissive system of regulation, vesting substantial autonomy with local officials to grant or deny requests, "in its substance and in operation," the ordinance really "differs little from a notification system."[88] The Court held that the "granting of permission is almost imperative, and rejection, under strict restriction only under very rare circumstances," namely, when a clear and present danger of public harm exists.[89] The majority also rejected objections to the regulation of speech activity on nonpublic property, noting that the harms associated with mass demonstrations did not differ based on the ownership of the property.[90]

The Japanese Supreme Court was comfortable vesting significant discretion with local authorities, subject to the admonition that this discretion should not be exercised absent an immediate threat of substantial harm. Thirteen of the Supreme Court's fifteen Justices endorsed the opinion of the Court; two Justices dissented. The decision represented a major expansion of the limitations upheld in the *Niigata Ordinance Decision.* It is also doubtful that the United States Supreme Court would have reached a similar conclusion on the facts presented.[91]

In dissent, Justice Hachiro Fujita emphasized that "the full guarantee of the freedom of expression provided in Article 21 . . . is one of the most important basic principles of [a] democratic form of government."[92] Fujita noted that the majority in the *Niigata* decision had sanctioned only a system of prior notification, not a "general permissive system."[93] In his view, Article 21 precluded local authorities from assuming a censorial role, even if that role were strictly limited.[94] He went on to cite *Hague v. CIO*[95] and *Saia v. New York*[96] for the proposition that freedom of speech is inconsistent with discretionary permitting schemes administered by local functionaries.[97]

Justice Katsumi Tarumi also authored a dissent.[98] Tarumi objected to the ordinance's attempt to regulate speech on both public and private property,[99] and to the drafters' use of vague standards[100] and definitions.[101] He also objected to the majority's attempt to place a limiting construction on the Tokyo ordinance in order to save it from being declared unconstitutional: "As long as it relates to the control of freedom of expression, it seems highly improper to render construction in such a way as to make it constitutional as . . . was done in the majority opinion."[102]

Notwithstanding the significant cultural differences that separate the United States and Japan, Justice Tarumi's dissent echoes the main themes of Justice Holmes's dissent in *Abrams*:[103]

> Every individual is capable of thinking freely of what is true, good and beautiful through his concept in the fields of religion, creed, morals, sciences, the world, and human existence; or in his respective fields of endeavor in society, such as in politics, economics, culture and arts. . . . If law and the government do not exercise control over speech, and permit free competition of expression, truth would finally prevail, and it may even be possible for all the varieties of flowers to bloom in profusion and bear fruits in amity. A complete unanimity of mind should be rejected.[104]

Justice Tarumi plainly embraced Holmes's marketplace of ideas metaphor. In turn, this intellectual commitment led him to reject the majority's decision to leave the Tokyo ordinance in place. Any doubts in this regard can be resolved by reference to his subsequent argument that freedom of speech does not guarantee any particular outcomes.

After setting forth the litany of horrors associated with Soviet-style communism, Justice Tarumi concluded that freedom of speech required the government to tolerate those who advocated such a system.[105] As Justice Tarumi explained, in Japan "[p]eople may listen to such a talk to their heart's content. Such is the tolerance of thought embodied in the liberal Constitution."[106]

Both the majority and dissenting Justices in the *Tokyo Ordinance Decision* fully embraced freedom of expression. Moreover, both sides defined the debate about the proper scope of Article 21 in terms immediately familiar to students of the First Amendment. The majority embraces Meiklejohn's community-based vision of the freedom of expression, justifying the protection of freedom of speech by reference to its role in facilitating democratic self-governance. Justice Tarumi's dissent, on the other hand, invokes the Holmesian marketplace of ideas metaphor. Notwithstanding the significant differences in culture, the Justices framed the free speech issues in largely the same terms that the United States Supreme Court would have used if faced with deciding the case.

Unlike the United States Supreme Court, however, the Supreme Court of Japan more fully embraced a community-based theory of freedom of speech. It is not the individual's interest in self-expression but, rather, the community's interest in overseeing the government, which is paramount.

Turning from theory to doctrine, the majority's opinion in the *Tokyo Ordinance* case places free expression at risk by trusting in the good faith of local authorities to grant permission absent a clear and present danger of public harm. The Japanese Supreme Court's rejection of a "bad tendency" test, however, is far more intriguing than the inconsistency of the majority's result with *Hague* and *Saia*. That is to say, not a single Justice endorsed the proposition that government may regulate speech deemed potentially harmful to the public because of its ideological content. Yet, less than a century ago, the United States Supreme Court sustained criminal convictions on just such a theory.[107] As recently as 1951, the Supreme Court sustained the conviction of a group of Communists based on a perilously overbroad "bad tendencies" theory of the First Amendment.[108]

The *Tokyo Ordinance* majority's formulation of the problem also implicitly reflects a commitment to the project of viewpoint neutrality. Only danger to the public—not hostility toward the content of a particular speaker's message—can serve as a basis for denying access to public property for speech-related activities. As Professor Sunstein has explained, "[w]hen government regulates on the basis of viewpoint, it will frequently be acting for objectionable reasons."[109] By prohibiting local officials from refusing permission for speech activities based on the viewpoint or content of the speaker's message, the Supreme Court of Japan conferred substantial protection on would-be speakers.[110]

Indeed, rather than snipe at the Japanese Supreme Court's work product, one should marvel at the fundamental transformation worked by the Constitution of 1947: In the space of less than two decades, a nation that had never recognized an unqualified legal right to freedom of expression or participatory democracy embraced both concepts.[111] This represents a remarkable accomplishment. By way of comparison, the United States Congress passed the Alien and Sedition Act of 1798 only seven years after the adoption of the First Amendment, and the Supreme Court did not definitively reject the view that the state could punish seditious libel until 1964, in *New York Times Co. v. Sullivan*.[112] In relative terms, then, the Japanese free speech tradition should be viewed as a success.

C. Democratic Self-Government and the Meiklejohn Theory in Other Political Speech Decisions of the Supreme Court of Japan

The Japanese Supreme Court, like its United States counterpart, has tied freedom of expression to the project of democratic self-governance in contexts other than public forum cases. Take, for example, *Japan v. Kanemoto*,[113] also known as the *Kanemoto Pamphlet Case*. A number of radicals distributed pamphlets advocating the violent overthrow of the Japanese government and were arrested, tried, and convicted of violating the Subversive Activities Prevention Law.[114] The Nagoya High Court, the intermediate appellate court, reversed the convictions on the ground that mere advocacy of the violent overthrow of the government was not a criminal act in the absence of a clear and present danger of concrete acts against the state.[115] The prosecutor appealed this reversal to the Supreme Court of Japan.

The Supreme Court affirmed the Nagoya High Court's decision, holding that the mere advocacy of insurrection against the government was not a criminal act. In so doing, the Court expressly rejected the prosecutor's argument that "speech whose very contents are contrary to the public welfare . . . clearly constitute[s] notable abuse of freedom of expression beyond the bounds of Article 21 guarantees."[116] This ruling is consistent with the Supreme Court's rejection of the "bad tendency" test in the *Niigata Ordinance* and *Tokyo Ordinance* cases.

A more recent decision involving the use of the Narita Airport for protest activities demonstrates the Supreme Court's continuing embrace of the clear and present danger standard for the restriction of protest activity. In *Sanrizuka-Shibayama Anti-Airport League v. Okuda*,[117] the Supreme Court sustained a statute limiting protest activities at the new Tokyo International Airport.[118] The new airport had proven controversial, and radical elements had attempted to impede its progress; these efforts included acts of violence, such as driving a blazing vehicle into the airport, throwing Molotov cocktails into the airport, and destroying equipment inside the airport.[119] In response to these acts of terrorism, the Diet enacted a law to prohibit violent protest activities at the new airport.[120] Entitled "Law on Emergency Measures for the Security of the New Tokyo International Airport," the measure empowered the Minister of Transport to prohibit speech activity at the airport when "violent and destructive activities" might be imminent.[121] Would-be anti-airport protestors challenged the constitutionality of this law, arguing that it infringed their Article 21 right to freedom of expression.

The Japanese Supreme Court sustained the law, but imposed a limiting construction on its rather open-ended terms. Although the provisions of the law did not specify the level of danger required to close the airport to speech activities, the majority read the law to require a clear and present danger of violence: "[I]t can be inferred that the phrase 'anyone who engages in, or is suspected of engaging in, violent and destructive activities' in Article 2(2) of the Law should be interpreted as 'anyone who actually engages in, or is highly likely to engage in, violent and destructive activities.' "[122] In addition, the Supreme Court read the phrase "when the structure is used, or is suspected of being used" for prohibited activities to mean "when the structure is actually used, or is found highly likely to be used" for such activities.

As written, the law appeared to confer virtually limitless discretion on the Minister of Transport. The Supreme Court's gloss, however, adroitly avoided a conflict between the law and Article 21 by strictly limiting the Minister's authority to restrict speech activity under the law's provisions.

Though the United States Supreme Court would probably have insisted on a system of independent review to ensure that the Minister did not arbitrarily apply the law to discriminate against a particular group or viewpoint,[123] it is virtually certain that it would sustain a statute aimed at ensuring that airports remain open and accessible for those wishing to travel (which would necessarily imply an airport free of protestors tossing about Molotov cocktails).[124]

Perhaps more important than the Japanese Supreme Court's limiting construction of the statute was its frank recognition of the importance of freedom of speech in a democratic society. The Supreme Court began its analysis of the protestors' Article 21 claim by acknowledging the linkage of freedom of speech to a functioning democracy:

> In a modern democratic society, assembly by the people is needed in order for them to develop and form their views and personalities by being exposed to a variety of opinions and information, and by conveying and exchanging opinions, information and the like. It is also an effective means by which they may make their views known to the general public. Hence, the freedom of assembly guaranteed by Article 21(1) of the Constitution should be especially respected as one of the fundamental human rights in a democratic society.[125]

Alexander Meiklejohn himself could have authored these words; they embrace and embody his conception of freedom of speech.[126] The *New Narita Airport Decision* not only demonstrates the extent to which the Japanese judiciary has embraced freedom of expression as a preferred freedom under the Japanese Constitution but also reflects the Justices' essentially communitarian conception of the right.

D. The Importance of Community

Although recognizing the importance of the free flow of ideas and information to democratic self-government,[127] the Japanese Supreme Court has been very solicitous of communal interests. This is reflected, in part, in its case law considering the constitutionality of the Election Law's restrictions on candidate canvassing. It is also reflected in *Yamagishi v. Japan*,[128] a case involving the use of public utility poles for posters promoting a conference supporting a nuclear weapons ban.[129] The protestors were charged with and convicted of a misdemeanor for hanging the posters without obtaining prior permission from the poles' owners.[130] They appealed their convictions to the Supreme Court, arguing that the convictions violated their Article 21 right to free expression.[131] Because the anti-war activists had not sought permission to use the poles, the question of what standard to apply to a state actor's denial of permission to use the poles for posting political messages was not presented for decision. Rather, the issue before the Supreme Court was whether publicly and privately owned poles could be unilaterally commandeered for speech activity.

The Supreme Court affirmed the convictions, observing that "a means for outwardly expressing one's ideas has never been permissible if that means is such as to do unfair damage to the property rights of other persons."[132] Accordingly, the appellants failed to state a viable Article 21 claim. The *Yamagishi* decision reaches the same result as a similar United States Supreme Court decision, *City Council v. Taxpayers for Vincent.*[133] Moreover, it does so for similar reasons: freedom of speech does not imply an unqualified right of access to public or private property for use incidental to speech activities.

III. The Case of Defamation: Balancing the Personal and the Political

Defamation provides another area of law in which the Japanese Supreme Court has borrowed, at least to some extent, from the United States. In *Judgment Upon Case of Defamation,*[134] the Supreme Court broadly construed an exceptions clause to create a right of fair comment concerning matters of public concern. The defendant, Katsuyoshi Kawachi, published a newspaper, the *Yukan Wakayama Jiji.* On February 18, 1963, he accused the publisher of a rival publication of extorting monies from local officials.[135]

The Japanese law at issue, which dated from the turn of the century, punished defamation strictly: "A person who defames another by publicly alleging facts shall, regardless of whether such facts are true or false, be punished with imprisonment at forced labor or imprisonment for not more than three years or a fine of not more than 1,000 yen."[136] However, if a trial court found that the otherwise defamatory statement had been "committed solely for the benefit of the public and regarding matters of public concern and when, upon inquiry into the truth or falsity of the facts, the truth is proved, punishment shall not be imposed."[137] Thus, the exceptions clause appears to require a defendant to establish the literal truth of the allegedly defamatory statement in order to avoid liability; however, the Supreme Court of Japan saw it differently.

Reversing the judgments of the trial and appellate courts, the Supreme Court opined that freedom of expression and protection from defamation had to be balanced in order to protect both "personal security to honour of an individual and the freedom of speech provided for in Article 21 of the Constitution."[138] Accordingly, the Supreme Court construed the exceptions clause broadly to protect commentary on matters of public concern:

> Giving thought to the reconciliation and balance of these two interests, it should be construed that, even if there is no proof of the existence of the facts . . . , no crime of defamation was committed because of the absence of *mens rea,* when the publisher believed mistakenly in the existence of the facts and there was good reason for his mistaken belief on the basis of reliable information and grounds.[139]

Because the record showed that the publisher had established a reasonable basis in fact for believing the allegations to be true, he could not be held liable for defamation.[140]

Significantly, the Supreme Court did not declare any part of Article 230 of the Penal Code contrary to the Japanese Constitution; instead, it simply rewrote the exceptions clause to make it compatible with Article 21's guarantee of freedom of speech. In so doing, it was able to achieve two seemingly incompatible goals: protecting and enforcing freedom of expression without upsetting harmonious relations between the judicial and legislative branches. Of course, one could object to the Supreme Court's decision to revise unilaterally the text of the statute's exemptions clause. This course of action arguably constituted a more aggressive—and less legitimate—form of judicial activism than simply declaring Article 230 unconstitutional on its face.

Although the Japanese Supreme Court has recognized that freedom of expression must at times take precedence over protection of an individual's reputation, it has drawn the boundary between these two interests decidedly in favor of protecting reputation. In *Hoppo Journal Co. v. Japan,*[141] a divided Supreme Court affirmed an injunction against the distribution of the *Hoppo Journal.*[142] The trial court issued the injunction because the magazine contained defamatory statements about Kozo Igarashi, a local mayor who was preparing to run for governor of Hokkaido.[143] The

April 1979 issue of the magazine contained a story entitled "An Authoritarian's Temptation," which described Igarashi as "skillful at lying, bluffing and cheating," "a born liar," and "an opportunist without scruples, doing anything for his own interest and his own success."[144] With regard to Igarashi's personal life, the article asserted that "he divorced his innocent wife by dastardly means and caused her to commit suicide in order to win a new woman."[145] Nor were the editors content to malign poor Kozo. They also went after his family: "His father was a bold businessman famous in Asahikawa who had once been a roadhouse man. He blindly loved a beautiful young prostitute in his old age and the masterpiece of the two was [Igarashi]."[146] Suffice it to say that the *Hoppo Journal* pulled no punches.

Igarashi sought and obtained, on an ex parte basis, an injunction against the distribution of the magazine. Igarashi argued that the statements were defamatory per se as a matter of law and, if released, would cause him irreparable harm. The Sapporo High Court affirmed and the *Hoppo Journal* brought an appeal to the Supreme Court. Before the Supreme Court, the *Hoppo Journal* argued that the injunction constituted an unlawful form of censorship and that the magazine enjoyed the right to publish its news story on Igarashi under Article 21.

The Supreme Court rejected the magazine's argument that the injunction constituted "censorship" for purposes of Article 21's prohibition against government censorship. It emphasized that censorship, for purposes of Article 21, constituted viewpoint discrimination based on ideological or political grounds.[147] Because the magazine contained materials that were defamatory as a matter of law, the lower court simply had vindicated Igarashi's preexisting legal right without regard to the magazine's motivations for writing the story.[148]

This approach differs significantly from *New York Times Co. v. Sullivan*.[149] Alabama argued that application of its common law of torts did not constitute state action; accordingly, the First Amendment simply did not apply to the dispute between Commissioner Sullivan and the newspaper. Justice Brennan rejected this argument, explaining that "[t]he test is not the form in which state power has been applied but, whatever the form, whether such power has in fact been exercised."[150] Similarly, the fact that the injunction issued was based on a finding that Igarashi's legal rights were in jeopardy should not have resolved the issue of censorship.

Instead, the Japanese Supreme Court should have directly addressed the conflict between the censorial effect of the injunction and the legal claim at issue. At bottom, the *Hoppo Journal* was arguing that Article 21 protects defamatory statements. The Supreme Court could have rejected this argument directly: prohibiting the distribution of defamatory materials is not censorship because defamatory statements are not protected under Article 21 unless made in good faith and with a reasonable basis for belief in their veracity.[151]

Turning to the magazine's generalized claim of Article 21 protection, the Supreme Court noted that freedom of speech is critical to the survival of democracy:

> In a democratic nation where sovereign power resides with the people[152] the following is the foundation of its existence. That is, the people as constituents of that nation may express any doctrine, advocacy of doctrine and the like as well as receive such information from each other, and by taking whatever he believes rightful from among them of his own free will, majority opinion is formed, and government administration is determined through such process.[153]

Thus, when matters of public interest are at issue, speech must be protected even if false, provided that the speaker reasonably believes the speech to be truthful.[154] Consistent with the Meiklejohn approach, speech associated with the project of democratic self-government must be protected from government abridgment—not because everyone "has an unalienable right to speak whenever, wherever, however he chooses" but, rather, because "[t]he welfare of the community requires that those who decide issues shall understand them."[155] In the case at hand, however, the Justices concluded that the magazine had intended to publish the statements without the requisite good faith belief in their truth. Accordingly, the magazine could be enjoined, on an ex parte basis, from distributing the magazines containing the defamatory materials.

Returning to the theme of prior restraint, the Court noted that "it should be said that in light of the purport of Article 21 of the Constitution which guarantees the freedom of expression and prohibits censorship, prior restraint on acts of expression is allowed only under strict and definite requirements."[156] The Court later spelled out these requirements: "[A]n injunction should be exceptionally allowed only when it is obvious that the contents of expression are not true or its objectives are not solely in the public interest, and, moreover, when the victim may suffer serious and irreparable damage."[157] Igarashi satisfied these conditions and the Court therefore affirmed the district court's injunction.[158]

For the most part, the Supreme Court's logic is sound. To the extent that defamatory statements are not protected under Article 21, it is perfectly appropriate to provide injunctive relief burdening the publication of such statements. The problem lies in the Court's argument that the statements were obviously defamatory: if the statements were so obviously false, then no one would believe them; if no one believes the statements, then Igarashi suffers no harm. Indeed, the *Hoppo Journal's* exercise in attack journalism compares favorably with news stories in the United States taking up the public and private character of prominent national officials, such as Presidents Nixon and Clinton, and Speakers of the House Newt Gingrich and Jim Wright.

Arguably, the United States case most directly on point is *Hustler Magazine v. Falwell.*[159] In the now-infamous "Campari Ad," Larry Flynt's pornographic magazine suggested that Jerry Falwell, a prominent Baptist minister, first experienced sexual intercourse "during a drunken incestuous rendezvous with his mother in an outhouse."[160] In addition, the "ad" suggested that Falwell abused alcohol regularly and preached only when intoxicated. Falwell sued, and a jury found *Hustler Magazine* liable for intentional infliction of emotional distress.[161] The U.S. Court of Appeals for the Fourth Circuit affirmed.[162]

The United States Supreme Court reversed, holding that *Hustler's* parody of Falwell came within the protection of the First Amendment. Writing for a unanimous court, Chief Justice Rehnquist observed:

> The sort of robust political debate encouraged by the First Amendment is bound to produce speech that is critical of those who hold public office or those public figures who are "intimately involved in the resolution of important public questions or, by reason of their fame, shape events in areas of concern to society at large."[163]

In a fit of understatement, he then noted that "[s]uch criticism, inevitably, will not always be reasoned or moderate; public figures as well as public officials will be subject to vehement, caustic, and sometimes unpleasantly sharp attacks."[164]

The United States Supreme Court repeated its prior holding that false statements made with knowledge of their falsity or with reckless disregard for their truth or falsity remain actionable.[165] Speech aimed at inflicting emotional harm or holding an officeholder up to public ridicule, however, enjoys First Amendment protection. "[I]n the world of debate about public affairs, many things done with motives that are less than admirable are protected by the First Amendment."[166] In order to recover against a publisher, a plaintiff must show "that the publication contains a false statement of fact which was made with 'actual malice.'"[167]

If one read the *Hoppo Journal* story literally—and the Japanese Supreme Court so read the story—the result in the *Hoppo Journal Co.* case is not inconsistent with *Falwell* and *New York Times Co.* It is difficult, however, to understand how the Supreme Court of Japan could have read the story literally. The story made no attempt to be objective or to justify its wildest assertions; moreover, it was sprinkled with political invective: Igarashi is "an ugly character hiding behind a beautiful mask," a "cockroach," an "opportunist," a "magician with words and a street vendor quack," "a born liar," a "mayor like the rump of the bitch," and a "viperous Dosan." The imagery is fantastical, not factual.[168] Perhaps most important, the main point of the piece is political, not personal: Igarashi is "a useless and pernicious person to Hokkaido" and "the Japan Socialist Party should change the candidate for governorship immediately if reform is earnestly sought."[169]

No reasonable person reading the *Hoppo Journal*'s attack on Igarashi would take it literally. Although in the form of a news story, in substance the piece is an editorial. Nevertheless, the Supreme Court took the article at face value. "This issue of [the] magazine, having an expected first issue circulation of twenty-five thousand, was considered to be capable of seriously and almost irreparably defaming the said Appellee [Igarashi]. . . ."[170]

One is left with the firm conclusion that something in the *Hoppo Journal*'s catalog of insults and epithets truly irked the Justices. Yet, it is difficult to identify a specific statement that explains the result.[171]

It is certainly true that the Japanese traditionally have placed a very high premium on their good name and honor.[172] Professor Benedict argues that *giri* (duty) to one's name is a core component of Japanese social ethics. Although Japanese society is highly structured and marked by strong hierarchical patterns, personal insult invites—and perhaps even demands—revenge, even at the cost of breaching preexisting duties to social superiors.[173] Perhaps the Supreme Court's decision simply reflects an implicit recognition of the salience of *giri* to one's name and an assumption that a less protective rule would merely encourage resort to extralegal means of obtaining satisfaction. Whatever the precise motivations for the decision, it is difficult to believe that any reasonable reader would have taken the accusations against Igarashi literally.

Even the concurring Justice with the most expansive vision of freedom of speech joined the majority's conclusion that the article was not protected speech. Justice Masataka Taniguchi argued that in the context of an election, "the circulation of information which is necessary and useful to decision-making has priority over protection of reputation of the public servants or the candidates for elective public offices."[174] In order to avoid self-censorship and "to enable debate and decision-making on public matters, it is necessary to permit false speech as well."[175]

For Justice Taniguchi, as a general proposition, the solution to the problem of false speech is not censorship, but counterspeech:

> [E]ven if the contents of speech are false and statement of opinion is based on such false facts, presentation of the opinion and free debate will only compel reconsideration and re-examination of the dissenting opinion, and bring about deeper recognition of the reason to support such opinion and better understanding of the meaning of it.[176]

If false speech is made with actual malice (e.g., knowledge of its falsehood), however, it loses its protected status. Justice Taniguchi agreed with the majority that the *Hoppo Journal*'s article included knowingly false statements and was, therefore, not protected by Article 21.[177]

The defamation cases establish at least two important points: (1) the Japanese Supreme Court views freedom of speech as an essential corollary of democratic self-governance, and (2) the Justices are prepared to draw clear lines between protected and unprotected speech activity. The two positions need not be contradictory. In the United States, the Supreme Court's commitment to viewpoint neutrality and its related anti-censorship project have led the Justices to afford even marginal speech activity significant First Amendment protection.[178] The United States Supreme Court essentially has overprotected marginal speech activities in order to avoid creating a "chilling effect"[179] on protected speech activities.

The Japanese Supreme Court has taken the opposite tack. Although embracing freedom of expression insofar as speech relates to self-governance, it has refused to protect speech that does not directly further this effort. From the Supreme Court's perspective, a gross parody of a candidate for political office does not facilitate considered debate of his relative merits for office. In consequence, the parody should not enjoy Article 21 protection. Conversely, a newspaper reporting a story about corruption in city hall should be immune from liability if the story turns out to be false

—provided that the newspaper had a good faith belief in the truth of the story at the time it made its decision to publish it.

Implicit in the Japanese position is a rejection of the Holmesian marketplace model of free expression in favor the Meiklejohn and Brandeis conception of the town hall. If a person behaves in a rude, obnoxious, or obscene fashion during a town hall meeting, the person is escorted from the chamber, not tolerated.[180] Such behavior is antithetical to the consideration of the issues facing the community.

The marketplace of ideas, by way of contrast, potentially belongs to those with the deepest lungs or the fattest wallets, regardless of the merits of their contributions. In a true marketplace, Larry Flynt is as free to peddle his pornographic and scatological wares as a candidate for political office is to distribute her position papers. Government may not restrict Flynt's speech in order to enhance the relative voice of other speakers[181] nor may it do so because Flynt's speech is genuinely perceived to present a threat of harm to the community.[182] Under this view, as Justice Holmes explains, freedom of speech "is an experiment, as all life is an experiment."[183] It implies toleration of speech, including "the expression of opinions that we loathe and believe to be fraught with death."[184] The Supreme Court of Japan has protected the expression of ideas that it probably "loathes,"[185] but has been unwilling to prohibit government action aimed at restricting speech that is demonstrably harmful to the community or potentially disruptive of normal political processes.

The Japanese Supreme Court's defamation cases seem to reflect Meiklejohn's observation that "[t]he town meeting, as it seeks for freedom of public discussion of public problems, would be wholly ineffectual unless [disruptive and counterproductive] speech were thus abridged."[186] For the Supreme Court of Japan, as for Meiklejohn, freedom of speech is not "a dialectical free-for-all" but, rather, is "self-government."[187]

Indeed, community values permeate the Japanese Supreme Court's Article 21 jurisprudence. That is not to say that the Supreme Court has stood idly by while government officials silenced unpopular political minorities. Rather, the Supreme Court consistently has demonstrated a concern for public values when articulating the scope of Article 21 rights.

Both the defamation and political speech cases reflect a strong commitment to freedom of expression as it relates to democratic self-governance but not as a means of individual self-actualization or liberty. The community's interest in self-government justifies protecting speech related to self-government, but not ancillary—much less wholly unrelated—speech.

Thus, the Justices of the Supreme Court of Japan would undoubtedly agree with Meiklejohn's assertion that

> [a]nyone who would . . . irresponsibly interrupt the activities of a lecture, a hospital, a concert hall, a church, a machine shop, a classroom, a football field, or a home, does not thereby exhibit his freedom. Rather, he shows himself to be a boor, a public nuisance, who must be abated, by force if necessary.[188]

The Supreme Court of Japan has permitted government to "abate" such free speech "nuisances," whether in the form of pesky candidates canvassing door-to-door or, rather, in the form of a hyperbolic, counterfactual attack on a regional politician in a local magazine.

In short, the Justices of the Supreme Court of Japan have embraced Meiklejohn's vision of freedom of speech as a means and not an end. In so doing, they have laid bare some of the implicit costs and benefits associated with Meiklejohn's theory of freedom of expression. Perhaps most important, they have demonstrated the communitarian, group-oriented cast of Meiklejohn's philosophy of free speech.[189]

In a society that can reach basic agreement about who shall serve as the "parliamentarian" and what the rules of the debate shall be, Meiklejohn's democratic self-government theory of free expression seems to function effectively. The question remains, however, whether a pluralistic society could agree on a common set of "floor rules." To the extent that the Japanese experience demonstrates the viability of the Meiklejohn theory for a group-oriented society that functions on the basis of establishing community consensus,[190] it should lead one to question the viability of such a theory in a society committed to individualism and respect for cultural pluralism.

At the same time, one should not underestimate the costs associated with government regulation of the modalities of speech—small, unpopular minorities may be effectively silenced. Arguably, minority rights should not be subjugated solely because the minority is really small. Yet, a truly communitarian speech ethic will be hard pressed to avoid just such a result.[191]

It also requires something of a leap of faith to assume that communitarian speech regulations will relate solely to the modalities of speech without bleeding over into issues of content and viewpoint. A small, unpopular minority committed to engaging in highly offensive forms of speech activity is unlikely to find the Japanese courts particularly receptive to its Article 21 claims. The communitarian impulse that justifies the regulation of how one engages in speech activity is likely also to affect judicial consideration of the content of speech activity.

IV. The Problem of Obscenity

Although U.S. free speech values have made strong inroads in Japan, the Japanese High Court has certainly established a distinctly Japanese free speech tradition. As noted above, one common theme is a concern for the tranquility of the community and the protection of its values.

In this regard, the Japanese Supreme Court's treatment of obscenity reflects a strong concern for maintaining the viability of Japanese cultural values related to sexuality and gender relations. In a series of cases beginning in the 1950s, the Japanese Supreme Court has endorsed government efforts to restrict salacious materials—even when these materials have significant and well-recognized artistic or literary value. Beginning with its opinion in the *Lady Chatterly's Lover Decision,*[192] the Supreme Court of Japan has adopted the position that obscene materials fall outside the scope of Article 21.[193]

The facts of the case are straightforward. Local prosecutors sought to suppress the sale and distribution of a Japanese translation of D. H. Lawrence's *Lady Chatterly's Lover.* Citing Article 175 of the Penal Code of Japan, which prohibits the distribution, sale, or public display of an "obscene writing, picture, or other object,"[194] the prosecution argued that the translator and publisher of *Lady Chatterly's Lover* should be punished for disseminating an obscene writing.[195] The trial court found the novel obscene as a matter of law and convicted the defendants. On appeal, the defendants argued that *Lady Chatterly's Lover* was not obscene because it had significant and well-recognized literary value, that Article 21 privileged their sale and distribution of the work, and that even if the novel was obscene and did not enjoy Article 21 protection, they could not be convicted because they did not know that the novel was obscene. The Supreme Court rejected all three contentions.

With respect to the definition of obscenity, the Supreme Court cited the earlier holdings of its predecessor, the Court of Cassation, interpreting Article 175. Under these precedents, the term "obscene writings" as used in Article 175 "refers to a writing, picture, and everything else which tends to be an obscene matter" and "it must be such that it causes man to engender feeling[s] of shame and loathsomeness."[196] The Court of Cassation later refined this rather circular and vague definition: obscenity includes any material " 'which unnecessarily excites or stimulates sexual desire, injures the normal sense of embarrassment commonly present in a normal ordinary person, and runs counter to the good moral concept pertaining to sexual matters.' "[197]

The Supreme Court then concluded that *Lady Chatterly's Lover* met this definition of obscenity, based on twelve sexually explicit passages.[198] The Court explained that "the translation of the passages under consideration far exceeds the bound of propriety generally accepted in society."[199] This conclusion stood, notwithstanding the fact that "unlike the usual type of pornographic writings, it [the novel] is not entirely without literary characteristics."[200] Describing the passages at issue as "too bold, detailed, and realistic," the Court rejected the defendants' free speech defenses, noting that "[a]rt, even art, does not have the special privilege of presenting obscene matters to the public."[201]

Moreover, the fact that the defendants did not have prior knowledge that the novel violated Article 175 did not insulate them from liability.[202] "Whether the writer had a complete knowledge as to the obscene nature of his work or had only a vague recognition, or whether he had no knowledge whatsoever, merely goes to the question of mitigation."[203]

Finally, the Justices turned to Article 21. They squarely rejected any suggestion that Article 21 protects legally obscene materials. Invoking Article 12's "public welfare" limitation, the Supreme Court characterized the production and sale of obscene materials as an "abuse" of freedom of expression.[204] Nor did the prohibition of obscene material constitute a form of censorship, also prohibited by Article 21.[205] Although a number of Justices penned concurring opinions, not a single member of the fifteen-Justice Supreme Court dissented from the view that *Lady Chatterly's Lover* constituted obscenity.

In 1969, the Supreme Court revisited the issue of obscenity in *Ishii v. Japan,*[206] also known as the *de Sade Case.* The defendants argued that the work in question, the Marquis de Sade's *In Praise of Vice,* was not obscene because it had significant literary value. Restating its prior holding in the *Lady Chatterly's Lover Case,* the Supreme Court held that the book in question was legally obscene, even though de Sade's work possessed significant literary value.[207] "When writings of artistic and intellectual merit are obscene, then to make them the object of penalties in order to uphold order and healthy customs in sexual life is of benefit to the life of the whole nation."[208] Thus, the Supreme Court strongly reaffirmed its position that the fact that a work has significant literary, artistic, or scientific value does not save it from prohibition under Article 175 of the Penal Code.

Commentators, both in Japan and abroad, have been highly critical of these decisions.[209] Some have even predicted that the Supreme Court would eventually reverse itself, at least insofar as it has sanctioned the prohibition of works that possessed serious social value.[210] Nevertheless, the Supreme Court has declined to oblige these critics. On the contrary, the Court reaffirmed the validity of *Lady Chatterly's Lover* and *de Sade* within the past twenty years,[211] citing its earlier precedents and again reiterating its position that "[w]hen viewed from the standpoint of maintaining and securing sound sexual morals in our country, prevention of the unnecessary influx of matters of obscene expression from abroad is in conformity with the public welfare."[212]

What should one take from *Lady Chatterly's Lover* and its progeny? Plainly, the Supreme Court's decisions do not fit into an overall governmental commitment to protect the community from erotic or sexually explicit speech—the commodification of sex is a *fait accompli* in Japan.[213] Nor has the Japanese Supreme Court, like its Canadian counterpart, made a conscious decision to elevate gender equality above freedom of expression.[214] Although Japanese women increasingly are challenging traditional stereotypes[215] about their proper role in society,[216] the Supreme Court's decisions do not invoke the equal protection guarantee contained in Article 14, nor has the Court framed its decisions in terms of avoiding the degradation of women. Perhaps this is just as well, given the widespread availability of socially correct pornography in Japan—pornography that is thoroughly Japanese in its outlook on proper sexual behaviors.[217]

If the *Lady Chatterly's Lover* line of cases cannot be explained in terms of a general social concern about pornography, nor in terms of a commitment to gender equality that supersedes the protection of freedom of expression, what then explains the Japanese Supreme Court's willingness to cast a blind eye on state-sponsored censorship? Why has the Japanese Supreme Court given its blessing to the state's efforts to bowdlerize pornography (an oxymoronic task, to be sure)?

Arguably, the *Lady Chatterly's Lover* line of cases reflects an attempt to protect the community from "bad ideas" about sex and sexual relationships. It is not the sexually explicit nature of the materials that caused the state to prohibit them; rather, it was their un-Japanese worldview coupled with their primal subject matter.[218] The Supreme Court's approach seems to embrace the logic that the average Japanese citizen can safely be exposed to foreign political ideas, and even to foreign cultural materials; these materials can be incorporated into Japanese society without altering its basic chemistry. Foreign ideas about sex and gender relations, however, are another matter entirely.

The Justices of the Japanese Supreme Court apparently believe that foreign ideas about sex and gender relations are somehow potentially more dangerous to the community. Not only foreign pornography but even foreign works containing a substantial erotic element need not be tolerated;[219] traditional taboos and social mores must be maintained.[220]

Needless to say, this kind of censorship is hardly consistent with the marketplace of ideas model of freedom of speech. Moreover, it is also inconsistent with most iterations of the Meiklejohn theory of the First Amendment. Alexander Meiklejohn himself argued that art, literature, and science are needed to make the citizenry capable of meaningful participation in democratic self-governance.[221] Such works also help to frame the terms of public debate.[222] He also disapproved of viewpoint-based censorship.[223]

Professor Meiklejohn's attempts to extend his democratic self-government paradigm to encompass artistic, literary, and scientific expression produced recurring criticism. As Professor Marty Redish explained, "[a]lthough Meiklejohn in later years appeared to soften the rigidity of his lines of demarcation by effectively extending his doctrine—in a somewhat less than persuasive manner—to many forms of apparently nonpolitical speech, other commentators have adopted his initial premise and kept within its logical limits."[224] Meiklejohn's attempt to expand his theory led to attacks from "those who believe that the first amendment has no special political basis and by political 'purists' who accept Meiklejohn's initial premise about the relationship between the first amendment and the political process, but question the logic of his extension."[225]

The Japanese Supreme Court's free speech jurisprudence amply demonstrates that it is possible to protect political speech without protecting nonpolitical speech and, moreover, that such an approach is not inconsistent with the maintenance of a functioning democratic polity. Viewed in this light, the *Lady Chatterly's Lover* line of decisions demonstrates the limits of Meiklejohn's theory of the proper scope of freedom of expression.

On the other hand, most of Meiklejohn's intellectual descendants have not endorsed the proposition that the government can attempt to protect the citizenry from dangerous ideas about sex or gender roles.[226] Even Catharine MacKinnon, who endorses the proposition that the government should be permitted to punish the advocacy of certain bad ideas,[227] does not embrace the view that government can attempt to impose orthodoxy in matters of intimate human relationships and gender roles.[228]

The Japanese Supreme Court's approach is perhaps consistent with Robert Bork's theory of the First Amendment. Formerly a U.S. Circuit Judge on the D.C. Circuit and also a failed nominee to the Supreme Court of the United States, Bork seems to subscribe to the cultural *jihad* thesis set forth by Justice Scalia;[229] he has argued that communities should be permitted to determine the level of deviancy that they will tolerate,[230] and to impose punishments on those who insist on transgressing the established limits.[231]

Ironically, however, Japanese sexual mores have not been static; they have evolved and changed over time. One concurring Justice in the *Lady Chatterly's Lover Case* notes that once upon a time, Japanese men and women regularly engaged in orgies at a sacred mountain.[232] He even notes references to the practice in traditional folk songs: "[i]n regard to this 'uta-gaki,' there is a song in Mannyoshu which goes, 'in kagau-kagai, may I also participate in intercourse with another's wife, and let others commune with my wife.' "[233] Of course, "it must be remembered that these functions were regular affairs practiced in the spring and autumn in the sacred compound with divine permission."[234]

Rather than demonstrating a lack of principle on the part of Justice Mano, I think that these observations tend to confirm that the Supreme Court's principal concern in this line of cases is preserving Japanese attitudes and mores regarding sexuality and gender roles. Indeed, Justice Mano explained that the ancient practices he described "must be considered as revealing a glimpse of ancient marriage customs based upon group sentiment and group conscience of that time"; accordingly, "it cannot be adjudged simply by the concept of eroticism or obscenity as we understand it today."[235] What Justice Mano is really saying is that unlike *Lady Chatterly's Lover* or the writings of the Marquis de Sade, erotic Japanese literature may not reflect contemporary social values or morals but still retains its Japanese essence; because it is Japanese it can be tolerated, if not embraced, notwithstanding its eroticism.

Before assuming the mantel of cultural/legal superiority, would-be American critics should take care to remember that the United States Supreme Court has not been consistently vigilant against efforts to enforce orthodoxy through government actions designed to suppress ideas or doctrines that it disfavors. In fact, the Supreme Court has from time to time turned a blind eye on efforts to enforce political orthodoxy, by discouraging —if not prohibiting—access to persons and materials deemed dangerous.

In the 1970s, for example, the Supreme Court sustained legislation prohibiting the issuance of visas to foreign nationals who had been identified as advocates of communism.[236] In practice, of course, this meant persons who identified with Soviet-style socialism.[237] Surely Justice Marshall was correct in observing that "[n]othing is served—least of all our standing in the international community—" by excluding foreign writers and scholars based on their political views.[238]

More recently, the United States Supreme Court sustained the Reagan Justice Department's efforts to discourage the dissemination of foreign books and films deemed undesirable by the government.[239] Invoking a law passed in the 1930s in response to the perceived dual threats of communism and Nazism and recodified during the Red Scare of the 1950s, the Justice Department required a would-be distributor of foreign films designated "political propaganda" by the department to warn potential recipients of the films that they had been disseminated by "agents" of "foreign principals."[240] A would-be distributor challenged the labeling and notification requirements, arguing that he did not wish to be tagged with distributing "foreign political propaganda" at the behest of the agents of foreign principals.[241]

The Supreme Court concluded that the labeling requirement did not constitute a prior restraint or undue burden on the dissemination of the materials in question.[242] Instead, the majority opined, the law at issue simply required would-be distributors to share the government's official view that the materials in question might reflect a foreign government's official party line.

In many respects, attempts to fence out political ideas are more reprehensible than attempts to preserve common cultural understandings. As Justice Douglas observed in *Mandel*, "[t]hought control is not within the competence of any branch of government."[243] Yet, the results in *Mandel* and *Keene* are hard to square with this proposition.

The Japanese Supreme Court's rather broad obscenity decisions will probably do little harm in the long run because Japan maintains a viable system of political pluralism. If political pluralism exists, cultural pluralism should necessarily follow. As Professor MacKinnon and other feminists have noted, the personal is political; one cannot divorce civic life from social life.[244] On the other hand, cultural pluralism can be suppressed in a society that lacks political pluralism. A totalitarian regime that prohibits the free exchange of political ideas can easily annex efforts to control popular culture to its program of repression.[245]

The Japanese effort to maintain a sexual Maginot line is arguably misguided and, in any event, probably ineffectual, but it is hardly the stuff from which dictatorships are forged.[246] Moreover, the Japanese government does not maintain active and ongoing censorial efforts—with the possible exception of aggressive customs inspectors bent on ferreting out the latest copy of *Hustler*.[247] Whatever its precise motivations, the Japanese Supreme Court obviously views governmental efforts to preserve Japanese cultural norms as constitutionally permissible in some instances, even if such efforts ultimately prove to be largely unsuccessful.

If the Supreme Court were to broaden the scope of its censorial project to include all erotic materials, the *Lady Chatterly's Lover* line of cases could be made consistent with the "purist" version of the Meiklejohn theory of freedom of expression.[248] As former-Judge Bork once put it, the objection to excluding nonpolitical speech from constitutional protection arguably "confuses the constitutionality of laws with their wisdom."[249] The absolutist approach to applying Meiklejohn's theory of free expression relies upon "the enlightenment of society and its elected representatives" to protect nonpolitical speech, a state of affairs that Bork characterizes as "hardly a terrible fate."[250] Thus, at a minimum, should the Supreme Court ultimately elect to maintain its stance that erotic speech does not merit Article 21 protection, it should apply this rule to both foreign and domestic materials: "spring books," "spring movies," and similar fare should not enjoy formal legal privilege based solely on their domestic origins.[251]

On the other hand, it is difficult not to be sympathetic toward Meiklejohn's attempt to extend his theory to encompass artistic, literary, and scientific speech.[252] Can a people be politically free but intellectually and culturally repressed? Even if one posits the arts, sciences, and humanities as independent social goods,[253] their relationship to democracy cannot be denied: a society of illiterates will prove incapable of self-governance.[254] Indeed, Thomas Jefferson repeatedly drew the connection between education, enlightenment, and democratic self-government.[255]

Democracy presupposes the wisdom, intelligence, and humanity to make meaningful and informed decisions about who shall govern and what they shall do. To protect political speech without affording broad protection to artistic, literary, and scientific speech necessarily constitutes an incomplete and imperfect project; Alexander Meiklejohn came to recognize this and, accordingly, modified his democratic self-government paradigm. One would hope that the Justices of the Japanese Supreme Court, like Alexander Meiklejohn, will one day come to eschew the Borkian approach and instead embrace Meiklejohn's "new and improved" democratic self-governance paradigm for freedom of expression.

V. Freedom of Expression, Social Consensus, and Judicial Review

Examination and analysis of the Japanese Supreme Court's principal decisions involving freedom of speech presents a mixed picture. The Supreme Court has been moderately protective of political speech and the use of public property for mass demonstrations. At the same time, however, it has proven extremely deferential to governmental authorities—whether local or national, whether legislative or executive. An American observer cannot help but wonder why the Supreme Court of Japan has failed to enforce Article 21 more aggressively. What explains the reluctance of the Supreme Court to challenge directly legislative and executive branch actions that burden freedom of expression?

It would be impossible to demonstrate conclusively that a single reason, or even a group of reasons, explains this pattern of behavior. There are, however, at least four possible explanations that merit consideration. Even if they cannot provide a conclusive resolution to the question, considered individually and collectively they provide plausible rationales for the Japanese Supreme Court's course of action.

First, the ghost of Japan's civil law past haunts the common law Constitution and its ostensible guardian, the Supreme Court. Strong judicial review simply was not a part of the civil law system that existed prior to 1945. Moreover, since 1945, the Supreme Court has failed to assert routinely its authority to "say what the law is."[256] No strong Chief Justice has articulated a clear vision of a robust form of judicial review. Nor has the Supreme Court attempted to carve out a coequal constitutional status with the Diet and ministries. On the contrary, "[t]he Court has never played the unique role in the country's political and social life that the United States Supreme Court has played."[257]

The civil law tradition historically has not placed judges at the apex of government structure. Instead, most civil law traditions include a healthy dose of legislative supremacy as a core constitutional precept.[258] Thus, even the adoption of written constitutions in many civil law jurisdictions did not necessarily affect the relative authority of judges vis-à-vis legislatures because "[l]egislative supremacy and a flexible constitution are companion concepts."[259] It is possible to maintain a constitutional system in which the legislature, rather than the courts, retains primary responsibility for considering and implementing constitutional values.[260] In many respects, this was the situation that existed in Japan under the Meiji Constitution.

Professor Merryman reports that although "[t]he trend toward judicial review of the constitutionality of legislation in the civil law world has been strong, particularly in this century,"[261] the results have not been particularly encouraging in many jurisdictions. "The tendency has been for the civil law judge to recoil from the responsibilities and opportunities of constitutional adjudication."[262] Indeed, Professor Merryman questions whether it is possible for civil law judges to raise their sights because "[t]he tradition is too strong, the orthodox view of the judicial function too deeply ingrained, the effects of traditional legal education and career training too limiting."[263] All that said, however, the trend within civil law jurisdictions is toward the adoption of what Merryman characterizes as "formal, rigid constitutions" that vest a power of judicial review in a judicial or quasi-judicial organ.[264]

Through its cases considering freedom of expression claims, one can see how the Supreme Court of Japan has experienced the difficulties associated with making a transition from a civil law to a common law model. Given the limited role posited for courts in traditional civil law constitutionalism, it is not at all surprising that the Supreme Court of Japan has not adopted an aggressive posture with respect to its relatively new powers of judicial review.

Professor Okudaira has argued that the Supreme Court's reticence is self-reinforcing: "Because the Court does not venture to challenge another branch of the government, its authority is not augmented and its prestige does not increase."[265] He labels this state of affairs a kind of "vicious circle."[266] Thus, one explanation for the Supreme Court's relative quiescence is a lack of raw political power coupled with a lack of social consensus regarding the legitimacy of a strong, perhaps confrontational, form of judicial review. As Professor Okudaira has put it, "[p]erhaps our Court knows it has neither enough authority nor enough prestige to hand down decisions such as *INS v. Chadha* or *Texas v. Johnson,* which strike hard blows at the U.S. Congress or at the executive administration."[267]

A perceived lack of power or concerns about the legitimacy of judicial review in a democratic polity could support a general posture of deference.[268] This explanation, however, is plainly incomplete. The fact of the matter is that the Japanese Supreme Court has struck down legislation from time to time; indeed, one commentator has noted that in comparative terms, the Japanese Supreme Court has proven far more aggressive in its exercise of judicial review than did the United States Supreme Court in its early years of existence.[269] The Court not only possesses but actually exercises the power of judicial review; its scruples about overriding the decisions of the political branches have not proven to be a controlling consideration in all cases.[270]

A second possible explanation for the Supreme Court's cautious nature relates to the selection process for members of the Japanese Supreme Court. Dean Luney reports that most scholars attribute the Supreme Court's "conservative trend to the political dominance in postwar Japan of the Liberal Democratic Party (LDP) and to the Supreme Court appointment process."[271] No doubt, the composition of the Supreme Court and the manner in which Justices are selected contribute to the Supreme Court's institutional conservatism.

The LDP selects the persons (to date always men) to be appointed to the Supreme Court of Japan. More often than not, the nominees share a common understanding of the institutional role of the Supreme Court and its proper place in Japan's constitutional scheme. This is not to say that they are ideological clones, nor that they have identical backgrounds. Obviously, individual Justices have different philosophical and jurisprudential leanings. Moreover, the LDP historically has selected Justices from a variety of constituencies within the legal community, including academia, the lower courts, prosecutor's offices, and the practicing bar.[272]

Nevertheless, as in Great Britain, persons appointed to the Supreme Court tend to share a common understanding of Japan's courts and their proper role in the political system.[273] "Most Supreme Court justices have been appointed by the leadership of the LDP or its conservative forerunners and, for the most part, reflect the social, economic, cultural, and political values of the party membership."[274] Just as federal judges appointed during the Reagan and Bush years tended to share a common ideological point of view,[275] so too judges selected by the LDP's leadership are likely to have common attitudes and approaches to constitutional interpretation.

At the same time, however, this explanation seems too thin to explain the astonishing consistency in the Supreme Court's behavior over the past fifty years. Even the most zealous ideological selection process occasionally goes awry.[276] The Justices have maintained a unanimity of style and approach that cannot be attributed to a remarkable string of "good picks" by the LDP. Something more is afoot here. Perhaps a more complete explanation is that the Justices' attitudes are generally indicative not only of the LDP but also of Japanese society more broadly.

A perceived lack of relative authority provides a third potential explanation for the Japanese Supreme Court's caution. Simply put, the Japanese Supreme Court does not perceive itself to be a powerful institution vis-à-vis the Diet or bureaucracy—with good reason. Historically, the Japanese courts have simply enforced the legal rules established by others. In the Meiji period, this meant the edicts of the Emperor and his ministers. In the postwar era, this means the laws promulgated by the Diet and the rules and regulations established by the career bureaucrats in the various government ministries.

Neither the Diet nor the bureaucracy would take kindly to more active interventions by the Supreme Court in their affairs. Dean Luney goes so far as to argue that "[t]he judiciary is not in a position to be an instrument for social, economic, or political change; instead, it performs the conservative task of preserving basic civil liberties guaranteed by the Constitution and recognized by the Diet and a majority of the population."[277]

Moreover, the Justices' professional behavior tends to reinforce their relative lack of power vis-à-vis the political branches. The Justices of the Japanese Supreme Court keep a low profile; they do not seek out confrontations with the political branches of government.

Before condemning the Japanese Supreme Court's lack of institutional chutzpah,[278] one would do well to bear in mind that the United States Supreme Court has not always stepped willingly and boldly into the breach.[279] In fact, United States history is littered with instances in which the United States Supreme Court walked to the edge of the abyss, peeked over, and quickly stepped back. *Marbury v. Madison*,[280] Andrew Jackson's defiance of the Supreme Court's decision in *Worcester v. Georgia*,[281] the *Legal Tender Cases*,[282] and the *Gold Clause Cases*[283] all provide instances of artful dodging by the Supreme Court to avoid crossing the President or Congress. Indeed, to some extent, even *Brown v. Board of Education*[284] fits into this overall pattern: in *Brown I*, the Court punted away the question of the proper remedy,[285] and, in *Brown II*, the Supreme Court adopted its infamous "all deliberate speed" mandate to dismantle de jure segregation in the public schools.[286] The lack of a firm remedy, the lack of a definite timetable for implementation, and the Court's subsequent unwillingness to fill in these blanks significantly muted the social and political impact of the decision.[287] Thus, after some reflection, its seems clear that the United States Supreme Court has established a relatively consistent pattern, if not a practice, of attempting to avoid creating constitutional crises.[288]

In some circumstances, this strategy of prudent avoidance can make a great deal of sense. Consider that just thirty years ago, there was more than a little doubt about whether then-President Nixon would comply with the Supreme Court's order—should it decide to affirm the district court's subpoena requiring him to hand over the tape recordings of his oval office conversations.[289] Lacking both power of purse and power of sword, the judiciary is by nature the "least dangerous branch" in a constitutional democracy.[290]

The Japanese Supreme Court's efforts to avoid direct confrontation with the political branches probably reflect, at least in part, concerns about the ability of the Court to enforce its will. The malapportionment cases are telling in this regard. Over a period of thirty years, the Supreme Court has demanded that the Diet reduce the relative disparity that existed in citizens' voting power. Ultimately, it settled upon a ratio of 3:1 as a constitutional standard.

When presented with a challenge to a district with a 3.18:1 ratio, however, it indicated that the 3:1 ratio was not set in stone and that its application would be flexible enough to accommodate shifts in population.[291] Once again, the Supreme Court of Japan demonstrated its willingness to compromise principles in order to avoid interbranch conflict.

Fourth, and perhaps most important, conflict avoidance is an important Japanese cultural norm. Forty years ago, Professor Nathanson severely criticized the Supreme Court of Japan, arguing that "[w]hile it has generally paid lip service to the principles of Chapter III of the Constitution, it has not struck any resounding blows for their effective implementation."[292] This observation reflects a gross misconception of the fundamental nature of Japanese society; "striking resounding blows," thereby rushing into direct and open conflict with other branches of the government, would be profoundly un-Japanese. Neither institutions nor individuals gain much ground in Japan by rocking the *wa,* or social harmony.[293] Direct confrontation is to be avoided and mediation of disputes is to be preferred over formal court adjudication.[294]

In many respects, the Japanese Supreme Court attempts to mediate, rather than decide, constitutional disputes. As Justice Sonobe of the Japanese Supreme Court has explained, "there is a tendency to emphasize the aspect of balance, that is, of harmony and collaboration, in applying the principle of checks and balances."[295] Rather than broadly endorsing the positions of either the government or the challengers, it often finds a third way that splits the difference: "[a]s to the specific exercise of the power of judicial review, the courts have been keen to balance many competing claims."[296] The *Tokyo* and *Niigata Ordinance* decisions reflect this sort of approach, as do the Court's cases on defamation.

One should be careful, of course, about accepting at face value culturally-based explanations for legal rules and institutions in Japan. Professor Mark Ramseyer, in particular, rejects the idea of an " 'essence' of Japanese law," " 'core' of the Japanese legal system," or "generalization about the gist of Japanese law that distinguishes it from other advanced capitalist systems."[297] Why? "We offer no essence, no core, no gist—because there is none."[298] Applying a pure law and economics approach, Ramseyer argues that Japanese law and the Japanese legal system "reflect[ ] nothing more than the accumulated exigencies of lawmaking by legislatures, courts, and administrative agencies over time."[299]

Even Ramseyer, however, acknowledges the prevalence of cultural explanations for the relative weakness of both formal law in Japan and Japanese legal institutions.[300] Moreover, scholars who think culture plays an important role in shaping contemporary Japanese legal institutions do not suggest that it has a talismanic explanatory power. Professor Haley, for example, focuses on comparative institutional competence and design far more than on abstract cultural generalizations.[301] Similarly, Professor Mark West has observed that many scholars of Japanese law and the Japanese legal system have looked to Japanese culture for explanations and understanding. He explains that "[f]or Japan, in particular, scholars have explained law and the position of law in society as an outgrowth of Japan's unique cultural history."[302]

Although Professor Ramseyer is undoubtedly correct to question facile cultural explanations for differences in law and legal institutions in Japan, it seems equally problematic simply to ignore the effect of culture on those laws and legal institutions. In this regard, Professor Haley's approach, which emphasizes comparative institutional competencies, potentially seems to have greater explanatory power than a pure law and economics approach. Accordingly, I think some consideration of cultural values can be relevant to understanding why Japanese legal institutions look and act as they do.

A radically revisionist account of the Supreme Court of Japan's behavior is also tenable. One could view the Supreme Court's practice of providing limiting constructions as a form of judicial activism, rather than as the product of extreme judicial deference. At least arguably, the Supreme Court has a bad habit of simply rewriting constitutionally problematic laws to suit its liking. Perhaps the Diet or, for that matter, the general electorate, would prefer no law to the watered-down statute that the Supreme Court has drafted. If a statute lacks a constitutionally necessary limiting principle, then arguably the Supreme Court should simply strike down the legislation and tell the Diet to try again.

The revisionist account accurately identifies a substantial activist streak in the Supreme Court of Japan's overall posture of deference. It misplaces, however, the proper point of emphasis.

The Supreme Court of Japan wishes to avoid interbranch conflict and the use of limiting constructions provides a convenient means of enforcing constitutional limitations without ever having to declare a specific legislative work product invalid. The Court's motivation is not the covert exercise of legislative power but, rather, an escape from what the Justices view as a Hobson's choice: abandoning constitutional principles or directly challenging the authority of the political departments of government.

As it happens, Professor Merryman predicts just such judicial behavior in his seminal work on the civil law. In jurisdictions featuring a "flexible" constitution, Merryman posits that "[w]here a possible conflict between a constitutional provision and a statute appears to have occurred without conscious legislative consideration, the tendency of the courts will be to interpret the provision and the statute in such a way as to avoid the conflict."[303] According to Merryman, this and similar kinds of devices permit the courts in a civil law system to respect constitutional commitments without upsetting settled understandings of the proper relationship between the courts and the political branches of government.[304]

In the final analysis, the Japanese Supreme Court probably knows its institutional limitations much better than an American observer does. Undoubtedly, the Japanese Supreme Court's non-confrontational approach stems from more than one source or rationale, but the end result seems to reflect an institutional reality rather than a consistent and endemic lack of courage or fortitude on the part of the Justices.[305]

VI. Conclusion

Notwithstanding the Supreme Court's "careful and cautious"[306] approach to enforcing Article 21, freedom of speech is a meaningful reality in Japan. This observation has been almost universally endorsed for the past forty years.[307] Simply put, the Japanese government does not engage in regularized attempts to squelch freedom of expression. Accordingly, the Supreme Court's failure to issue opinions striking "resounding blows" in favor of freedom of expression has not adversely affected the social landscape, even if it has left more constitutional questions dangling than some commentators think wise.[308] Even in the case of pornography, the Supreme Court's failure to protect serious literary or artistic works featuring erotic themes has not seriously impeded access to such materials.[309]

The Japanese Supreme Court's Article 21 cases are, nonetheless, quite important. Time and again, the Supreme Court has drawn the connection between democratic self-governance and freedom of expression; indeed, it is almost a reflexive gesture. Given the Court's inherent caution, it would not repeatedly invoke this observation were it not consistent with the prevailing views of the political branches of government and the general public. Thus, one can view the Supreme Court of Japan's free speech opinions as both reflecting and ratifying the Japanese people's embrace of free expression as a necessary incident of democracy. The government's general laissez-faire approach to regulating speech and speech-related activities also seems consistent with this conclusion.

To the extent that freedom of speech faces challenges in Japan, they tend to stem from nongovernmental sources. As Professor Beer has noted, strong social traditions and cultural values militate against the expression of individualism.[310] "Japanese culture values individual reticence and, in many contexts, views aggressive assertion of personal opinion as reprehensible."[311] Professor Haley argues that this "groupism" is not genetic but, rather, stems from the complex systems of mutual interdependence that characterized both traditional Japanese villages in the past and modern Japanese corporations in the present.[312]

Once again, it is possible to learn from the Japanese example. Although the United States is undoubtedly a more individualistic society than is Japan, freedom of speech in the United States also suffers from informal economic and social forms of control. A worker employed by Lockheed-Martin probably will not march in a mass protest demanding an immediate nuclear freeze and unilateral disarmament. Similarly, a teacher in a

Catholic high school may be more than a little reticent to share her view that abortion on demand should remain legal, not only with her students and colleagues but also with members of the general community. To speak out on this issue would jeopardize her social standing within her workplace—if not her job. To be sure, these informal mechanisms of control are less pervasive and operate less effectively in the United States than in Japan. They do, however, exist.

In conceptualizing freedom of expression, American commentators tend to ignore nongovernmental pressures. As a matter of formal legal analysis, this is entirely understandable, given the state action doctrine.[313] Because the federal courts have cast the Constitution as a charter of negative rights, that is, a set of freedoms from rather than affirmative rights to particular things, Americans naturally overlook corporate and community power over freedom of speech.[314] Professor Owen Fiss has questioned the rationality of this approach, arguing that the state could be seen as the friend of free speech rather than its enemy: "At the core of my approach is a belief that contemporary social structure is as much an enemy of free speech as is the policeman."[315] I would argue that the Japanese example demonstrates the salience of Fiss's concerns about the dangers of defining the free speech project solely in terms of prohibiting governmental censorship.

A second, and arguably more important, potential lesson from this exercise in comparative law relates to the vitality and power of Alexander Meiklejohn's theory of the First Amendment. In the space of a half century, the Supreme Court of Japan has articulated a clear and coherent vision of freedom of expression. For the most part, it embodies Alexander Meiklejohn's vision of freedom of speech as a necessary corollary of democratic self-governance. The Supreme Court of Japan also has extended this vision of freedom of speech beyond the obvious examples of direct government censorship to include elements of private law, such as tort, that burden the free exchange of information and ideas.

On the other hand, the Holmesian "marketplace of ideas" model has not really taken hold in Japanese legal thought. The Supreme Court of Japan consistently relates free expression to matters of self-governance, not individual freedom or autonomy. Moreover, it has observed that restrictions on commercial speech "do not ipso facto impair freedom of thought and freedom of conscience."[316] This result comports with the Meiklejohn theory of the First Amendment but not with the contemporary understanding of Holmes's marketplace of ideas.

The Japanese Supreme Court's apparent rejection of the marketplace of ideas paradigm may in part reflect cultural values that emphasize community over individualism.[317] Political pluralism requires that citizens be permitted to meet and discuss issues of civic concern. It does not require the community to tolerate speech activities unrelated to democratic self-governance, such as dial-a-porn services or hard-core pornography.[318] Given the importance of consensus and harmony in contemporary Japanese society, it is easy to see why the notion of an open and unregulated marketplace does not fit: the community both wants and expects the ability to maintain decorum.[319]

The Japanese Supreme Court's concern for community potentially explains not only its embrace of Meiklejohn's essentially communitarian vision of freedom of expression but also its relatively sparing use of the power of judicial review. In a democratic state, the elected branches of government should generally establish major social policies. Moreover, judicial review need not inexorably lead to a state of constant conflict between the judiciary and the citizen's elected representatives.

More than one hundred years ago, Harvard law professor James Thayer argued that judicial review should be limited to instances of "clear error," in which the legislature has not only transgressed, but badly transgressed, a particular constitutional limitation.[320] Professor Mark Tushnet has noted that Thayer's vision of limited or "minimalist" judicial review has not proven persuasive in the United States.[321] Thayer's argument, however, has more than a little logic: if courts exercise restraint in exercising judicial review, then legislative and executive branch personnel should be more attuned to constitutional values; they will not be able to rely on the judiciary to correct their constitutional transgressions.[322] To some extent, Great Britain's system of parliamentary supremacy, coupled with a limited (if not nonexistent) system of judicial review resembles Thayer's model.[323] It may be overly optimistic, however, to expect individual legislators to elevate constitutional responsibilities over short-term political opportunities.

One could view the Japanese Supreme Court's approach to judicial review as largely consistent with Thayer's "minimalist" approach. The Japanese Supreme Court works to avoid finding incompatibility between legislative or executive work product and the Constitution because of a strong belief that this approach will best protect community values—if not constitutional values. Moreover, this approach also respects the community's decision to vest legislative and executive responsibilities with a particular set of officeholders. As Professor Tushnet has put it, "[m]inimal judicial review docs, almost by definition, provide a wider domain within which legislators and the public have an opportunity to articulate constitutional norms."[324] The exercise of judicial review to strike down legislative work product or an executive action necessarily entails displacing decisions made by persons elected by the community to make precisely those decisions. Although a written constitution should cabin the discretion of elected officials, the question of an appropriate balance of power remains open.[325]

In a fashion consistent with Thayer's maxim, the Supreme Court of Japan simply declines to interpose its will over the will of the Diet absent an extraordinarily compelling reason for doing so. This is not to say that the Supreme Court makes no effort to protect or defend constitutional rights. On the contrary, the Supreme Court has repeatedly used interpretative devices, such as limiting constructions, to minimize the impact of government regulation on constitutionally protected rights. This approach to the judicial function does not reflect contemporary practice in the U.S. federal courts, but it is certainly a defensible theory of judicial review.[326]

At the same time, the Supreme Court of Japan's approach to enforcing Article 21 also reflects a communitarian cast. By locating freedom of expression as an incident of democratic self-government, the Justices have effectively linked freedom of speech to the citizenry's sovereign status. The Japanese Constitution makes it quite plain that the "sovereign power" resides with the people.[327] As Alexander Meiklejohn explained almost fifty years ago, effective popular sovereignty necessarily entails the ability to discuss and debate questions regarding who should hold office and the policies that those persons should pursue once in office.[328] Consistent with this approach, it is not the individual's interest in self-expression but, rather, the community's interest in a full and robust debate that undergirds Japanese society's protection of freedom of expression.

The Japanese Supreme Court and the other branches of the Japanese government have achieved remarkable success at incorporating freedom of expression as a basic tenet of Japan's civic faith.[329] When one considers the near complete absence of rights consciousness among the Japanese citizenry in pre-war Japan,[330] this achievement seems all the more amazing.

Moreover, it would be wrong of Americans to expect the Japanese people to have incorporated U.S. constitutional values in a lockstep fashion. As Professor Ruth Benedict cautioned in the immediate aftermath of World War II, "[i]t is not easy to work out new assumptions and new virtues."[331] Accordingly, she concluded, "[t]he Western world can neither suppose that the Japanese can take these [new democratic values] on sight and make them truly their own, nor must it imagine that Japan cannot ultimately work out a freer, less rigorous ethics."[332] History has borne out Professor Benedict's prophecy. Although the United States could not "create by fiat a free, democratic Japan,"[333] the Japanese people themselves have elected to establish and maintain such a polity, a polity in which freedom of speech is an integral component of their experiment in democratic self-government.

Seven years after the adoption of the First Amendment, Congress passed the Alien and Sedition Act.[334] Needless to say, this marked an inauspicious beginning for the nation's experiment with freedom of expression. It took the better part of two hundred years (166 years to be exact) for the Supreme Court of the United States to hold that good-faith criticism of government officials could not serve as the basis for criminal or civil sanctions.[335] The Japanese Supreme Court reached this conclusion a scant twenty-two years after Article 21 came into force.

It is certainly true that the Japanese conception of free speech differs in material respects from the prevailing marketplace paradigm in the United States. But "difference" does not imply a lack of dedication or concern for the freedom of speech. Over the course of almost sixty years, the Supreme Court of Japan has demonstrated a consistent commitment to protecting free expression as an essential incident of democratic self-government.

6

Freedom of Expression in the United Kingdom

Free Speech and the Limits of a Written Constitution

Some jurists and legal scholars have posited that the existence of a written constitution places certain rights, obligations, and duties in a preferred place within a nation's legal constellation.[1] Thus, the existence of the First Amendment, with an express guarantee of speech and press rights, should provide (at least nominally) greater protection for those liberties than would otherwise exist in the absence of such a provision. Quite often, this seemingly unobjectionable proposition holds true.[2]

The proposition is not, however, as self-evident as one might assume. Counterexamples exist.[3] The presence of a written constitutional guarantee of a particular right does not automatically mean that courts will afford the right greater solicitude, and the absence of a written constitutional provision does not preclude the protection of a particular liberty.[4] This is not to suggest that the absence of a specific textual provision protecting freedom of speech and the press has no effect on the disposition of cases raising such claims.[5] The point is more limited—the presence or absence of a textual guarantee of speech and press rights is not as sure a predictor of actual outcomes as one might expect.[6]

The United Kingdom presents a particularly good opportunity for the study of the freedom of speech in the context of an unwritten constitution. To be sure, Parliament has enacted the Human Rights Act of 1998 (Act),[7] which codifies certain provisions of the European Convention on Human Rights and Fundamental Freedoms.[8] Prior to 1998, the citizens of the United Kingdom did not enjoy any textual guarantee to the freedom of speech under domestic British law. This has changed now, at least as a formal matter: the Human Rights Act of 1998 requires public authorities to respect freedom of speech[9] and specifically authorizes judicial relief against executive officials who have violated the free speech rights of British citizens.[10] The Act took effect on October 2, 2000, by order of the United Kingdom's secretary of state.[11]

Significantly, the Act does not authorize the British courts to exercise a power of judicial review over domestic legislation; instead, the Human Rights Act requires judges to attempt to render a saving construction of ambiguous laws or regulations that could be, but need not be, interpreted as transgressing European Convention rights.[12] If a saving construction is simply not possible, the Act instructs a reviewing court to issue a "declaration of incompatibility," which puts Parliament on notice that, at least by judicial lights, its legislative handiwork transgresses Convention rights.[13]

Following the issuance of a declaration of incompatibility, Parliament, at least in theory, will consider enacting corrective legislation that addresses the incompatibility between British domestic law and the United Kingdom's international obligations under the European Convention. If "compelling reasons" exist, a Crown minister may unilaterally order amendments to the offending legislation "as he considers necessary to remove the incompatibility."[14] The same power exists with respect to secondary legislation (i.e., laws passed by the local parliaments for Wales, Scotland, or Northern Ireland and administrative rules and regulations).[15] Finally, the Act requires the sponsors of any piece of legislation to make a statement that the provisions of the bill are compatible with the European Convention or, if such a statement cannot be made, that she wishes for the bill to be considered anyway.[16]

The Human Rights Act thus provides an express and textual guarantee of the freedom of speech in Great Britain by making Article 10 of the European Convention domestically enforceable. In relevant part, Article 10 provides that "[e]veryone has the right to freedom of expression," including "freedom to hold opinions and to receive and impart information and ideas without interference by public authority and regardless of frontiers." This does not "prevent States from requiring the licensing of broadcasting, television, or cinema enterprises."

Significantly, Article 10 also directly limits the scope of the right to freedom of expression by mandating balancing exercises that weigh other social values against the free speech right:

The exercise of these freedoms, since it carries with it duties and responsibilities, may be subject to such formalities, conditions, restrictions or penalties as are prescribed by law and are necessary in a democratic society, in the interests of national security, territorial integrity or public safety, for the prevention of disorder or crime, for the protection of health or morals, for the protection of the reputation or rights of others, for preventing disclosure of information received in confidence, or for maintaining the authority and impartiality of the judiciary.[17]

Obviously, a sufficiently censorial government could deploy these limitations to justify very broad restrictions on the exercise of the right to free speech.

In theoretical terms, then, one would expect the adoption of the Human Rights Act, and the codification of Article 10, to transform the status of free speech in the United Kingdom. For a variety of reasons, such predictions are likely to prove wide of the mark.

In reality, British judges have been sensitive to free speech claims for many years. Moreover, the principal new judicial power, a mandate to render saving constructions whenever it is feasible to do so, merely ratifies the prior practice of the British courts. Similarly, prior to the enactment of the HRA when British judges could not render a saving construction, they were hardly precluded from formally noting the incompatibility of the statute with a proper understanding of Article 10 rights. As will be demonstrated below, the protection afforded the freedom of speech may have a great deal more to do with the salience of the right within a given culture than with the formal codification of a free speech guarantee as part of a Bill of Rights (or similar instrument).

Professor Frederick Schauer has argued that rights do not come into existence in a cultural vacuum; rather, rights exist in part because they incorporate and reflect preexisting community norms.[18] He suggests that "rights are constitutional in the familiar sense, but also . . . are constitutional in the sense that they constitute who and what we are."[19] Rights reflect and help to define a society and exist as a kind of cultural mirror. "Without going anywhere near the implausible claim that rights are all of what we are, one can still venture that rights are some of what we are, and for some people may be much of what they are."[20]

If this is so, then judges would not necessarily need the formal imprimatur of a legal text in order to recognize and enforce rights thought to exist by the general community. This is not to say that text is irrelevant to the recognition and enforcement of constitutional rights, nor that formal sources of law are mere smoke and mirrors for the enforcement of preexisting social norms. Instead, I am merely suggesting that text might not be an essential condition for the recognition and enforcement of a right. Similarly, the existence of a legal text ostensibly guaranteeing a right might not matter if the community's traditions (or at least the judges' traditions) are utterly unsympathetic to the precise claim at bar.

The Blair government's proposal for the creation of a new Supreme Court of the United Kingdom could have brought about an important change in process of rights enforcement in Great Britain. On June 12, 2003, the United Kingdom announced its intention to create a "Supreme Court." The proposed change did not reflect dissatisfaction with the incumbent Law Lords serving the House of Lords but, rather, the thought that, all things being equal, it would be desirable to separate formally judicial and legislative functions.[21] The proposal would transfer the twelve incumbent Law Lords of the Appellate Committee of the House of Lords to a "Supreme Court," a new judicial entity separate and distinct from the legislative branch.[22] Significantly, the proposed new judicial entity would not enjoy the power of judicial review and would not serve as a constitutional court (as does the German Federal Constitutional Court).[23]

Even though the proposed Supreme Court would not really radically change the scope or meaning of judicial review in the United Kingdom, the idea met with sustained opposition, both within Parliament and within the British judiciary. Six of the incumbent Law Lords have opposed the proposal; only four supported it (with two Law Lords declining to stake out public positions).[24] Moreover, on March 8, 2004, the House of Commons defeated the bill that would establish the new institution, by a vote of 216-183. Meanwhile, the House of Lords also opposed the bill and engaged in a series of delaying tactics to impede, if not prevent, its adoption.[25] Although its chief legislative sponsor, Lord Falconer, finally succeeded in securing passage of the Constitution Reform Act of 2005 on March 21, 2005, the newly created (but not yet established) "Supreme Court of the United Kingdom" will enjoy only those institutional powers currently exercised by the Appellate Committee of the House of Lords.[26]

If Great Britain established a new Supreme Court with the power of judicial review, the status of human rights could be significantly affected. At present—and for the immediate future—the system remains one of Parliamentary supremacy, meaning that Parliament can enact any law that it desires and the British courts lack any power to invalidate properly enacted legislation. Creation of a true constitutional court, vested with the power of judicial review, would be a revolutionary change in the British Constitution.

The United Kingdom's extraordinarily weak courts make consideration of human rights law at the constitutional level significantly less important than in Canada, Germany, Japan, and the United States. Of course, statutory human rights laws exist, and many of these laws regulate speech to promote equality. That said, a full examination of British domestic law statutory enactments prohibiting hate speech and pornography would not be particularly useful.

First, British law is not materially different from Canadian or German law on these matters. Accordingly, a detailed examination of the domestic law of the U.K. on these topics would not add much additional perspective on the problem of balancing free speech with a strong commitment to equality, civility, or human dignity—and, this would be true even if the British domestic courts had the authority to invalidate these enactments on free speech grounds, which they do not.

A second, and larger, reason for abjuring a detailed treatment of the substance of British speech regulations (as opposed to a focus on structure) is that Britain, alone of the five nations examined, lacks any judicially enforceable limits on the scope of Parliament's legislative powers. The HRA does not in any way bind a contemporary majority of the House of Commons; indeed, Tony Blair could repeal the HRA tomorrow, if he decided it would be politically useful to do so.

Of course, political realities would make it difficult, if not impossible, for Blair to repeal the Human Rights Act (HRA). But he really would not have to repeal the HRA in order to enact laws that violate it: the British judiciary (unlike the judiciaries in the United States, Canada, Germany, and Japan) lacks the power of judicial review. This was true before passage of the HRA, and it remains true today. The same ability to amend or abolish the HRA extends to hate speech regulations and all other aspects of British domestic law.

Accordingly, the most interesting aspect of British free speech law—its most salient characteristic—is the near-total reliance on cultural norms to check the abuse of government power to restrict or ban expression. The lack of judicial review also makes consideration of legislation regulating speech less compelling: the question in any given case will be how to interpret and apply the law, not whether the law is itself invalid. To be sure, free speech principles can and will seep into the process of statutory construction (something that the HRA endorses), but the main point remains the near-total reliance on Parliament's self-control to protect the freedom of speech.

Previous chapters have taken the relevance of constitutional text as a given—this assumption merits some sustained consideration. Free speech in the United Kingdom prior to the enactment of the Human Rights Act provides an excellent means of considering the relevance of text to the recognition and enforcement of constitutional rights.

Indeed, a pair of cases from the British House of Lords and the Supreme Court of the United States demonstrate quite concretely the limits of written constitutional provisions.[27] Examined in conjunction, these cases show that the protection of free speech or a free press may not be as extensive as one would assume under a written constitution and may, surprisingly, be more extensive than one would expect in the absence of such a document.

In February 1991, in *Regina v. Secretary of State for the Home Dep't, Ex parte Brind*,[28] the British House of Lords upheld a ban on broadcasts featuring in-person appearances by representatives of several designated political affiliates of allegedly terrorist organizations. The ban went into effect in 1988, pursuant to an administrative order issued by then-Home Secretary Douglas Hurd.[29]

In the summer of that same year, the Supreme Court of the United States decided *Rust v. Sullivan*,[30] a case involving policy concerns largely similar to those at issue in *Brind*. In *Rust*, the Court reached a result parallel with that reached in *Brind*, the First Amendment notwithstanding.[31]

One should note that the precise questions presented in *Brind* and *Rust* were not identical. Nevertheless, the approach that the Supreme Court and the House of Lords took in deciding the respective cases belies the proposition that the existence or absence of a written free speech guarantee prefigured the result in either case. A comparison of *Brind* and *Rust* shows that the existence of a written constitution may not always be a safe predictor of outcomes in actual cases.[32]

In *Brind*, the House of Lords, sitting as a court of law in a nation with no written constitution, appeared to import a "compelling state interest" test into a routine review of an administrative regulation, all in the name of protecting the "fundamental right" of free speech.[33] More or less concurrently, the United States Supreme Court, hearing an appeal challenging the legality of a federal regulation, declined to apply seemingly well-settled First Amendment law,[34] and in the process weakened both the scope and strength of the First Amendment.[35]

As will be explained more fully below, the ironic results in *Brind* and *Rust* do not appear to have been in any way contingent on the presence or absence of a written constitutional guarantee of free speech. Reasons beyond the presence or absence of text appear to account for the level of solicitude accorded free speech claims in the United States and Great Britain. This conclusion obviously has some bearing on the indeterminacy argument advanced by some in the legal academy.

In their effort to disprove the claim that judges decide cases in neutral, nonpolitical ways, adherents of the Critical Legal Studies (CLS) movement have identified the "indeterminacy problem" as one of the central bulwarks of their argument that law is mostly politics.[36] Some within the CLS movement argue that law is not simply indeterminate in particular applications but, rather, indeterminate at its "core."[37] A legal system's foundational principles should be the surest place to find stability and determinism; thus, *Brind* and *Rust* lend some support to the CLS claim that law is fundamentally "indeterminate." The better view, however, is that written constitutional provisions, coupled with strong community traditions, can at least constrain indeterminacy.

I. *Brind and* Rust*: Similar Cases, Similar Results*

The United States and Great Britain are distinct societies.[38] Despite a common legal heritage, the legal systems of the two nations have developed quite differently.[39] The historic absence of a written constitution, or a statutory bill of rights in Great Britain, is perhaps one of the most salient differences between the two legal systems. Since the enactment of the HRA, the citizens of United Kingdom have enjoyed a written compendium of rights formally protected under domestic law—albeit rights that are not really judicially enforceable.

Before the HRA came into effect, and given the historical absence of a textual guarantee of free speech rights in British domestic law, one would not expect the British House of Lords to decide a free speech case in the same manner as would the United States Supreme Court.[40] Quite reasonably, one would expect the Supreme Court to treat invocations of the right of free speech with greater solicitude than the House of Lords, an appellate court that operates in a nation where the legislature is sovereign[41] and the power of judicial review can charitably be described as "weak."[42] Paradoxically, in spite of its institutional limitations, the House of Lords has demonstrated a willingness to push at the margins to protect free speech,[43] whereas the United States Supreme Court from time to time permits the federal government to purchase speech rights through the creative exercise of Congress's taxing and spending powers.[44]

Madison once observed that a Bill of Rights is "useful" but not "essential."[45] *Brind* and *Rust* together suggest that Madison's observation may be more accurate than one might think.

A. *Brind*: Incorporating Free Speech Values Absent a Constitutional Mandate

The United Kingdom, unlike the United States, has no written constitution.[46] Consequently, British courts do not possess a direct constitutional command to consider free speech claims. The HRA now establishes a statutory right to the freedom of speech (by incorporating Article 10 of the European Convention on Human Rights and Fundamental Freedoms), but only time will tell if it makes a real difference in cases raising free speech claims against the government. As one observer has noted, "[t]he United Kingdom's Human Rights Act represents the partial, but only partial, Americanization of the British constitution."[47]

Since the HRA went into operation in October 2000, British trial courts have issued fifteen declarations of incompatibility and appellate courts have sustained ten of these declarations.[48] The ten declarations of incompatibility have addressed a wide variety of legal issues, but none has involved a free speech claim. Although five years is a relatively short temporal span, the British judiciary's initial enforcement efforts seem to suggest that the HRA will not have a radical effect on domestic laws that burden the exercise of freedom of speech.

The absence of a written constitution containing a guarantee of free speech explains, at least in part, the English judiciary's historical failure to vindicate free speech and free press claims routinely prior to the enactment of the HRA.[49] But other important factors are also at work. As Professor Gearty has observed:

> The assumption is that to enact a measure purporting to guarantee "human rights" is necessarily to enhance their protection. But how justified is this belief? In particular, since this inevitably involves a judicialization of rights-disputes, why should we now expect the judicial branch suddenly to change its spots and become the protector of civil liberties?

This is, after all, a role that it has carefully avoided discharging properly for the entire democratic era.[50]

Thus, the British judiciary always has avoided playing an active role in the resolution of contentious social policy questions—unlike the U.S. Supreme Court, which willingly has played such a role at least since *Brown v. Board of Education*[51] and arguably since *Marbury v. Madison*.[52] However, this explanation may be too facile.[53]

1. Free Speech as a Canon of Statutory Interpretation and as a Restraint on Administrative Discretion

In Great Britain, prior to the enactment of the HRA, the citizen's interest in freedom of speech stemmed from community tradition rather than legal fiat.[54] Given the structural weaknesses of the HRA, this may continue to hold true, at least over the short term. Although prior to October 2, 2000, no written provision of domestic law secured a "right" of free speech, the British judiciary had demonstrated a willingness to address free speech claims substantively. Thus, the casual observer would be mistaken if, upon discovering the absence of a written guarantee of the freedom of speech, she immediately drew the conclusion that freedom of speech as an autonomy interest would lack all currency.

The absence of a textual provision made it much easier for the British judiciary to justify its failure to vindicate speech interests.[55] But this circumstance tells only part of the story. Historically, the British courts have deferred to Parliamentary acts regardless of the judiciary's appraisal of the wisdom of Parliament's action.[56] Nor will the HRA really change this practice. Beyond the issuance of potentially ineffectual "statements of incompatibility," the British judiciary cannot remedy even facial violations of the HRA. As the great U.S. Chief Justice John Marshall once observed, "it is a general and indisputable rule that, where there is a legal right, there is also a legal remedy," and that "every right, when withheld, must have a remedy, and every injury its proper redress."[57] Chief Justice Marshall was speaking, of course, of a *judicial*, not *legislative*, remedy. It seems very odd indeed to tell a person suffering a legal wrong to seek formal redress from the very entity that committed the wrong in the first place.

Consistent with the doctrine of Parliamentary supremacy, the British judiciary does not possess the constitutional authority to reject an act of Parliament, so long as Parliament promulgated the act properly.[58] And this remains true even *after* the enactment of the HRA and its coming into force in October 2000.[59] Judicial review, in the strong form observed in the United States,[60] simply does not exist in Britain.

Accordingly, the British judiciary, in the absence of a Parliamentary command to vindicate speech rights, is limited to considering the tradition of favoring speech rights only at the margins—for example, as a consideration in issues involving statutory interpretation.[61] The HRA now directs the judiciary to consider such claims directly—at least in certain cases involving government actors[62]—but Parliament could repeal the statute tomorrow if it wished to do so. Moreover, such a course of action would not itself be subject to challenge under domestic law.

Any serious analysis of the strength of the freedom of speech in the United Kingdom must therefore begin with the frank recognition that if Parliament acts clearly and unambiguously, a claim of privilege under some notion of free speech will fail in the British domestic courts.[63] This illustrates the most obvious effect of a constitutional speech clause: such a provision legitimates, and often necessitates, judicial review of legislative enactments for consistency with the asserted speech right. At the outset, then, one must concede that the utter absence of an analogue to the First Amendment in British domestic law prior to the HRA substantially restricted the ability of the British judiciary to consider free speech claims on the merits. In the vast majority of cases arising before the HRA, any claim that an act of Parliament unduly infringed legitimate speech rights was heard (if at all) by the European Court of Human Rights in Strasbourg, France.[64]

However, there were (and are) exceptions to these general propositions. First, if an act of Parliament is ambiguous, the British courts are free to interpret the act consistently with the European Convention on Human Rights and Fundamental Freedoms (ECHR).[65] In fact, the HRA now expressly directs the British domestic courts to do just this. Article 10 of the ECHR safeguards the freedom of expression,[66] which, in conjunction with the HRA, may be raised in the British domestic courts as a textual basis for the vindication of free speech claims. Thus, when a statutory provision is ambiguous, British courts will have recourse to Article 10 of the ECHR to help determine the proper meaning of the provision.

The question at hand, however, is whether the existence of a written constitutional provision actually serves as a safe predictor of outcomes in cases involving the freedom of speech. Recourse to Article 10 of the ECHR, whether directly or indirectly via the HRA, does not address this question.

An analysis of the effectiveness of the HRA's incorporation of Article 10 of the European Convention in the British domestic courts fails to demonstrate that the British courts could—and would—consider speech interests in the absence of any textual command.

The British judiciary possesses the power to consider speech claims in another context: review of administrative regulations. Indeed, this power predates enactment of the HRA and therefore provides a better test of this chapter's hypothesis. Parliamentary acts sometimes require implementing regulations,[67] and those regulations are subject to judicial review. In Britain, judicial review of administrative regulations is not plenary.[68] A reviewing court's discretion is either limited by the terms of the act conferring the authority on the agency to promulgate regulations, or, in the absence of a textual statutory limitation, to a standard of reasonableness.[69]

Before the HRA, when a British court reviewed an exercise of administrative discretion, recourse to the ECHR was not mandatory.[70] Thus, unlike cases in which a court engaged in statutory interpretation—in such circumstances, both before and after the HRA, the British domestic courts must consider compatibility with the ECHR when resolving statutory ambiguities—recourse to the ECHR was entirely within the discretion of the administrative decision maker.[71] In consequence, when a British court reviewed an administrative regulation, there was no textual source for the protection of the freedom of speech, and therefore no formal basis for a reviewing court to consider it incident to review of the regulation. Nevertheless, the British judiciary seemingly incorporated free speech values into its review of administrative regulations many years prior to the HRA's enactment.

2. *Brind* and Judicially Created Speech Interests

In *Brind,* the British House of Lords had to decide whether administrative regulations proscribing the in-person broadcast of any message by an official representative of certain allegedly terrorist political organizations[72] exceeded the lawful authority of the government[73] minister who promulgated the regulations.

Then-Home Secretary Douglas Hurd promulgated the directive pursuant to the Broadcasting Act of 1981,[74] which authorized the Home Secretary to establish restrictions on domestic publicly owned broadcasters. The directive required the British Broadcasting Corporation (BBC) and the Independent Broadcasting Authority (IBA) to refrain from broadcasting any matter which consists of or includes—any words spoken, whether in the course of an interview or discussion or otherwise, by a person who appears or is heard on the programme in which the matter is broadcast where—(a) the person speaking the words represents or purports to represent an organisation specified in paragraph 2 below or (b) the words support or solicit or invite support for such an organisation, other than any matter specified in paragraph 3 below.[75]

The ban applied only to certain organizations:

The organisations referred to in paragraph 1 above are—(a) any organisation which is for the time being a proscribed organisation for the purposes of the Prevention of Terrorism (Temporary Provisions) Act 1984 or the Northern Ireland (Emergency Provisions) Act 1978; and (b) Sinn Fein, Republican Sinn Fein and the Ulster Defence Association.[76]

Finally, paragraph three limited the applicability of paragraph one:

The matter excluded from paragraph 1 above is any words spoken—(a) in the course of proceedings in Parliament, or (b) by or in support of a candidate at a parliamentary, European parliamentary or local election pending that election.[77]

The ban also did not apply to purely fictional works.[78]

Consistent with the terms of the directive, the broadcast media could report the words of an official representative of a proscribed organization; indeed, using actors, they were even free to re-create the statement.[79] The directive thus erected a prior restraint[80] against the broadcasting of statements by certain persons, unless the statements were made incident to an election, in a parliamentary body, or were part of a fictional work.

The standard of review applicable to the House of Lords' review of the Home Secretary's regulations was quite modest: the sole question before the court was whether a reasonable administrator could reasonably have promulgated the regulations at issue.[81] The House of Lords does not exercise plenary review over an administrator's choice among policy options; rather, the Lords are limited to reviewing a decision to ensure that it was not wholly arbitrary.[82] Lord Ackner explained that unlike run-of-the-mill legal cases in which the courts exercise "appellate" jurisdiction, that is, the power to review a trial court's decision on the merits without regard to the lower court's disposition of the legal issues, the court's review of an administrator's exercise of discretion is merely "supervisory."[83]

Despite the court's admittedly modest scope of review, four of the five Law Lords[84] hearing the case strongly suggested in dicta that they would reject a regulation regulating speech more aggressively; a more stringent regulation of speech[85] would be sufficiently "perverse" to fail the "reasonableness" test.[86]

Among the Law Lords, Lord Bridge was the strongest proponent of free speech as a substantive value in the process of judicial review of the exercise of discretionary administrative authority.[87] After noting that the House of Lords lacked authority to consider whether the regulation was consistent with Article 10 of the ECHR, Lord Bridge explained that "I do not accept that this conclusion means that the courts are powerless to prevent the exercise by the executive of administrative discretions, even when conferred, as in the instant case, in terms which are on their face unlimited, in a way which infringes fundamental human rights."[88] He continued:

> In exercising the power of judicial review we have neither the advantages nor the disadvantages of any comparable code [referring to the ECHR] to which we may refer or by which we are bound. But again, this surely does not mean that in deciding whether the Secretary of State, in the exercise of his discretion, could reasonably impose the restriction he has imposed on the broadcasting organisations, we are not perfectly entitled to start from the premise that any restriction of the right to freedom of expression requires to be justified and that nothing less than an important competing public interest will be sufficient to justify it.[89]

Lord Bridge observed that the "primary judgment as to whether the particular competing public interest justifies the particular restriction imposed" is within the administrative decision maker's province.[90] The British courts, however, "are entitled to exercise a secondary judgment by asking whether a reasonable Secretary of State, on the material before him, could reasonably make that primary judgment."[91] Applying the test he proposed, Lord Bridge, joined by Lord Roskill, concluded that the restriction at issue furthered an important public interest, and that a reasonable administrator therefore could adopt the regulation.[92]

Although ostensibly cabined within the confines of the "reasonable administrator/reasonable conclusion" test, Lord Bridge's opinion promulgates a relatively stout framework for applying that test: "an important competing public interest" is necessary to justify "*any* restriction" on "the right to freedom of expression."[93] This test sounds somewhat like the Supreme Court's "compelling state interest" test, used in cases such as *Boos v. Barry*.[94] To be sure, Lord Bridge's "important competing public interest" test appears to be at least marginally less protective than the "compelling state interest" test, insofar as "compelling" connotes a sense of urgency not inherent in the words "important competing." Regardless of the relative strength of the test, Lord Bridge's opinion is significant because it demonstrates that absent any written document providing a textual basis for the protection of speech interests, a Law Lord was prepared to promulgate de novo a standard for the protection of speech interests, and moreover, a standard with potential bite.

Lord Bridge and Lord Roskill were not the only members of the *Brind* panel who gave voice to concerns over the protection of free speech. Lord Templeman expressed what Lord Bridge merely implied: "My Lords, freedom of expression is a principle of every written and unwritten democratic constitution."[95] Lord Templeman ultimately concluded that "the interference with freedom of expression" caused by the regulation was "minimal" and that "the reasons given by the Home Secretary were compelling."[96] Like Lord Bridge, Lord Templeman decried engaging in judicial review beyond ensuring that the "reasonable administrator/reasonable decision" standard has been satisfied.[97] According to Lord Templeman, however, the context in which the reasonableness analysis occurs must take account of the value British society places on free expression.[98]

Lord Lowry's opinion also reflected concern for the protection of free expression:

> [T]he inspiration for the applicants' argument, if not perhaps the facts on which the argument is based, is closely linked with the principle of freedom of speech in a democratic society, so far as compatible with the safety of the state and the well-being of its citizens, which may provide a reason for me to say something.[99]

Lord Lowry concluded that the restrictions at issue imposed at most a "modest" burden on freedom of expression.[100] He emphasized, however, that "administrative acts" that severely burdened free expression "might well be justified, but they would certainly deserve the closest scrutiny."[101]

The remaining panel member, Lord Ackner, noted that "[i]n a field which concerns a fundamental human right—namely that of free speech —close scrutiny must be given to the reasons provided as justification for interference with that right."[102] Lord Ackner found that "the extent of the interference with the right to freedom of speech is a very modest one,"[103] and concluded that it was therefore reasonable.

Significantly, Lord Ackner appeared to place considerable reliance on Parliament's subsequent affirmation of the Home Secretary's regulation.[104] Thus, for Lord Ackner, Parliament's overt approval of the directive counted heavily against finding that the regulation was unreasonable.[105] That said, Lord Ackner's ultimate conclusion probably stems as much from his view that the directive's interference with the right to free expression was minimal as from his respect for Parliament's imprimatur.[106]

3. *Brind* and the Limits of Unwritten Protections of Civil Liberties

Brind demonstrates that the absence of a written provision protecting free expression does not bar consideration of speech interests as either a "right" or a decisional "principle."[107] In *Brind*, three of the five Law Lords view free expression as a fundamental "right." All five Lords believe that when an administrator promulgates a regulation that impinges on free expression, the regulation must receive "close" or the "closest scrutiny" and/or further an "important public interest." Although one may quibble with the result that the Lords reach, the language they use along the way closely parallels the language of Supreme Court cases interpreting the First Amendment.[108]

The limited scope of review applicable to the regulation at issue in *Brind* did not prevent the Lords from expounding on the administrator's need to have an important reason for exercising his discretion as he did.[109] Moreover, the Law Lords placed considerable emphasis on the limited nature of the restriction at issue; the regulation merely precluded certain persons, under certain conditions, from directly spreading their message via broadcast media. Neither the message nor the messenger were completely barred from the marketplace of ideas. Particularly compelling from the Lords' perspective was the potential for furthering acts of terrorism through in-person presentations by representatives of the affected organizations.

Brind shows that the existence of a written legal provision protecting free expression is not a necessary condition for judicial consideration or vindication of speech rights in a democratic society. Nor is *Brind* unique in British case law. As early as 1882, a British court considered the importance of the freedom of speech when deciding a criminal appeal.[110] And, as recently as 1999, a year before the effective date of the HRA, the House of Lords tortured the law of trespass in order to overturn trespass convictions for a group celebrating the summer solstice at Stonehenge.[111]

Brind demonstrates that the Law Lords were—and probably remain—prepared to hold as an abuse of discretion the most ambitious attempts by administrative decision makers to impose limits on free expression.[112] To be sure, *Brind* affords only a modicum of protection to free expression; Parliament is always free either to write a statute that expressly confers discretion on an administrator to regulate expression or simply to codify a particular restriction on free speech. And, *nothing* in the HRA would preclude Parliament from taking such action. To be clear: *Brind* offers no relief whatsoever in the face of an unambiguous Parliamentary enactment.[113]

Nevertheless, *Brind* remains quite significant not because it represents a "strong" free expression case but, rather, because it shows that the British judiciary, left to its own devices, is both willing and able to embrace free expression as a decisional norm without any prodding from Parliament. Community tradition, rather than legal fiat, provided the British judiciary with sufficient justification to create and police barriers against enforcement of restrictions on free expression absent overt approval by Parliament.[114] The strong and longstanding British community tradition in favor of permitting any citizen to speak his piece constitutes, at least in the abstract, a viable partial alternative to a legal right stemming from a textual source. This was true prior to the enactment of the HRA, and it remains true today.

In an important sense, then, the HRA simply codified a preexisting practice of the British judiciary. Parliament's blessing might lead judges to be more aggressive in applying the free speech norm, but there is no reason to believe that British judges will necessarily alter their behaviors one whit. The British domestic courts already had considered the effects of government action on the freedom of speech before the HRA went into effect and, under the HRA, they will undoubtedly continue to do so. Given the inability of the British courts to offer any relief for Parliamentary violations of the freedom of speech (other than a toothless "Declaration of Incompatibility"), the domestic protection of free speech will largely occur (as it does in Japan) through the process of creative statutory and regulatory interpretation, rather than through broad judicial pronouncements along the lines of *Brandenburg* or *New York Times Company*.

Ultimately, then, the United Kingdom presents an interesting analogue to Japan. The Japanese Supreme Court possesses a textual mandate to protect the freedom of expression and a strong, textually mandated, power of judicial review.[115] Yet, the history of parliamentary supremacy has led to judicial reticence to exercise this power directly and boldly. By way of contrast, the British courts lack both a strong textual mandate to protect freedom of expression and a strong power of judicial review. Yet, the British judiciary appears willing to defend the free speech principle from either parliamentary or ministerial abuse. Moreover, the British courts resort to the same techniques deployed by the Supreme Court of Japan—albeit for very different reasons. The Japanese Supreme Court, at least on paper, possesses a power that it fears using. The House of Lords, by way of contrast, is using a power that it claims not to possess.

B. *Rust v. Sullivan* and Limits of the First Amendment

Both theoretically and in practice, free speech enjoys much greater protection in the United States than in Great Britain. The Supreme Court's somewhat reflexive vindication of First Amendment claims in many modern cases[116] reflects a solicitude for free speech not necessarily shared in other countries—including Great Britain. The Court's willingness to vindicate speech rights undoubtedly reflects, at least to some degree, the presence of the Speech Clause of the First Amendment.[117]

The existence of the First Amendment, however, does not necessarily mean that the federal courts will always or predictably vindicate speech claims.[118] The First Amendment certainly requires the U.S. Supreme Court to consider a speech claim on the merits,[119] but it does not foreclose a result adverse to the vindication of the claim.[120] The natural question, then, is how much bite a textual provision entrenching speech rights actually has. Put differently, absent the First Amendment, would the Supreme Court have decided a significant number of its more important First Amendment precedents differently, or rather, would the Court have vindicated the speech claims under some other constitutional theory?[121]

The House of Lords' decision in *Brind* suggests that speech rights relate to sufficiently important community traditions to warrant solicitude by courts *regardless* of the precise source of the interest in free speech. Moving in the opposite direction, however, the Supreme Court's decision in

Rust suggests that even where a community's tradition of support for the freedom of speech is both strong and codified in the foundational legal document, a sufficiently politicized Court is quite capable of ignoring the textual provision.

1. *Rust* and the Failure of the Supreme Court to Vindicate Free Expression

Rust v. Sullivan presented the question of whether certain administrative regulations promulgated by the Reagan administration's Department of Health and Human Services (HHS) were consistent with the Free Speech Clause of the First Amendment.[122] The facts are relatively straightforward.

In 1970, Congress adopted a restriction on the expenditure of federal family planning appropriations.[123] Codified at section 300a-6 of Title 42, the provision states that "[n]one of the funds appropriated under this subchapter shall be used in programs where abortion is a method of family planning."[124]

In 1988, HHS reinterpreted this provision and promulgated a revised code of conduct for physicians and staff participating in the Title X program.[125] Under the new regulations, a doctor could not mention the availability of abortion to women who participated in the Title X program.[126] Even if a pregnant patient asked about the availability of abortion as a possible course of treatment, the attending physician could not counsel her in his best professional judgment.[127] Rather, the regulations required the doctor to say that "the project does not consider abortion an appropriate method of family planning and therefore does not counsel or refer for abortion."[128] Interestingly, the regulations expressly authorized physicians to refer pregnant women for prenatal care.[129] Thus, the regulations prohibited any discussion of abortion, ostensibly because abortion was outside the terms of the project. At the same time, participating clinics were required to refer patients for prenatal care, making untenable any claim that the Title X program's services ended once a woman became pregnant.

Rust presented two discrete questions for review. The first related to HHS's decision to change its interpretation of section 300a-6.[130] The second issue, the question of the regulation's consistency with the First Amendment, need have been reached only if the Supreme Court concluded that HHS had justified adequately its change of policy.[131] The majority concluded that HHS had justified its change of policy under section 300a-6,[132] and therefore proceeded to reach the First Amendment claims.

The First Amendment issue was relatively simple: Could the federal government condition participation in the Title X program on compliance with the administration's speech regulations? The Supreme Court answered in the affirmative.[133]

Chief Justice Rehnquist, writing for the majority, reasoned that the government was not required to subsidize all speech equally.[134] He opined that "[t]he Government can, without violating the Constitution, selectively fund a program to encourage certain activities it believes to be in the public interest, without at the same time funding an alternate program which seeks to deal with the problem in another way."[135] The Chief Justice observed that in exercising its taxing and spending powers, Congress could legitimately favor one kind of speech over another to further an otherwise legitimate policy choice.[136]

The *Rust* majority also rejected the petitioners' argument that the regulations violated the unconstitutional conditions doctrine.[137] Under the doctrine, government may not condition the conferral of a valuable governmental benefit on the ceding of some otherwise protected right or liberty.[138] Put differently, the government may not use its largesse "to produce a result which it could not command directly."[139]

The petitioners argued that the regulations at issue impermissibly required participating clinics to cede their speech rights regarding the availability of abortion as an alternative to pregnancy and childbirth in order to obtain the valuable benefit of Title X funds.[140] The *Rust* Court turned this objection aside simply by noting that participating clinics were free to exercise their speech rights as they wished, so long as they did not use Title X funds to promote abortion.[141]

The Court also rejected the petitioners' argument that the regulations unduly burdened physicians' ability to discharge in good conscience their professional duties.[142] The majority declined to decide whether doctors possessed a protected First Amendment interest in communicating with their patients because the regulations did not require the doctors to represent the forced speech as their own.[143] According to the majority, women who relied on Title X clinics for competent, professional medical advice did not rely on the clinic doctors or staff for comprehensive medical counseling because "the doctor-patient relationship established by the Title X program is not sufficiently all-encompassing so as to justify an expectation on the part of the patient of comprehensive medical advice."[144]

Finally, the majority determined that a woman's Fifth Amendment right to an abortion was not implicated by the government's decision not to subsidize abortion counseling incident to family planning services.[145] Because the government is not obliged to subsidize a woman's fundamental right to choose abortion, the government is likewise not required to subsidize counseling services related to that right.[146]

Justice Blackmun, in dissent, took issue with every step of the majority's analysis.[147] For present purposes, however, one need consider only his dissent's analysis of the majority's treatment of the speech-related claims.[148]

First, Justice Blackmun found that the regulations violated the unconstitutional conditions doctrine by conditioning a valuable governmental benefit on the ceding of protected speech rights.[149] His principal objection was with the majority's assertion that the government was simply subsidizing certain kinds of services and speech incident to those services.[150] The regulations did not prohibit—indeed they encouraged[151]—speech favorable to carrying the fetus to term. Thus, the regulations only prohibited speech by Title X clinics relating to abortion and abortion services.[152] In this respect, the speech regulations were entirely viewpoint based and, therefore, presumptively invalid on First Amendment grounds.[153]

Second, Justice Blackmun took issue with the majority's analysis of a medical doctor's interest in providing full medical disclosure to her patients.[154] He reasoned that if the government could circumscribe a doctor's professional speech as a condition of receiving government funds, "the First Amendment could be read to tolerate any governmental restriction upon an employee's speech so long as that restriction is limited to the funded workplace."[155]

2. *Rust* and the Nonapplicability of the First Amendment

For present purposes, *Rust* is significant primarily for its holding that the government's gag on a physician's professional speech to further a policy favoring childbirth was constitutional.[156] More specifically, the question of the level of scrutiny brought to bear on the restriction deserves close attention. Presumably, the First Amendment must have mandated that the Court examine with "closest scrutiny"[157] such a restriction. Alternatively, the Court could have required the secretary of Health and Human Services to justify the restriction on a physician's professional speech under a slightly less rigorous test—perhaps the Secretary need only have proffered "an important competing public interest."[158]

Careful review of the majority's decision reveals that the government had virtually *no* burden to meet—the government was free to pursue the policy without any constitutional impediment, even though the method of implementing the policy had a profound impact on the speech rights of physicians participating in the Title X program.[159] Justice Blackmun failed to target the most troubling turn of logic in the majority's approach: the absence of any statement regarding the level of scrutiny to which the Court would subject the proposed regulation as it related to a physician's professional speech.[160]

Apparently, the government is free, incident to a policy choice to subsidize family planning but not abortion, to restrict professional speech incident to the subsidized services without meeting *any* level of scrutiny. "[T]he general rule that the Government may choose not to subsidize speech applies with full force."[161] Thus, if the government elects to restrict the speech of a person working in a federally subsidized environment incident to an otherwise legitimate governmental program, that person has no First Amendment interest in maintaining his or her speech rights while on duty. If the government subsidizes A, and a person paid by the government to provide A feels a professional obligation to tell the putative recipient of A that he or she might wish to consider the possibility of B, that is just too bad. The government has no obligation to explain or to justify why it chose to preclude any discussion of B, even if in the professional judgment of the person providing A, mention of B seems mandatory.[162] Likewise, a patient has no protected First Amendment interest in hearing the speech.[163]

Where is the First Amendment in all this? Apparently, it simply has no application on these facts.[164] Under the First Amendment, "Congress shall make no law . . . abridging the freedom of speech."[165] It necessarily follows that Congress cannot delegate to the executive branch the task of making a law abridging the freedom of speech and thereby achieve indirectly what it could not itself do. Yet, this is precisely the action the Supreme Court sanctioned in *Rust*.[166] Thus, a written constitutional provision that ostensibly protects both the right to speak and the right to hear may be abrogated at will if the government is subsidizing the forum in which the speech-squelching restriction is to apply. *Rust* strongly demonstrates the limits of a written constitution; a textual right is only as powerful as the resolve of those charged with enforcing it.

Viewing the case somewhat more charitably, one could take the view that government should enjoy a relatively freer hand when subsidizing speech than when directly regulating private speech.[167] As Professor Post has noted, "[l]ike many First Amendment issues, they [subsidized speech problems] demand complex and contextual normative judgments about the boundaries of distinct constitutional domains in social space."[168]

If one views the speech as essentially private, the government scheme at issue in *Rust* was patently unconstitutional; conversely, if one could plausibly claim that only the government itself was speaking, the majority's attenuated free speech analysis becomes a more tenable approach. Government may itself participate in the marketplace of ideas and, to a large extent, may decide for itself the content of its message.

Professor Post suggests that "[t]he criteria for establishing whether speech ought to be characterized as public discourse are complex, contextual, and obscure, and particularly so in cases of subsidized speech."[169] He asserts that "there can be no simple empirical or descriptive line of demarcation," and that instead "speech will be assigned to public discourse on the basis of normative and ascriptive judgments as to whether particular speakers in particular contexts should constitutionally be regarded as autonomous participants in the ongoing process of democratic self-governance."[170] Professor Post cautions that "[w]hether explicitly addressed or not, such judgments are essential predicates to all cases of subsidized speech."[171]

I do not disagree with any of these observations but (like Post) believe that *Rust* presents a context in which characterizing the speech at issue as "government speech" requires either willful blindness or bad faith on the part of Chief Justice Rehnquist. In largely analogous contexts involving professors at public colleges and universities, the Supreme Court strongly has rejected the government's claim that it has a right to control the message of an instructor in her classroom.[172] Similarly, the Justices have disallowed efforts to control the professional speech of lawyers, even when the government itself employs the lawyers.[173] Simply put, the *Rust* majority never seriously addresses the principled distinction that justifies wildly different rules for government-employed university professors and government-employed Legal Services Corporation lawyers, on the one hand, and merely government-subsidized medical doctors and their professional staff, on the other.

Post argues that "[t]he Court's response to the plaintiffs' unconstitutional conditions argument is unconvincing."[174] He notes that "[i]t would be unconstitutional for the government to condition access to the 'subsidy' of second-class mailing privileges on the waiver of all advocacy of abortion within the mailed matter, even if magazines were free to advocate abortion outside 'the scope of' the United States mail." Moreover, "[i]t is far from clear . . . that physicians, even if they have accepted employment in a Title X clinic, occupy roles defined by reference to a purely organizational logic, particularly in situations where that logic seems to override the necessary exercise of independent professional judgement."[175]

The idea that patients in Title X clinics do not expect to receive comprehensive medical advice, premised on the physician's best professional judgment, "can properly be said to border on the 'disingenuous.' "[176] As Post explains, "[i]n a world where physicians routinely exercise independent judgment, patients come to expect and rely upon that judgment."[177] Yet, the regulations at issue in *Rust* utterly and completely displaced the ability of a physician to offer her patient the benefit of her best professional judgment when asked a direct question about the availability of and medical issues associated with an abortion. Post is surely correct when he asserts that "[e]xcept in the most unusual of circumstances, patients expect the independent judgment of their physicians to trump inconsistent managerial demands."[178]

The question that begs to be asked and answered is "Why did the *Rust* majority work so hard to avoid finding a First Amendment violation?" In my view, the answer has much to do with the antipathy of some of the Justices to abortion rights and very little to do with the First Amendment.

II. Brind, Rust, *and the Limits of Written Constitutional Provisions*

Viewing *Brind* and *Rust* in juxtaposition, one might wonder which tribunal was working with a stronger legal protection of free speech. The House of Lords subjected the Home Secretary to a far more probing review of the broadcasting restriction than the Supreme Court required of the Secretary of the Department of Health and Human Services (HHS) in *Rust*. This result is at least mildly surprising, especially if one has faith in the power of written constitutional protections.

The restrictions on freedom of expression at issue in *Brind* and *Rust* are not much different qualitatively. Both involve administrative regulations used to implement ambiguous statutes; both proscribe certain kinds of speech deemed unworthy of government subsidy; and both in a concrete way deny the right of free expression to those regulated. Finally, the results are roughly analogous. The shock value of studying the two cases in tandem stems from the absence of a written constitutional protection for free speech in the case of *Brind* and the existence of such a provision in *Rust*.

Beyond irony, *Rust* and *Brind* invite two questions: First, upon what legal basis did the House of Lords import the value of free expression evidenced in the *Brind* decision? Second, upon what legal basis did the Supreme Court abdicate its responsibilities under the First Amendment in *Rust*?

A. *Brind* and Judicial Activism

The opinions in *Brind* reflect a rare burst of judicial activism by the Law Lords. On their own and without Parliamentary sanction,[179] the Lords took upon themselves the task of safeguarding the British citizenry's right to free expression by incorporating a moderate-to-strong free speech value into the rational basis test used to review administrative acts.[180] Despite their protestations to the contrary, the Lords required more than mere rationality to justify the regulation. In doing this, however, the Lords acted legitimately.

Although there was no written provision in British law that guaranteed freedom of speech, there was, and is, a tradition in Britain of respecting a citizen's interest in free expression. This is not to say that this tradition has always prevailed over popular sentiments favoring the abrogation of the right.[181] Nor is it to suggest that the tradition favoring free speech is a sure substitute for a written guarantee of free speech; it is not.[182] Rather, it would seem that the absence of a written guarantee of freedom of expression does not mean that the British domestic courts will refuse to recognize the individual's interest in free expression routinely and without recourse. Moreover, there is reason to believe that the absence of a written guarantee of freedom of expression may be irrelevant in some cases, provided that an independent judiciary is prepared to consider on the merits the society's tradition favoring free expression. To be sure, a written provision guaranteeing freedom of expression should afford British citizens a greater and more predictable degree of protection.[183] The question, however, relates to the scope or degree of the right, rather than to its very existence.

B. *Rust* and Judicial Abdication

A written constitutional provision guaranteeing freedom of speech is of little use if the judiciary charged with enforcing the provision abdicates its responsibilities. *Rust* is an example of such judicial abdication. Regardless of where one stands on the merits of the HHS regulation, one cannot plausibly deny that the restriction on a doctor's right to impart truthful, nonmisleading medical information and the patient's interest in receiving such information merited closer scrutiny by the majority under the First Amendment. Indeed, some ten years later in 2001, a majority of the Justices joined an opinion very much at odds with the reasoning in *Rust*.[184] In 1991, however, the *Rust* majority was content to apply a de facto rational basis standard of review when examining the speech limitations applicable to medical doctors and other clinic personnel.

The *Rust* majority did not misconstrue the First Amendment—it simply decided not to apply it to the case at hand. Using faulty factual premises and non sequiturs, the majority decided that neither the physician nor the patient had any free speech interest in speech related to abortion in a government-sponsored family planning clinic.[185]

To be sure, subsidized speech cases are complex and require careful attention to context. Professor Post suggests that, as a preliminary matter, such cases require a "characterization of speech" as within the realm of "public discourse," and, if the speech satisfies this condition, a further inquiry into whether the regulation represents an appropriate "managerial" decision to define a program's parameters.[186] Applying his own test, Post concludes that "I do not see how the regulations can be supported by any convincing justifications."[187]

A convincing justification for the *Rust* majority's decision does exist—but it has much more to do with judicial politics over abortion rights than with the freedom of speech. Chief Justice Rehnquist has consistently opposed the constitutional protection of abortion rights. He dissented in *Roe v. Wade*[188] and, since that decision, has insisted that it was wrongly decided and should be overruled.[189] A mere two years prior to *Rust*, in *Webster*, Chief Justice Rehnquist fell one vote short of lowering the standard of review applicable to state abortion regulations to mere rationality.[190] Justice O'Connor declined to join Chief Justice Rehnquist's plurality opinion and instead wrote a concurring opinion that applied an "undue burden" test to Missouri's abortion regulations.[191]

Both the majority and dissenting Justices in *Rust* viewed the case through the prism of abortion rights, rather than free speech rights. If one holds the view that a complete criminal proscription against abortions would be constitutionally valid, then a government restriction on speech advocating criminal conduct—particularly in the context of a government-funded medical clinic—presents a very easy question. Of course, government can refuse to subsidize speech that relates to a subject that the government could, if it desired, criminalize.[192]

Accordingly, one would be mistaken to accuse Chief Justice Rehnquist of being hostile to free speech principles in *Rust*. It is not hostility to free speech but to abortion itself that provides the rationale for the majority's decision to denigrate the professional speech of physicians, while safeguarding the professional speech of college and university professors and lawyers. Free speech principles were a casualty of the Justices' longstanding feud over abortion rights. Other free speech cases involving picketing and pamphleting reflect the same sort of phenomenon.

In *Hill v. Colorado*, for example, a majority composed of Justices normally thought to be strong advocates of free speech principles sustained moving bubbles of prior restraint applicable to a public sidewalk—a classic public forum.[193] The majority's framing device for the case—a conflict between the speech rights of the protestors and the right of family planning clinic patients and staff to exercise their fundamental right to procreative freedom—was (and remains) nonsensical.[194] Neither the state of Colorado nor any other state actor had attempted to impede access to family planning clinics offering abortion services; the burden on the exercise of the fundamental right of privacy was entirely a function of *private* action. The only constitutional right being burdened was the right of anti-abortion protestors to picket the clinics. But, the majority's commitment to the pro-choice cause led it to abandon jurisprudential principle by equating state and purely private action for purposes of "balancing" the interests involved.

As I have noted in another context, this abdication of free speech principles has not gone unnoticed by members of the Supreme Court: "Justice Scalia has established a pattern of voting against granting certiorari in abortion protest decisions because 'experience suggests that seeking to bring the First Amendment to the assistance of abortion protesters is more likely to harm the former than help the latter.' "[195] Justice Scalia's objection is well founded. If the protesters in *Hill* had been advocating racial equality, it is unthinkable that the Supreme Court would have sustained the speech restrictions at issue.[196]

When renormalized in the context of the Justices' continuing disagreements over abortion rights, the *Rust* majority's decision begins to take on a palpable practical logic (just as *Hill* makes sense when viewed from the perspective of a pro-choice partisan). If one characterizes the case as being more about abortion rights than about free speech, the decision fits very nicely into a decisional framework that encompasses both government funding cases, like *Maher*[197] and *Harris*,[198] and decisions addressing abortion regulation more directly.

At the end of the day, then, I would argue that *Rust* does not reflect hostility to free speech but, rather, manifests hostility to abortion. Free speech principles were simply collateral damage in a case perceived as part of the overall battle over the scope and meaning of *Roe v. Wade.* The fact that the dissenting Justices in *Rust* would so willingly disregard free speech concerns in *Hill,* tends to confirm, rather than refute, the suggestion that abortion cases are not good exemplars of free speech jurisprudence in action.

Thus, the *Rust* majority's approach to the free speech claim reflects a different kind of activism from that in *Brind*—namely judicial abdication.[199] By refusing to apply the Court's well-settled First Amendment analysis, the majority was able to reach the result it desired (limiting abortion rights) in the most expeditious fashion. In the majority's haste to uphold the gag rule and sustain an abortion regulation, the First Amendment became an irrelevancy.

C. Critical Legal Studies and Indeterminacy

The novelty of *Brind* and *Rust* may have some currency beyond the straightforward point that written constitutions have their limits, and unwritten societal traditions can help inform decisional principles in appropriate cases. One of the main projects of the Critical Legal Studies (CLS) movement has been the indeterminacy problem. "[T]he indeterminacy argument [holds] that within the standard resources of legal argument [are] the materials for reaching sharply contrasting results in particular instances."[200] According to some in the CLS movement, "law is indeterminate at its core, in its inception, not just in its applications."[201]

Brind and *Rust* seem to support the CLS assertion that "law is indeterminate at its core." After all, if law at the constitutional level is little more than the expressed policy preferences of a handful of elites wearing black robes, then there is little hope for determinacy at any level.[202] Arguably, a legal system's constitutional provisions—its foundational principles— should be the surest place to find stability and determinism. If judges are free to disregard fundamental laws at will, then they are likely to be free to disregard more mundane ordinances with impunity.

A reexamination of *Brind* and *Rust* with an eye toward the CLS indeterminacy argument will carry the main thesis of this chapter—that written constitutions are helpful but unnecessary to vindication of the freedom of speech—a step further. Moreover, the indeterminacy argument helps to explain, at least in part, the results in *Brind* and *Rust*.

1. The Indeterminacy Argument

Some members of the CLS school argue that legal rules are indeterminate,[203] and that principled decision making cannot exist because its foundation—neutral, normative rules—does not exist.[204] CLS holds that because the participants in the present legal system have a vested interest in maintaining the status quo, they refuse to recognize that the system of rules constituting the law is nothing but a subjective exercise by judges, who rely on the intellectual equivalent of smoke and mirrors to reach politically pleasing results. As Professor Girardeau Spann has explained, for many non-CLS adherents "any lingering dissonance between faith in the system's general fairness and perceptions of unfairness in particular cases is resolved through the conviction that while unjust results may constitute imperfections in practice, they do not undermine the theory of principled decision making itself."[205] The process of legal decision making confers legitimacy on the decision; a particular case may be resolved in any number of ways, so long as proper process is observed.

Under this worldview, those who maintain a belief in principled decision making have failed to accept the basic truth that the legal system is actually a chaotic place where principle routinely falls to ideological or, worse yet, political preference.[206] As a result, such persons are guilty of complicity in the continuing disempowerment of various groups, including women, minorities, and the poor.[207] Not only is the law indeterminate but the fiction of principled decision making is merely a ruse used to hide the exercise of political power.

Finally, but perhaps most important, many (although far from all) in CLS circles generally reject the construct of "rights" as a helpful means of identifying and protecting discrete minority interests.[208] CLS adherents seem to view rights as merely one more tool for vindicating the policy preferences of the established ruling caste.[209] More subtly, some within the CLS movement argue that rights discourse emphasizes and helps to perpetuate an impersonal world in which individuals are needlessly alienated from the community of which they are inextricably a part.

Given the foregoing premises, one may hypothesize that a CLS critique of *Brind* and *Rust* would probably run along the following lines:

1. Because the law is fundamentally indeterminate and judges are

essentially political policymakers, judges are unconstrained and are unconstrainable;

2. It follows necessarily that it is not in the least surprising that the Supreme Court would largely ignore the First Amendment in *Rust,* nor is it surprising that the House of Lords would give voice to free speech values absent a textual referent compelling consideration of such values;

3. *Brind* and *Rust* merely demonstrate that law is largely a function of politics, a point that CLS has been explaining for years.

A CLS critique of *Brind* and *Rust* certainly raises troubling possibilities about the nature of judges and judging. Judges free to ignore a constitutional provision they dislike or free to create a provision they deem desirable do not fit the Legal Process ideal of the neutral adjudicator. But does the play inherent in legal rules, even those with constitutional pedigrees, necessarily mean that the rules are not "rules" or that blessing them with a constitutional mandate is at best superfluous and at worst ludicrous? There is reason for some optimism that law is not merely politics.

2. Living with Indeterminacy in Constitutional Adjudication

Even if courts remain theoretically free to disregard constitutional mandates, such action does not entirely devalue the use of written decisional rules.[210] Moreover, the recognition and application of strong community traditions when applying legal rules need not be a cause for alarm. This is true for at least two reasons.

First, the existence of a written provision forces the judiciary to act, to respond to the provision, however disingenuously. Even when a court seemingly refuses to apply a particular constitutional provision fairly, a court faced with a constitutional claim is obliged to explain itself. That is to say, the existence of a written constitutional provision at least nominally circumscribes judicial policy making by requiring the judge to make an effort, however forced, to apply the ostensibly controlling provision; a written constitutional provision establishes a process through which the claim to a particular right may be raised and heard (if not vindicated).[211] In more ideal circumstances, the judiciary will simply enforce the provision in good faith.[212] Thus, the existence of the written provision, whether it is enforced in good faith or is merely an impediment to a result the court deems desirable, has a predictable and reliable effect on the outcome of concrete cases. To the extent indeterminacy exists, it is cabined.[213]

Second, there is nothing inherently indeterminate or illegitimate about judges relying on well-established traditions in society when applying and developing legal rules.[214] Problems of legitimacy and indeterminacy arise only when judges resort to tradition as the primary means of discerning the relevant decisional principle, even in the face of an ostensibly relevant and controlling written legal command.[215]

Reconsidered in light of the foregoing, *Rust* appears to be a poorly crafted decision. Even if the result in *Rust* is correct as a matter of First Amendment law,[216] the majority did not explain or justify its failure to take up the primary First Amendment question on the merits. However, the radical indeterminacy suggested by some in the CLS school is not entirely borne out. First, the majority was constrained to at least explain (however unconvincingly) why the First Amendment was not implicated by either the physician's professional relationship with his patient or by the patient's interest in hearing the speech.[217] Second, the lack of indeterminacy in this area of the law is precisely what allows the disinterested observer to see the error in the majority's analysis. If the law were truly indeterminate, a "correct" result should not be obvious. That a given case may be wrongly decided for ideological or political reasons does not prove that the law itself is fundamentally unprincipled. Rather, it demonstrates that although the law is itself not fundamentally indeterminate, those charged with enforcing it may create indeterminate results by declining to decide a given case consistently with the law.[218]

From a Legal Process perspective, *Brind* fares considerably better than *Rust.* In *Brind*, the Lords did not stray from the discrete task at hand: deciding whether a reasonable Home Secretary could reasonably adopt the regulation.[219] After having identified the correct decisional principle, i.e., the "reasonableness" test, the Lords had to decide how that principle should be applied on the facts of the case. When applying the requisite legal test, the Lords had recourse to the English tradition in favor of freedom of expression.[220] Tradition did not supplant the decisional principle but, rather, informed its application. Thus, the Lords were not creating a new right out of thin air but, rather, were attempting to apply the law in a fashion consistent with community norms, in the absence of a contrary legal command. Such action should lead to predictable results in similar cases, assuming the Lords access the community's tradition at the same level of generality.[221] In any event, one cannot fairly characterize *Brind* as an example of a wild-eyed judiciary making up the law to suit its tastes;

Brind is an example of conscientious judges attempting to find an acceptable context in which to place a decisional rule.

III. Conclusion

Brind and *Rust* together help to show the limits of a written constitution and the possibilities of an unwritten constitution. Along the way, they also help to highlight the importance of principled decision making by judges if there is to be determinacy in the law. To the extent that *Rust* is disturbing for its lack of principled decision making, *Brind* is to the same degree a cause for hope.

Accordingly, the presence of a written guarantee protecting the freedom of speech is not a panacea. By itself, such a guarantee will do little to protect free expression in the absence of judges committed to enforcing the provision. At the same time, the absence of a written free speech guarantee need not be fatal to the recognition or vindication of free speech claims against the government. In the end, judges are far more important than text in securing human rights.

This is perhaps an obvious lesson, but one that bears repeating in light of the optimism surrounding the HRA. In the absence of a strong commitment on the part of the British judiciary to give meaningful enforcement to the HRA, the status of civil liberties in the United Kingdom is not likely to change a great deal. In the meantime, the European Court of Human Rights, sitting in Strasbourg, France, remains open to citizens of the United Kingdom who come away dissatisfied from the British domestic courts.

7

Free Speech and the Culturally Contingent Nature of Human Rights

Some Concluding Observations

At the outset of this book, I suggested that a comparative law analysis of free speech rights in Western industrial democracies might shed some important insights into the relationship between the freedom of speech and democratic self-government. At an even more theoretical level, I posited that a comparative law analysis might yield useful perspectives from which to evaluate universalist claims about the fundamental nature of the freedom of speech. The foregoing materials *do* yield such insights but, for the most part, in the direction of rights pluralism rather than a single working definition of "the freedom of speech."

I. *"Free Speech" Lacks a Common, or Universal, Definition*

Free speech rights are highly culturally contingent, and universalist claims about the proper outcomes in free speech cases simply do not bear up upon closer inspection. This holds true with respect to societies that are overtly committed to maintaining the freedom of speech as an essential component of the project of democratic self-government. Accordingly, defenders of the free speech orthodoxy currently observed in the United States should be prepared to concede that free speech absolutism is not the only model for a society committed to safeguarding the freedom of speech.

The routine exclusion of certain disfavored kinds of speech, such as child pornography and hard-core forms of erotica (in all five nations, to some degree or another), as well as the protection of low-value speech like commercial speech (the United States and Canada, but not Germany, Japan, or the United Kingdom) inevitably reflect highly subjective normative value judgments. There is nothing intrinsically good or bad about this, but such a state of affairs effectively belies any claim to some Platonic idea or Natural Law definition of free speech that judges, regardless of cultural influences, will reflexively identify and intuitively apply to reach largely identical results in cases presenting more-or-less similar facts. To the extent that international law makes safeguarding the freedom of speech an objective of the international human rights regime,[1] a great deal of leeway with regard to a nation-state's definition of "free speech" appears to be entirely unavoidable.

With those caveats, certain themes, elements, and leitmotifs about the purpose or role of free speech in a democratic polity *do* seem to exist. The *ideology* of free speech seems to have serious transnational salience. All five legal cultures—and the judges who serve as the apex of the legal pyramid —find it tremendously important to proclaim their commitment to the freedom of speech as an important component of the project of democratic self-government. Indeed, democratic self-governance, personal autonomy, self-actualization, and facilitating dissent all receive serious and regular consideration in the free speech case law of all five legal systems, even if the concrete results in particular cases vary wildly.

II. *Constitutional Text Matters*

Another potentially relevant conclusion that one might draw is that text matters. The most protective free speech regimes exist in the two nations with the most textually unqualified protections of the freedom of speech. Neither the First Amendment nor Article 21 of the Japanese Constitution directly invites rights balancing. The First Amendment simply states that "Congress shall make no law . . . abridging the freedom of speech."[2] Article 21 guarantees to all citizens "[f]reedom of assembly and association as well as speech, press, and all other forms of expression" and provides that "[n]o censorship shall be maintained, nor shall the secrecy of any means of communication be violated."[3] Unlike the German and Canadian Constitutions, or the British Human Rights Act, neither the United States Constitution nor the Japanese Constitution invites judges overtly to balance free speech against other interests (whether of a constitutional magnitude or not).

To be sure, the absence of constitutional text protecting the freedom of speech might not preclude courts from considering such claims on the merits—the United Kingdom prior to the enactment of the Human Rights Act provides an instructive example. Nevertheless, the presence of such text plainly facilitates judicial protection of free expression. Moreover, the nature of the constitutional text makes a difference too. The unqualified protection of a right seems to embolden courts to interpret the right more broadly than does more qualified language. Indeed, this comparative exercise shows a descending order of protection that certainly appears to track constitutional text very nicely. Again, one should not discount other important factors, such as a general culture that values the right in question and the presence of an independent judiciary vested with the power of judicial review. But, holding these conditions more or less constant, the precise articulation of a right seems to have an important effect on its implementation; in a word, text matters and drafters of constitutional instruments should be careful to bear this in mind.

Text does not happen by magic, of course. In particular, the drafters of the Japanese Constitution and the Basic Law provided, quite intentionally, very different levels of relative protection for the freedom of speech. The Japanese free speech guarantee is unqualified and, with respect to political speech, the Supreme Court of Japan has interpreted and enforced Article 21 in this way. The German Basic Law's protection of free speech, by way of contrast, is itself highly qualified and, moreover, totally subordinated to other constitutional interests (notably including human dignity (Article 1) and free development of the personality (Article 2)).

Although the First Amendment has remained textually unchanged since 1791, the amendment's jurisprudential meaning has evolved significantly over time. It was not until the twentieth century—and arguably the 1960s, with the Warren Court's expansive free speech decisions—that it came to provide political advocacy virtually unlimited protection. Thus, constitutional text probably mirrors culture as much as it shapes it. Canada, Germany, and the United Kingdom feature highly conditional protections of free speech precisely because the citizens of those polities value free speech somewhat less highly than the citizens (and judges) of the United States and Japan.

Of course, some degree of rights balancing is probably inevitable, even in the United States and Japan. But it does seem significant that the absence of conditional language appears to track a more robust construction of the freedom of speech. Other factors, such as an independent judiciary with the power of judicial review are obviously important too. But Canada, Germany, and the United Kingdom feature independent judiciaries, and both the Canadian Supreme Court and the German Constitutional Court possess and use the power of judicial review to invalidate legislation and executive actions deemed inconsistent with constitutional rights.

Thus, constitutional text tracks social values even as it helps to shape them. For example, both the Canadian and German free speech guarantees are limited on their face. Section 1 of the Canadian Charter of Rights and Freedoms conditions the rights and freedoms that the Charter guarantees by expressly permitting "reasonable limits prescribed by law" that "can be demonstrably justified in a free and democratic society."[4] Article 2 rights are thus subject to generic limitations, provided that the limits are both "reasonable" and "demonstrably justified in a free and democratic society."

The German Basic Law establishes a hierarchy of rights, with dignity, protected in Article 1, residing, quite literally, at the top of the list.[5] Moreover, Article 5, which protects the freedom of speech, contains numerous provisos and limitations, including an express limitation protecting personal honor and reputation. In light of the highly conditional nature of the free speech rights in Canada and Germany, one should not be surprised to see the Supreme Court of Canada and the Federal Constitutional Court overtly balancing away the freedom of speech in order to advance other important interests—interests that themselves enjoy express constitutional protection too.

The United Kingdom provides an important cautionary note regarding the limits of text as a means of safeguarding human rights. But the status of free speech in the United Kingdom seems consistent with the overall picture sketched above. British courts certainly take free speech claims seriously but always measure this interest carefully against the traditional rule of parliamentary supremacy. This structural feature of the British Constitution has a higher priority than any specific human right, be it free speech or privacy rights.[6] This was true before enactment of the Human Rights Act of 1998 and it remains equally true today.

III. *Freedom of Speech as an Essential Condition for Democratic Self-Government and the Countervailing Problem of Rights Pluralism*

The transcultural salience of the freedom of speech as an essential element of a just government constitutes another potential lesson one may draw from this comparative law exercise. In all five nations, when citizens bring free speech claims, courts generally recognize that these claims implicate, to some degree at least, important social values related to the project of democratic self-government. This does not mean, of course, that advancing these values ultimately will take precedence over competing values, such as the protection of personal dignity (Germany) or the maintenance of a viable pluralist, multicultural society (Canada). But it does show that the conceptualization of free speech as a human right reflects some transculturally valid common ground.

Disagreement seems to arise not so much about the values that free speech advances but, rather, over the relative importance of these values when measured against other competing social goals and objectives. Thus, the particular implementation of shared concerns about the value of free speech does not allow for predictable results across legal cultures; different nations implement their commitment to "free speech" in unique and severable ways. For international human rights law, this would suggest the need for a very wide "margin of appreciation" when determining whether a particular country's laws and practices adequately discharge the obligation to respect "the freedom of speech."[7] Some concrete examples will demonstrate the point.

Campaign finance limits might or might not exist in a given nation (although the trend is fairly clear that most constitutional democracies maintain such measures and view them as entirely consistent with "the freedom of speech"). A regime that permits or disallows campaign finance laws should, accordingly, be deemed consistent with a commitment to free speech. A meaningful commitment to respecting "the freedom of speech" simply does not prefigure any specific approach to this problem.

Similarly, a constitutional court might—or might not—construe the freedom of speech to reach certain forms of erotica. Again, the diverse approaches that constitutional democracies committed to the freedom of speech have adopted regarding erotica suggests that a meaningful commitment to the freedom of speech says absolutely nothing about the protection of erotica. Both systems protecting and withholding protection from these materials may legitimately claim to respect the freedom of speech. As with the presence or absence of campaign spending limits, either choice on this question should be seen as consistent with adherence to the principle of free speech.

Perhaps most significantly, the spectrum of protected *political* speech also might be less than unlimited. Canada, Germany, and the United Kingdom *all* restrict core political speech, generally in efforts to protect either personal dignity or the dignity and well-being of racial, religious, and ethnic minorities within their polities. The reasons for these practices vary from country to country.

Canada features an ideology of pluralism and multiculturalism that makes Canada different from the United States. Restrictions on free speech that advance the multiculturalist program seem entirely reasonable to the Canadian Supreme Court. In Canada, efforts to promote equality outweigh, at least in some circumstances, an individual or group's interest in free expression.

Germany's commitment to dignity values certainly reflects the historical fact of the Holocaust. But the German legal system's concern for individual dignity, honor, and reputation significantly predates the Holocaust and World War II. To be sure, the National Socialist period represents a complete cultural meltdown. That neither the German government nor the German citizenry wishes to take chances going forward should not really come as a surprise. If the United States had undergone a similar recent experience, it would not be surprising if the Supreme Court limited free speech principles in order to promote human dignity, both for the individual and for minority groups.

On the other hand, it would be mistaken to view the Federal Constitutional Court's commitment to protecting dignity values as solely a product of postwar reforms. In fact, German society has taken good manners seriously for a very long time indeed.[8] Therefore, one should not be surprised that the freedom of speech, even with respect to core political speech, must give way when a free speech claim conflicts with the protection of personal honor and dignity. This does not mean that Germany lacks an appreciation for the freedom of speech; it simply reflects a different relative priority regarding the importance of speech vis-à-vis the importance of human dignity.

In the United Kingdom, historical accidents largely associated with the doctrine of parliamentary supremacy work to limit the ability of courts to vindicate free speech claims. This was true prior to the adoption of the

Human Rights Act of 1998, and it will remain true for some time to come. The protection of human rights in the United Kingdom largely rests with Parliament, and not the courts. To the extent that Parliament wishes to displace free speech in favor of national security, the protection of the deity against blasphemous utterances, or to make the community a more welcoming place for racial and ethnic minorities, Parliament is free to do so and the British domestic courts will not stand in the way.

Great Britain's principal constitutional value is an unlimited commitment to the idea of majority rule, and this, by definition, implies bad things for minorities. Existing legal rules privilege the cultural and political majority at the expense of cultural and political minorities—but this might change as the Human Rights Act takes greater hold over time.

One should, however, bear in mind that the doctrine of parliamentary supremacy does not stop the courts from reading free speech values into ambiguous statutory or regulatory language. And the British courts have not shirked from doing just this. The social commitment to free speech— the shared social expectation that citizens will enjoy free speech to some degree—informs and influences the British judiciary's work.

Perhaps surprisingly, Japan's formal free speech doctrine looks the most like the free speech law of the United States. The Supreme Court of Japan has more or less adopted the Warren Court's free speech orthodoxy. To be sure, it has accepted greater limits on free speech to protect personal reputation than has the United States Supreme Court. The Supreme Court of Japan also has conceptualized the free speech project in terms of supporting the project of democratic self-government, rather than personal autonomy or freedom.

The marketplace of ideas metaphor receives occasional lip service from the Supreme Court of Japan, but the results in concrete cases reflect a commitment to protecting speech associated with democratic self-government. Hence, erotica, commercial speech, and political speech that involves strong personal insult do not receive protection. But speech critical of the government or its officers enjoys very broad protection.

In sum, these myriad restrictions on the freedom of speech coexist cheek by jowl with generalized expectations of freedom of speech in Western-style industrial democracies. The portrait that emerges reflects tremendous diversity as to means, if not ends. At bottom, a commitment to free speech implies merely a willingness to balance the burden of a particular law on an individual's right to self-expression against the social objectives the law in question advances; it does not imply (much less guarantee) any particular outcomes.

IV. *Freedom of Speech Probably Cannot Be Cabined by Any Single Operative Definition or Set of Conditions*

Professor Michael Perry has observed that differences in the conceptualizations of human rights do not, by themselves, negate the possibility of a meaningful international discourse regarding the existence and scope of universal human rights. "To say that human beings *are* all alike in at least some respects such that some things are good and some things are bad for *every* human being is not to deny that human beings are *not* all alike in many other respects; it is not to deny that some things are good and some things are bad for *some* human beings *but not for others*."[9] Thus, "a concrete way of life good for one or more human beings might not be good for every human being, and a way of life bad for one or more human beings might not be bad for every human being."[10] These facts about human nature mandate some degree of difference among nations and cultures in conceptualizing human rights: "Undeniably, then, any plausible conception of human good must be pluralist."[11] But, one should take care to note that pluralism does not necessarily imply utter moral relativism. A conception of human good "can acknowledge sameness as well as difference, commonality as well as variety."[12]

Some practices, such as slavery and torture, present easy cases. "Practices transculturally agreed to be moral abominations—slavery and genocide, for example—are, typically, explicitly proscribed."[13] For other rights, such as freedom of speech, great differences of opinion exist as to whether particular laws and practices transgress the right. This sort of value pluralism is unavoidable and the product of cultural difference. In such cases, "[i]t makes good sense that some human rights are, as established by international law, not only conditional, because some human rights—like the right to freedom of expression—are, as a moral matter, nonabsolute."[14]

The natural and inescapable consequence of varying conceptualizations of specific rights is a degree of indeterminism in setting the metes and bounds of the right in question. As Perry observes, "some provisions of the international law of human rights [are] at least somewhat indeterminate in some contexts in which the provisions are implicated" precisely because it is necessary to "leav[e] room for a reasonable difference of judgment about whether, given all the relevant particularities, the necessary conditions exist."[15]

Once again, the observation seems inescapable that a strong "margin of appreciation"[16] must needs apply when analyzing whether a given national legal system adequately protects "the freedom of speech." Broad discretion to define and shape the meaning of free speech seems essential. Unlike some rights, free speech simply is not the subject of broad transnational consensus as to either its shape or scope.

We would probably all agree that a government's use of thumb screws or electric shock to a prisoner's genitals constitutes "torture." Similarly, proscriptions against slavery and murder seem relatively easy to define and enforce. Cultural deviation as to these practices is far more circumscribed. Consensus generally exists across a wide swath of jurisprudential territory.[17] By way of contrast, whether commercial speech advances important social values or whether money equals speech are *not* propositions on which broad transnational agreement exists. Accordingly, it should be easier to achieve international consensus on the substance of a prohibition against torture or slavery than on the substance of an affirmative right to the freedom of speech.

There is an important domestic tension here too: the meaning of free speech is hardly fixed or immutable. The proper scope of free speech is both contestable and contested. Recourse to a comparative law survey conclusively shows that, unlike the law of physics, the laws governing free speech exhibit tremendous variability both across and within legal cultures. This should give both defenders and opponents of free speech orthodoxy pause—neither camp can lay claim to any more ground than persuasive argumentation can win for it.

Workplace harassment laws, campus speech codes, and campaign finance reform are *all* arguably consistent with a meaningful commitment to the freedom of speech. Similarly, one can plausibly claim that measures such as these go too far and, accordingly, cannot be squared with the First Amendment. The scope of the freedom of speech is and will always remain a work in progress, a kind of permanent legal construction zone.

This conclusion, moreover, should not be a cause for alarm. It seems entirely fitting that the free speech project itself should serve as an object of national—and international—debate. A commitment to free speech without a commitment to discourse and debate on the substance of the right would be more than a little bit ironic. Indeed, it would be a betrayal of the free speech principle itself.

Notes

1. U.S. Const. amend. 1.

2. *See, e.g., Wisconsin v. Mitchell*, 508 U.S. 476 (1993) (upholding, against free speech challenge, a state law enhancing sentences for crimes in which the defendant selects victim because of the victim's race); *R.A.V. v. St. Paul*, 505 U.S. 377 (1992) (invalidating on free speech grounds a St. Paul, Minnesota, city ordinance that prohibited speech or expressive conduct causing fear or alarm on the part of another person based on race, gender, or religion); *Meritor Savings Bank v. Vinson*, 477 U.S. 57 (1986) (recognizing a claim of action under Title VII for the creation and maintenance of a hostile work environment); *American Booksellers Association, Inc. v. Hudnut*, 771 F.2d 323 (7th Cir. 1985) (invalidating on free speech grounds an Indianapolis, Indiana, ordinance that prohibited pornography that degraded or subordinated the models on the basis of gender), *summarily aff'd*, 475 U.S. 1001 (1986).

3. By "equality of citizenship," I mean the ability to participate fully in the political, economic, and social life of the community without regard to one's race, gender, religion, sexual orientation, or similar characteristics.

4. *Printz v. United States*, 521 U.S. 898, 977 (1997) (Breyer, J., dissenting).

5. *Atkins v. Virginia*, 536 U.S. 304, 347 n.21 (2002); *see also Thompson v. Oklahoma*, 487 U.S. 815, 830 & 831 n.31 (1988) (taking into consideration legal views of "other nations that share our Anglo-American heritage" and "the leading members of the Western European community" in analyzing Eighth Amendment question).

6. *Atkins*, 536 U.S. at 352 (Rehnquist, C.J., dissenting).

7. *Id.* at 353.

8. 539 U.S. 558 (2003).

9. *See id.* at 576–77 (noting that "[o]ther nations, too, have taken action consistent with an affirmation of the protected right of homosexual adults to engage in intimate, consensual conduct" and that "the right petitioners seek in this case has been accepted as an integral part of human freedom in other countries").

10. *Id.* at 576.

11. *Id.* at 577.

12. *See id.* at 604 (Scalia, J., dissenting) (referencing recognition of same-sex marriage under the Canadian Charter of Rights and Freedoms equal protection doctrine).

13. *See, e.g.,* Symposium, "New Directions in Comparative Law," 46 *Am. J. Comp. L.* 597 (1998); Symposium, "New Approaches to Comparative Law," 1997 *Utah L. Rev.* 255.

14. Catherine A. Rodgers, "Gulliver's Troubled Travels, or The Conundrum of Comparative Law," 67 *Geo. Wash. L. Rev.* 149, 150 (1998).

15. *See infra* Chapter 3.

16. *See* Mari J. Matsuda et al., *Words That Wound: Critical Race Theory, Assaultive Speech, and the First Amendment* (1993); Mari J. Matsuda, "Public Response to Racist Speech: Considering the Victim's Story," 87 *Mich. L. Rev.* 2320 (1989).

17. *See* Richard Delgado & Jean Stefancic, *Must We Defend Nazis? Hate Speech, Pornography, and the New First Amendment* (1997); Richard Delgado, "Words That Wound: A

Tort Action for Racial Insults, Epithets, and Name-Calling," 17 *Harv. C.R.-C.L. L. Rev.* 133 (1982).

18. *See* Catharine A. MacKinnon, *Sexual Harassment of Working Women* (1979); *see also* Catharine A. MacKinnon, *Only Words* (1993).

19. *See* Leslye Amede Obiora, "Toward an Auspicious Reconciliation of International and Comparative Legal Analyses," 46 *Am. J. Comp. L.* 669, 671–78 (1998) (suggesting that the search for wholly abstract universal human rights truths may be hopelessly "utopian" and arguing for a renewed effort at informing international human rights law norms with carefully researched comparative legal studies of rights in action).

20. Michael J. Perry, *The Idea of Human Rights: Four Inquiries* 73 (1998).

21. *Id.* at 75.

22. *See* John Chipman Gray, *The Nature and Sources of the Law* (2d ed. 1921); John Austin, *Lectures on Jurisprudence* (5th ed. 1885); Wesley Newcomb Hohfeld, "Some Fundamental Legal Conceptions as Applied to Judicial Reasoning," 23 *Yale L.J.* 16 (1913).

23. Frederick Schauer, "The Boundaries of the First Amendment: A Preliminary Exploration of Constitutional Salience," 117 *Harv. L. Rev.* 1765, 1767 (2004).

24. *Id.*

25. *Id.* at 1787.

26. *Id.*

27. *See id.* at 1784–86 (describing these theories and providing citations to major works by the principal proponents of each theory).

28. *See Brandenburg v. Ohio*, 395 U.S. 444 (1969) (strictly limiting government restrictions on speech to circumstances in which the speech presents a "clear and present danger of imminent lawlessness," a test that has proven to be highly protective of intemperate and offensive speech).

29. *See* Schauer, *supra* note 23, at 1766–68 (noting that courts and commentators often simply assume, without careful reflection or justification, the boundary lines of the Free Speech Clause).

30. *See* Stanley Fish, *Is There a Text in This Class? The Authority of Interpretive Communities* 305-321, 328–34, 338–55 (1980) [hereinafter Fish, *Text in This Class*] (arguing that words derive their meaning within interpretative communities and that this meaning inheres not from any objective connection between words and things or ideas but, rather, from a set of shared assumptions that confer meaning on symbols); *see also* Stanley Fish, *Doing What Comes Naturally: Change, Rhetoric, and the Practice of Theory in Literary and Legal Studies* 120–60 (1989) [hereinafter Fish, *Doing What Comes Naturally*]. For analysis and criticism of Professor Fish's theories, see Peter Schanck, "The Only Game in Town: An Introduction to Interpretive Theory, Statutory Construction, and Legislative Histories," 38 *Kan. L. Rev.* 815, 830–37 (1990); Pierre Schlag, "*Fish v. Zapp:* The Case of the Relatively Autonomous Self," 76 *Geo. L.J.* 37, 42–45 (1987).

31. By way of example, consider the culturally specific nature of various speech idioms, e.g., "We had a ball last night." Taken literally, this sentence could convey any number of meanings: (1) the group possessed a round, spherical object of some sort, but lost it, (2) the group put on an elaborate dance, (3) it could constitute a kind of scatological reference, (4) it could mean something else. As it happens, most users of American English would select option (4): the sentence means that the group had a pleasant evening, without any reference to precisely what the group did. Legal language is no different and is, therefore, culturally contingent. *See* Dan F. Henderson, "Japanese Law in English: Reflections on Translation," 6 *J. Japanese Stud.* 117 (1980) (noting that problems of comparative legal studies not only include difficulties of connotation and denotation of particular terms but also encompass systemic difficulties associated with differing views about the nature of precedent and the proper operation of the rule of law).

32. *See* Fish, *Doing What Comes Naturally, supra* note 30, at ix, 436–67; Fish, *Text in This Class, supra* note 30, at 13–17; *see also* Stanley Fish, "Still Wrong After All These Years," 6 *Law & Phil.* 401, 405–07 (1987); Stanley Fish, "Work-

ing on the Chain Gang: Interpretation in Law and Literature," 60 *Tex. L. Rev.* 551, 562 (1982).

33. *See* Ruth Benedict, *The Chrysanthemum and the Sword: Patterns of Japanese Culture* 13–16 (1946); *see also* Daniel H. Foote, "The Roles of Comparative Law," 73 *Wash. L. Rev.* 25 (1998).

NOTES TO CHAPTER 2

1. *See* David M. Rabban, *Free Speech in Its Forgotten Years* (1997).

2. 376 U.S. 254 (1964).

3. 395 U.S. 444 (1969).

4. *See infra* text and accompanying notes 58 to 63.

5. *See* Ronald J. Krotoszynski, Jr., "An *Epitaphios* for Neutral Principles in Constitutional Law: *Bush v. Gore* and the Emerging Jurisprudence of Oprah!" 90 *Geo. L.J.* 2087, 2093–2104 (2002) (arguing that Supreme Court's claim to institutional legitimacy rests on proposition that Justices will decide cases in principled, rather than political, fashion).

6. Frederick Schauer, "The Boundaries of the First Amendment: A Preliminary Exploration of Constitutional Salience," 117 Harv. L. Rev. 1765, 1785 (2004).

7. *Id.* at 1786.

8. *See Abrams v. United States,* 250 U.S. 616, 624–31 (1919) (Holmes, J., dissenting).

9. *See Gitlow v. New York,* 268 U.S. 652, 672–73 (1925) (Holmes, J., dissenting).

10. *Abrams,* 250 U.S. at 630 (Holmes, J., dissenting). Justice Brennan coined the phrase "marketplace of ideas" in *Lamont v. Postmaster Gen.,* 381 U.S. 301, 308 (1965). *See* Owen M. Fiss, *Liberalism Divided: Freedom of Speech and the Many Uses of State Power* 160 n.25 (1996).

11. *Gitlow,* 268 U.S. at 673 (Holmes, J., dissenting).

12. *See* John Stuart Mill, *On Liberty* (Elizabeth Rapaport ed., Hackett Publ'g Co. 1978) (1859).

13. *See* Frederick Schauer, *Free Speech: A Philosophical Enquiry* 15–34 (1982); Rodney A. Smolla, *Free Speech in an Open Society* 6–11 (1992).

14. *See* Joel Achenbach et al., "Group Awaited Spacecraft Behind Comet," *Wash. Post,* Mar. 28, 1997, at A1; Frank Bruni, "Death in a Cult: The Personality," *N.Y. Times,* Mar. 28, 1997, at A1; Todd S. Purdum, "Death in a Cult: The Scene," *N.Y. Times,* Mar. 30, 1997, § 1, at 1.

15. *Gitlow,* 268 U.S. at 673 (Holmes, J., dissenting).

16. *See* Smolla, *supra* note 13, at 6–7; Cass R. Sunstein, *Democracy and the Problem of Free Speech* 17–22, 34–38, 72–73, 249–52 (1993).

17. *See* Steven H. Shiffrin, *Dissent, Injustice, and the Meanings of America* 24–31, 57–67 (1999); Owen M. Fiss, "Free Speech and Social Structure," 71 *Iowa L. Rev.* 1405, 1410–21 (1986).

18. *See, e.g., Reno v. ACLU,* 521 U.S. 844 (1997); *McIntyre v. Ohio Elections Comm'n,* 514 U.S. 334, 341, 348 n.11 (1995); *Texas v. Johnson,* 491 U.S. 397, 418, 429 (1989); *American Booksellers Ass'n v. Hudnut,* 771 F.2d 323, 330 (7th Cir. 1985), aff'd, 475 U.S. 1001 (1986); *FCC v. Pacifica Found.,* 438 U.S. 726, 745–46 (1978); *Virginia State Bd. of Pharmacy v. Virginia Citizens Consumer Council, Inc.,* 425 U.S. 748, 760 (1976); *id.* at 781 (Rehnquist, J., dissenting); *Miami Herald Publ'g Co. v. Tornillo,* 418 U.S. 241, 248, 251 (1974); *Lamont v. Postmaster Gen.,* 381 U.S. 301, 308 (1965); Martin H. Redish, *Freedom of Expression: A Critical Analysis* 45–48 (1984).

19. *See* Ronald J. Krotoszynski, Jr., "Dissent, Free Speech, and the Continuing Search for the 'Central Meaning' of the First Amendment," 98 *Mich. L. Rev.* 1613, 1625–29 (2000) (arguing that content-neutral rules benefit minorities because judges drawn from the dominant cultural group by democratically elected government officials will consistently exercise discretion in favor of the dominant group's interests and not for the benefit of marginalized dissenters belonging to subordinated minority groups); Alex Kozinski & Stuart Banner, "Who's Afraid of Commercial Speech?" 76 *Va. L. Rev.* 627 (1990) (arguing that government has neither the right nor the responsibility to control the free flow of information within the marketplace of ideas, whatever the motivations of the speaker).

20. *See* Krotoszynski, *supra* note 19, at 1635–44 (arguing that current free speech doctrine, which reflects the marketplace paradigm and a commitment to viewpoint neutrality, generally protects unpopular groups engaged in dissenting speech from a heckler's veto).

21. *See, e.g., Cohen v. California*, 403 U.S. 15, 22–26 (1971). *See generally* Ronald J. Krotoszynski, Jr., "*Cohen v. California*: 'Inconsequential' Cases and Larger Principles," 74 *Tex. L. Rev.* 1251 (1996).

22. *See* Shiffrin, *supra* note 17, at 41–48, 93, 112–13; *but cf.* Robert C. Post, *Constitutional Domains: Democracy, Community, Management* 272–89 (1995) (arguing that "collectivist" theories of freedom of expression, including the Meiklejohn theory, "impl[y] managerial control" and, at least to some degree, also entail the "discard [of] our commitment to democracy"); Kozinski & Banner, *supra* note 19, at 631–34, 651–53 (arguing that the problems associated with the subjectivity inherent in non-market-based approaches to protecting freedom of speech cannot be overcome and that a unitary theory of the First Amendment would avoid these difficulties); Paul G. Stern, Note, "A Pluralistic Reading of the First Amendment and Its Relation to Public Discourse," 99 *Yale L.J.* 925, 932–33 (1990) (noting the various definitional difficulties associated with Meiklejohn theory of the First Amendment).

23. *Compare Texas v. Johnson,* 491 U.S. 397, 403–10 (1989) (holding a Texas flag-desecration statute unconstitutional on First Amendment grounds, at least as applied to a political protest at which the protestors burned a United States flag) *with United States v. O'Brien*, 391 U.S. 367, 376–77 (1968) (upholding a statutory prohibition against the destruction of Selective Service registration certificates on the theory that the statutory prohibition against destroying the certificates was totally unrelated to the suppression of a particular viewpoint and was necessary to facilitate administration of the Selective Service system).

24. *See Barnes v. Glen Theatre, Inc.*, 501 U.S. 560 (1991).

25. *See 44 Liquormart, Inc. v. Rhode Island,* 517 U.S. 484 (1996).

26. *See* Ronald J. Krotoszynski, Jr., "Back to the Briarpatch: An Argument in Favor of Constitutional Meta-Analysis in State Action Determinations," 94 *Mich. L. Rev.* 302, 333–35, 342–46 (1995).

27. *See Reno v. ACLU*, 521 U.S. 844, 884–85 (1997) (invoking the marketplace metaphor); *44 Liquormart, Inc.*, 517 U.S. at 495–98, 503–04 (applying the marketplace metaphor to protect alcohol advertising); *id.* at 518–23 (Thomas, J., concurring in part and concurring in the judgment) (embracing the marketplace metaphor and arguing for equal treatment of all speech); *Virginia State Bd. of Pharmacy v. Virginia Citizens Consumer Council, Inc.*, 425 U.S. 748, 756–65 (1976) (invoking and applying the marketplace metaphor to justify affording commercial speech significant First Amendment protection); Smolla, *supra* note 13, at 6–8, 236–39 (describing merits of a market-based system of speech regulation and noting consanguinity of such an approach with a free market economy); Kozinski & Banner, *supra* note 19, at 651–53 (applying the marketplace metaphor to support an argument in favor of treating commercial speech no less favorably than noncommercial speech).

28. *See* Alexander Meiklejohn, *Free Speech and Its Relation to Self-Government* (1948) [hereinafter Meiklejohn, *Free Speech*]; Alexander Meiklejohn, *Political Freedom: The Constitutional Powers of the People* (1960) [hereinafter Meiklejohn, *Political Freedom*]; Alexander Meiklejohn, "The First Amendment Is an Absolute," 1961 *Sup. Ct. Rev.* 245.

29. Meiklejohn, *Political Freedom, supra* note 28, at 26.

30. *See* Owen M. Fiss, *The Irony of Free Speech* 15–26 (1996) [hereinafter Fiss, *Irony*]; Fiss, *supra* note 10, at 83–87, 117–20; Harry Kalven, Jr., *A Worthy Tradition: Freedom of Speech in America* 150–78 (Jamie Kalven ed., 1988); Sunstein, *supra* note 16, at 28, 34–43, 48–51, 121–29; Harry Kalven, Jr., "The New York Times Case: A Note on the 'Central Meaning' of the First Amendment," 1964 *Sup. Ct. Rev.* 191, 207–13, 221 & n.125 [hereinafter

Kalven, "Central Meaning"]; *cf.* Post, *supra* note 22, 278–89 (rejecting both Meiklejohn and his contemporary followers because so-called collectivist theories of free expression grossly overestimate the abilities of government to establish truly viewpoint-neutral, non–culturally contingent speech regulations and faulting the Meiklejohn camp for disregarding the value of individual autonomy, which traditional free speech theories greatly facilitate).

31. *See* Cass R. Sunstein, "Television and the Public Interest," 88 *Cal. L. Rev.* 499 (2000); Cass R. Sunstein, "The Privatization of Our Public Discourse," 12 *Cardozo Stud. L. & Lit.* 129 (2000); *but cf.* First Nat'l Bank v. Bellotti, 435 U.S. 765 (1978) (striking down state-imposed restrictions on the use of corporate monies to influence the outcome of elections); *Buckley v. Valeo,* 424 U.S. 1 (1976) (striking down federal spending limits on independent expenditures to influence the outcome of elections for federal office).

32. *See Red Lion Broad. Co. v. FCC,* 395 U.S. 367, 389–91 (1969); Stephen A. Gardbaum, "Broadcasting, Democracy, and the Market," 82 *Geo. L.J.* 373 (1993).

33. 274 U.S. 357 (1927).

34. *Id.* at 375 (Brandeis, J., concurring).

35. *Id.*

36. *See id.* at 377 ("To courageous, self-reliant men, with confidence in the power of free and fearless reasoning applied through the processes of popular government, no danger flowing from speech can be deemed clear and present, unless the incidence of the evil apprehended is so imminent that it may befall before there is opportunity for full discussion."); *see also De Jonge v. Oregon,* 299 U.S. 353, 364–65 (1937) ("The greater the importance of safeguarding the community from incitements to the overthrow of our institutions by force and violence, the more imperative is the need to preserve inviolate the constitutional rights of free speech, free press and free assembly in order to maintain the opportunity for free political discussion, to the end that government may be responsive to the will of the people and that changes, if desired, may be obtained by peaceful means.").

37. *Whitney,* 274 U.S. at 377 (Brandeis, J., concurring).

38. As Professor Cass Sunstein has noted, "[i]n Brandeis' conception, free speech is emphatically 'a means' insofar as it is connected to the achievement of a certain conception of democratic government." Sunstein, *supra* note 16, at 27–28.

39. *See Abrams v. United States,* 250 U.S. 616, 630–31 (1919) (Holmes, J., dissenting).

40. *See Gitlow v. New York,* 268 U.S. 652, 673 (1925) (Holmes, J., dissenting).

41. *Abrams,* 250 U.S. at 630 (Holmes, J., dissenting).

42. Professor Cass Sunstein has noted the dichotomy between the Holmes and Brandeis approaches to freedom of expression and endorsed Justice Brandeis's point of view because it is consistent with the Madisonian Civic Republican tradition. *See* Sunstein, *supra* note 16, at 23–28.

43. *See* Robert H. Bork, "Neutral Principles and Some First Amendment Problems," 47 *Ind. L.J.* 1 (1971); *see also* Robert H. Bork, *Slouching Towards Gomorrah: Modern Liberalism and American Decline* 98–102, 146–50 (1996) [hereinafter Bork, *Slouching Towards Gomorrah*]; Robert H. Bork, *The Tempting of America: The Political Seduction of the Law* 333–36 (1990) [hereinafter Bork, *The Tempting of America*].

44. *See* Bork, *Slouching Towards Gomorrah, supra* note 43, at 193–225 (attacking modern feminism as antifamily and elitist); *id.* at 123–29 (denouncing modern culture and art as violent, scatological, and obscene); Bork, *The Tempting of America, supra* note 43, at 110–26 (decrying substantive due process as a form of unjustifiable judicial activism).

45. In this regard, consider Title VII, 42 U.S.C. § 2000e-2, which prohibits discrimination in the workplace. The federal courts have held that Title VII prohibits the creation or maintenance of a "hostile environment" in the workplace. *See Meritor Sav. Bank v. Vinson,* 477 U.S. 57 (1986); *Bundy v. Jackson,* 641 F.2d 934 (D.C. Cir. 1981); *Rogers v. EEOC,* 454 F.2d 234 (5th Cir. 1971); *see also* Joshua F. Thorpe, Note, "Gender-Based Harassment and the Hostile Work Environment," 1990

Duke L.J. 1361, 1362–63. This obviously has an impact on the ability of individuals in a given workplace to express themselves; automobile mechanics might wish to festoon their workplace with sexually explicit photographs and muse about the relative desirability of sexual relations with their female colleagues. If this conduct were sufficiently pervasive, it could give rise to liability under Title VII. Thus, Title VII constitutes a kind of content-based, government-imposed restriction on free speech in the nation's workplaces. Nevertheless, it is quite doubtful that the Supreme Court would sustain a First Amendment challenge to Title VII. We have decided as a society not to tolerate unfettered freedom of speech in the workplace. Logically, we could value equality above free expression in other contexts, such as college and university campuses. *See* Catharine A. MacKinnon, *Only Words* (1993); Richard Delgado & David H. Yun, "Pressure Valves and Bloodied Chickens: An Analysis of Paternalistic Objections to Hate Speech Regulation," 82 *Cal. L. Rev.* 871 (1994).

46. Robert B. Reich, *Locked in the Cabinet* 108 (1998).

47. *See* Stern, *supra* note 22, at 933. Professor Robert Post has suggested that another significant drawback of the Meiklejohn theory is a failure to appreciate the important role free speech plays in facilitating individual autonomy. *See* Post, *supra* note 22, at 274–76, 282–86, 288–89.

48. *See* Meiklejohn, *supra* note 28, at 256–57.

49. *See* U.S. Const. art. I, § 8, cl. 8 (conferring upon Congress the power to encourage "science and useful arts").

50. Martin H. Redish & Kevin Finnerty, "What Did You Learn in School Today? Free Speech, Values Inculcation, and the Democratic-Educational Paradox," 88 *Cornell L. Rev.* 62, 74 (2002).

51. *Id.* at 73.

52. *See* Redish, *supra* note 18, at 11–14 (making a strong argument that the ultimate purpose of the First Amendment is to enhance "individual self-realization," including individual self-fulfillment as well as auton-

omy in making decisions about one's own destiny); *see also* Robert C. Post, "Equality and Autonomy in First Amendment Jurisprudence," 95 *Mich. L. Rev.* 1517 (1997); Thomas M. Scanlon, Jr., "Freedom of Expression and Categories of Expression," 40 *U. Pitt. L. Rev.* 519, 531 (1979); *Consolidated Edison Co. v. Public Serv. Comm'n,* 447 U.S. 530, 534 n.2 (1980) (arguing that the Free Speech Clause "protects the individual's interests in self-expression"); *First Nat'l Bank v. Bellotti,* 435 U.S. 765, 777 n.12 (1978) ("The individual's interest in self-expression is a concern of the First Amendment separate from the concern for open and informed discussion."); *Cohen v. California,* 403 U.S. 15, 24 (1971) (characterizing the Free Speech Clause's protections as essential to facilitating individual dignity and choice).

53. *See* Shiffrin, *supra* note 17, at 10–18, 40–48, 110–13.

54. *See Milk Wagon Drivers Union of Chicago, Local 753 v. Meadowmoor Dairies,* 312 U.S. 287, 293 (1941) (free speech averts "force and explosions"); *see also* Steven Shiffrin, "Defamatory Non-Media Speech and First Amendment Methodology," 25 *UCLA L. Rev.* 915, 949 (1978) (advancing social safety valve thesis); Thomas I. Emerson, *The System of Freedom of Speech* 7 (1970) (same).

55. Justice Black professed to hold this view, stating that the First Amendment means literally what it says "without any 'ifs' or 'buts' or 'whereases.'" *Beauharnais v. Illinois,* 343 U.S. 250, 275 (1952) (Black, J., dissenting). Nevertheless, Justice Black wrote and joined opinions that would allow some restrictions. For example, he joined a dissent in *Cohen v. California,* 403 U.S. 15 (1971), in which the majority refused to allow a criminal prosecution based on Cohen's wearing a jacket emblazoned with "Fuck the Draft," *id.* at 26; the dissent argued that wearing the message on the jacket was conduct, not speech. *Id.* at 27. Professor Melville Nimmer claims that those holding the absolutist position use conduct as a code word for speech that they find to be undeserving of First Amendment protections. Melville B. Nimmer, *Nimmer on Freedom of Speech: A Treatise on the Theory of the*

First Amendment § 2.01, at 7 (1984). *See, e.g.,* Kinsley R. Browne, "Title VII as Censorship: Hostile-Environment Harassment and the First Amendment," 52 *Ohio St. L.J.* 481 (1991) (noting that because Title VII permits some statements about race or sex and disapproves of others, it violates the principle that the government may not prohibit the expression of an idea because it finds it offensive); Robert W. Gall, "The University as an Industrial Plant: How a Workplace Theory of Discriminatory Harassment Creates a 'Hostile Environment' for Free Speech in America's Universities," 60 *Law & Contemp. Probs.* 203, 210–11 (Autumn 1997) (arguing that colleges and universities should not import the hostile environment theory into their speech codes because of the threat it poses to the free speech rights of faculty and students); Steven G. Gey, "The Case Against Post-Modern Censorship Theory," 145 *U. Pa. L. Rev.* 193 (1996) (arguing that efforts to balance speech rights against other constitutional values inevitably devolve into arguments in favor of government censorship against disfavored viewpoints); Eugene Volokh, "Freedom of Speech and Workplace Harassment," 39 *UCLA L. Rev.* 1791, 1793 (1992) (arguing that the hostile work environment theory imposes impermissible content- and viewpoint-based restrictions on workplace speech); Eugene Volokh, "Freedom of Speech, Permissible Tailoring and Transcending Strict Scrutiny," 144 *U. Pa. L. Rev.* 2417 (1996) (same).

56. *See, e.g.,* Browne, *supra* note 55, at 481 (arguing that certain applications of Title VII violate the Free Speech Clause in the workplace); Nadine Strossen, "Regulating Racist Speech on Campus: A Modest Proposal?" 1990 *Duke L.J.* 484, 494 (maintaining "that equality will be served most effectively by continuing to apply traditional speech-protective precepts to racist speech because a robust freedom of speech ultimately is necessary to combat racial discrimination"); Volokh, "Permissible Tailoring," *supra* note 55, at 2417–18 (arguing that content-based restrictions on fully protected speech should be invalidated); Eugene Volokh, "Freedom of Speech and Appellate Review in Workplace

Harassment Cases," 90 *Nw. U. L. Rev.* 1009, 1011–12 (1996) (arguing that trying to achieve Title VII's broad rule of workplace equality by applying the hostile environment theory of discrimination in the workplace threatens the First Amendment freedom of workers and employers); Eugene Volokh, "How Harassment Law Restricts Free Speech," 47 *Rutgers L. Rev.* 563, 574–79 (1995) (arguing that some balancing of interests may be necessary in free speech cases and further arguing that any balancing should be closely cabined by adherence to formal rules designed to protect free speech values); *but cf.* Richard Delgado, "Campus Anti-racism Rules: Constitutional Narratives in Collision," 85 *Nw. U. L. Rev.* 343 (1991); Jessica M. Karner, "Political Speech, Sexual Harassment, and a Captive Workforce," 83 *Cal. L. Rev.* 637 (1995); Charles R. Lawrence, III, "If He Hollers Let Him Go: Regulating Racist Speech On Campus," 1990 *Duke L.J.* 431; MacKinnon, *supra* note 45, at 45–48; Mari J. Matsuda, "Public Response to Racist Speech: Considering the Victim's Story," 87 *Mich. L. Rev.* 2320 (1989); Suzanne Sangree, "Title VII Prohibitions against Hostile Environment Sexual Harassment and the First Amendment: No Collision in Sight," 47 *Rutgers L. Rev.* 461 (1995).

57. *See, e.g., Burson v. Freeman,* 504 U.S. 191 (1992) (allowing restrictions on plainly political speech in order to serve government's "compelling interest" in allowing voters to be free from polling place intimidation).

58. *See* Catharine A. MacKinnon, *The Sexual Harassment of Working Women* (1979); *see also Meritor Sav. Bank v. Vinson,* 477 U.S. 57, 73 (1986) (holding that Title VII creates a cause of action based on the maintenance of a hostile work environment); *Aguilar v. Avis Rent-A-Car System, Inc.,* 980 P.2d 846 (Cal. 1999) (holding constitutional, against a free speech challenge, an injunction that enjoined a manager from making racist remarks), *cert. denied,* 529 U.S. 1138 (2000).

59. *See* Delgado, *supra* note 56; Richard Delgado, "Words That Wound: A Tort Action for Racial Insults, Epithets, and Name Calling," 17 *Harv. C.R.-C.L. L. Rev.* 133 (1982);

Matsuda, *supra* note 56; *see also Bridges v. California,* 314 U.S. 252, 282 (1941) (Frankfurter, J., dissenting) ("Free speech is not so absolute or irrational a conception to imply paralysis of the means for effective protection of all the freedoms secured by the Bill of Rights.").

60. *See* Akhil Reed Amar, "The Case of the Missing Amendments: *R.A.V. v. City of St. Paul,*" 106 *Harv. L. Rev.* 124, 151–55 (1992); *see also* Leonard Levy, *Legacy of Suppression: Freedom of Speech and Press in Early American History* 176–248 (1960) (discussing the origins of the First Amendment and its original purpose—the creation of a free press). Other examples also exist. For example, we value the right of all individuals to vote. If an individual sets up a display offensive to women in front of a local voting booth, clearly his right to freedom of speech should not automatically trump the interest of women who use that voting booth to exercise their right to vote.

61. *See* Kenneth L. Karst, "Equality as a Central Principle in the First Amendment," 43 *U. Chi. L. Rev.* 20, 20–21 (1976); Scanlon, *supra* note 52, at 520–21; Frederick Schauer, "Categories and the First Amendment: A Play in Three Acts," 34 *Vand. L. Rev.* 265 (1981); Paul B. Stephan III, "The First Amendment and Content Discrimination," 68 *Va. L. Rev.* 203, 203–07 (1982); *see also* Owen M. Fiss, "The Supreme Court and the Problem of Hate Speech," 24 *Cap. U.L. Rev.* 281, 283 (1995) (stating that the freedom of speech never has received absolute protection from the Court); Richard A. Posner, "Free Speech in an Economic Perspective," 20 *Suffolk U.L. Rev.* 1, 7 (1986) (arguing that the Framers of the First Amendment would not have wanted to "tie the hands of government" from stopping the spread of "worthless and vicious ideas").

62. *See Olivieri v. Ward,* 801 F.2d 602, 605 (2d Cir. 1986) (citing *Heffron v. International Soc'y for Krishna Consciousness,* 452 U.S. 640, 647 (1981)); *see also Barenblatt v. United States,* 360 U.S. 109, 126 (1959) ("Where First Amendment rights are asserted . . . resolution of the issue always involves a balancing by the courts of the competing private and public interests at stake in the particular circumstances shown.").

63. Certainly the contemporaneous actions of the Congress support such an inference. In 1798, Congress passed the Alien and Sedition Act, a law establishing content-based restrictions on core political speech. *See* Sedition Act, ch. 74, 1 Stat. 596 (1798); Alien Enemies Act, ch. 66, 1 Stat. 577 (1798) (current version at 50 U.S.C. § 21–23 (2001)); Alien Act, ch. 58, 1 Stat. 570 (1798); Naturalization Act, ch. 54, 1 Stat 566 (1798). These laws represented a wartime effort to deport threatening aliens and silence attacks on the government. *See New York Times v. Sullivan,* 376 U.S. 254, 273–75 (1964); Zechariah Chaffee, *Freedom of Speech* 1, 29 (1920); Levy, *supra* note 60, at 197–200; *see also Frohwerk v. United States,* 249 U.S. 204, 206 (1919) ("We venture to believe that neither Hamilton nor Madison, nor any other competent person then or later, ever supposed that to make criminal the counseling of a murder within the jurisdiction of Congress would be an unconstitutional interference with free speech."); Martin H. Redish, "Advocacy of Unlawful Conduct and the First Amendment: In Defense of Clear and Present Danger," 70 *Calif. L. Rev.* 1159, 1165 n.25 (1982) ("There can be little doubt that whatever the framers intended, it was not absolute protection.").

64. *See Watts v. United States,* 394 U.S. 705, 707–08 (1969) (holding that hyperbolic threat of violence against the president constituted protected speech because not seriously intended, construing criminal statute prohibiting threats against the president narrowly to avoid coverage of such statements, and noting that criminal liability for a "true 'threat' " would be both within scope of statute and constitutionally permissible); *see also Virginia v. Black,* 538 U.S. 343, 358–60, 362–63 (2003) (applying *Watts* to a Virginia statute prohibiting cross burning with intent to convey threat and holding that Virginia's ban on cross burning, when applied to targeted threats, did not violate the First Amendment).

65. Stanley Fish, *There's No Such Thing as Free Speech and It's a Good Thing Too* 102–19

(1994); *see also* Schauer, *supra* note 6, at 1767–74, 1784–87 (arguing that contemporary free speech theory in the United States has largely failed to engage, in a serious way, the source and scope of free speech boundary lines and suggesting that "political, sociological, cultural, historical, psychological, and economic" factors play an important, if not dispositive, role in the construction of "the freedom of speech").

66. *See* Bork, *The Tempting of America, supra* note 43, at 128; Andrea Dworkin, *Pornography: Men Possessing Women* (1989); Andrea Dworkin, "Against the Male Flood: Censorship, Pornography, and Equality," 8 *Harv. Women's L.J.* 1 (1985); MacKinnon, *supra* note 45, at 71–110; Sunstein, *supra* note 16, at 210–26.

67. 492 U.S. 115 (1989).

68. *See id.* at 126–31.

69. *See Winters v. New York,* 333 U.S. 507, 510 (1948) ("We do not accede to appellee's suggestion that the constitutional protection for a free press applies only to the exposition of ideas. The line between the informing and the entertaining is too elusive for the protection of that basic right."). Indeed, the U.S. Court of Appeals for the Seventh Circuit has even extended this reasoning to protect graphically violent video games marketed to children. *See Am. Amusement Machine Ass'n v. Kendrick,* 244 F.3d. 572, 577–78 (7th Cir.) (noting that "[m]ost of the video games in the record of this case, games that the City believes violate its ordinances, are stories" and holding that violent video games enjoy full protection under the Free Speech Clause), *cert. denied,* 534 U.S. 994 (2001).

70. *See, e.g.,* Bork, *The Tempting of America, supra* note 43, at 128; Fiss, *supra* note 10, at 83–87; Meiklejohn, *Free Speech, supra* note 28, at 22–27; Sunstein, *supra* note 16, at 215–26.

71. *See* Redish, *supra* note 18, at 68–76, 259–64; William W. Van Alstyne, *Interpretations of the First Amendment* 21–22, 40–49 (1984).

72. 517 U.S. 484 (1996).

73. *See id.* at 489, 506–16.

74. *See id.* at 502–08

75. *See 44 Liquormart, Inc. v. Rhode Island,* 39 F.3d 5, 7–8 (1st Cir. 1994), *rev'd,* 517 U.S. 484 (1996); *Dunagin v. City of Oxford,* 718 F.2d 738, 747–51 & 748 n.8 (5th Cir. 1983) (en banc). *See generally Virginia State Bd. of Pharmacy v. Virginia Citizens Consumer Council, Inc.,* 425 U.S. 748 (1976). I suppose one could argue that virtuous Civic Republican citizens might use the savings realized through lower alcohol prices resulting from active price competition to underwrite political causes they support or perhaps to go to an ennobling form of entertainment, such as the opera or ballet. If one could make this argument with a straight face, *44 Liquormart* could be brought within the Meiklejohn vision of the First Amendment. Of course, it seems far more likely that most consumers will simply buy more alcohol, or cigarettes, or perhaps both. Indeed, advertising not only promotes competition between suppliers of a good or service but also promotes consumption of the good or service being advertised. *See Penn Advertising, Inc. v. Mayor of Baltimore,* 63 F.3d 1318, 1321, 1325–26 (4th Cir. 1995), *vacated and remanded,* 518 U.S. 1030 (1996), *modified,* 101 F.3d 332 (4th Cir. 1996), and *cert. denied* 520 U.S. 1204 (1997); *Anheuser-Busch, Inc. v. Schmoke,* 63 F.3d 1305, 1309–10, 1314–17 (4th Cir. 1995); *Dunagin,* 718 F.2d at 748 n.8; *see also* Regulations Restricting the Sale and Distribution of Cigarettes and Smokeless Tobacco to Protect Children and Adolescents, 61 Fed. Reg. 44,396 (1996) (to be codified at 26 C.F.R. § 801).

76. 478 U.S. 328 (1986).

77. *See* Shiffrin, *supra* note 17, at 32–48.

78. *Liquormart,* 517 U.S. at 510.

79. *Id.* at 512.

80. *See generally* William W. Van Alstyne, "To What Extent Does the Power of Government to Determine the Boundaries and Conditions of Lawful Commerce Permit Government to Declare Who May Advertise and Who May Not?" 51 *Emory L.J.* 1513, 1545–55 (2002) (describing Supreme Court cases since *Posadas* and arguing that these subsequent cases have fatally, and correctly, undermined the validity of the *Posadas* "greater power to regulate commerce necessarily includes the lesser power to regulate speech" theory).

81. *See Greater New Orleans Broad. Ass'n v. United States,* 527 U.S. 173, 182–84, 188–95 (1999) (rejecting the *Posadas* "lesser-includes-the-greater" analysis and requiring government to use direct regulations rather than restrictions on speech activity to achieve regulatory objectives).

82. *See, e.g.,* Shiffrin, *supra* note 17, at 32–48, 53–57.

83. *See New York Times Co. v. Sullivan,* 376 U.S. 254, 282 (1964); Kalven, *supra* note 30, at 162–63; Kalven, "Central Meaning," *supra* note 28, at 208–10. Justice Brennan was more explicit in his later opinions and writings. *See Board of Educ. v. Pico,* 457 U.S. 853, 867 n.20 (1982) (plurality opinion); William J. Brennan, Jr., "The Supreme Court and the Meiklejohn Interpretation of the First Amendment," 79 *Harv. L. Rev.* 1 (1965). Other members of the Supreme Court also have invoked Meiklejohn's theory from time to time. *See Consolidated Edison Co. v. Public Serv. Comm'n,* 447 U.S. 530, 534 n.3 (1980); *CBS, Inc. v. Democratic Nat'l Comm.,* 412 U.S. 94, 122 (1973).

84. *Barnes v. Glen Theatre, Inc.,* 501 U.S. 560, 566 (1991); *see also Sable Communications v. FCC,* 492 U.S. 115, 128 (1989); *First Nat'l Bank v. Bellotti,* 435 U.S. 765, 777–78 (1978); *Doran v. Salem Inn, Inc.,* 422 U.S. 922, 932 (1975); *California v. LaRue,* 409 U.S. 109, 118 (1972).

85. *See Miller v. California,* 413 U.S. 15, 23–25 (1973).

86. *See Osborne v. Ohio,* 495 U.S. 103, 108–111 (1990); *New York v. Ferber,* 458 U.S. 747, 756–62 (1982); *but cf. Ashcroft v. Free Speech Coalition,* 535 U.S. 234 (2002) (holding that nonobscene child pornography that features only "virtual" models or youthful-looking adults, rather than real children, enjoys full First Amendment protection and cannot be prohibited).

87. *See City of Erie v. Pap's A.M.,* 529 U.S. 277, 289–301 (2000); *Barnes v. Glen Theatre, Inc.,* 501 U.S. 560, 564–72 (1991).

88. *See* Amy Adler, "The Perverse Law of Child Pornography," 101 *Colum. L. Rev.* 209 (2001) (noting intellectual inconsistencies in the Supreme Court's approach to laws restricting speech because it encompasses sexual materials related to minors); Amy Adler, "Inverting the First Amendment," 149 *U. Pa. L. Rev.* 921 (2001) (arguing that the Supreme Court has reversed the usual presumption against viewpoint-based restrictions on speech in the context of materials presenting nude children).

89. Another possible exception to this general rule involves speech that creates or maintains a hostile work environment. *See Meritor Sav. Bank v. Vinson,* 477 U.S. 57, 72–73 (1986) (recognizing claim under Title VII for hostile work environments).

90. 394 U.S. 557 (1969) (holding that the First Amendment, in conjunction with other provisions of the Bill of Rights, protects the possession and display of obscene materials for noncommercial purpose within a private residence).

91. 492 U.S. 115 (holding unconstitutional on First Amendment grounds a statutory provision criminalizing the distribution of certain indecent communications over telephone systems).

92. 517 U.S. 484 (holding unconstitutional on First Amendment grounds a state law prohibiting price advertising for alcoholic beverages).

93. *See* Redish & Finnerty, *supra* note 50, at 74–75 (noting that "[u]nder the First Amendment, the Supreme Court has said, there is 'no such thing as a false idea' and arguing that government censorship of speech should be avoided because "[b]y distorting the free flow of information and opinion to favor one viewpoint or to burden another, government would interfere with the exercise of the electorate's ultimate self-governing function").

94. *See, e.g.,* R. H. Coase, "Advertising and Free Speech," 6 *J. Legal Stud.* 1, 32–33 (1977); R. H. Coase, "The Economics of the First Amendment: The Market for Goods and the Market for Ideas," 64 *Am. Econ. Rev.* 384 (1974); Kozinski & Banner, *supra* note 19.

95. *See* Kozinski & Banner, *supra* note 19, at 628; Steven H. Shiffrin, "The First Amendment and Economic Regulation: Away from a General Theory of the First Amendment," 78

Nw. U. L. Rev. 1212, 1216 (1983); *cf.* William Van Alstyne, "Remembering Melville Nimmer: Some Cautionary Notes on Commercial Speech," 43 *UCLA L. Rev.* 1635, 1638–48 (1996) (arguing that political speech deserves a higher degree of First Amendment protection than commercial speech).

96. *See* Van Alstyne, *supra* note 95, at 1638–40, 1654–57.

97. *See, e.g., Reno v. ACLU,* 521 U.S. 844 (1997); *City of Cincinnati v. Discovery Network, Inc.,* 507 U.S. 410 (1993).

98. *See* Fiss, *Irony, supra* note 30, at 1–26; Sunstein, *supra* note 16, at 17–51, 241–52.

99. *See* Sunstein, *supra* note 16, at 23–28.

100. *See* Plato, *The Apology,* in Five Dialogues 23, at 41, para. 38 (G. M. A. Grube trans., 1981).

101. *See, e.g.,* Bork, *The Tempting of America, supra* note 43, at 333–36 (arguing that the Supreme Court's free speech case law is grossly overprotective of speech unworthy of even minimal protection); MacKinnon, *supra* note 45, at 71–110 (arguing that a genuine commitment to the principle of equality precludes the protection of sexist and racist speech); Sunstein, *supra* note 16, at 241–52 (arguing that government should be permitted to enact viewpoint-neutral laws aimed at improving the social and political culture of the United States).

102. Notwithstanding the current vogue of balancing away the intrinsic value of freedom of expression, a number of distinguished legal scholars have continued to advocate broad protection for expressive activity, even expressive activity that is offensive or hurtful to particular segments of the community. *See, e.g.,* Redish, *supra* note 18, at 259–64; Schauer, *supra* note 13, at 154–63, 184–88; Smolla, *supra* note 13, at 15–17, 43–65, 330–42; Nadine Strossen, *Defending Pornography: Free Speech, Sex, and the Fight for Women's Rights* 14–15, 244–50 (1995); Van Alstyne, *supra* note 71, at 40–49.

NOTES TO CHAPTER 3

1. *See* Part I of the Constitution Act, 1982, Canada Act, 1982, ch. 11, sch. B, art. 2 (U.K.)

(containing the Canadian Charter of Rights and Freedoms) [hereinafter Charter]. For a discussion of the history surrounding the adoption of the Charter and some of its primary differences with the Bill of Rights, *see* Paul Bender, "The Canadian Charter of Rights and Freedoms and the United States Bill of Rights: A Comparison," 28 *McGill L.J.* 811 (1983).

2. *See generally* Richard Moon, *The Constitutional Protection of Freedom of Expression* 32–42, 54–70 (2000). Professor Moon's book is an excellent and remarkably comprehensive guide to free speech principles in Canada. I strongly recommend it to those seeking an evaluation of Canadian free speech doctrine across the spectrum of facts that give rise to free speech claims.

3. *See* Kathleen E. Mahoney, "Hate Speech: Affirmation or Contradiction of Freedom of Expression," 1996 *U. Ill. L. Rev.* 789, 797–803 (describing with approval the general practice of the Supreme Court of Canada of elevating equality concerns over the unfettered exercise of free speech).

4. Mahoney, *supra* note 3, at 797.

5. *R. v. Keegstra,* [1990] 3 S.C.R. 697, 787.

6. Charter, § 27.

7. *Keegstra,* [1990] 3 S.C.R. at 743.

8. *See* Justice Frank Iacobucci, "The Supreme Court of Canada: Its History, Powers, and Responsibilities," 4 *J. App. Prac. & Process* 27, 31–33 (2002) (describing history of constitutional adjudication in Canada and effect of Charter on role and function of the Supreme Court of Canada).

9. Charter, § 2.

10. *See generally* Bender, *supra* note 1, at 858–65 (discussing text of Section 2 and suggesting questions that Supreme Court will have to address in defining scope of Section 2 rights).

11. *See* Donald L. Beschle, "Clearly Canadian? *Hill v. Colorado* and Free Speech Balancing in the United States and Canada," 28 *Hastings Const. L.Q.* 187, 188 (2001) ("The Canadian Charter explicitly instructs courts to engage in a form of balancing.").

12. Charter, § 1.

13. For a detailed examination of *R. v.*

Oakes, [1986] 1 S.C.R. 103, *see infra* pp. 41 to 45. *See also* Peter W. Hogg, *Constitutional Law of Canada* ch. 35, at 851–89 (3rd ed. 1992).

14. U.S. Const. amend. I ("Congress shall make no law . . . abridging the freedom of speech").

15. *See infra* pp. 37 to 41.

16. *See* Janet L. Hiebert, *Limiting Rights: The Dilemma of Judicial Review* 126–49 (1996).

17. Kent Greenawalt, "Free Speech in the United States and Canada," 55 *Law & Contemp. Probs.* 5, 10 (Winter 1992).

18. *See Retail, Wholesale and Department Store Union, Local 580 v. Dolphin Delivery Ltd.*, [1986] 2 S.C.R. 573 (holding that only state action violates the Charter but noting that scope of Section 2 rights extends to all expressive activities other than violence).

19. *Id.* at 578–79.

20. *See id.* at 580–81.

21. *See id.* at 581.

22. *Id.* at 583.

23. *Id.*

24. *Id.*

25. *See id.* at 584–86.

26. *Id.* at 588. For a very trenchant evaluation of the Supreme Court's *Dolphin Delivery* opinion, *see* J. A. Manwaring, "Bringing the Common Law to the Bar of Justice: A Comment on the Decision in the Case of *Dolphin Delivery Ltd.*," 19 *Ottawa L. Rev.* 413, 415 (1987) ("In *Dolphin Delivery,* the Supreme Court of Canada does not provide persuasive reasons for its decision.").

27. *Dolphin Delivery,* [1986] 2 S.C.R. at 588.

28. Manwaring, *supra* note 26, at 415.

29. *See* Moon, *supra* note 2, at 32–34.

30. *Id.* at 597; *see also* Bender, *supra* note 1, at 823 (noting that "despite its affirmative cast" most likely reading of Charter rights "is that negative rights are all that are intended").

31. *Dolphin Delivery,* [1986] 2 S.C.R. at 599; *see* Greenawalt, *supra* note 17, at 8–9 (noting that "[a]ccording to present interpretation, common law rules enforcing private rights do not present Charter issues").

32. *Id.* at 600.

33. *Id.*

34. *Id.* at 603; *but cf.* Bender, *supra* note 1, at 826–32 (arguing that any nexus with the government, including judicial enforcement of common law doctrines, should be sufficient to trigger application of Charter rights).

35. *See, e.g., New York Times Co. v. Sullivan,* 376 U.S. 254, 265 (1964). For a discussion of the state action doctrine in the United States, *see* Ronald J. Krotoszynski, Jr., "Back to the Briarpatch: An Argument in Favor of Constitutional Meta-Analysis in State Action Determinations," 94 *Mich. L. Rev.* 302 (1995).

36. *See Eldridge v. British Columbia (Attorney General),* [1997] 3 S.C.R. 624; *see also* P. Macklem et al., *II Canadian Constitutional Law* 221–46 (1994).

37. *See Godbout v. Longueuil (Ville),* [1997] 3 S.C.R. 844.

38. *See Hill v. Church of Scientology of Toronto,* [1995] 2 S.C.R. 1130; *see also* Lorraine E. Weinrib & Ernest J. Weinrib, "Constitutional Values and Private Law in Canada," in *Human Rights in Private Law* 43–72 (Daniel Friedmann & Daphne Burak-Erez, eds. 2001).

39. *See infra* Chapter 4.

40. *But cf.* Manwaring, *supra* note 26, at 433–43 (criticizing soundly the Canadian approach and suggesting that state action is present whenever a court creates a substantive rule of the common law).

41. *Attorney General (Quebec) v. Irwin Toy Ltd.,* [1989] 1 S.C.R. 927.

42. Consumer Protection Act, R.S.Q., c.P-40.1, § 248.

43. *Id.* at § 249.

44. *Irwin Toy Ltd.,* [1989] 1 S.C.R. at 967.

45. *Id.*

46. *Id.* at 968.

47. *Id.* at 968–69 (internal citation omitted).

48. *Id.* at 969.

49. *Id.* at 970.

50. *Id.* (emphasis in the original).

51. *Id.*

52. *Id.*

53. *See* Moon, *supra* note 2, at 64–65, 76–83 (examining and questioning the rationales

offered for including commercial speech within the scope of Section 2).

54. *Id.* at 33.

55. *Irwin Toy Ltd.,* [1989] 1 S.C.R. at 971.

56. *See* Ronald J. Krotoszynski, Jr., "Identity, Privacy, and the New Information Scalpers: Recalibrating the Rules of the Road in the Age of the Infobahn," 33 *Ind. L. Rev.* 233, 235–36 (1999) (discussing Kaczynski and his ideologically motivated campaign of terror against those associated with new technologies).

57. *Irwin Toy Ltd.,* [1989] 1 S.C.R. at 971.

58. *See* Moon, *supra* note 2, at 65–75 (noting the analytical shortcomings of the Supreme Court's analysis of commercial speech issues).

59. *Irwin Toy Ltd.,* [1989] 1 S.C.R. at 972.

60. *Id.* at 976.

61. *Id.*

62. *Id.* at 977; *see also id.* at 979 ("To make this claim, the plaintiff must at least identify the meaning being conveyed and how it relates to the pursuit of truth, participation in the community, or individual self-fulfillment and human flourishing.").

63. *Id.* at 977.

64. *See id.* at 977, 979.

65. *See generally* Moon, *supra* note 2, at 32–42 (criticizing Canadian Supreme Court's failure to ground Section 2 analysis firmly in public values free speech thought to advance).

66. *See infra* pp. 41 to 45.

67. *Irwin Toy Ltd.,* [1989] 1 S.C.R. at 980–86.

68. *Id.* at 986–91.

69. *Id.* at 987.

70. *Id.* at 991–1000.

71. *See id.* at 1005–1010 (McIntyre, J., dissenting).

72. *Id.* at 1007.

73. *Id.* at 1007–08 ("A total prohibition of advertising aimed at children below an arbitrarily fixed age makes no attempt at the achievement of proportionality.").

74. *Id.* at 1009.

75. *See* Ronald J. Krotoszynski, Jr., "Celebrating Selma: The Importance of Context in Public Forum Analysis," 104 *Yale L.J.* 1441

(1995) (noting reluctance of federal courts to declare new public spaces to be "public forums" because of potential severe adverse effects on intended uses of public property).

76. *See* Hiebert, *supra* note 16, at 138–40.

77. Macklem et al., *supra* note 36, at 191.

78. *Id.* Professor Hiebert explains that "Quebec was the only province that refused to agree to the constitutional reforms in 1981 which included an entrenched Charter of Rights." Hiebert, *supra* note 16, at 131. The authors of the Charter included Section 33 as an accommodation to Quebec. *See id.* at 130–32.

79. *Id.* at 139.

80. *Id.* at 145.

81. *Id.*

82. Charter, § 33(1).

83. *See* Charter, § 33(2) ("A declaration made under subsection (1) shall cease to have effect five years after it comes into force or on such earlier date as may be specified in the declaration.").

84. *See* Charter, § 33(4) ("Parliament or the legislature may re-enact a declaration made under subsection (1)."). The same five-year sunset provision applies to reenactment of notwithstanding declarations. *See* Canadian Charter, § 33(4) ("Subsection (3) applies in respect of a re-enactment made under subsection (4).").

85. *See* Charter, § 33(2) ("An Act or provision of an Act in respect of which a declaration made under this section is in effect shall have such operation as it would have but for the provision of this Charter referred to in the declaration.").

86. *Cf. City of Boerne v. Flores,* 521 U.S. 507 (1997) (invalidating federal law that attempted to extend by statute scope of religious free exercise rights).

87. Hiebert, *supra* note 16, at 139.

88. *Id.* at 181 n.42.

89. *See* An Act Respecting the Constitution Act, S.Q. 1982, ch. 21. The law amended preexisting provincial statutes to include a provision that stated "[t]his Act shall operate notwithstanding the provisions of sections 2 and 7 to 15 of the Constitution Act, 1982." *Id.*

90. *See Ford v. Quebec (Attorney General),* [1988] 2 S.C.R. 712, 739–41.

91. *Id.* at 741.

92. *Id.*

93. *See* Alexander M. Bickel, *The Least Dangerous Branch: The Supreme Court at the Bar of Politics* 16–33 (1962).

94. Charter, § 33 ("notwithstanding a provision included in section two or sections seven to fifteen").

95. *See* Hiebert, *supra* note 16, at 138–47.

96. Letter from Professor Grant Huscroft, July 11, 2003 (on file with author).

97. Hiebert, *supra* note 16, at 145.

98. Charter, § 1.

99. U.S. Const. amend. I ("Congress shall make no law . . . abridging the freedom of speech").

100. *Oakes,* [1986] 1 S.C.R. 136–37.

101. *Id.* at 137.

102. *Id.*

103. *Id.*

104. *Id.*

105. *Id.* at 138.

106. *Id.* (internal quotations and citations omitted).

107. *Id.* at 138–39.

108. *Id.* at 139.

109. *Id.* (emphasis in the original).

110. *Id.* at 140.

111. Hiebert, *supra* note 16, at 61.

112. Id. at 62.

113. This has not gone without notice or criticism among Canadian commentators— and even sitting members of the Supreme Court. *See, e.g.,* Justice Bertha Wilson, "Constitutional Advocacy," 24 *Ottawa L. Rev.* 265, 267–69 (1992) (conceding that "I think it is now fair to say that, although the Court continues to pay lip service to the strict *Oakes* test, in many of its judgments it has in fact applied it in a less rigorous fashion").

114. Hiebert, *supra* note 16, at 62.

115. *See RJR-MacDonald, Inc. v. The Attorney General of Canada,* [1995] 3 S.C.R. 199, 344–50 (invalidating complete ban on advertising for tobacco products).

116. *See Rocket v. Royal College of Dental Surgeons of Ontario,* [1990] 2 S.C.R. 232, 247–51 (invalidating complete ban on advertising by medical professionals, including dentists).

117. *See Ford v. Quebec (Attorney General),* [1988] 2 S.C.R. 712, 779–80 (invalidating ban on all use of English on commercial signage and indicating in dicta that rules favoring use of French language on commercial displays would be sustained under Section 1 analysis).

118. *See Butler v. R.,* [1992] 1 S.C.R. 452, 491–510.

119. *See R. v. Keegstra,* [1990] 3 S.C.R. 697, 771–794.

120. *See R. v. Butler,* [1992] 1 S.C.R. 452.

121. Criminal Code, R.S.C., 1985, C-46, § 163(8).

122. *See Butler,* [1992] 1 S.C.R. at 488–90.

123. *Id.* at 502.

124. *See id.* at 502–04.

125. *See* Wilson, *supra* note 113, at 269.

126. *See Irwin Toy Ltd. v. Quebec (Attorney General),* [1989] 1 S.C.R. 927, 986–99.

127. *See R. v. Keegstra,* [1990] 3 S.C.R. 697, 767–88.

128. *But see* James B. Kelly & Michael Murphy, "Confronting Judicial Supremacy: A Defence of Judicial Activism and the Supreme Court of Canada's Legal Rights Jurisprudence," 16 *Canadian J.L. & Soc'y* 3, 15–23 (2001) (arguing that Supreme Court of Canada has been relatively strict in enforcing Charter rights associated with police search and seizure and has not been particularly deferential to legislative enactments in this area of its rights jurisprudence).

129. *Irwin Toy Ltd.,* [1989] 1 S.C.R. at 993.

130. *Id.* at 999.

131. 319 U.S. 624 (1943).

132. *Id.* at 642.

133. *See id.* ("We think the action of the local authorities in compelling the flag salute and pledge transcends constitutional limitations on their power and invades the sphere of intellect and spirit which it is the purpose of the First Amendment to our Constitution to reserve from all official conduct.").

134. *Id.* at 647 (Frankfurter, J., dissenting).

135. *Id.*

136. *Id.*

137. *Id.* at 663.

138. *Id.* at 661.

139. *Id.* at 661–62.

140. *See, e.g., R. v. Butler,* [1992] 1 S.C.R. 452, 501–502 (upholding restrictions on "de-

humanizing" and "degrading" erotica notwithstanding lack of dispositive social science evidence establishing that such materials cause harm because Parliament "had a *reasonable* basis" for enacting the ban based on inconclusive social science evidence).

141. *See United States v. O'Brien*, 391 U.S. 367 (1968).

142. *See Central Hudson Gas v. PSC*, 447 U.S. 557 (1980).

143. *Connick v. Meyers*, 461 U.S. 138 (1983).

144. *See Ward v. Rock Against Racism*, 491 U.S. 781 (1989).

145. Charter, § 1 ("The Canadian Charter of Rights and Freedoms guarantees the rights and freedoms set out in it subject to only such reasonable limits prescribed by law as can be demonstrably justified in a free and democratic society.").

146. Beschle, *supra* note 11, at 188.

147. *Id.*

148. *Oakes*, [1986] 1 S.C.R. at 135.

149. *Id.*

150. *Id.* at 136.

151. *Id.*

152. *See Miller v. Johnson*, 515 U.S. 900 (1995); *Adarand Constructors, Inc. v. Pena*, 515 U.S. 200 (1995); *Shaw v. Reno*, 509 U.S. 630 (1993); *City of Richmond v. J. A. Croson Co.*, 488 U.S. 469 (1989).

153. 529 U.S. 598 (2000).

154. 531 U.S. 356 (2001).

155. *See* Ruth Colker & James Brudney, "*Dissing Congress*," 100 *Mich. L. Rev.* 80 (2001).

156. *See Beauharnais v. Illinois*, 343 U.S. 250 (1952) (sustaining, against First Amendment challenge, Illinois group libel statute that prohibited racial vilification).

157. One should take care not to essentialize Canadian thought on the question of hate speech regulation. Considerable debate about the topic exists and, in all probability will continue to exist, not only between Canadian and U.S. commentators but also between Canadians themselves. *Compare* Terry Heinrichs, "Censorship as Free Speech!: Free Expression Values and the Logic of Silencing in *R. v. Keegstra*," 36 *Alberta L. Rev.* 835 (1998) (criticizing *Keegstra* severely and suggesting

that the decision is fundamentally inconsistent with a proper appreciation of free speech rights in a democratic polity) *with* Mahoney, *supra* note 3, at 797–804 (arguing forcefully that *Keegstra* and *Butler* reflect a crucial government effort to create and maintain a political community in which minorities and women feel comfortable participating as equals).

158. *Brandenburg v. Ohio*, 395 U.S. 444 (1969).

159. *Virginia v. Black*, 538 U.S. 343, 359–61 (2003) (holding that state may criminalize cross burning when circumstances and context of event affirmatively establish intent to communicate threat of racial violence).

160. Mahoney, *supra* note 3, at 799.

161. *R. v. Butler*, [1992] 1 S.C.R. 452, 484–85.

162. [1990] 3 S.C.R. 697.

163. Criminal Code, R.S.C., 1985, c. C-46, § 319. For a brief historical review of this statute and its predecessors, *see* Mayo Moran, "Talking About Hate Speech: A Rhetorical Analysis of American and Canadian Approaches to the Regulation of Hate Speech," 1994 *Wis. L. Rev.* 1425, 1481–82.

164. *Keegstra*, [1990] 3 S.C.R. at 714.

165. *Id.*

166. *Id.*

167. Heinrichs, *supra* note 157, at 837–38.

168. *Id.* at 837.

169. Criminal Code of Canada, R.S.C., 1985, c. C-46, § 319(2).

170. *See id.* at § 319(3)(a)–(d).

171. *Id.* at § 319(6) ("No proceeding for an offence under subsection (2) shall be initiated without the consent of the Attorney General.").

172. *Keegstra*, [1990] 3 S.C.R. at 713.

173. *Id.* at 719–22.

174. *Id.* at 729.

175. *Id.* at 732.

176. *Id.*

177. *See Irwin Toy Ltd. v. Quebec (Attorney General)*, [1989] 1 S.C.R. 927, 970.

178. *Keegstra*, [1990] 3 S.C.R. at 733.

179. *Id.*

180. *See id.* at 744–87.

181. See generally Robert A. Kahn, "How

Americans and Canadians Justify Their Positions on Hate Speech" (May 21, 2002) (draft on file with author) (arguing that commitment to multiculturalism and pluralism provides an important distinguishing characteristic for Canadians and that these values are used to distinguish Canadian democracy from its neighbor to the south). Kahn notes that "when Canadians defend hate speech laws, they are not simply defending what they see as a Pareto-optimal approach to a difficult problem." *Id.* at 24. Instead, "[t]hey are defending a legal tradition by which they distinguish themselves from the United States." *Id.*

182. *See Keegstra,* [1990] 3 S.C.R. at 747–49 (discussing legislative history of the statute); *cf.* Heinrichs, *supra* note 157, at 855 (arguing that "with all due respect to the Court, the fact remains that we have no more *hard* evidence of the exact relationship between hate speech and target group attitudes or behaviour than we have of the relationship between pornography and the behaviour of its supposed 'targets' —women and children.").

183. *Keegstra,* [1990] 3 S.C.R. at 743.

184. *See id.* at 746.

185. *Id.* at 793.

186. *Id.*

187. Heinrichs, *supra* note 157, at 855 (emphasis in the original).

188. *See infra* text and accompanying notes 370 to 390.

189. *Keegstra,* [1990] 3 S.C.R. at 756.

190. *Id.; see also* Mahoney, *supra* note 3, at 792 ("People who are targeted by hate propaganda respond to it by being fearful and withdrawing from full participation in society. They are humiliated and degraded, and their self-worth is undermined. They are silenced and their credibility is eroded. The more they are silenced, the deeper their inequality grows.").

191. Mahoney, *supra* note 3, at 793.

192. *See United States v. Morrison,* 529 U.S. 598 (2000).

193. *See Buckley v. Valeo,* 424 U.S. 1 (1976).

194. *See R.A.V. v. City of St. Paul,* 505 U.S. 377 (1992).

195. *Cf. Cohen v. California,* 403 U.S. 15 (1971) (holding that jacket emblazoned with "Fuck the Draft" enjoys substantial First Amendment protection and noting that because emotional impact and connotative meaning vary with precise form of expression, those aspects of speech activity enjoy full First Amendment protection as much as basic idea or thought itself).

196. *Keegstra,* [1990] 3 S.C.R. at 764; *see also* Mahoney, *supra* note 3, at 792–93 (describing why hate speech is antithetical to a functioning democracy).

197. *See Keegstra,* [1990] 3 S.C.R. at 764–65.

198. *See* Mahoney, *supra* note 3, at 792–94, 797–803.

199. *Keegstra,* [1990] 3 S.C.R. at 769.

200. *Id.*

201. *See id.* at 783.

202. *Id.*

203. Mahoney, *supra* note 3, at 800.

204. *See Little Sisters Book and Art Emporium v. Canada (Minister of Justice),* [2000] 2 S.C.R. 1120, 1136–42 (describing discriminatory enforcement of obscenity standards to censor materials featuring gay and lesbian themes); *see also infra* text and accompanying notes 300 to 340.

205. *See* DeNeen L. Brown, "Native Leader in Canada Apologizes for Hitler Remark," *Washington Post,* Dec. 18, 2002, at A24. For additional discussion of this incident, and its contrast to the approach Canadian authorities have taken when racist speech by Quebec separatists has been at issue, *see infra* pp. 82–89.

206. Heinrichs, *supra* note 157, at 848–49.

207. *See id.* at 849 ("Indeed, given the history of government efforts in this regard, they should be considered much less capable.").

208. *See Keegstra,* [1990] 3 S.C.R. at 828–29, 849–50 (McLachlin, J., dissenting).

209. *Id.* at 849.

210. *Id.* at 859.

211. *Id.* at 862.

212. *Taylor v. Canadian Human Rights Comm'n,* [1990] 3 S.C.R. 892.

213. *See id.* at 903–04.

214. Canadian Human Rights Act, S.C. 1976–1977, c. 33, § 13(1).

215. *See id.* at § 2.

216. *See Taylor,* [1990] 3 S.C.R. at 904–05.

217. *Id.* at 905.

218. *See id.*

219. *See id.* at 908–10.

220. *See id.* at 913–15.

221. *Id.* at 915.

222. *See id.* at 916–40.

223. *See id.* at 918–19; *cf.* Heinrichs, *supra* note 157, at 855 (questioning the Supreme Court's empirical basis for finding that hate speech and pornography are at the root of great social harms).

224. *Taylor,* [1990] 3 S.C.R. at 919.

225. *Id.* at 922.

226. *See id.* at 922–23.

227. *See* Moon, *supra* note 2, at 32–42, 56–70.

228. *See Taylor,* [1990] 3 S.C.R. at 953–54 (McLachlin, J., dissenting).

229. *Id.* at 953.

230. *See id.* at 957–59.

231. *Id.* at 962.

232. *Id.* at 964.

233. *See id.* at 967–68.

234. *Id.* at 969.

235. *Id.* at 968–69.

236. *Id.* at 969.

237. [1992] 3 S.C.R. 731.

238. Criminal Code, R.S.C., 1985, C-46, § 181.

239. *Zundel,* [1992] 3 S.C.R. at 743–44.

240. *Id.* at 743.

241. *Id.*

242. *See id.* at 751–59; *id.* at 801–03 (Iacobucci, J., dissenting) (finding that booklet enjoys Section 2 protection but concluding that section 181 is saved by operation of Section 1).

243. *Id.* at 764.

244. *See id.* at 765–66.

245. *Id.*

246. *See id.* at 774–76.

247. *Id.* at 776.

248. *See id.* at 805–07.

249. *Id.* at 806.

250. *Id.* at 808 (citing and quoting Mari J. Matsuda, "Public Response to Racist Speech: Considering the Victim's Story," 87 *Mich. L. Rev.* 2320, 2379 (1989)).

251. *Id.*

252. *Id.* at 810.

253. *See id.* at 810–24.

254. *Id.* at 824.

255. *Id.* at 825.

256. *Id.* at 826.

257. *See infra* Chapter 4.

258. 403 U.S. 15 (1971).

259. *Id.* at 16–17.

260. *Id.* at 22.

261. *Id.* at 24.

262. *Id.*

263. *Id.* at 25.

264. *Id.* at 26.

265. *Id.*

266. *Id.* at 27 (Blackmun, J., dissenting).

267. Ronald J. Krotoszynski, Jr., "*Cohen v. California*: 'Inconsequential' Cases and Larger Principles," 74 *Tex. L. Rev.* 1251, 1253 n.24 (1996).

268. *Cohen,* 403 U.S. at 25.

269. *Id.*

270. *See R. v. Keegstra,* [1990] 3 S.C.R. 697, 743 ("in my view the international commitment to eradicate hate propaganda and, most importantly, the special role given equality and multiculturalism in the Canadian Constitution necessitate a departure from the view, reasonably held in America at present, that the suppression of hate propaganda is incompatible with the guarantee of free expression"); *see also* International Convention on the Elimination of All Forms of Racial Discrimination, Can. T.S. 1970; International Covenant on Civil and Political Rights, 999 U.N.T.S. 171 (1966).

271. *Keegstra,* [1990] 3 S.C.R. at 754.

272. [1992] 1 S.C.R. 452.

273. *Id.* at 461.

274. *Id.* at 462.

275. *Id.* at 462.

276. Criminal Code, R.S.C., 1985, c. C-46, § 163(1)(a).

277. *See id.* at § 163(2).

278. *Id.* at § 163(8).

279. *Id.* at § 163(6).

280. *Id.* at § 163(3).

281. *Butler,* [1992] 1 S.C.R. at 462–69.

282. *See id.* at 476–80.
283. *Id.* at 478.
284. *Id.* at 479.
285. *Id.* at 479–80.
286. *Id.* at 484.
287. *Id.* at 485.
288. *Id.* at 484–85.
289. *Id.* at 485.
290. *Id.* at 485–86.
291. *See id.* at 486–87.
292. *See id.* at 496–98 ("As outlined above, s. 163(8) criminalizes the exploitation of sex and violence, when, on the basis of the community test, it is undue. The determination of when such exploitation is undue is directly related to the immediacy of a risk of harm to society which is reasonably perceived as arising from its dissemination.").
293. *See id.* at 499–504.
294. *See id.* at 504–06.
295. *See id.* at 509.
296. *Id.*
297. *Id.*
298. *Id.*
299. *See id.* at 509–10.
300. [2000] 2 S.C.R. 1120.
301. *See id.* at 1135 ("The store carried a specialized inventory catering to the gay and lesbian community which consisted largely of books that included, but was not limited to, gay and lesbian literature, travel information, general interest periodicals, academic studies related to homosexuality, AIDS/HIV safe sex advisory material and gay and lesbian erotica.")
302. *Id.* at 1135–36.
303. *See* Customs Tariff, S.C. 1987, c. 49, sch. VII, Code 9956(a).
304. *See Little Sisters,* [2000] 2 S.C.R. at 1136–37.
305. *Id.* at 1137.
306. *Id.*
307. *Id.* at 1138–39.
308. *See id.* at 1139–41.
309. *See id.* at 1149.
310. *See id.* at 1150.
311. *Id.* at 1154.
312. *Id.* at 1155.
313. *Id.* at 1160.
314. *Id.* at 1162.

315. *Id.* at 1170.
316. *See id.* at 1172–96.
317. *Id.* at 1200.
318. *Id.*
319. *See id.* at 1181 ("I would therefore declare that s. 152(3) is not to be construed and applied so as to place on an importer the onus to establish that goods are not obscene within the meaning of s. 163(8) of the Criminal Code."). Thus, the Supreme Court issued a binding interpretation of the Customs Act that requires the agency to refrain from requiring an importer to prove at trial that the materials may be lawfully imported, and instead places the burden of proof on the government to show that they may not, at least in obscenity cases. *Cf.* Customs Act, R.S.C., 1985, c. 1, § 152(3) (providing that "in any proceeding under this Act, the burden of proof in any question" that relates to compliance with the Act "in respect of any goods" will lie "on the person, other than Her Majesty, who is a party to the proceeding or the person who is accused of an offence, and not on Her Majesty").
320. *See id.* at 1203–04.
321. *Id.* at 1207 (Iacobucci, J., dissenting).
322. *See id.* at 1212–13.
323. *Id.* at 1215 (quoting letter from DOJ to senior legal counsel at the Customs Service).
324. *See id.* at 1216–17.
325. *Id.* at 1217.
326. *See id.* at 1217–21 (describing various incidents involving incorrect seizures over a prolonged temporal period involving a wide variety of materials, including books, films, and photographs, and discriminatory treatment visited on selected importers, like Little Sisters).
327. *See id.* at 1223–24.
328. *Id.* at 1225–26.
329. *Id.* at 1226.
330. *Id.* at 1238–40.
331. *Id.* at 1243.
332. *Id.*
333. *Id.* at 1243.
334. *Id.*
335. *Id.* at 1247.
336. *Id.*
337. *Id.* at 1247–48.

338. *Id.* at 1260.
339. *Id.* at 1252.
340. *Id.* at 1257.
341. [2001] 1 S.C.R. 45.
342. *See id.* at 62.
343. *See* Criminal Code, R.S.C. 1985, c. C-46, § 163.1.
344. *Id.* at § 163.1(4)(a).
345. *Id.* at § 161.1(1).
346. *Id.*
347. *Sharpe,* [2001] 1 S.C.R. at 65–66.
348. *Id.* at 66.
349. *See id.* at 66–67.
350. *See id.* at 68 ("On the first issue the Crown concedes that the law intrudes upon the guarantee of free expression in s. 2(b) of the Charter.").
351. *Id.* at 71–72.
352. *Id.* at 72–73.
353. *See R. v. Butler,* [1992] 1 S.C.R. 452, 485.
354. *See Osborne v. Ohio,* 495 U.S. 103 (1990); *New York v. Ferber,* 458 U.S. 747 (1982). In the United States, materials featuring real children need not meet the test of legal obscenity to be proscribable under state or federal law.
355. *Sharpe,* [2001] 1 S.C.R. at 93.
356. *See id.* at 93–94, 110–13, 119.
357. *Id.* at 111, 119.
358. *Id.*
359. *Id.* at 112.
360. *Id.* at 81.
361. *Id.* at 82.
362. *Id.* at 87.
363. *Id.*
364. *Id.*
365. *Id.* at 92.
366. *See id.* at 90–91.
367. *See id.* at 89.
368. *See Osborne v. Ohio,* 495 U.S. 103 (1990); *New York v. Ferber,* 458 U.S. 747 (1982).
369. *See Ashcroft v. Free Speech Coalition,* 535 U.S. 234 (2002) (invalidating federal statute that criminalized virtual depictions of naked children as well as materials created with adults who appear to be under 18 years of age).
370. *See* DeNeen L. Brown, "Native Leader in Canada Apologizes for Hitler Remark,"

Wash. Post, Dec. 18, 2002, at A2. Tribal leaders immediately condemned Ahenakew's remarks and sought to distance themselves from him. *See id.* ("Perry Bellegarde, chief of the Federation of Saskatchewan Indian Nations, said the group passed three motions denouncing Ahenakew's comments. 'We apologize for comments made by one of our own. . . . We know what racism is and we feel that pain.").
371. Craig Turner, "Quebec Separatism Brings Fear of Intolerance," *L.A. Times,* Nov. 10, 1995, at A12.
372. Charles Trueheart, "Premier To Resign in Quebec; Separatists Promise Renewed Campaign," *Wash. Post,* Nov. 1, 1995, at A1.
373. Christopher J. Chipello & John Urquhart, "Quebec Rejects Separatist Plan in Close Vote," *Wall St. Journal,* Oct. 31, 1995, at A3.
374. Craig Turner, "Quebec Rejects Bid to Secede From Canada," *L.A. Times,* Oct. 31, 1995, at A1.
375. *Id.*
376. Turner, *supra* note 371, at A12.
377. Trueheart, *supra* note 372, at A21.
378. Anne Swardson, "Quebecers Who Spurned Sovereignty Fear Rift, Assert Patriotism," *Wash. Post,* Nov. 2, 1995, at A21.
379. Trueheart, *supra* note 372, at A21.
380. Charles Trueheart, "Quebecer Damages Separatist Cause With Remark on Low Province Birthrate," *Wash. Post,* Oct. 18, 1995, at A26.
381. *Id.*
382. *Id.*
383. *See* Edison Stewart, "Minister Upset Over 'Racist Remark,'" *Toronto Star,* Oct. 18, 1995, at A10.
384. Turner, *supra* note 374, at A12.
385. *Id.*
386. *Id.*
387. Swardson, *supra* note 378, at A21.
388. *Id.*
389. Truehart, *supra* note 380, at A26.
390. *See* Stewart, *supra* note 383, at A10.
391. *See* Brown, *supra* note 370, at A24.
392. *Id.*
393. *Id.*; *see also* Reuters, "Native Leader Charged With Promoting Hate," *N.Y. Times,*

June 12, 2003, at A10 ("David Ahenakew, a re-
tired leader of the Assembly of First Nations,
Canada's main aboriginal group, was charged
with promoting hatred for praising Hitler's
slaughter of Jews in World War II, the
Saskatchewan Justice Department said.").

394. Brown, *supra* note 370, at A24.

395. *See* Tim Cook, "Former Native
Leader Guilty of Hate Crime," *Toronto Star,*
July 9, 2005, at A 20 (reporting on
Ahenakew's conviction and his view that the
hate crime prosecution was racially motivated); "For the Record," *Wash. Post,* June 12,
2003, at A24 (reporting that "David
Ahenakew, a Canadian aboriginal leader who
praised Adolf Hitler for ordering the deaths
of 6 million Jews during World War II, was
charged with promoting hatred, the
Saskatchewan Justice Department said.").

396. Mahoney, *supra* note 3, at 807.

397. Even if sexual minorities are marginalized in Canada, they are obviously less marginalized than in many other places, notably
including the United States. Canada is poised
to recognize formally, on a nationwide basis,
same-sex marriage—something that represents a material and significant validation of
such relationships. *See* Associated Press,
"Canadian high court rules in favor of same-
sex marriage," *USA Today,* Dec. 10, 2004, at
14A; Doug Struck, "High Court In Canada
Backs Gay Marriage," *Wash. Post,* Dec. 10,
2004, at A1. The push for recognizing same-
sex marriage began with a ruling by an Ontario appellate court mandating marriage
rights for same-sex couples. *See* Tom Cohen,
"Dozens in Canada Follow Gay Couple's
Lead; Same Sex Partners Apply for Marriage
Licenses After Landmark Court Ruling,"
Wash. Post, June 12, 2003, at A25. The Martin
government promised to enact a federal law
that would recognize same-sex unions; until
July 20, 2005, same-sex marriage licenses
were available in eight of Canada's ten
provinces and two of its three territories. *See*
Struck, *supra,* at A30. On July 20, 2005,
Canada's Parliament gave final approval to
legislation authorizing same-sex marriage on
a nationwide basis. "Canada Gay Marriage
Approved," *N.Y. Times,* July 21, 2005, at A6;

"Canada Legalizes Same-Sex Marriage," *L.A.
Times,* July 21, 2005, at A8.

398. Moran, *supra* note 163, at 1477–78.

399. *Id.* at 1478–79.

400. Betsy Powell, "Rapper Eminem Performs Here Despite Protest," *Toronto Star,*
Oct. 27, 2000, at 1.

401. *Id.*

402. *Id.*

403. *Id.*

404. *See* Nui Te Koha, "Group Says Eminem Too Hateful," *Herald Sun,* June 27, 2001,
at 13 ("In Canada, city leaders in Toronto
have banned Eminem from performing at
the New Muzik Festival on Sunday.").

405. *See* Jason Tchir & Maria McClintock,
"Politics Show Biz 'For Ugly People': Doesn't
Like U.S.? Parrish the Thought," *Toronto Star,*
Mar. 4, 2003, at 4 (reporting on Carolyn Parrish's comments and her subsequent observation that "I can't even promise it won't happen again"); Tim Harper, " 'Damn Americans' Accused By Angry MP," *Toronto Star,*
Feb. 27, 2003, at A1.

406. DeNeen Brown, "Canadian Apologizes For Expletive About U.S.," *Wash. Post,*
Feb. 28, 2003, at A17.

407. *Id.*

408. Bob McDonald, "The Gall of Them:
How Dare Chretien, Chirac Sit on the Side-
lines and Call for UN Action," *Toronto Sun,*
Mar. 23, 2003, at 29.

409. *Id.*

410. *Id.*

411. *See* Rachel Sa, "Thobani's an Insult to
Western Feminists," *Toronto Sun,* Oct. 6, 2001,
at 16.

412. *Id.*

413. *See* Jim Lynch & Julie Sullivan, "A Relationship Bordering on Hostile," *Cleveland
Plain Dealer,* Nov. 4, 2001, at 5.

414. Greg Joyce, "Furore Grows Over
'Hateful' Speech," *Toronto Star,* Oct. 3, 2001,
at A6.

415. *See* Turner, *supra* note 374, at A1.

416. Andrew J. Petter & Patrick J. Mona-
han, "Developments in Constitutional Law:
The 1986–1987 Term," 10 *Sup. Ct. L. Rev.* 61,
66 (1988).

417. Commentators have noted that the

Supreme Court of Canada has been less generous in applying Section 1 in the context of arrest, search, and seizure cases. Thus, *Oakes* balancing does not result in pro-government decisions across all Charter rights. *See* James B. Kelly & Michael Murphy, "Confronting Judicial Supremacy: A Defence of Judicial Activism and the Supreme Court of Canada's Legal Rights Jurisprudence," 16 *Can. J. Law & Soc'y* 3, 15–24 (2001).

418. *See* Heinrichs, *supra* note 157, at 849 (noting that government lacks superior insights into truth and suggesting that "it seems much wiser policy to leave to each individual the task of sorting out the true from the false, the right from the wrong, and the good from the bad or evil").

419. *See infra* Chapter 4.

420. It bears noting that, in the absence of legislation proscribing racist or sexist utterances, Section 2 would protect such expression. The Canadian Supreme Court has not held racist or sexist speech to be outside the free speech guarantee but, rather, has sustained laws abridging the freedom of speech, insofar as the speech at issue constitutes hate speech.

421. 403 U.S. 15 (1971).

422. *Id.* at 24.

NOTES TO CHAPTER 4

1. Grundgesetz [Basic Law] (F.R.G.) [hereinafter Basic Law]. For a brief history of the Basic Law, including its creation and adoption, *see* David P. Currie, *The Constitution of the Federal Republic of Germany* 8–24 (1994), and Donald P. Kommers, *The Constitutional Jurisprudence of the Federal Republic of Germany* 7–10, 30–49 (2nd ed. 1997).

2. *See* Ernst Benda, "The Protection of Human Dignity (Article I of the Basic Law)," 53 *SMU L. Rev.* 443, 445–46 (2000). As one commentator noted at the time of the vote "I am not sure how to grasp the symbolic meaning of this date. This 8th of May, in essence, is the most tragic and questionable paradox in our history. Why? Because we have, at the same time, been redeemed and destroyed." *Id.* at 445.

3. *See* Basic Law, art. 1(1) ("Human dignity shall be inviolable. To respect and protect it shall be the duty of all state authority.").

4. *See* Benda, *supra* note 2, at 444.

5. *See* Basic Law, art. 21(2) ("Parties that, by reason of their aims or the behavior of their adherents, seek to impair or abolish the free democratic basic order to endanger the existence of the Federal Republic of Germany are unconstitutional. The Federal Constitutional Court shall decide on the question of unconstitutionality.").

6. *See* Basic Law, art. 5(2) ("These rights find their limits in the provisions of general statutes, in statutory provisions for the protection of youth, and in the right to respect for personal honor.").

7. *Cf. Keyishian v. Board of Regents*, 385 U.S. 589 (1967) (finding that academic freedom enjoys constitutional protection as a penumbral right associated with the Free Speech Clause of the First Amendment).

8. Dieter Grimm, "The European Court of Justice and National Courts: The German Constitutional Perspective After the *Maastricht* Decision," 3 *Colum. J. Eur. L.* 229, 233 (1997).

9. *See Lüth*, 7 BVerfGE 198 (1958), *reprinted in 2 Federal Constitutional Court, Decisions of the Bundesverfassungsgericht— Federal Constitutional Court—Federal Republic of Germany (Part I)* at 1 (1992) [hereinafter *2 Decisions of the Federal Constitutional Court (Part I)*]; *see also* Peter E. Quint, "Free Speech and Private Law in German Constitutional Theory," 48 *Md. L. Rev.* 247, 252–89 (1989) (discussing the *Lüth* case). As Professor Quint has stated the matter, the German Constitutional Court has

> emphasized that the Basic Law establishes "an objective order of values," and indicated that the introduction of this concept in constitutional doctrine represents a fundamental strengthening of the effectiveness of the basic rights and a certain extension of those rights beyond their traditional realm.

Id. at 261 (quoting *Lüth* internally).

10. Edward J. Eberle, "Human Dignity, Privacy, and Personality in German and

American Constitutional Law," *1997 Utah L. Rev.* 963, 967.

11. Dieter Grimm, "Human Rights and Judicial Review in Germany," *in Human Rights and Judicial Review: A Comparative Perspective* 267, 273 (David M. Beatty, ed. 1994).

12. *Id.*

13. *Id.*

14. Basic Law, art. 79(3); *see also* Currie, *supra* note 1, at 10–11.

15. *See* U.S. Const., art. V (generally permitting amendments to the Constitution, except that "no State, without its consent, shall be deprived of its equal suffrage in the Senate").

16. Basic Law, art. 5(1).

17. Basic Law, art. 5(3).

18. Basic Law, art. 5(2).

19. Basic Law, art. 5(3).

20. Basic Law, art. 8.

21. Basic Law, art. 8(2).

22. Basic Law, art. 9(1).

23. Basic Law, art. 9(2).

24. Basic Law, art. 17.

25. Basic Law, art. 21(1).

26. *Id.*

27. Basic Law, art. 21(2).

28. *Id.*

29. Basic Law, art. 18.

30. *Id.*

31. Basic Law, art. 21(1).

32. Basic Law, art. 20(4).

33. *See* 5 BVerfGE 85 (1956); *see also* Kommers, *supra* note 1, at 37–38, 222–24 (discussing application of Article 21 ban on anti-democratic political parties).

34. 395 U.S. 444 (1969).

35. 458 U.S. 886 (1982).

36. For a comprehensive discussion of free speech doctrine and theory in Germany, see Dieter Grimm, *Die Meinungsfreiheit in der Rechtsprechung des Bundesverfassungsgericht* [Freedom of Speech Precedents of the Federal Constitutional Court], 48 *Neue Juristiche Wochenschrift* 1697 (1995).

37. *See* Ronald J. Krotoszynski, Jr., "Back to the Briarpatch: An Argument in Favor of Constitutional Meta-Analysis in State Action Determinations," 95 *Mich. L. Rev.* 302, 303–21 (1995).

38. For example, suppose that a high school operated by the Roman Catholic Church fires a religion teacher after learning that the religion teacher belongs to NARAL (the National Abortion Rights Action League). The decision to fire would not raise any serious free speech issues, precisely because the high school, a private actor, is not obliged to respect the First Amendment. *See, e.g., Rendell-Baker v. Cohn,* 457 U.S. 830, 837–38 (1982). A county sheriff, on the other hand, could not engage in the same behavior; the First Amendment would protect an employee who spoke out regarding a matter of public concern. *See Rankin v. McPherson,* 483 U.S. 378 (1987).

39. Professor Erwin Chemerinsky has advocated such an approach. *See* Erwin Chemerinsky, "Rethinking State Action," 80 *Nw. U.L. Rev.* 503–11, 536–42 (1985).

40. *Id.* at 503–07, 524–27, 535–57.

41. Grimm, *supra* note 11, at 276.

42. Dieter Grimm, "Judicial Activism," *in Judges in Contemporary Democracy: An International Conversation* 17, 21 (Robert Badinter & Stephen Breyer, eds. 2004).

43. *See* Nigel Foster, *German Legal System & Laws* 153–56 (2d ed. 1996); *see also* Christian Starck, "Human Rights and the Private Law in German Constitutional Development and in the Jurisdiction of the Federal Constitutional Court," *in Human Rights in Private Law* 97–112 (Daniel Friedmann & Daphne Barak-Erez, eds. 2001).

44. Grimm, *supra* note 42, at 21.

45. *Id.* at 47.

46. Edward J. Eberle, "Public Discourse in Contemporary Germany," 47 *Case W. Res. L. Rev.* 797, 813 (1997).

47. Grimm, *supra* note 11, at 277.

48. *See id.* at 277–82 (explaining how the values of the Basic Law require both negative and affirmative government action to ensure that human rights are effectively enjoyed by all persons in Germany).

49. Quint, *supra* note 9, at 262.

50. 376 U.S. 254 (1964).

51. *Id.* at 265 (citation omitted).

52. Eberle, *supra* note 46, at 813; *see* Starck, *supra* note 43, at 97–112.

53. Grimm, *supra* note 11, at 279.

54. *Id.* at 283.

55. *Id.*

56. *Id.*; *see also* Grimm, *supra* note 42, at 20–22 (discussing the doctrine of *Schutzpflicht* and the obligation of government to secure fundamental rights against social or economic barriers created or maintained by third parties).

57. Grimm, *supra* note 11, at 283.

58. Quint, *supra* note 9, at 339.

59. *See* Eberle, *supra* note 46, at 811.

60. Eberle, *supra* note 10, at 971 (noting that "[h]uman dignity is the central value of the Basic Law"); *see also id.* at 972 (noting that "dignity is the highest legal value in Germany"). For a definition of the concept of "dignity" in German constitutional law jurisprudence, *see id.* at 975–76.

61. Eberle, *supra* note 46, at 805.

62. *Mephisto,* 30 BVerfGE 173 (1971).

63. *Soraya,* 34 BVerfGE 269 (1973).

64. *Lebach,* 35 BVerfGE 202 (1973).

65. *Strauss,* 75 BVerfGE 369 (1987).

66. 485 U.S. 46 (1988). For a discussion and thoughtful critique of the *Falwell* case, *see* Robert C. Post, *Constitutional Domains: Democracy, Community, Management* 119–51 (1995). Post argues that "[t]he individualist methodology of First Amendment doctrine ultimately means that individuals must be free within public discourse from the enforcement of all civility rules, so as to be able to advocate and to exemplify the creation of new forms of communal life in their speech." *Id.* at 151. The German approach generally *enforces* civility norms against iconoclasts, precisely because maintaining a common culture that safeguards personal honor constitutes a more pressing social objective for the German legal system than facilitating transgressive self-expression. *See infra* text and accompanying notes 74 to 158.

67. Currie, *supra* note 1, at 237.

68. *Id.* at 237.

69. *See R.A.V. v. City of St. Paul,* 505 U.S. 377 (1992).

70. *See, e.g.,* Friedrich Kübler, "How Much Freedom for Racist Speech? Transnational Aspects of a Conflict of Human Rights," 27 *Hofstra L. Rev.* 335, 340–47 (1998) (discussing German laws protecting reputation and prohibiting fighting words and hate speech).

71. Eberle, *supra* note 46, at 805.

72. *See* Stanley Fish, *There's No Such Thing as Free Speech and It's a Good Thing, Too* 102–19 (1994).

73. *See* Currie, *supra* note 1, at 242–43 ("In all of this there is much food for thought as to the proper role of a constitutional court as well as the proper scope of free expression and of those cognate rights that help to make it a reality. And that, in addition to the more modest but equally worthy goal of better understanding, is what comparative law is all about."); *see also* Richard Delgado, "Words That Wound: A Tort Action for Racial Insults, Epithets, and Name-Calling," 17 *Harv. C.R.-C.L. L. Rev.* 133 (1992); Mari J. Matsuda, "Public Response to Racist Speech: Considering the Victim's Story," 87 *Mich. L. Rev.* 2320 (1989); *cf.* Stephen G. Gey, "The Case Against Post-Modern Censorship Theory," 145 *U. Pa. L. Rev.* 193, 194–96 (1996) (arguing that efforts to limit speech rights to advance other values constitutes impermissible government censorship).

74. 30 BVerfGE 173 (1971), reprinted and translated in *The Federal Constitutional Court, 2 Decisions of the Bundesverfassungsgericht—Federal Constitutional Court—Federal Republic of Germany (Part I: Freedom of Speech)* 147–80 (1992); *see also* Kommers, *supra* note 1, at 301–04.

75. *Mephisto, 2 Decisions of the Bundesverfassungsgericht (Part I), supra* note 74, at 148–49.

76. Klaus Mann, *The Turning Point* 281 (1942). The Federal Constitutional Court cites this work and quotes Mann's identification of the fictional character with Gründgens. *Mephisto, 2 Decisions of the Bundesverfassungsgericht (Part I), supra* note 74, at 148–49.

77. *Id.* at 149.

78. *Id.* at 150.

79. *See id.* at 151.

80. *See id.* at 153. Ironically, Mann died prior to the Federal Constitutional Court's decision in the case. The *Mephisto* case there-

fore tested a dead author's interest in free expression against another dead man's reputational rights.

81. *Id.* at 155.
82. *Id.*
83. *Id.* at 156.
84. *Id.* at 158.
85. *See id.* at 158–61.
86. *Id.* at 161. Because Article 5(3) provides a more specific textual home for Mann's claim, the Federal Constitutional Court declined to apply Article 5(1). *See id.* ("Artistic statements, even if they contain statements of opinion, mean something other than those statements.").
87. Quint, *supra* note 9, at 295.
88. *Mephisto, supra* note 74, at 162–63 (Stein, J., dissenting).
89. *Id.* at 166.
90. *Id.* at 167.
91. *Id.* at 173.
92. *Id.* at 175 (Rupp-von Brünneck, J., dissenting).
93. *Id.* at 179 (internal citation omitted).
94. Kommers, *supra* note 1, at 124.
95. 34 BVerfGE 269, 283–84 (1973), *translated in* Currie, *supra* note 1, at 198.
96. *Id.* at 286, *translated in* Currie, *supra* note 1, at 198 n.95.
97. *Id.* at 283–84.
98. *Princess Soraya,* 34 BVerfGE 269 (1973), *translated in* Kommers, *supra* note 1, at 419–20.
99. *Lebach,* 35 BVerfGE 202 (1973).
100. Currie, *supra* note 1, at 199 n.96 (emphasis in the original).
101. *Lebach,* 35 BVerfGE 202 (1973), translated in Kommers, *supra* note 1, at 417.
102. *Id.* at 418.
103. *Id.*
104. *Id.* at 419.
105. *Id.*
106. Quint, *supra* note 9, at 301.
107. James Q. Whitman, "The Two Western Cultures of Privacy: Dignity Versus Liberty," 113 *Yale L.J.* 1151, 1195 n.202 (2004).
108. *See Lebach II,* BVerfG, 1 BvR 348/98, 1 BvR 755/98, v. 25.11.1999.
109. Gebhard Rehm, "Just Judicial Activism? Privacy and Informational Self-De-

termination in U.S. and German Constitutional Law," 32 *U. West L.A. L. Rev.* 275, 292 n.82 (2001).
110. *Id.*
111. *Id.*
112. Eberle, *supra* note 10, at 1009.
113. *Id.*
114. *Id.*
115. *See* Donald Kommers, "The Jurisprudence of Free Speech in the United States and in the Federal Republic of Germany," 53 *S. Cal. L. Rev.* 657, 691–93 (1980).
116. Currie, *supra* note 1, at 206.
117. *Id.*
118. *Id.*
119. *See* Kommers, *supra* note 1, at 420–21.
120. *See Böll,* 54 BVerfGE 208 (1980), *reprinted in* 2 *Decisions of the Federal Constitutional Court (Part I)* 189 (1998).
121. *Id.* at 191.
122. *Id.* at 195.
123. *Id.* at 196.
124. *See id.* at 197–98.
125. Quint, *supra* note 9, at 337.
126. *See Bose v. Consumers' Union,* 466 U.S. 485, 501 (1983) (requiring independent appellate review of questions of constitutional fact resolved adversely to media defendant); *see also* Betsy Wilborn Malloy & Ronald J. Krotoszynski, Jr., "Recalibrating the Cost of Harm Advocacy: Getting Beyond Brandenburg," 41 *Wm. & Mary L. Rev.* 1159, 1236 (2000) ("Moreover, the Supreme Court has noted that the First Amendment entitles a speaker to an independent examination of a court or jury determination that the speech is subject to regulation.").
127. In fairness to Professor Currie, he acknowledges these cases, even as he asserts that the Constitutional Court has afforded "broader protection" to the freedom of speech. *See* Currie, *supra* note 1, at 206.
128. 75 BVerfGE 369 (1987).
129. *Strauss Caricature,* 75 BVerfGE 369 (1987), reprinted in part, 2 *German Constitutional Court, Decisions of the Bundesverfassungsgericht—Federal Constitutional Court—Federal Republic of Germany: Freedom of Speech, Part II* 420, 420–21 (Karlsruhe 1998).
130. *Id.* at 421.

131. *Id.* at 423.

132. *See id.* at 424–25.

133. *Id.* at 425.

134. *Id.*

135. *Id.*

136. *Id.* (emphasis in original).

137. *Cf. Hustler v. Falwell,* 485 U.S. 46, 51–53 (1988); *New York Times Co. v. Sullivan,* 376 U.S. 254, 279–82 (1964).

138. Frederick Schauer, "Can Public Figures Have Private Lives?" 17 *Soc. Phil. & Pol'y* 293, 306 (2000).

139. *Id.* at 306–07.

140. *See, e.g., Saia v. New York,* 334 U.S. 558, 562 (1948) ("Courts must balance the various community interests in passing on the constitutionality of local regulations of the character involved here. But in that process they should be mindful to keep the freedoms of the First Amendment in a preferred position."); *Prince v. Massachusetts,* 321 U.S. 158, 164 (1944) ("If by this appellant seeks for freedom of conscience a broader protection than for freedom of the mind, it may be doubted that any of the great liberties insured by the First Article can be given a higher place than the others. All have preferred position in our basic scheme."); *Murdock v. Pennsylvania,* 319 U.S. 105, 115 (1943) ("Freedom of the press, freedom of speech, freedom of religion are in a preferred position.").

141. *See* Edmond Cahn, "The Firstness of the First Amendment," 65 *Yale L.J.* 464 (1956); *see also United States v. Carolene Prods. Co.,* 304 U.S. 144, 152 n.4 (1938) (arguing that "[t]here may be narrower scope for operation of the presumption of constitutionality when legislation appears on its face to be within a specific prohibition of the Constitution, such as those of the first ten Amendments, which are deemed equally specific when held to be embraced within the Fourteenth").

142. *Thomas v. Collins,* 323 U.S. 516, 529–30 (1945); *see Marsh v. Alabama,* 326 U.S. 501, 509 (1946) ("When we balance the Constitutional rights of owners of property against those of the people to enjoy freedom of the press and religion, as we must here, we re-main mindful of the fact that the latter occupy a preferred position.").

143. *See, e.g., Roth v. United States,* 354 U.S. 476 (1957) (rejecting First Amendment defense to prosecution for obscenity, holding that hard-core pornography does not implicate the Free Speech Clause at all); *id.* at 514 (1957) (Douglas, J., dissenting) (arguing that the materials should enjoy constitutional protection because "[t]he First Amendment puts free speech in a preferred position."); *but cf. Employment Div. v. Smith,* 494 U.S. 872, 895 (1990) (O'Connor, J., concurring) ("The compelling interest test effectuates the First Amendment's command that religious liberty is an independent liberty, that it occupies a preferred position, and that the Court will not permit encroachments upon this liberty, whether direct or indirect, unless required by clear and compelling government interests of the highest order." (internal quotations and citations omitted)).

144. *See* Lillian R. BeVier, "Intersection and Divergence: Some Reflections on the Warren Court, Civil Rights, and the First Amendment," 59 *Wash. & Lee L. Rev.* 1075, 1084–86, 1091–93 (2002).

145. 485 U.S. 46 (1988).

146. Basic Law, art. 5(3).

147. Basic Law, art. 2(1).

148. James Q. Whitman, "Enforcing Civility and Respect: Three Societies," 109 *Yale L.J.* 1279, 1381 (2000).

149. *See id.* at 1295–1300, 1313–30.

150. *Id.* at 1328–29 (emphasis in the original).

151. *Id.* at 1384.

152. *Id.* at 1387, 1391.

153. *Id.* at 1312.

154. *See Flag Desecration,* 81 BVerfGE 278 (1990), *reprinted in 2 Decisions of the Federal Constitutional Court (Part II)* 437 (1992). One should note that the Constitutional Court invalidated criminal convictions for flag desecration only on an "as applied basis." The Court explained that although "complainants' actions fall in the area of artistic freedom protection" that this conclusion "does not, from the outset, actually stand in the way of punishment under § 90a of the

Criminal Code for disparaging the federal flag." *Id.* at 443.

155. *See German National Anthem,* 81 BVerfGE 298 (1990), *reprinted in 2 Decisions of the Federal Constitutional Court (Part II)* 450 (1992). In this case, the magazine *Howler* published a parody of the German national anthem. *See id.* at 451 (providing text of the parody). A local court convicted the publisher of an offense under § 90a(1) of the German Criminal Code and the appellate courts affirmed the conviction. The Federal Constitutional Court reversed on Article 5(3) grounds, finding that the lower courts had failed to properly balance the publisher's interest in using the national anthem to parody social contradictions against the government's interest in preserving the dignity of the national anthem. *See id.* at 455–57. Here, the value of the satire outweighed, at least in context, the state interest in protecting the national anthem. As in the *Flag Desecration* case, the Constitutional Court invalidated the convictions only on an "as applied" basis.

156. *See Tucholsky* (Soldiers are Murderers Case), 93 BVerfGE 266 (1995), *reprinted in 2 Decisions of the Federal Constitutional Court (Part 2)* 659 (1998). The Federal Constitutional Court held that Article 5(1) protected a citizen who published the words "Soldiers Are Murderers," provided that the statement is not directed at any particular soldier or group of soldiers. *See id.* at 676–77. "Instead, they expressed a judgment about soldiers and about the profession of soldier, which in some circumstances compels the killing of other people." *Id.* at 677.

157. *Tucholsky, 2 Decisions of the Federal Constitutional Court (Part II)* at 678.

158. *Id.*

159. *Id.*

160. *Id.* at 680.

161. *Id.*

162. *See id.* at 682–88.

163. *Id.* at 698 (Haas, J., dissenting).

164. *Id.*

165. *See* Eberle, *supra* note 46, at 825.

166. *Lüth,* 7 BVerfGE 198, 208 (1958).

167. Currie, *supra* note 1, at 175.

168. *See Physician Advertising,* 71 BVerfGE 162 (1985); *Pharmacy Advertising,* 53 BVerfGE 96 (1980). These results stand in stark contrast with cases like *Edenfield v. Fane,* 507 U.S. 761 (1993) and *Virginia State Board of Pharmacy v. Virginia Consumer Council,* 425 U.S. 748 (1976), which protect the ability of accountants and pharmacies, respectively, to advertise their products and services.

169. *See, e.g., Communist Party,* 5 BVerfGE 85 (1956); *Socialist Reich Party,* 2 BVerfGE 1 (1952).

170. *See, e.g., The "Auschwitz Lie" (Holocaust Denial),* 90 BVerfGE 241 (1994).

171. Whitman, *supra* note 148, at 1310.

172. *Id.*

173. *Id.*

174. *See id.* at 1310–12.

175. 7 BVerfGE 198 (1958), *reprinted in 2 Decisions of the Federal Constitutional Court (Part I)* 1 (1998); *see also* Kommers, *supra* note 1, at 361–69 (excerpting and translating case).

176. Grimm, *supra* note 42, at 25.

177. *See* Kommers, *supra* note 1, at 361. Professor Grimm also notes *Lüth's* jurisprudential significance, explaining that "the Court began to conceive of fundamental rights not only as subjective rights enabling the individual to defend himself or herself against government acts affecting a constitutionally protected freedom." Grimm, *supra* note 42, at 21. Instead, "[i]n the Court's view, fundamental rights are at the same time objective principles (or 'values,' in the earlier terminology) permeating the whole legal order and guiding lawmaking as well as the application of the law." *Id.*

178. *See supra* text and accompanying notes 36 to 58.

179. Kommers, *supra* note 1, at 361.

180. The provision, section 826, provides that "[w]hoever causes damages to another person intentionally and in a manner offensive to good morals is obliged to compensate the other person for the damage." *See id.* at 362.

181. *Lüth, 2 Decisions of the Federal Constitutional Court (Part I)* at 3.

182. *Id.* at 3–4.

183. *Id.* at 5.

184. *Id.*

185. *Id.*

186. *Id.* at 7.

187. *Id.* at 6–7.

188. *Id.* at 7.

189. *Id.* at 9.

190. *Id.*

191. *Id.* at 11.

192. *Id.*

193. *Id.* at 13.

194. *Id.* at 14.

195. *Id.* at 14; *see also id.* at 14–18 (describing the findings of the Court of Assizes, which found Harlan had no choice but to make the Nazi films and that he attempted, to the extent possible, to sabotage his work product for the National Socialist government).

196. *Id.* at 17.

197. *Id.* at 18.

198. *Id.* at 2.

199. *Id.* at 20.

200. 2 BVerfGE 1 (1952).

201. 5 BVerfGE 85 (1956).

202. Basic Law, art. 9(2).

203. Basic Law, art. 18.

204. Basic Law, art. 21(2). For a very helpful discussion of political parties and their role in the constitutional order that the Basic Law establishes, *see* Currie, *supra* note 1, at 207–13.

205. Kommers, *supra* note 1, at 219. The Federal Constitutional Court has not offered translations of either the *SRP* or *Communist Party* cases. Accordingly, citations are to the Kommers translations.

206. *Id.*

207. *Id.*

208. *Id.* at 220.

209. *See id.* at 220–22.

210. *Id.* at 222.

211. *Id.* at 223.

212. 5 BVerfGE 85, 142 (1956), *translated in* Kommers, *supra* note 1, at 223.

213. *Id.* at 139, *translated in* Kommers, *supra* note 1, at 223.

214. *See id.*

215. *See* Kommers, *supra* note 1, at 223.

216. *See id.* at 224–29.

217. *Id.* at 236.

218. *See id.* at 236–37.

219. *See* Currie, *supra* note 1, at 221.

220. 90 BVerfGE 241 (1994), *translated in 2 Decisions of the Federal Constitutional Court (Part II)* 620 (1998) & in Kommers, *supra* note 1, at 382.

221. *Gertz v. Robert Welch, Inc.,* 418 U.S. 323, 339 (1974).

222. Martin H. Redish & Kevin Finnerty, "What Did You Learn in School Today? Free Speech, Values Inculcation, and the Democratic-Educational Paradox," 88 *Cornell L. Rev.* 62, 74–75 (2002).

223. *Gertz,* 418 U.S. at 339–40.

224. *See 2 Decisions of the Federal Constitutional Court (Part II)* at 621.

225. *Id.* at 624.

226. *Id.* at 625.

227. *Id.*

228. *Id.*

229. *Id.*; *cf. Gertz,* 418 U.S. at 339–40 (holding that the government may not endeavor to declare truth and suppress falsehoods, but must instead rely on the marketplace of ideas to resolve any problems that false statements might cause if the speech involves a public figure or matter of public concern).

230. *Auschwitz Lie, 2 Decisions of the Federal Constitutional Court (Part II)* at 626.

231. *See id.* at 626–30. For a comprehensive review of Germany's laws prohibiting Holocaust denial and their history, *see* Eric Stein, "History Against Free Speech: The New German Law Against the 'Auschwitz'—and Other 'Lies,' " 85 *Mich. L. Rev.* 277 (1986).

232. 82 BVerfGE 1 (1990), *translated in 2 Decisions of the Federal Constitutional Court (Part II)* 458 (1998).

233. *Id.* at 459.

234. *See id.*

235. *Id.*

236. *See id.* at 459–60.

237. *Id.* at 461.

238. *Id.*

239. *Id.* at 462.

240. *See* Peter Finn, "Neo-Nazi Web Site Moving to U.S.," *Wash. Post,* Dec. 12, 2000, at A1.

241. *See id.*; *see also* John F. McGuire,

Note, "When Speech Is Heard Around the World: Internet Content Regulation in the United States and Germany," 74 *N.Y.U. L. Rev.* 751, 768–71 (1999) (describing contemporary efforts by the German government to regulate Internet content both domestically and with regard to Web sites located abroad but accessible by German citizens).

242. *See* David A. Jacobs, "Recent Developments, The Ban of Neo-Nazi Music: Germany Takes on the Neo-Nazis," 34 *Harv. Int'l L.J.* 563, 563–64, 567–68 (1993) (noting that "Germany has recently experienced an alarming rise in neo-Nazi and right-wing violence against foreigners and Jewish memorials" and reporting recent statistics involving hate crimes in Germany).

243. *See* Currie, *supra* note 1, at 221.

244. Grimm, *supra* note 11, at 295.

245. *See generally* McGuire, *supra* note 241, at 753 & 753 n.10 (collecting cases and noting that "[i]n both theory and practice, speech is considered the most fundamental of rights in the United States").

246. Eberle, *supra* note 10, at 1049.

247. *See, e.g.,* Cass R. Sunstein, *Democracy and the Problem of Free Speech* (1993) (arguing that private market forces may not serve democratic self-government very well and that government might need to assume some responsibility for regulating, and hence shaping, the marketplace of ideas); Owen Fiss, *The Irony of Free Speech* (1996) (arguing that government regulations are necessary to ensure that monied interests do not use wealth to essentially buy up the marketplace of ideas).

248. *See* David E. Weiss, "Striking a Difficult Balance: Combatting the Threat of Neo-Nazism in Germany While Preserving Civil Liberties," 27 *Vand. J. Transnat'l L.* 899, 912–13 (1994) (describing the Rostock anti-immigrant riots of 1992 and the German government's response to the riots).

249. *See* Steven Erlanger, "Bill Easing Immigration Passes First Test in German Parliament," *N.Y. Times,* March 2, 2002, at A5.

250. *Id.*

251. Jacobs, *supra* note 242, at 576.

252. *Id.* at 576 n.85 (collecting and citing

cases); *see also* Kay Hailbronner, "Fifty Years of the Basic Law—Migration, Citizenship, and Asylum," 53 *SMU L. Rev.* 519, 527 (2000) (noting that "[t]he Constitutional Court, in a landmark decision of October 31, 1990 . . . struck down the Hamburg law [extending voting rights to resident noncitizens] as unconstitutional" and observing that "[b]y reforming the citizenship law, the legislature can react to factual changes in the population of the Federal Republic").

253. Jacobs, *supra* note 242, at 577; *see also* Ediberto Roman, "An Examination of the Models of United States Citizenship As Well As Questions Concerning European Union Citizenship," 9 *U. Miami Int'l & Comp. L. Rev.* 81, 112 (2000/2001) ("Germany has a history of onerous and restrictive naturalization laws for foreigners.").

254. Jacobs, *supra* note 242, at 577; *see* Edmund L. Andrews, "German Immigration Bill Wins Disputed Vote," *N.Y. Times,* Mar. 23, 2002, at A3 ("For decades, even when Germany recruited millions of 'guest workers' in the 1950s and 1960s, German leaders insisted that theirs was not 'an immigration country' and made it nearly impossible for foreigners to become citizens. Now, with more than seven million resident foreigners, or 9 percent of the total population, Germany is already a nation of immigrants.").

255. Richard Cohen, "The German 'Volk' Seem Set to Let Outsiders In," *N.Y. Times,* Oct. 16, 1998, at A4, col. 3.

256. Jacobs, *supra* note 242, at 577; *see also* Cohen, *supra* note 255, at A4 (" 'Many people have a rooted image of Germany as a blood community,' said Hartmut Esser, a sociologist.").

257. *See* David A. Martin, "New Rules On Dual Nationality For a Democratizing Globe: Between Rejection and Embrace," 14 *Geo. Immigr. L.J.* 1, 3 (1999) (noting that the reform bill "triggered such heated opposition that it was generally blamed for the Social Democrats' defeat in a state election in Hesse in February 1999" and observing that this loss cost the party control of the Bundesrat, or upper house of the German federal Parliament, which in turn required that the provisions of

the naturalization reform bill be weakened in order to pass in the upper house).

258. *See* Daniel Boettcher, "Current Development, German Government Considers Changing Citizenship Laws, But Original Proposals Meet Fierce Opposition," 13 *Geo. Immigr. L.J.* 339, 339–40 (1999).

259. Staatsangehörigkeitsgesetz (Citizenship Law), art. 1, BGB1 I S.1618; *see* Kay Hailbronner, "Labor Transfer Schemes—in Whose National Interest? Globalization and the Transfer of Labor—the European Experience," 16 *Geo. Immigr. L.J.* 773, 775 (2002); Hailbronner, *supra* note 252, at 529–34 (discussing reforms and possible effects on German political community and noting that "[t]he extension of German citizenship to children born on German territory to foreigners means a substantial conceptual change").

260. Hailbronner, *supra* note 252, at 530.

261. Id.; *see also* Martin, *supra* note 257, at 3 n.6 (describing substantive changes in German citizenship law, including forced election of nationality by age 23 for jus soli German citizens).

262. Professor Hailbronner explains that "[f]oreigners may now acquire German citizenship after eight years of lawful residence in Germany, provided that they: 1) have a residence permit or a residence entitlement; 2) are not dependent on social welfare; 3) have no criminal record; and 4) have sufficient knowledge of the German language." Hailbronner, *supra* note 259, at 775; *see also* Hailbronner, *supra* note 252, at 530–31 ("Foreigners with a secure residence permit have a right to acquire German citizenship after eight years of residence instead of the fifteen-year wait period for those without secure residence permits. This right is dependent on a sufficient knowledge of the German language and a formal commitment to respect the Basic Law.").

263. Hailbronner, *supra* note 259, at 775.

264. Hailbronner, *supra* note 252, at 531.

265. Id. at 533–34.

266. *See* Roman, *supra* note 253, at 112 ("Foreign individuals seeking German citizenship have historically had to demonstrate cultural integration, which included fluency in written and spoken German."); Karin Scherner-Kim, "The Role of the Oath of Renunciation in Current U.S. Nationality Policy— to Enforce, to Omit, or Maybe to Change?" 88 *Geo. L.J.* 329, 344–47 (2000) (observing importance of "need to foster national cohesion to common values" but also noting the importance of functional aspects of citizenship and the negative effect demands for cultural integration might have on voluntary naturalization). Given this historical demand for cultural integration as a condition of full citizenship, it is odd that "[f]or decades, German political leaders have avoided developing effective initiatives geared toward long-term integration of Turkish and Kurdish immigrants." Vera Eccarious-Kelly, *Radical Consequences of Benign Neglect: The Rise of the PKK in Germany*, 24 *Fletcher F. World Affairs* 161, 161 (2000). Eccarious-Kelly reports that "[t]his lack of official recognition has prompted descendants of Kurdish and Turkish immigrants to organize politically in order to increase their domestic influence." *Id.* Presumably, this sort of effort to create permanent ethnic voter blocs is exactly the sort of development that Professor Hailbronner most fears. At least arguably, however, the creation (or maintenance) of an ethnic identity simply represents a rational response to the fact of racism and discrimination in contemporary German society.

267. Martin, *supra* note 257, at 9.

268. *See generally* Shlomo Avineri, "Comment: Remarks on Michelman and Breyer," 21 *Cardozo L. Rev.* 1085, 1087 (arguing that "the current German debate over citizenship law and naturalization is equally characterized by the lack of solidarity with the ethnic Turkish population" and noting that "Turkish people, even if born in Germany, are to many Germans outside the pale of effective solidarity, and hence the debate is not really about rights, but about identity").

269. *See* U.S. Const. amend. XIV, § 1 ("All persons born or naturalized in the United States, and subject to the jurisdiction thereof, are citizens of the United States and of the State wherein they reside.").

270. *See* Marshall Frady, *Wallace: The Classic Portrait of Alabama Governor George Wallace* 289 (1996) (describing Wallace's 1979 visit to the Dexter Avenue Baptist Church in Montgomery, Alabama, to apologize for his past behavior and seek forgiveness from those he had wronged in the past); Art Harris, "George Wallace's Visions & Revisions; Wooing Alabama's Voters Away From His Own Past," *Wash. Post,* Sept. 1, 1982, at B1 (describing Wallace's pilgrimage to an African American Baptist church seeking spiritual and political salvation); *see also* Caroline Rand Herron et al., "George Wallace Leads the Pack in Alabama Vote," *N.Y. Times,* Sept. 12, 1982, at § 4, p. 4 (noting Wallace's efforts to "court[ ] Alabama blacks, apologizing for his past race-baiting ways" and reporting that Wallace, seeking "an unprecedented fourth term as Governor," secured the electoral support of "nearly a third of the state's black voters" in the 1982 Democratic Party state primary election).

271. *See* Ronald J. Krotoszynski, Jr., "Celebrating Selma: The Importance of Context in Public Forum Analysis," 104 *Yale L.J.* 1411, 1414–20, 1426–28 (1995) (describing genesis of Voting Rights Act of 1965 and its effects on minority participation in federal, state, and local government after enactment).

272. Germany has experienced significant immigration from ostensibly "temporary" guest workers since the 1960s. *See* Boettcher, *supra* note 258, at 339–40. These workers "were expected to return home after several years' labor in Germany, so neither the Germans or the Turks made great efforts to integrate." *Id.* at 340.

273. *See* Whitman, *supra* note 148, at 1295–1312, 1327–32, 1381–90.

274. *Id.* at 1384.

275. *Id.* at 1385 (emphasis deleted).

276. *See id.* at 1303, 1310–11.

277. *Id.* at 1311.

278. *See id.* at 1296–97 ("In fact, every German knows that anybody who is the target of *any* such gesture—for example, 'the finger' or 'the fig'—has the right to call the cops."). For an amusing compendium of potentially actionable insults, *see id.* at 1305–06 n.70.

279. *See* LG Mannheim [Trial Court of Mannheim], 32 NJW 504 (1979). The case and the principles informing its decision are discussed in Whitman, *supra* note 148, at 1295–97, 1305 n.70, & 1312 n.88, and in Andreas Hohnel, *"Doppelvogel" und Andere Beleidigungen* 6–7 (1997).

280. Whitman, *supra* note 148, at 1312.

281. *See* Kübler, *supra* note 70, at 375–76 (observing that understandings of free speech differ across national legal systems and suggesting that "a shared understanding that a reasonable interpretation of free speech guarantees will allow the prohibition of the most threatening emanations of racial hatred and dehumanizing propaganda").

282. Whitman, *supra* note 148, at 1382.

283. *Id.*

284. Currie, *supra* note 1, at 237.

285. *See* Whitman, *supra* note 148, at 1395–98.

NOTES TO CHAPTER 5

1. *But cf.* Frank K. Upham, "The Place of Japanese Legal Studies in American Comparative Law," 1997 *Utah L. Rev.* 639 (noting the relative lack of interest in Japan among American comparative law scholars and positing the possible explanations for this state of affairs).

2. *See Japan's Commission on the Constitution: The Final Report* 24–31, 207–44 (John M. Maki ed. & trans., 1980); *see also* Kyoko Inoue, *MacArthur's Japanese Constitution: A Linguistic and Cultural Study of Its Making* 6–37 (1991). Notwithstanding the historical circumstances surrounding the adoption of the Constitution of 1947, the Japanese people have never amended it, and today the Constitution enjoys a very high degree of popular legitimacy. *See* John M. Maki, "The Constitution of Japan: Pacifism, Popular Sovereignty, and Fundamental Human Rights," *in Japanese Constitutional Law* 39, 52–53 (Percy R. Luney, Jr. & Kazuyuki Takahashi eds., 1993); *see also* Yasuhiro Okudaira, "Forty Years of the Constitution and Its Various Influences: Japanese, American, and European," *in Japanese Constitutional Law, supra,* at 1, 6–20, 25–32.

3. *See* Nihonkoku Kenpō, [Constitution] [Kenpō] art. 21, para. 1 ("Freedom of assembly and association as well as speech, press and all other forms of expression are guaranteed."").

4. In Japan, although the Meiji Constitution of 1889 ostensibly guaranteed the citizenry certain basic rights, in practice these guarantees were generally not judicially enforceable and even when nominally enforceable, the judiciary lacked the power to provide meaningful remedies to successful litigants. *See Constitutional Systems in Late Twentieth Century Asia* 135–40, 156, 225, 230 (Lawrence W. Beer ed., 1992); J. W. Dower, *Empire and Aftermath* 52–54, 318–29, 349–57 (1988); John W. Dower, "Sensational Rumors, Seditious Graffiti, and the Nightmares of the Thought Police," *in Japan in War and Peace* 101, 101–54 (1993); John Owen Haley, *Authority Without Power: Law and the Japanese Paradox* 77–80, 134 (1991); *The Japanese Legal System* 637–41 (Hideo Tanaka ed., 1976); Lawrence W. Beer, "Freedom of Expression: The Continuing Revolution," 53 *Law & Contemp. Probs.* 39, 45 (Winter and Spring 1990); Takeshi Ishida, "Fundamental Human Rights and the Development of Legal Thought in Japan," 8 *Law in Japan* 39, 62–66 (Hiroshi Wagatsuma & Beverly Braverman trans., 1975). One should keep in mind, however, that the Meiji Constitution on its face made the rights of the citizenry subject to legislative abrogation. In this sense, then, the failure to respect constitutional rights was less a failure of the Japanese judiciary than of the foundational document itself.

5. For an excellent history of the framing of the Japanese Constitution of 1947, see Koseki Shoichi, *The Birth of Japan's Postwar Constitution* (Ray A. Moore ed. & trans., 1997).

6. *See* Inoue, *supra* note 2, at 53–54. At the same time, however, the rule of law did exist during the Meiji period. Courts of law applied the statutes and regulations issued in the emperor's name and, in some instances, exhibited a fair amount of independence. For example, judicial review of administrative regulations for consistency with legislative

delegations took place, with the courts of law striking down regulations that departed from legislative mandates or general principles of statutory construction. *See* Haley, *supra* note 4, at 83–104; John Owen Haley, "The Myth of the Reluctant Litigant," 4 *J. Japanese Stud.* 359, 373–78 (1978). Indeed, even in the years of the Tokugawa Shogunate, the idea of enforcing formal duties, as opposed to rights, existed. *See* Ruth Benedict, *The Chrysanthemum and the Sword: Patterns of Japanese Culture* 70–71 (1946). On the other hand, actually lodging a formal claim with the Shogun against a superior could have dire consequences. *See id.* at 65–67 (describing how a Tokugawa Shogun granted a farmers' petition for relief against their local *daimyo,* or overlord, only to then order the farmers put to death for insubordination).

7. *See* Lawrence W. Beer, "Freedom of Expression: The Continuing Revolution," *in Japanese Constitutional Law* 221, 224–26, 245–47 (Percy R. Luney, Jr. & Kazuyuki Takahashi eds., 1993) [hereinafter Beer, "Freedom of Expression"]; Lawrence W. Beer, "The Public Welfare Standard and Freedom of Expression in Japan," *in The Constitution of Japan: Its First Twenty Years, 1947–67,* at 205, 210–20 (Dan Fenno Henderson ed., 1968) [hereinafter Beer, "Public Welfare"]; Chin Kim, "The Law of the Subtle Mind: The Traditional Japanese Conception of Law," *in Selected Writings on Asian Law* 41, 48 (1982); Chie Nakane, *Japanese Society* 26–40, 83–84, 103, 147–51 (1970); Clyde V. Prestowitz, Jr., *Trading Places: How We Allowed Japan to Take the Lead* 82–86 (1988); Paul Lansing & Tamra Domeyer, "Japan's Attempt at Internationalization and Its Lack of Sensitivity to Minority Issues," 22 *Cal. W. Int'l L.J.* 135, 139–40 (1991); Toni M. Massaro, "Shame, Culture, and American Criminal Law," 89 *Mich. L. Rev.* 1880, 1906–10 (1991); Richard B. Parker, "Law, Language, and the Individual in Japan and the United States," 7 *Wis. Int'l L.J.* 179, 183–93 (1989); Mark D. West, Note, "Prosecution Review Commissions: Japan's Answer to the Problem of Prosecutorial Discretion," 92 *Colum. L. Rev.* 684, 709–11 (1992); *cf.* Haley, *supra* note 4, at 108–18, 170–91, 196–200 (re-

jecting traditional view that Japanese citizens are inherently conformists in favor of view that complex and highly evolved systems of economic and social interdependence cabin the ability of individuals to engage in iconoclastic behavior and arguing that Japan enjoys "a special type of pluralism" characterized by active competition and interplay between well-defined social, political, and economic interest groups); Haley, *supra* note 6, at 378–90 (arguing that institutional incapacity and limited authority to provide relief, rather than a general social aversion to litigation, best explains Japan's relatively low per capita incidence of lawsuits).

8. *See generally* Owen M. Fiss, *Liberalism Divided: Freedom of Speech and the Many Uses of State Power* 20–30 (1996) (arguing that nongovernmental constraints on speech activity can be just as harmful to meaningful public discourse as ham-handed attempts at state-imposed censorship).

9. My citation conventions for decisions of the Supreme Court of Japan are as follows: (1) whenever available, I have cited to the official English language translation of the decisions of the Supreme Court of Japan, which are published by the General Secretariat of the Supreme Court of Japan; (2) when official translations are not available, I have cited to unofficial translations prepared and published by legal academics and have provided a parallel citation to the official Japanese reporter in which the case may be found.

10. This observation does not hold true for the lower Japanese courts. Japanese district and intermediate appellate courts have struck down both local and federal regulations based on Article 21's guarantee of freedom of expression. *See, e.g., Judgment on the Enshrinement of a Dead SDF Officer to Gokoku Shrine, Series of Prominent Judgments of the Supreme Court of Japan upon Questions of Constitutionality No. 25,* at 1 (General Secretariat, Supreme Court of Japan, 1991) (decided June 1, 1988) (reversing district and high court rulings that Shinto enshrinement of a dead SDF officer violated Article 20's prohibition of mandatory religious obser-

vances); *Judgment Upon Case of Constitutionality on Customs Inspection, Series of Prominent Judgments of the Supreme Court of Japan upon Questions of Constitutionality No. 20,* at i (General Secretariat, Supreme Court of Japan, 1985) (decided Dec. 12, 1984), 38 Minshū 12, at 1308, *reprinted in* Lawrence W. Beer & Hiroshi Itoh, *The Constitutional Case Law of Japan, 1970 through 1990* at 453 (1996) [hereinafter *Customs Inspection Case*] (reporting and later reversing district court's holding that certain customs inspection laws violated freedom of speech); *Judgment Upon Case of the So-Called "Popolo Theatrical Group Case," Series of Prominent Judgments of the Supreme Court of Japan upon Questions of Constitutionality No. 8,* at 1 (General Secretariat, Supreme Court of Japan, 1965) (decided May 22, 1963) (reversing district court ruling that academic freedom justified students' decision to beat undercover police who had infiltrated their organization); *Judgment Upon Case of the Metropolitan Ordinance, Series of Prominent Judgments of the Supreme Court of Japan upon Questions of Constitutionality No. 5,* at 1–2 (General Secretariat, Supreme Court of Japan, 1962) (decided July 20, 1960) (reversing the initial decision of the district court striking down Tokyo's mass demonstration ordinance); *see also* Lawrence Ward Beer, *Freedom of Expression in Japan: A Study in Comparative Law, Politics, and Society* 377–78 (1984) (reporting the split among the lower courts regarding the constitutionality of various provisions of the Election Law's speech restrictions). There are at least two possible explanations for this phenomenon. Because the lower courts do not have the last word, they may feel less of an institutional constraint on exercising the power of judicial review. *See, e.g., Quill v. Vacco,* 80 F.3d 716 (2d Cir. 1996), *rev'd,* 521 U.S. 793 (1997); *Compassion in Dying v. Washington,* 79 F.3d 790 (9th Cir. 1996) (en banc), *rev'd sub nom., Washington v. Glucksberg,* 521 U.S. 702 (1997). There are also age differences at work. Supreme Court Justices are usually in their sixties when appointed, whereas lower court judges are often appointed at a considerably younger age. *See* Percy R. Luney,

Jr., "The Judiciary: Its Organization and Status in the Parliamentary System," *in Japanese Constitutional Law, supra* note 2, at 123, 129–37. Thus, "youthful exuberance" may also help to account for the Japanese lower courts' relatively bold approach to constitutional adjudication.

11. *See, e.g., Customs Inspections Case, supra* note 10, at 6–10 (reading an authorization to prohibit the import of materials that injure "the public morals" to restrict only obscene materials); *Judgment Upon Case of Defamation, Series of Prominent Judgments of the Supreme Court of Japan upon Questions of Constitutionality No. 11,* at 2 (General Secretariat, Supreme Court of Japan, 1970) (decided June 25, 1969) (interpreting broadly an exemption to liability for defamatory statements regarding matters of public concern when such statements, although false, are made without reckless disregard for truth); *Judgment Upon Case of the Metropolitan Ordinance, supra* note 10, at 4 (reading Tokyo ordinance to require issuance of permission for mass demonstrations absent a clear and present danger of imminent lawlessness).

12. As George Wallace once wryly remarked in his 1968 independent presidential quest, at least arguably "there ain't a dime's worth of difference" between Democrats and Republicans. John H. Aldrich, *Why Parties? The Origin and Transformation of Political Parties in America* 11 (1995). To a large extent, this is true. *See* Robert Reich, *Locked in the Cabinet* 59–65, 118–19, 146–48 (1998) (describing the Clinton Administration's decision to pursue policies endorsed by Wall Street investment firms rather than the human capital and physical infrastructure investment programs set forth by then-candidate Bill Clinton during the 1992 election campaign). Consider, for example, the 1996 presidential election. The policy differences between President Clinton and Senator Dole were not pronounced; both endorsed fiscal responsibility and sustainable growth as the paramount national objectives. Notwithstanding Ross Perot's "success" in 1992 and with the possible exception of Theodore Roosevelt's "Bull Moose" party in 1912, third

parties have not enjoyed significant support in the United States for more than one hundred years. By way of contrast, "marginal" parties in Japan, like the Communists, regularly elect members to the Diet. *See* Hitoshi Abe et al., *The Government and Politics of Japan* 115–38 (James W. White trans., 1994); Gerald L. Curtis, *The Japanese Way of Politics* 18–44, 174 (1988); *see also* T. R. Reid, "Maverick Takes Over in Japan," *Wash. Post,* Aug. 7, 1993, at A14. On the other hand, the Liberal Democratic Party's historic dominance in the Diet, coupled with a parliamentary system of government, significantly mutes the real-world impact of Japan's multiparty electoral system. *See* Abe et al., *supra,* at 115–71, 182–89; Maki, *supra* note 2, at 44–46; Okudaira, *supra* note 2, at 29–31, 33; *see also* Norma Field, *In the Realm of a Dying Emperor* 27 (1993) ("Thus, the great Socialist victory in the upper house elections of July 1989 created a painfully hopeful moment when it almost seemed as if one-party rule, which had already blanketed four decades, did not have to stretch into infinity.").

13. *See* J. Mark Ramseyer, "The Puzzling (In)dependence of Courts: A Comparative Approach," 23 *J. Legal Stud.* 721, 740–41 (1994).

14. As one commentator has put it, "[t]he status of the freedom of expression in Japan may be explained by the statement that 'Japan is politically free, but socially not free.'" Okudaira, *supra* note 13, at 10; *see also* Haley, *supra* note 4, at 183–86; James J. Nelson, "Culture, Commerce, and the Constitution: Legal and Extra-Legal Restraints on Freedom of Expression in the Japanese Publishing Industry," 15 *UCLA Pac. Basin L.J.* 45 (1996). Professor Lawrence Beer, a noted expert on freedom of expression in Japan, has offered similar observations: "In Japan . . . homogeneity, group orientation, social hierarchy, quasi-parental-filial relationships (*oyabun-kobun*), reciprocal dependency patterns (*amae*), and ethnic separatism join the civil law, common law, and conciliation traditions to affect freedom and restraint of expression." Beer, "Freedom of Expression," *supra* note 7, at 224; *see also* John O. Haley, "Intro-

duction: Legal vs. Social Controls," 17 *Law in Japan* 1, 3–5 (1984).

15. *See* Owen M. Fiss, "Silence on the Street Corner," 26 *Suffolk U. L. Rev.* 1, 2–3, 14–20 (1992) (arguing that the Supreme Court's public forum decisions fail to provide sufficient public space for speech activities by those who lack access to private property or capital); Owen M. Fiss, "Why the State?" 100 *Harv. L. Rev.* 781, 787–89, 793–94 (1987) [hereinafter Fiss, "Why the State"] (noting the ability of wealthy and powerful interests to limit meaningful public debate and arguing in favor of state efforts to ameliorate these untoward effects in order to ensure full and robust public debate on matters of community concern); *see also The Japanese Legal System, supra* note 4, at 758 (noting that in Japan "every motion picture" is subject to review by a "Committee for the Maintenance of Ethics in Motion Pictures" and explaining that this system of film censorship "is maintained by motion picture companies without any government participation").

16. *See* Field, *supra* note 12, at 44–47, 132–36 (describing the informal social pressure placed on dissidents in Japanese society); Owen Fiss, *The Irony of Free Speech* 1–4, 15–26 (1996) (describing the dangers that concentrations of wealth and media power can pose to deliberative democracy); Edwin M. Reingold, *Chrysanthemums and Thorns: The Untold Story of Modern Japan* 162–63 (1992) (describing the censorial efforts of the Burakumin Liberation League). *See generally* Bill Carter, "TV Sponsors Heed Viewers Who Find Shows Too Racy," *N.Y. Times,* Apr. 23, 1989, § 1, at 1; Allen R. Myerson, "Southern Baptist Convention Calls for Boycott of Disney," *N.Y. Times,* June 19, 1997, at A18; Allen R. Myerson, "Baptists Boycott the Magic Kingdom," *N.Y. Times,* June 22, 1997, § 4, at 2; Bruce Selcraig, "Reverend Wildmon's War on the Arts," *N.Y. Times,* Sept. 2, 1990, § 6, at 22.

17. Kenpō, art. 21, para. 1.

18. *Id.* at art. 21, para. 2.

19. *See, e.g., Judgment Upon Case of Defamation, supra* note 11 (balancing interest in freedom of expression and a free press against private interest in preserving good name and reputation).

20. *See, e.g., Customs Inspection Case, supra* note 10, at 8 (balancing right to freedom of expression against community interest in "sexual order and maintenance of a minimum sexual morality").

21. *See* Alexander Meiklejohn, "The First Amendment Is Absolute," 1961 *Sup. Ct. Rev.* 245, 251–52; *see also* Eugene Volokh, "Freedom of Speech, Permissible Tailoring and Transcending Strict Scrutiny," 144 *U. Pa. L. Rev.* 2417, 2438–44 (1996) (discussing the uses and abuses of balancing in the Supreme Court's First Amendment strict scrutiny analyses).

22. Consider, for example, the right to a fair trial and the right of the press to report on pending cases. *See* Ronald J. Krotoszynski, Jr., "Fundamental Property Rights," 85 *Geo. L.J.* 555, 611 n.354 (1997).

23. Kenpō, art. 12; *see Judgment Upon Case of Translation and Publication of Lady Chatterly's Lover and Article 175 of the Penal Code, Series of Prominent Judgments of the Supreme Court of Japan upon Questions of Constitutionality No. 2,* at 11–12 (General Secretariat, Supreme Court of Japan, 1958) (decided Mar. 13, 1957) [hereinafter *Lady Chatterly's Lover*] (discussing and applying Article 12); Beer, "Public Welfare," *supra* note 7, at 207–10 (discussing the operation of Article 12).

24. *See Judgment Upon Case of the Metropolitan Ordinance, supra* note 10, at 2–3, 5–6 (invoking Article 12 incident to a balancing analysis that weighed the interest of the general public in using streets and other public spaces for their intended uses against interest of protestors in using such properties for their speech-related activities); *see also* Christopher A. Ford, "The Indigenization of Constitutionalism in the Japanese Experience," 28 *Case W. Res. J. Int'l L.* 3, 22–29 (1996) (discussing and analyzing Japan's evolving "abuse of rights" doctrines).

25. *See, e.g., Japan v. Kanemoto,* 396 Hanrei Jihō 19 (Sup. Ct., Dec. 21, 1964), *reprinted in* Hiroshi Itoh & Lawrence Ward Beer, *The Constitutional Case Law of Japan: Selected Supreme Court Decisions, 1961–70,* at 242

(1978) (rcjccting State's argument that Article 12 balancing justified suppression of allegedly subversive political tracts).

26. *See* Chapter 3; *see also* Kent Greenawalt, *Fighting Words: Individuals, Communities, and Liberties of Speech* 12–16, 64–70 (1995); Catharine A. MacKinnon, *Only Words* 97–107 (1993); Nadine Strossen, *Defending Pornography: Free Speech, Sex, and the Fight for Women's Rights* 229–46 (1995); *see also* Franklin R. Liss, Comment, "A Mandate to Balance: Judicial Protection of Individual Rights Under the Canadian Charter of Rights and Freedoms," 41 *Emory L.J.* 1281, 1283–92, 1296–1306 (1992).

27. Kenpō, art. 81; *see* Hanreishū, VI, No. 9, at 783 (The Suzuki Decision) (Sup. Ct., Oct. 8, 1952), *reprinted* in John M. Maki, *Court and Constitution in Japan: Selected Supreme Court Decisions, 1948–60,* at 362, 363–64 (Ikeda Masaaki et al. trans., 1964); *cf. Marbury v. Madison,* 5 U.S. (1 Cranch) 137 (1803) (discerning a power of judicial review in the system of separated and divided powers created by the United States Constitution).

28. *See* Hanreishū, V, No. 5, at 214 (Sup. Ct., Apr. 4, 1951), *reprinted in* Maki, *supra* note 27, at 285, 287 (holding that "limitations on such freedoms by obligations freely contracted under special public or private law are unavoidable"); *see also Judgment on the Enshrinement of a Dead SDF Officer to Gokoku Shrine, supra* note 10, at 8–11 (rejecting Article 20 claim against state-sponsored religious observances because ostensibly private veterans' association maintained shrine and oversaw Shinto ceremony); *id.* at 18–21 (Nagashima, J., concurring) (arguing that nexus between veterans' association and government officials was too attenuated to attribute Shinto enshrinement ceremony to government).

29. *Cf. Jackson v. Metropolitan Edison Co.,* 419 U.S. 345 (1974) (holding that a private utility company's decision to terminate services to customer for nonpayment of bills did not constitute state action and, therefore, the customer could not claim a deprivation of due process incident to the termination).

30. *See* Beer & Itoh, *supra* note 10, at 49–52; Hiroshi Itoh, *The Japanese Supreme Court: Constitutional Policies* 186 (1989); Itsuo Sonobe, "Human Rights and Constitutional Review in Japan" (Masako Kamiya trans.), *in Human Rights and Judicial Review: A Comparative Perspective* 135, 174 n.60 (David M. Beatty ed., 1994). Professor Haley suggests the Japanese Supreme Court's failure to enforce Article 21 through the exercise of judicial review could reflect a dearth of cases rather than a lack of institutional commitment to freedom of expression. *See* Interview with Professor John O. Haley, University of Washington (July 9, 1998). Professor Haley posits that because instances of the government directly restricting or censoring speech activities are relatively uncommon in Japan, litigation asking the Supreme Court of Japan to enforce Article 21 has been correspondingly infrequent. *See id.* This theory certainly provides a partial explanation for the lack of Supreme Court decisions enforcing Article 21 by striking down legislative or executive actions that burden speech activity. On the other hand, seeking out judicial decisions featuring unqualified rejections of legislative or executive actions might be the wrong inquiry. Many Supreme Court opinions nominally rejecting free speech claims actually feature the judiciary imposing substantial restrictions on the government's discretion to restrict speech activity. In such circumstances, the Supreme Court of Japan's technical refusal to find a violation of Article 21 arguably is a matter of semantics rather than substance.

31. *See Japan v. Ienaga,* 51 Minshū 2921–3618 (Sup. Ct., Aug. 29, 1997); Sonni Efron, "Japan's High Court Rules Government May Not Tamper With Truth in Textbooks," *Wash. Post,* Aug. 30, 1997, at A28; Nicholas D. Kristof, "Japan Bars Censorship of Atrocities in Texts," *N.Y. Times,* Aug. 30, 1997, at A4. For additional background on Professor Ienaga's travails in the Japanese court system, see Reingold, *supra* note 16, at 54, 56–57 (describing Japanese history textbooks' "whitewashing" of "Japanese colonial depredations in China and Korea, Singapore, and else-

where"); Ginko Kobayashiu et al., "Changing Screening System," *Daily Yomiuri* (Tokyo), Sept. 15, 1997, at 16; Sayuri Saito, "Reconsidering History Education," *Daily Yomiuri* (Tokyo), Sept. 18, 1997, at 3. For a history of Professor Ienaga's battles against the Ministry of Education's censors, see Lawrence W. Beer, "Education, Politics and Freedom in Japan: The Ienaga Textbook Review Cases," 8 *Law in Japan* 67 (1975); *see also* Saburo Ienaga, *Japan's Last War: World War II and the Japanese, 1931–1945,* at 247–56 (1979).

32. *See Hiraguchi v. Hiraguchi,* 41 Minshū 3, at 408 (Sup. Ct., Apr. 22, 1987), *reprinted in* Beer & Itoh, *supra* note 10, at 327 (invalidating restriction on the division of real property based on Article 29's protection of private property rights); *Judgment Upon Case of the Constitutionality of the Provisions of the Public Offices Election Law on Election Districts, Series of Prominent Judgments of the Supreme Court of Japan upon Questions of Constitutionality No. 17* (General Secretariat, Supreme Court of Japan, 1981) (decided Apr. 14, 1976) (striking down the apportionment of seats in the Diet on equal protection grounds); *Judgment Upon Case of Constitutionality of the Act to Regulate Location of Pharmacies, Series of Prominent Judgments of the Supreme Court of Japan upon Questions of Constitutionality No. 16* (General Secretariat, Supreme Court of Japan, 1976) (decided Apr. 30, 1975) (holding unconstitutional legislation proscribing the operation of unapproved pharmacies as violative of the Article 22's guarantee of freedom of choice of occupation); *Judgment Upon Case of Constitutionality of Article 200 of the Penal Code Providing Killing an Ascendant, Series of Prominent Judgments of the Supreme Court of Japan upon Questions of Constitutionality No. 13* (General Secretariat, Supreme Court of Japan, 1975) (decided Apr. 4, 1973) (striking down on equal protection grounds a provision of the Japanese criminal code that made the killing of a lineal ascendant an aggravating factor for purposes of punishment and overruling its earlier decision upholding this provision against an equal protection challenge); *Nakamura v. Japan,* 16 Keishū 11, at 1593 (Sup. Ct.,

Nov. 28, 1962), *reprinted in* Itoh & Beer, *supra* note 25, at 58 (invoking Article 31 due process guarantee and Article 29 protection of property rights to strike down legislation permitting, without prior notice or hearing, government seizure of innocent third-party's goods or property when such goods or property are used in an illegal smuggling operation); *see also* Beer & Itoh, *supra* note 10, at 24 (noting five instances of judicial invalidation of legislative work product); Sonobe, *supra* note 30, at 167–68, 172–73; *cf.* Beer & Itoh, *supra* note 10, at 50–51 (arguing that there have been only "three instances of judicial activism" in which the Supreme Court struck down legislation on constitutional grounds).

33. *See Judgment Upon Case of Constitutionality of the Provisions of the Public Offices Election Law, Series of Prominent Judgments of the Supreme Court of Japan upon Questions of Constitutionality No. 21,* at 8–9 (General Secretariat, Supreme Court of Japan, 1986) (July 17, 1985) (holding apportionment ratios for seats in the Diet to be unconstitutional); *Judgment Upon Case of Constitutionality of the Provisions of the Public Offices Election Law on Election Districts, supra* note 32, at 8–10 (same); *Koshiyama v. Chairman, Tokyo Metro. Election Supervision Comm'n,* 18 Minshū 2, at 270 (Sup. Ct., Feb. 5, 1964), *reprinted in* Itoh & Beer, *supra* note 25, at 53; *see also* Beer & Itoh, *supra* note 10, at 38–41 (describing the series of cases in which the Japanese Supreme Court found malapportioned electoral districts to be unconstitutional, but in each instance declining to void the election results).

34. *See Judgment Upon Case of Constitutionality of the Provisions of the Public Offices Election Law, supra* note 33, at 9–11; *Judgment Upon Case of the Constitutionality of the Provisions of the Public Offices Election Law on Election Districts, supra* note 32, at 10–13; *see also* Haley, *supra* note 4, at 189; *Koshiyama,* 18 Minshū 2, at 270, *reprinted in* Itoh & Beer, *supra* note 25, at 53, 54–55. For an examination of the Supreme Court's ineffective remedial efforts and the practical and institutional constraints under which the Supreme Court of Japan operated, *see* Haley, *supra* note 6, at 387–88.

35. *See, e.g., Judgment Upon Case of the Metropolitan Ordinance, supra* note 10, at 3–6 (upholding Tokyo ordinance requiring notification of police before engaging in mass parades or demonstrations).

36. *See The Japanese Legal System, supra* note 4, at 772–74.

37. *See* Haley, *supra* note 4, at 189.

38. *See* Beer & Itoh, *supra* note 10, at 7–8; *The Japanese Legal System, supra* note 4, at 686–87; *cf.* John O. Haley, Comment, 53 *Law & Contemp. Probs.* 201–02 (1990).

39. *See* Okudaira, *supra* note 2, at 2–4.

40. *See* Itoh, *supra* note 30, at 9–12, 204–12; Luney, *supra* note 10, at 125–26; Okudaira, *supra* note 2, at 7–9.

41. *See* Kenpō, art. 81; *see also* Itoh, *supra* note 30, at 159–62; Percy R. Luney, Jr., *Introduction to Japanese Constitutional Law, supra* note 2, at viii, x–xi; John O. Haley, "Judicial Independence in Japan Revisited," 25 *Law in Japan* 1, 17–18 (1995). As Professor Merryman has put it, "[b]oth the civil law and the common law traditions, to the extent that they are in force in Japan, are of course imposed on a prior legal tradition that retains some force but is in no way related to either the civil law or the common law." John Henry Merryman, *The Civil Law Tradition: An Introduction to the Legal Systems of Western Europe and Latin America* 5 (2d ed. 1985).

42. This may be something of an understatement, given that the Supreme Court of Japan has directly overturned legislative work-product on constitutional grounds on only five occasions. *See supra* note 32.

43. *See* Alexander M. Bickel, *The Least Dangerous Branch* (1962); John Hart Ely, *Democracy and Distrust: A Theory of Judicial Review* (1980).

44. *See* Beer & Itoh, *supra* note 10, at 49–53; Itoh, *supra* note 30, at 278–79.

45. As Professor Hiroshi Itoh has put it, "[i]n the vast majority of constitutional cases, the Court has upheld governmental actions." Beer & Itoh, *supra* note 10, at 49; *see, e.g., Judgment Upon Case of the So-Called "Sunakawa Case," Series of Prominent Judgments of the Supreme Court of Japan upon Questions of Constitutionality No. 4*

(General Secretariat, Supreme Court of Japan, 1960) (decided Dec. 16, 1959) (sustaining United States/Japan mutual defense treaty arrangements, including military bases on Japanese soil, against challenge pursuant to Article 9's renunciation of "war as a sovereign right of the nation and the threat or use of force as a means of settling international disputes"). Moreover, the Japanese Supreme Court "has also sustained administrative discretion in sublegislation in most cases." Beer & Itoh, *supra* note 10, at 49. This behavior may reflect a calculated effort at self-preservation: "The Supreme Court might have acted the way it did as self-defense and self-preservation against the much stronger political branches." Itoh, *supra* note 30, at 278; *cf. Marbury v. Madison,* 5 U.S. (1 Cranch) 137 (1803) (featuring amusing and important intellectual acrobatics by Chief Justice Marshall to avoid finding that Madison had a duty to present Marbury with his commission, perhaps because Marshall feared that Madison would simply ignore such an order); Donald O. Dewey, *Marshall Versus Jefferson: The Political Background of* Marbury v. Madison 97–99 (1970) (describing Madison's failure to respond to Marbury's suit). Professor Itoh has argued that by "minimiz[ing] conflicts with the Diet and the executives" the Supreme Court of Japan has "consolidated itself in the Japanese political system." Itoh, *supra* note 30, at 278.

46. As Norma Field has explained, to undertake civil rights or civil liberties litigation in contemporary Japan requires great fortitude. *See* Field, *supra* note 12, at 132–34; *see also* Rokumoto Kahei, "The Law Consciousness of the Japanese," 9 *Japan Foundation Newsletter* 5, 9–10 (1982) (describing a community's hostile reaction to a lawsuit challenging restrictions on student hairstyles in the local public school). Field explains that, "[t]o create an awkward moment is a sin in Japan; to cause disruption puts one beyond the pale." Field, *supra* note 12, at 75. On the other hand, as Professor Haley has noted, so-called "cause" lawyers do not hesitate to take cases designed to challenge the status quo

ante through litigation intended to embarrass the government and promote social change. *See* Haley, *supra* note 4, at 189; Haley, *supra* note 14, at 5–6.

47. Of course, this could be more reflective of the Japanese Supreme Court's assumption about what rights matter most to American lawyers; that is to say, the Supreme Court has translated its major freedom of expression cases based on the assumption that Americans care most about this right. Even if this rationale explains the Supreme Court's decision to publish Article 21 cases in English, it does not explain why litigants continue to expend time and money pressing such claims under Article 21.

48. Both individuals and organizations in Japan view the loss of face, or *kao*, as a very serious matter, to be avoided if at all possible. *See* Mark Zimmerman, *How to Do Business With the Japanese* 65–67 (1985); *see also* Haley, *supra* note 4, at 176, 183; John O. Haley, "Sheathing the Sword of Justice in Japan: An Essay on Law Without Sanctions," 8 *J. Japanese Stud.* 265, 275–76 (1982).

49. Haley, *supra* note 4, at 183; *see also* Haley, *supra* note 48, at 275–76 (describing the importance of reputation to both private and government entities in Japan).

50. Haley, *supra* note 4, at 183.

51. *See id.* at 189. As Professor Haley explains in the context of "hopeless" litigation challenging the constitutionality of Japan's military "self-defense" forces, "[s]o long as the issue continues to be litigated in well-publicized cases, a political consensus against the Self-Defense Forces may be forged or at least one favoring their legitimacy remains in doubt." *Id.*; *see also* Field, *supra* note 12, at 97, 131–36.

52. *See* Nakane, *supra* note 7, at 49–50, 65, 144–46.

53. *See id.* at 145.

54. *Id.*

55. *See* Benedict, *supra* note 6, at 34–35. She quotes the following illustrative newspaper editorial, which appeared in print in July 1944:

In these few years, the people have not been able to say frankly what they think. They have been afraid that they might be blamed if they spoke certain matters. They hesitated, and tried to patch up the surface, so the public mind has really become timid. We can never develop the total power of the people in this way.

Id. at 34. Another contemporaneous speaker noted that under the wartime military government, "[f]reedom of speech has been denied" and opined that "[t]his is certainly not a proper way to stimulate [the Japanese people's] will to fight." *Id.*

56. Haley, *supra* note 4, at 189.

57. Ito Masami, Foreword to Beer, *Freedom of Expression in Japan*, *supra* note 10, at 13, 14.

58. *See* Koshoku senkyohō [Public Offices election law], Law No. 100 of 1950; *see also Takatsu v. Japan*, 35 Keishū 5, at 568 (Sup. Ct., July 21, 1981), *reprinted in* Beer & Itoh, *supra* note 10, at 598; *Nonaka v. Japan*, 33 Keishū 7, at 1074 (Sup. Ct., Dec. 20, 1979), *reprinted in* Beer & Itoh, *supra* note 10, at 604; *Taniguchi v. Japan*, 21 Keishū 9, at 1245 (Sup. Ct., Nov. 21, 1967), *reprinted in* Itoh & Beer, *supra* note 25, at 149; Beer, *supra* note 10, at 372–78; Taisuke Kamata, "Adjudication and the Governing Process: Political Questions and Legislative Discretion," *in Japanese Constitutional Law*, *supra* note 2, at 151, 154–56.

59. *See* Beer, *supra* note 10, at 373–74; Kamata, *supra* note 58, at 154–56; Okudaira, *supra* note 2, at 35 n.52. For a description of the operation of the Election Law and its attempt to establish a line of demarcation between "political activities," which are largely unregulated, and "election activities," which are highly regulated, see Curtis, *supra* note 12, at 165–75.

60. *See* Beer, *supra* note 10, at 377–78 & nn.100–04 (citing cases reported in Japanese language source materials).

61. 310 U.S. 296 (1940).

62. 424 U.S. 1 (1976).

63. *See* Fiss, Irony, *supra* note 16, at 79–83; Fiss, *supra* note 8, at 18–23, 28–30; Cass Sunstein, *Democracy and the Problem of Free Speech* 85, 97–101 (1993); Owen M. Fiss,

"Money and Politics," 97 *Colum. L. Rev.* 2470, 2476–83 (1997).

64. *See* Curtis, *supra* note 12, at 167–69.

65. *Id.* at 174.

66. *See* Haley, *supra* note 4, at 186–90; Zimmerman, *supra* note 48, at 26, 90–94.

67. *Cf. McConnell v. Fed. Comm. Comm'n,* 540 U.S. 93, 189–211 (2003) (sustaining broad restrictions that Bipartisan Campaign Reform Act of 2002 imposed on so-called "electioneering communications," in an apparent —and substantial—departure from the *Buckley* standards); *but see id.* at 272–75, 277–83 (Thomas, J., dissenting) (objecting to majority's decision to sustain limits on issue-oriented political speech).

68. Curtis, *supra* note 12, at 171.

69. Again, the effectiveness of the non-media restrictions is very much open to question; Curtis reports that "there has been a virtual institutionalization of patterns of evasion and circumvention of many of the law's restrictions." *Id.* at 173.

70. *See Hague v. CIO,* 307 U.S. 496 (1939).

71. *See United States v. Kokinda,* 497 U.S. 720 (1990); *see also* Ronald J. Krotoszynski, Jr., "Celebrating Selma: The Importance of Context in Public Forum Analysis," 104 *Yale L.J.* 1411 (1995).

72. *See Forsyth County v. Nationalist Movement,* 505 U.S. 123 (1992).

73. Hanreishū, VIII, No. 11, 1866 (Sup. Ct., Nov. 24, 1954), *reprinted* in Maki, *supra* note 27, at 70.

74. *See id.* at 71. Article I of the ordinance provided that "Parades, processions, and mass demonstrations . . . shall not be conducted without obtaining a license from the public safety commission which exercises jurisdiction over the area concerned." *Id.*

75. *See id.* at 71–72.

76. *See id.* at 72 (Article 4 of the Ordinance).

77. *See id.* at 74–75.

78. *Id.* at 75

79. *See id.* at 76–77. The United States Supreme Court maintains a similar tradition of using limiting constructions of statutes and regulations to avoid holding such enactments unconstitutional. *See Rust v. Sullivan,*

500 U.S. 173, 190–91 (1991); *id.* at 204–07 (Blackmun, J., dissenting); *New York v. Ferber,* 458 U.S. 747, 769 n.24 (1982); *Haynes v. United States,* 390 U.S. 85, 92 (1968). For a discussion of the reasons supporting this policy, see *Rust,* 500 U.S. at 223–25 (O'Connor, J., dissenting); *Ashwander v. TVA,* 297 U.S. 288, 348 (1936) (Brandeis, J., concurring). *See generally* Adrian Vermeule, "Saving Constructions," 85 *Geo. L.J.* 1945 (1997) (discussing and analyzing the federal judiciary's use of saving constructions and question avoidance).

80. *Judgment Upon Case of the Metropolitan Ordinance, supra* note 12.

81. *See* Metropolitan Ordinance, Law No. 44 of 1950, *reprinted in id.* at 38–39.

82. *See id.* at art. 1.

83. *Id.* at art. 3.

84. *See Judgment Upon Case of the Metropolitan Ordinance, supra* note 10, at 1–2.

85. *Id.* at 2.

86. *Id.*

87. *Id.* at 3.

88. *Id.* at 4.

89. *Id.*

90. *See id.* at 5–6; *cf. Brandenburg v. Ohio,* 395 U.S. 444 (1969) (holding that the Free Speech Clause of the First Amendment absolutely protects political or ideological speech activity on private property from governmental abridgement absent direct advocacy of lawlessness coupled with a clear and present danger of such lawlessness occurring and causing social harms of the highest order).

91. *See Forsyth County v. Nationalist Movement,* 505 U.S. 123, 133–36 (1992) (holding that a permitting system for speech activities cannot vest unrestricted discretion with local police authorities and that the exercise of viewpoint and content neutral, properly channelized discretion by local authorities must be subject to prompt judicial review). On the other hand, reflexive distrust of government is not a Japanese cultural trait. "The State, in all its domestic functions, is not a necessary evil as it is so generally felt to be in the United States." Benedict, *supra* note 6, at 86. Instead, "[t]he State comes nearer, in Japanese eyes, to being the supreme good."

Id. Accordingly, the idea of vesting substantial discretion with local police officials to regulate speech activities is less objectionable in Japan than in the United States.

92. *Judgment Upon Case of the Metropolitan Ordinance, supra* note 10, at 6 (Fujita, J., dissenting).

93. *Id.* at 7.

94. *See id.* at 8–10.

95. 307 U.S. 496 (1939).

96. 334 U.S. 558 (1948).

97. *See Judgment Upon Case of the Metropolitan Ordinance, supra* note 10, at 11 (Fujita, J., dissenting).

98. *See id.* at 11–30 (Tarumi, J., dissenting).

99. *See id.* at 10, 25–26.

100. *See id.* at 27–30.

101. *See* id. at 18–22.

102. *Id.* at 13.

103. *See supra* Chapter 2.

104. *Judgment Upon Case of the Metropolitan Ordinance, supra* note 10, at 15 (Tarumi, J., dissenting).

105. *See id.* at 16–17.

106. *Id.* at 17.

107. *See Abrams v. United States,* 250 U.S. 616, 623–24 (1919); *see also* William W. Van Alstyne, *Interpretations of the First Amendment* 29–37 (1984).

108. *See Dennis v. United States,* 341 U.S. 494, 510 (1951).

109. Sunstein, *supra* note 63, at 169.

110. *See* Rodney A. Smolla, *Free Speech in an Open Society* 45–54, 184–85, 208–11 (1992); *cf.* Sunstein, *supra* note 63, at 239–40 (arguing that other values may, from time to time, justify departures from content, or even viewpoint, neutrality in government regulation of speech activity). Of course, the clear and present danger test affords meaningful protection to speech activity if—and only if—the fact of public hostility to the speaker's message, the so-called "heckler's veto," does not count as a condition that satisfies the test. *See Forsyth County v. Nationalist Movement,* 505 U.S. 123, 133–36 (1992); *see also Gooding v. Wilson,* 405 U.S. 518 (1972); *Terminiello v. Chicago,* 337 U.S. 1 (1949). The *Tokyo* and *Niigata* cases do not speak to the problem of

the heckler's veto. Accordingly, further guidance from the Supreme Court will be necessary to ascertain the robustness of the clear and present danger test in Japan.

111. Of course, adoption of the Constitution of 1947 did not, as if by magic, alter the public values of the Japanese people. *See generally* Ronald J. Krotoszynski, "Building Bridges and Overcoming Barricades: Exploring the Limits of Law as an Agent of Transformational Social Change," 47 *Case W. Res. L. Rev.* 423, 424–32 (1997). Instead, the Constitution of 1947 provided a legal framework through which the transformation of Japan from a totalitarian regime in which the citizenry enjoyed its rights at the pleasure of the Emperor was replaced by a system of participatory democracy and constitutional rights. *See* Abe et al., *supra* note 12, at 3–13; Okudaira, *supra* note 2, at 1–32; Nobushige Ukai, "The Significance of the Reception of American Constitutional Institutions and Ideas in Japan," *in Constitutionalism in Asia: Asian Views of the American Influence* 111, at 114–15 (Lawrence Ward Beer ed., 1979). As Professor Benedict predicted, the Japanese have embraced rules of the new social order as reflected and embodied in the Constitution of 1947, albeit not in precisely the same forms as these rights existed (or currently exist) in the United States. *See* Benedict, *supra* note 6, at 295–96, 302–04.

112. 376 U.S. 254, 273–76, 282 (1964); *see* Harry Kalven, Jr., "The *New York Times* Case: A Note On 'The Central Meaning of the First Amendment,'" 1964 *Sup. Ct. Rev.* 191, 204–10.

113. 396 Hanrei Jihō 19 (Sup. Ct., Dec. 21, 1965), *reprinted in* Itoh & Beer, *supra* note 25, at 242.

114. *See id.* at 242.

115. *See id.*

116. *Id.* at 243. In this regard, the case represents a change of position from that reflected in Hanreishū, VI, No. 8, 1053 (Sup. Ct., Aug. 2, 1951), *reprinted in* Maki, *supra* note 27, at 123. In this case, a Communist protestor distributed handbills urging police to strike or "slowdown" the performance of their duties. *See id.* at 123–24. He was convicted of violating a provision of the Local Public Ser-

vice Law and appealed his case to the Supreme Court of Japan. The Supreme Court affirmed the conviction, holding that "abetment of this kind must be said to go beyond the limits of freedom of speech as guaranteed by the Constitution." *Id.* at 125. In order to avoid criminal liability, the defendant would have to offer proof that there was "absolutely no danger" that the police would adopt the course of action suggested in the handbill. *See id.* Obviously, this result is inconsistent with the result in the *Kanemoto* case. One can infer from the result in this earlier case that between the early 1950s and the early 1960s, freedom of expression gained significant ground in the Supreme Court of Japan.

117. *Judgment Upon Case of Constitutionality of the Provisions of the New Narita Airport Law, Series of Prominent Judgments of the Supreme Court of Japan upon Questions of Constitutionality No. 26* (General Secretariat, Supreme Court of Japan, 1993) (decided July 1, 1992).

118. *See id.* at 1–2.

119. *See id.* at 3–4

120. *See id.* at 4.

121. *Id.* at 5.

122. *Id.*

123. *See Forsyth County v. Nationalist Movement,* 505 U.S. 123, 132–36 (1992); *Cox v. New Hampshire,* 312 U.S. 569, 574–78 (1941); *see also* C. Edwin Baker, "Unreasoned Reasonableness: Mandatory Parade Permits and Time, Place, and Manner Regulations," 78 *Nw. U. L. Rev.* 937, 992–1007 (1983); Vince Blasi, "Prior Restraints on Demonstrations," 68 *Mich. L. Rev.* 1481, 1536–52 (1970). *But see Freedman v. Maryland,* 380 U.S. 51 (1965) (holding that procedural safeguards must be available to ensure fair application of licensing scheme for motion pictures).

124. *See International Soc'y for Krishna Consciousness v. Lee,* 505 U.S. 672 (1992) (upholding ban on solicitation in airports under a "reasonableness" standard of review, but striking down a prohibition on mere leafleting in airports, again relying on a "reasonableness" standard of review).

125. *Judgment Upon Case of Constitution-*

ality of the Provisions of the New Narita Airport Law, supra note 117, at 2–3.

126. *See* Alexander Meiklejohn, *Free Speech and Its Relation to Self-Government* 10–14, 25–27 (1948); Alexander Meiklejohn, *Political Freedom: The Constitutional Powers of the People* 115–20 (1960).

127. *See, e.g., Judgment Upon Case of Constitutionality of the Provisions of the New Narita Airport Law, supra* note 117, at 2–3.

128. 24 Keishū 6, at 280 (Sup. Ct., June 17, 1970), *reprinted in* Itoh & Beer, *supra* note 25, at 244.

129. *See id.* at 244–45. Yamagishi and his colleagues glued 84 posters to utility poles owned by the local telephone companies and located on public rights of way; the posters were emblazoned with messages such as "Let's Make A Great Success of the Tenth World Conference to Ban Nuclear Weapons! Aichi Gensuikyo." *See id.*

130. The utility poles at issue belonged to both publicly and privately owned utility companies. *See id.* at 245. With respect to the privately held utility poles, no state action existed and Article 21 simply would not apply, unless the Supreme Court construed Article 21 to create a free speech easement on privately owned property. *See, e.g., Pruneyard Shopping Ctr. v. Robins,* 447 U.S. 74 (1980). On the other hand, access to publicly owned utility poles presented a legitimate Article 21 question. *See, e.g., City Council v. Taxpayers for Vincent,* 466 U.S. 789 (1984).

131. *See Yamagishi,* 24 Keishū 6, *reprinted in* Itoh & Beer, *supra* note 25, at 244–45.

132. *Id.* at 245.

133. 466 U.S. 789 (1984).

134. *Series of Prominent Judgments of the Supreme Court of Japan upon Questions of Constitutionality No. 11* (General Secretariat, Supreme Court of Japan, 1970) (decided June 25, 1969).

135. *See id.* at 1. The story, entitled "Wicked Acts of Tokuichiro Sakaguchi, the Blood-sucker," reported that the publisher told an official in the public works section of the Wakayama City Office that "[i]f you made a due offer, we should shut our eyes to your deed." *Id.* Failing such an offer, Sak-

aguchi allegedly promised to publish allegations of corruption involving the public works office. *See id.*

136. Penal Code of Japan, Law No. 45 of 1907, art. 230-1, *reprinted in Judgment Upon Case of Defamation, supra* note 11, at 6.

137. *Id.* at art. 230–2, para. 1. A second exceptions clause excused liability when the statement at issue concerned "a public servant or a candidate for public office, and when, upon inquiry into the truth or falsity of facts, the truth is proved." *Id.* at art. 230–2, para. 3.

138. *Judgment Upon Case of Defamation, supra* note 11, at 2.

139. *Id.*

140. *See id.* at 2–3.

141. *Judgment Upon Case of Constitutionality of the Advance Injunctions Against Publication of a Magazine in Relation to the Freedom of Expression, Series of Prominent Judgments of the Supreme Court of Japan upon Questions of Constitutionality No. 22* (General Secretariat, Supreme Court of Japan, 1988) (decided June 11, 1986) [hereinafter *Judgment Upon Case of Constitutionality No. 22*].

142. *See id.* at 8–10.

143. *See id.* at 1, 7.

144. *Id.* at 7–8.

145. *Id.* at 8.

146. *Id.* at 24 (Nagashima, J., concurring).

147. *See id.* at 2–3.

148. On the other hand, had the *Hoppo Journal* published a complimentary story that grossly overstated Igarashi's merits for office, one wonders if the same result would have been obtained. Would the Supreme Court's solicitude for protecting the electorate from falsehoods extend to falsely *positive* news stories? As a matter of logic, a candidate competing with Igarashi for the prefectural governorship should enjoy the same right to an injunction on a theory that a false story praising Igarashi also constitutes a kind of fraud on the electorate. It is, however, rather doubtful that a magazine featuring a false, but positive, story on Igarashi would in fact be enjoined.

149. 376 U.S. 254 (1964).

150. *Id.* at 265.

151. *See Judgment Upon Case of Defamation, supra* note 11, at 2–3.

152. This, incidentally, reflects a major conceptual shift away from the Meiji Constitution. *See* Abe et al., *supra* note 12, at 3–13; Ann Waswo, *Modern Japanese Society 1868–1994*, at 8–34 (1996).

153. *Judgment Upon Case of Constitutionality No. 22, supra* note 141, at 4 (footnote added).

154. *See id.* at 5 ("Even if the truth is not proved, when there is good reason for the perpetrator of the act to have mistakenly believed that the article was true, the foregoing act should be construed to be not malicious or negligent.").

155. Meiklejohn, *Free Speech, supra* note 126, at 24–25.

156. *Judgment Upon Case of Constitutionality No. 22, supra* note 141, at 5.

157. *Id.* at 6.

158. *See id.* at 6, 9–10.

159. 485 U.S. 46 (1988).

160. *Id.* at 48.

161. *See id.* at 49.

162. *See Falwell v. Flynt*, 797 F.2d 1270 (4th Cir. 1986).

163. *Falwell*, 485 U.S. at 51 (quoting *Associated Press v. Walker*, 388 U.S. 130, 164 (1967) (Warren, C.J., concurring)).

164. *Id.* (internal quotation marks and citation omitted).

165. *See id.* at 51–52, 55–57; *see also New York Times Co. v. Sullivan*, 376 U.S. 254, 279–80 (1964).

166. *Falwell*, 485 U.S. at 53.

167. *Id.* at 56.

168. *See Judgment Upon Case of Constitutionality No. 22, supra* note 141, at 8 ("A goblin named Kozo is now wriggling on the earth of Hokkaido. It turns into a butterfly by day and a hairy caterpillar by night crying that (he) wants to live in the red brick (prefectural office) building.").

169. *Id.*

170. *Id.* at 9; *cf. Milkovich v. Lorain Journal Co.*, 497 U.S. 1, 14–16, 20–21 (1990); *Falwell*, 485 U.S. at 50; *Greenbelt Coop. Publ'g Ass'n v. Bresler*, 398 U.S. 6, 13–14 (1970).

171. *See* Beer, "Freedom of Expression,"

supra note 7, at 234–35 (acknowledging that the *Hoppo Journal's* article on Igarashi was "so extreme in its insults, vulgarity, and personal attack as obviously to lack credibility on a first reading," but arguing that the Supreme Court's resolution of the case was not entirely unreasonable because "[t]o the Court, character assassination trumped the public interest value of comment on a candidate for public office"); *cf. Texas v. Johnson*, 491 U.S. 397, 436–37 (1989) (Stevens, J., dissenting). Justice Stevens has generally been a strong supporter of broad and comprehensive First Amendment rights; his vote in *Johnson* is utterly inconsistent with his record in this area. *See, e.g., Reno v. ACLU*, 521 U.S. 844 (1997) (striking down portions of the Internet Decency Act on First Amendment grounds); *see also* Ronald J. Krotoszynski, Jr., "*Cohen v. California:* 'Inconsequential' Cases and Larger Legal Principles," 74 *Tex. L. Rev.* 1251, 1253–56 (1996).

172. *See* Benedict, *supra* note 6, at 145–76.

173. *See id.* at 146–48, 159–64, 199–205. The Koreans apparently have a similar social ethic and an even more protective rule of law regarding damaging truthful statements. *See* Nicholas D. Kristof, "News in U.S. Can Be 'Rumor' in Seoul, and Lead to Jail," *N.Y. Times,* Jan. 7, 1998, at A3.

174. *Judgment Upon Case of Constitutionality No. 22, supra* note 141, at 27 (Taniguchi, J., concurring).

175. *Id.* at 28.

176. *Id.*

177. *See id.* at 29–31.

178. *See, e.g., Sable Communications v. FCC*, 492 U.S. 115 (1989); *Miller v. California*, 413 U.S. 15 (1973).

179. *Reno v. ACLU*, 521 U.S. 844, 871–74 (1997); *Philadelphia Newspapers, Inc. v. Hepps*, 475 U.S. 767, 777 (1986); *Dombrowski v. Pfister*, 380 U.S. 479, 487 (1965); *New York Times Co. v. Sullivan*, 376 U.S. 254, 300 (1964) (Goldberg, J., concurring).

180. As Meiklejohn put it, in the context of democratic deliberation about matters of self-governance, "the talking must be regulated and abridged as the doing of the busi-

ness under actual conditions may require." Meiklejohn, *Free Speech, supra* note 126, at 23. Should a speaker "wander[ ] from the point at issue" or prove "abusive or in other ways threaten[ing] to defeat the purpose of the meeting, he may and should be declared 'out of order.' " *Id.* Ultimately, a disruptive person who persists in obstreperous conduct "may be 'denied the floor' or, in the last resort, 'thrown out' of the meeting." *Id.*

181. *See* Smolla, *supra* note 110, at 220–39; *cf.* Sunstein, *supra* note 63, at 93–105 (arguing that government attempts to limit the influence of wealth in elections should not be deemed unconstitutional); Fiss, *supra* note 8, at 5–6, 19–23, 42–45 (same); Fiss, *supra* note 63, at 2478–80 (same).

182. *See* MacKinnon, *supra* note 26, at 97–110.

183. *Abrams v. United States,* 250 U.S. 616, 630 (1919) (Holmes, J., dissenting).

184. *Id.*

185. *See Japan v. Kanemoto*, 396 Hanrei Jihō 19 (Sup. Ct., Dec. 21, 1964) *reprinted in* Itoh & Beer, *supra* note 25, at 242.

186. Meiklejohn, *Free Speech, supra* note 126, at 23.

187. *Id.*

188. *Id.* at 24.

189. *See* Robert C. Post, *Constitutional Domains: Democracy, Community, Management* 268–78, 288–89 (1995).

190. *See* Nakane, *supra* note 7, at 65–66, 143–51.

191. *See generally id.* at 103, 147–48; Benedict, *supra* note 6, at 219–20.

192. *Judgment Upon Case of Translation and Publication of Lady Chatterly's Lover and Article 175 of the Penal Code, Series of Prominent Judgments of the Supreme Court of Japan upon Questions of Constitutionality No. 2* (General Secretariat, Supreme Court of Japan, 1958) (decided Mar. 13, 1957), *reprinted in* Maki, *supra* note 27, at 3; *see also* Beer, *supra* note 10, at 347–49 (describing and discussing the *Lady Chatterly's Lover* decision); *cf. Kingsley Int'l Pictures Corp. v. Regents of the Univ.*, 360 U.S. 684, 688–89 (1959) (holding nonobscene as a matter of law a film version of *Lady Chatterly's Lover*).

193. *See Lady Chatterly's Lover, supra* note 23, at 10–13.

194. Japanese Criminal Code, art. 175, *reprinted in Lady Chatterly's Lover, supra* note 23, at 36.

195. *See Lady Chatterly's Lover, supra* note 23, at 1–3.

196. *Id.* at 3.

197. *Id.*

198. *See id.* at 3–9.

199. *Id.* at 7.

200. *Id.*

201. *Id.* at 7, 8. In a very similar case, the Supreme Court of the United States reached the opposite conclusion. *See Kingsley Int'l Pictures Corp. v. Regents of the Univ.,* 360 U.S. 684, 688–90. (1959). Writing for the majority, Justice Stewart characterized New York's effort to suppress a film version of *Lady Chatterly's Lover* as an attempt "to prevent the exhibition of a motion picture because that picture advocates an idea—that adultery under certain circumstances may be proper behavior." *Id.* at 688. Justice Stewart immediately rejected that proposition because "the First Amendment's basic guarantee is of freedom to advocate ideas." *Id.*

202. *See Lady Chatterly's Lover, supra* note 23, at 9–10; *cf. Smith v. California,* 361 U.S. 147 (1959) (holding that knowledge of a work's obscene nature was a prerequisite to prosecution of a bookstore owner because permitting California to impose liability without knowledge of a book's obscene content would unduly chill the availability of books to the public).

203. *Lady Chatterly's Lover, supra* note 23, at 10.

204. *See id.* at 11.

205. *See id.* at 12–13.

206. 23 Keishū 10, at 1239 (Sup. Ct., Oct. 15, 1969), *reprinted in* Itoh & Beer, *supra* note 25, at 183.

207. *See id.* at 184–85 ("[T]here is no obstacle to holding obscene a literary work with artistic and intellectual value.").

208. *Id.* at 186; *cf. Miller v. California,* 413 U.S. 15 (1973) (holding that works possessing serious artistic, literary, scientific, or other social value may not banned as obscenity,

notwithstanding sexually explicit content). *But see* Susan Paynter, "Two Police Chiefs, Two Views of Obscenity," *Seattle Post-Intelligencer,* July 18, 1997, at C1 (describing Oklahoma City police chief's decision to prosecute video rental stores offering customers *The Tin Drum* because of single scene involving attempted sexual activity between minors).

209. *See* Beer, *supra* note 10, at 233, 354–55; Masami Itoh, "The Rule of Law: Constitutional Development," *in Law in Japan: The Legal Order in a Changing Society* 205, 228 (Arthur Taylor von Mehren ed., 1963); Nathaniel L. Nathanson, "Human Rights in Japan: Through the Looking-Glass of Supreme Court Opinions," 11 *How. L.J.* 316, 322–23 (1965).

210. *See* Itoh, *supra* note 209, at 228; Interview with Professor John Haley, University of Washington (July 11, 1996).

211. *See Customs Inspection Case, supra* note 10, at 8. In this decision, the Supreme Court upheld the Customs Service's decision to seize certain 8mm films under a provision of the Customs Tariff Law prohibiting the importation of books or drawings that "injure the public morals." Unlike the *Lady Chatterly's Lover* and *de Sade* cases, however, the Supreme Court was divided. Four Justices of the 15 sitting issued a joint dissent, arguing that the "public morals" standard was too vague to survive Article 21 scrutiny. *See id.* at 18 (Ito, Taniguchi, Yasuoka, & Shimatani, JJ., dissenting).

212. *Id.* at 8.

213. In Japan, erotic materials are ubiquitous: "spring books" and "spring movies" are readily available, not to mention pornographic comic books. *See* Beer, *supra* note 10, at 339–40, 345–47 (discussing prevalence of sexually explicit films and books in Japan); Reingold, *supra* note 16, at 92–101 (describing the irony of the Japanese government's active censorship efforts against foreign erotica given the ubiquity of domestically produced smut); John Burgess, "Prostitute's Death From AIDS Alarms Japan," *Wash. Post,* Feb. 9, 1987, at A1 ("Pornographic comic books are standard fare for men commuting on sub-

ways.'"); David Remnick, "Tokyo After Dark," *Wash. Post,* June 16, 1985, Book World, at 7 (describing the Japanese sex industry). Beyond dirty pictures, movies, and books, one can readily obtain the real thing in Japan; prostitution is not uncommon and, while not officially sanctioned, is an established fact. *See* Burgess, *supra*; Mary Jordan, "In Okinawa's Whisper Alley, GIs Find Prostitutes Are Cheap and Plentiful," *Wash. Post,* Nov. 23, 1995, at A31. "Prostitution is so imbued in society that late-night TV programs feature live visits to establishments selling sex and interviews with the women there." Burgess, *supra.* In fact, recent press reports describe a disturbing trend of very young women selling their bodies in order to obtain the cash necessary to keep up with the latest in fashion trends. *See* Nicholas D. Kristof, "A Plain School Uniform as the Latest Aphrodisiac," *N.Y. Times,* Apr. 2, 1997, at A4.

214. *See R. v. Butler* [1992] S.C.R. 452 (Can.); Greenawalt, *supra* note 26, at 113–23; MacKinnon, *supra* note 26, at 100–05.

215. *See, e.g.,* Benedict, *supra* note 6, at 279–80 (describing the differences both in education and in formal and informal social status that stamp females as vastly inferior to males in traditional Japanese society).

216. *See* Reingold, *supra* note 16, at 103; Frank K. Upham, *Law and Social Change in Postwar Japan* 124–65, 215–18 (1987); Waswo, *supra* note 152, at 147–55; *see also* Kiyoko Kamio Knapp, "Still Office Flowers: Japanese Women Betrayed By the Equal Employment Opportunity Law," 18 *Harv. Women's L.J.* 83 (1995) (describing women's historical roles in Japanese society and their recent willingness to challenge traditional limitations and stereotypes); Andrew Pollack, "It's See No Evil, Have No Harassment in Japan," *N.Y. Times,* May 7, 1996, at D1 (describing increasing willingness of Japanese women to resist work-based sexual harassment and other forms of gender-based discrimination).

217. This presumably includes such publications as "Anatomical Illustrations of Junior High School Girls," and "V-Club" that feature "pictures of naked elementary school girls." *See* Kristof, *supra* note 213. *Cf. New York v.*

Ferber, 458 U.S. 747 (1982) (holding that, consistent with the First Amendment, government may ban any materials featuring nude pictures of children, regardless of their artistic or scientific value).

218. *See, e.g.,* Reingold, *supra* note 16, at 92–97 (describing the irony of active government censorship of foreign sexually explicit materials while turning a blind eye on domestic, socially conforming erotica).

219. *Cf. Kingsley Int'l Pictures Corp. v. Regents of the Univ.,* 360 U.S. 684, 689 (1959) ("[The First Amendment's free speech guarantee] is not confined to the expression of ideas that are conventional or shared by a majority. It protects advocacy of the opinion that adultery may sometimes be proper, no less than advocacy of socialism or the single tax.").

220. This approach is at least arguably consistent with the writings of Robert Bork, who argues that communities have a right to maintain minimum standards of decency, if necessary through projects of governmental censorship. *See* Robert H. Bork, *Slouching Towards Gomorrah: Modern Liberalism and American Decline* 140–53 (1996). It also comports with Justice Scalia's view that communities should be free to prohibit speech activity that is " 'contra bonos mores,' i.e., immoral." *Barnes v. Glen Theatre, Inc.,* 501 U.S. 560, 575 (1991) (Scalia, J., concurring).

221. *See* Meiklejohn, *supra* note 21, at 256–57. Subsequent critics have argued that this expansion of protected speech is not entirely justifiable. *See* Paul G. Stern, Note, "A Pluralistic Reading of the First Amendment and Its Relation to Public Discourse," 99 *Yale L.J.* 925, 932–33 (1990) (arguing that this rationale proves both too much and too little and suggesting that it lacks a logical limiting principle).

222. *See* Meiklejohn, *supra* note 21, at 257.

223. *See id.* at 261 ("Now if such ordinances are based upon official disapproval of the ideas to be presented at the meeting, they clearly violate the First Amendment. But if no such abridgment of freedom is expressed or implied, regulation or prohibition on other grounds may be enacted and en-

forced.""); *see also* Meiklejohn, *Political Freedom, supra* note 126, at 118–19:

> [W]hen we speak of the Amendment as guarding the freedom to hear and to read, the principle applies not only to the speaking or writing of our own citizens but also to the writing or speaking of everyone whom a citizen, at his own discretion, may choose to hear or to read.

224. Martin H. Redish, "The Value of Free Speech," 130 *U. Pa. L. Rev.* 591, 592 (1982) (footnote omitted); *see also* Stern, *supra* note 221, at 932–33.

225. Redish, *supra* note 224, at 597 (footnotes omitted).

226. *See* Sunstein, *supra* note 63, at 224–26; Owen M. Fiss, "Freedom and Feminism," 80 Geo. L.J. 2041, 2044, 2056–57 (1992); Owen M. Fiss, "State Activism and State Censorship," 100 *Yale L.J.* 2087, 2091–92, 2103–04 (1991); *cf.* Bork, *supra* note 220, at 99–102, 140–53 (arguing that some ideas are fundamentally inconsistent with democracy and therefore may be suppressed); Robert H. Bork, "Neutral Principles and Some First Amendment Problems," 47 *Ind. L.J.* 1, 20–35 (1971) (arguing that the state may suppress nonpolitical speech without violating the First Amendment).

227. *See* MacKinnon, *supra* note 26, at 103–07. MacKinnon embraces the Canadian Supreme Court's apparent rejection of the notion that "under the First Amendment, there is no such thing as a false idea." *Id.* at 106. According to MacKinnon, "[p]erhaps under equality law, in some sense there is." *Id.* In fairness, she attempts to create space for public discussion about the proper ordering of social relations, noting that the embrace of a First Amendment doctrine that permits the prohibition of the expression of hostile attitudes toward women and racial minorities should not preclude debate about or expression of "ideas to the contrary." *Id.* However, the terms of this debate would be delimited by the community's commitment to the equality ethic: debate or expression of ideas cannot impose "social inferiority." *Id.* Yet, as she describes the relationship of ideas and

actions, *see id.* at 25–29, 33–41, 74, 82–86, 98–100, the mere expression of viewpoints endorsing inequality based on gender, race, or religion both causes and helps to maintain social inferiority. Accordingly, MacKinnon's logic inexorably leads one to the conclusion that bad ideas exist and the state should be free to prohibit their dissemination as part of a larger project of ensuring social equality.

228. *See* Catharine A. MacKinnon, *Feminism Unmodified* 155–57, 165–66, 212–13 (1987).

229. *See Romer v. Evans,* 517 U.S. 620, 636 (1996) (Scalia, J., dissenting) ("The Court has mistaken a Kulturkampf for a fit of spite."); *id.* at 652 ("When the Court takes sides in the culture wars, it tends to be with the knights rather than the villains—and more specifically with the Templars, reflecting the views and values of the lawyer class from which the Court's Members are drawn.").

230. *See* Bork, *supra* note 220, at 3–4 (arguing that societies should be permitted to establish and maintain moral norms regarding acceptable behavior, with the assistance of state power if necessary).

231. *See id.* at 140–53 (arguing that government imposed censorship is necessary *right now* if Western civilization is to avoid moral ruination accompanied by total social, economic, and political collapse). In fairness to the Supreme Court of Japan, none of their decisions regarding the regulation of "obscenity" come anywhere close to justifying broad-based restrictions on speech based upon a Borkian "society is going to hell in a handbasket" thesis.

232. As Justice Mano describes it:

> According to the marriage customs and practices of old Japan, as may be perceived from such classic literature as Kojiki, Nihon, Shoki, Mannyohsu, Fudoki, etc., the method of selecting one's mate apparently was extremely liberal and completely incompatible with the punctilious method adopted later in the feudal period. In one particular, according to an ancient custom called "utagaki" or "kagai," it is said that a group of young men and

women went, hand in hand, up into a mountain, normally regarded as sacred, and there they feasted, sang, and danced; and at the height of pleasure, they engaged openly in indiscriminate group sex acts and indulged in the state of ecstasy.

Lady Chatterly's Lover, supra note 23, at 15 (Mano, J., concurring); *cf.* Reingold, *supra* note 16, at 103–04 (describing contemporary community enthusiasm for erotica and noting that "[t]oday, at the Tagata Shrine near Nagoya, regular festivals are held in which models of male and female genitals are paraded and genitalia-shaped souvenirs are sold to visitors").

233. *Lady Chatterly's Lover, supra* note 23, at 15–16.

234. *Id.*

235. *Id.*

236. *See Kleindienst v. Mandel,* 408 U.S. 753 (1972); *see also* 8 U.S.C. §§ 1182(a)(28)(D), (G)(v), & (d)(3)(A).

237. *See Mandel,* 408 U.S. at 771 (Douglas, J., dissenting); *see also Dennis v. United States,* 341 U.S. 494 (1951) (affirming convictions of Communist Party members for advocating violent overthrow of the United States government, notwithstanding the complete absence of any concrete actions to implement this point of view).

238. *Mandel,* 408 U.S. at 785 (Marshall, J., dissenting). Justice Marshall also lamented the Supreme Court's "depart[ure] from its own best role as the guardian of individual liberty in the face of governmental overreaching." *Id.* The excluded alien, Ernest E. Mandel, a prominent Belgian journalist and Marxist scholar, concluded that the government's decision demonstrated " 'a lack of confidence' on the part of our Government 'in the capacity of its supporters to combat Marxism on the battleground of ideas.' " *Id.* at 784.

239. *See Meese v. Keene,* 481 U.S. 465 (1987). The particular films at issue in *Keene* hailed from Canada and addressed the subjects of nuclear war and acid rain; one even received the 1983 Oscar for best documentary. *See id.* at 467–68, 475.

240. *See* 22 U.S.C. §§ 611, 614 (1994); *Keene,* 481 U.S. at 467–68.

241. *See Keene,* 481 U.S. at 467–68.

242. *See id.* at 480–85.

243. *Mandel,* 408 U.S. 753, 772 (Douglas, J., dissenting).

244. *See* MacKinnon, *supra* note 228, at 100; *see also* Linda J. Lacey, "Of Bread and Roses and Copyrights," 1989 *Duke L.J.* 1532, 1537 n.18; Elizabeth M. Schneider, "The Dialectic of Rights and Politics: Perspectives From the Women's Movement," 61 *N.Y.U. L. Rev.* 589, 601–02 (1986). As Professor MacKinnon puts it, "[t]he private is the public for those for whom the personal is the political." MacKinnon, *supra* note 228, at 100.

245. China under Mao provides a case study of the potential for success in such efforts. Not only did Mao control and define Chinese political life, he also kept tight control of Chinese cultural life. North Korea under Kim Il Sung provides a second example of this phenomenon.

246. In a rough sort of way, it parallels the French government's attempts to keep the French language pure and exclusive. *See, e.g.,* Anne Swardson, "French Groups Sue to Bar English-Only Internet Sites," *Wash. Post,* Dec. 24, 1996, at A1.

247. *See* Reingold, *supra* note 16, at 92–104; *see also* Beer, *supra* note 10, at 335–37; Kristof, *supra* note 213.

248. *See* Bork, *supra* note 220, at 99–102; Bork, *supra* note 226, at 27–28.

249. Bork, *supra* note 226, at 28.

250. *Id.*

251. *See generally* Herbert Wechsler, "Toward Neutral Principles of Constitutional Law," 73 *Harv. L. Rev.* 1 (1959) (arguing that principled constitutional decision making requires evenhanded application of doctrines across all cases involving similar facts).

252. *See* Meiklejohn, *supra* note 21, at 262–63.

253. *See* Stern, *supra* note 221, at 932–33.

254. *See* Thomas Jefferson, *Notes on Virginia, in* 4 *The Works of Thomas Jefferson* 64–65 (Paul Leicester Ford ed., 1904); *see also* Alexander Meiklejohn, "Education as a Factor in Post-War Reconstruction," *in Alexan-*

der Meiklejohn: Teacher of Freedom 185–89 (Cynthia Stokes Brown ed., 1981); Susan H. Bitensky, "Theoretical Foundations for a Right to Education Under the U.S. Constitution: A Beginning to the End of the National Education Crisis," 86 *Nw. U. L. Rev.* 550, 550–51, 588, 628–30 (1992); Susan P. Leviton & Matthew H. Joseph, "An Adequate Education for All Maryland's Children: Morally Right, Economically Necessary, and Constitutionally Required," *52 Md. L. Rev.* 1137, 1153–54, 1153 n.94 (1993).

255. *See* Letter from Thomas Jefferson to Joseph C. Cabell (Feb. 2, 1816), *in The Best Letters of Thomas Jefferson* 208–12 (J. G. de Roulhac Hamilton ed., 1926); Letter from Thomas Jefferson to Joseph C. Cabell (Sept. 9, 1817), *in* 17 *The Writings of Thomas Jefferson* 417, 423–24 (Andrew A. Lipscomb ed., 1904); Letter from Thomas Jefferson to William Charles Jarvis (Sept. 28, 1820), *in* 10 *The Writings of Thomas Jefferson* 160 (Paul Leicester Ford ed., 1899); Thomas Jefferson, "A Bill for the More General Diffusion of Knowledge," *in The Complete Jefferson* 1048 (Saul K. Padover ed., 1943); *see also* Bitensky, *supra* note 254, at 628–29.

256. *See* Okudaira, *supra* note 2, at 25 ("In Japan . . . there has been no tradition of judicial supremacy and no history of Supreme Court achievements."); *cf. Marbury v. Madison*, 5 U.S. (1 Cranch) 137, 177 (1803).

257. Okudaira, *supra* note 2, at 25; *see also* Luney, *supra* note 10, at 123, 144–45; Nathanson, *supra* note 209, at 323–24; Harold See, "The Judiciary and Dispute Resolution in Japan: A Survey," 10 *Fla. St. U. L. Rev.* 339, 349–50 (1982).

258. *See* Merryman, *supra* note 41, at 22–25, 28–38, 133–37.

259. *Id.* at 134–35.

260. *See id.* at 135.

261. *Id.* at 139.

262. *Id.*

263. *Id.*

264. *Id.* at 133–41.

265. Okudaira, *supra* note 2, at 25.

266. *Id.*

267. *Id.* (footnotes omitted).

268. *See, e.g.,* Sonobe, *supra* note 30, at 167–74.

269. *See* See, *supra* note 257, at 350 ("Whereas the United States Supreme Court used its power of judicial review to invalidate congressional acts only twice in its first sixty-eight years of existence, the Japanese Supreme Court has held five statutes unconstitutional in only half that time."). Of course, the utility of this observation should not be overstated. The United States Supreme Court had no preexisting role model to which it could look for guidance in articulating a meaningful vision of judicial review (other than perhaps the preexisting state supreme courts). In the latter half of the twentieth century, the United States Supreme Court itself could be seen as such a model. Moreover, other post–World War II constitutional courts in industrial democracies vested with the power of judicial review have not exhibited the Supreme Court of Japan's extreme form of judicial self-restraint. *See* Tom Farer, "Consolidating Democracy in Latin America: Law, Legal Institutions and Constitutional Structure," 10 *Am. U. J. Int'l L. & Pol'y* 1295, 1317–20 (1995); Donald P. Kommers, "German Constitutionalism: A Prolegomenon," 40 *Emory L.J.* 837, 837–45 (1991). The Constitutional Court of the Federal Republic of Germany provides perhaps the best example in this regard, especially given Germany's civil law tradition—indeed, the very civil law tradition Japan appropriated during the early years of the Meiji Restoration. *See* Chapter 4; *see also* Haley, *supra* note 4, at 67–80; Inoue, *supra* note 2, at 56–67; Donald P. Kommers, *The Constitutional Jurisprudence of the Federal Republic of Germany* 57–66 (1989).

270. Nor, for that matter, have Professor Nathanson's concerns about the lack of use of the power of judicial review leading to its "atrophy" come to pass. *See* Nathanson, *supra* note 209, at 324. At the same time, the Supreme Court's general posture of extreme deference to the political branches cannot be gainsaid. *Cf.* Haley, *supra* note 4, at 83–104 (arguing that, even during the Meiji and pre-

war periods, Japanese judges exhibited significant independence and worked successfully to maintain the rule of law).

271. Luney, *supra* note 10, at 145; *see also* Okudaira, *supra* note 2, at 24–25; Ramseyer, *supra* note 13, at 724–28, 734–38, 743–46. Indeed, Professor Ramseyer argues that politics not only influences the *selection* of judges in Japan but also affects their *behavior* once in office. *See id.* at 724–28. *But cf.* Haley, *supra* note 41 (arguing that the LDP does not maintain any effective system of control over members of the Japanese judiciary and that judicial selection is not really a function of LDP politics).

272. *See* Haley, *supra* note 41, at 8–12 (describing the selection process); Luney, *supra* note 10, at 132–36 (same).

273. *See* P. S. Atiyah & Robert S. Summers, *Form and Substance in Anglo-American Law* 45–47, 61–63, 222–39, 269–71 (1987).

274. Luney, *supra* note 10, at 145; *see also* Okudaira, *supra* note 2, at 24–25.

275. *See* Joan Biskupic, "Clinton Avoids Activists in Judicial Selections," *Wash. Post,* Oct. 24, 1995, at A1; David Johnston, "Bush Appears Set to Follow Reagan By Putting Conservatives on Bench," *N.Y. Times,* May 31, 1989, at B5; Neil A. Lewis, "In Selecting Federal Judges, Clinton Has Not Tried to Reverse Republicans," *N.Y. Times,* Aug. 1, 1996, at A20; Neil A. Lewis, "Selection of Conservative Judges Insures a President's Legacy," *N.Y. Times,* July 1, 1992, at A13; *see also* Carl Tobias, "Increasing Balance on the Federal Bench," 32 *Hous. L. Rev.* 137 (1995).

276. Consider, for example, the examples set by Justices David Souter, appointed by the first President Bush, and Harry Blackmun, appointed by President Nixon. Perhaps the most famous example of this phenomenon was President Eisenhower's decision to appoint then-New Jersey Supreme Court Justice William Brennan to the United States Supreme Court. Even if President Eisenhower realized that William Brennan was not a judicial conservative, it is doubtful that he realized just how liberal Brennan would prove to be. *See* Hunter R. Clark, *Justice Brennan: The*

Great Conciliator 78–84 (1995); Dwight D. Eisenhower, *Mandate for Change 1953–1956,* at 230 (1963).

277. Luney, *supra* note 10, at 145.

278. *Cf.* Leslye Amede Obiora, "Bridges and Barricades: Rethinking Polemics and Intransigence in the Campaign Against Female Circumcision," 47 *Case W. Res. L. Rev.* 275, 275–78, 284–85 (1997) (arguing that universalist assumptions regarding the transnational content and meaning of human rights and the proper roles of legal institutions in securing social reforms often reflects unjustifiable cultural elitism, if not a form of cultural imperialism).

279. *See, e.g., Vacco v. Quill,* 521 U.S. 793 (1997) (refusing to recognize a constitutional right to physician assisted suicide and opining that this question belongs more properly to the state legislatures); *Washington v. Glucksberg,* 521 U.S. 702 (1997) (same).

280. 5 U.S. (1 Cranch) 137 (1803).

281. 31 U.S. (6 Pet.) 515 (1832). President Jackson is reputed to have said of this decision that "John Marshall has rendered his decision, now let him enforce it." Grant A. Foreman, *Indian Removal: The Emigration of Five Civilized Tribes of Indians* 235 (2d ed. 1953); *see also* Larry Alexander & Frederick Schauer, "On Extrajudicial Constitutional Interpretation," 110 *Harv. L. Rev.* 1359, 1363–64 (1997); Girardeau A. Spann, "Expository Justice," 131 *U. Pa. L. Rev.* 585, 602 (1983); Kevin J. Worthen & Wayne R. Farnsworth, "Who Will Control the Future of Indian Gaming? 'A Few Pages of History Are Worth a Volume of Logic,'" 1996 *BYU. L. Rev.* 407, 423–24.

282. 79 U.S. (12 Wall.) 457 (1870); *see* David P. Currie, *The Constitution in the Supreme Court: The First Hundred Years, 1789–1888,* at 320–39 (1985).

283. *Perry v. United States,* 294 U.S. 330 (1935); *see also* David P. Currie, "The Constitution in Congress: Substantive Issues in the First Congress, 1789–1791," 61 *U. Chi. L. Rev.* 775, 806 n.178 (1994); Kenneth W. Dam, "From the Gold Clause Cases to the Gold Commission: A Half Century of American Monetary Law," 50 *U. Chi. L. Rev.* 504 (1983);

Frank H. Easterbrook, "Abstraction and Authority," 59 *U. Chi. L. Rev.* 349, 379 (1992).

284. 349 U.S. 294 (1955) [hereinafter *Brown II*] & 347 U.S. 483 (1954).

285. *See Brown,* 347 U.S. at 495–96.

286. *Brown II,* 349 U.S. at 301.

287. *See* Gerald N. Rosenberg, *The Hollow Hope: Can Courts Bring About Social Change?* (1991).

288. *See Ashwander v. TVA,* 297 U.S. 288, 346–48 (1936) (Brandeis, J., concurring). As Professor Neal Devins has put it, "[m]ost landmark Supreme Court decisions cannot be understood without paying attention to the politics surrounding them." Neal Devins, "Foreword," 56 *Law & Contemp. Probs.* 1, 2 (1993).

289. *See United States v. Nixon,* 418 U.S. 683 (1974); *see also* Archibald Cox, *The Role of the Supreme Court in American Government* 3–9 (1976); Alexander & Schauer, *supra* note 281, at 1364–65; Arthur S. Miller, "The President and Faithful Execution of the Laws," 40 *Vand. L. Rev.* 389, 397 (1987).

290. *See The Federalist No. 78,* at 522–23 (Alexander Hamilton) (Jacob E. Cooke ed., 1961).

291. *See Judgment Upon Case of Constitutionality of the Provisions of the Public Offices Election Law on Electoral Districts and the Apportionment of Seats, Series of Prominent Judgments of the Supreme Court of Japan upon Questions of Constitutionality No. 27* (General Secretariat, Supreme Court of Japan, 1996) (decided Jan. 20, 1993).

292. Nathanson, *supra* note 209, at 323.

293. *See* John L. Graham & Yoshihiro Sano, *Smart Bargaining: Doing Business With the Japanese* 25–27 (rev. ed. 1989); Kim, *supra* note 7, at 49–50, 52–53; Nakane, *supra* note 7, at 49–50; Rosalie L. Tung, *Business Negotiations With the Japanese* 46–49 (1984).

294. *See* Reingold, *supra* note 16, at 63.

295. Sonobe, *supra* note 30, at 138.

296. *Id.* at 173.

297. J. Mark Ramseyer & Minoru Nakazato, *Japanese Law: An Economic Approach* xi (1999); *cf.* John Owen Haley, *The Spirit of Japanese Law* (1998) (using a holistic approach, focusing on legal and political in-

stitutions and institutional constraints, to understand and explain the Japanese legal system and its operation).

298. Ramseyer & Nakazato, *supra* note 297, at xi.

299. *Id.; see also* J. Mark Ramseyer & Frances McCall Rosenbluth, *Japan's Political Marketplace* 2–3, 161–66 (1993) (arguing that the relative power imbalance between the courts and the Japanese Parliament better explains the relative reticence of the Japanese judiciary to confront the executive and legislative branches than cultural differences with the United States); J. Mark Ramseyer & Eric B. Rasmusen, *Measuring Judicial Independence: The Political Economy of Judging in Japan* (2003) (using law and economics analysis to explain relative institutional weakness of the Japanese judiciary and rejecting cultural difference as the basis for Japan's relatively weak judiciary); J. Mark Ramseyer, "The Reluctant Litigant Revisited: Rationality and Disputes in Japan," 14 *J. Japanese Stud.* 111, 114–15 (1988) (arguing that litigants and would-be litigants in Japan react rationally to design and power limitations of Japanese courts when deciding whether or not to pursue judicial relief for legal wrongs, rather than to some sort of social norm that discourages litigation in particular or conflict in general); *cf.* Haley, *supra* note 297 (applying a more comprehensive approach to understanding both Japanese law and Japanese legal institutions).

300. *See* Ramseyer & Nakazato, *supra* note 297, at 91, 147; *cf.* Haley, *supra* note 4, at 118, 159 (arguing that Japanese legal institutions differ significantly from those in the United States and these differences in design significantly impact institutional behavior).

301. *See, e.g.,* Haley, *supra* note 6, at 378–90 (arguing that institutional constraints, rather than abstract cultural norms, explain the relatively low litigation rates in Japan). For a discussion and application of comparative institutional analysis in the United States, see Neil Komesar, *Imperfect Alternatives: Choosing Institutions in Law, Economics, and Public Policy* (1994).

302. West, *supra* note 7, at 709.

303. Merryman, *supra* note 41, at 135.

304. *See id.* at 134–35.

305. *See, e.g.,* Sonobe, *supra* note 30, at 172 ("To my understanding, the description that the Japanese courts are taking 'a very careful and cautious approach' toward constitutional review seems to be more preferable and appropriate [than descriptions such as judicially passivist or restrained].") (footnote omitted).

306. *Id.* The judiciary's "cautious" approach also may reflect the lack of an effective and easily accessed system of formal enforcement of legal rules. As Professor Haley has explained, under such a system the effectiveness of new legal norms may "depend upon consensus and thus, as 'living' law, become nearly indistinguishable from nonlegal or customary norms." Haley, *supra* note 48, at 276. The Supreme Court may wish to avoid articulating legal norms that are unlikely to receive community support, for such rules are more likely to be honored in the breach than in the observance. *See id.* at 276–79.

307. *See, e.g.,* Beer, "Freedom of Expression," *supra* note 7, at 246–47 ("[I]rrepressible group actions involving workers, media companies, students, housewives, farmers, and other components of society seem as perennially essential to the nation's constitutional democracy as periodic elections and restraints on government power under law."); Masao Horibe, "Press Law in Japan," *in Press Law in Modern Democracies* 315, 316 (Pnina Lahav ed., 1985) (arguing Japanese citizens enjoy a high degree of personal freedom); Nathanson, *supra* note 208, at 323–24 (noting that "freedom of association and assembly, including demonstrations of social and political protest, have not been banished from the Japanese scene" and observing that "vigorous political debate and outspoken criticism of public officials continue"); Okudaira, *supra* note 2, at 26 ("[P]olitical freedom is greatly safeguarded and subjected to almost no direct restraint by the government. There is no legal impediment to criticism of the government, politicians, and bureaucrats.").

308. *See* Sonobe, *supra* note 30, at 173–74, 174 n.60.

309. *See* Burgess, *supra* note 213; Kristof, *supra* note 213; *see also* Beer, *supra* note 10, at 339–40, 345–47.

310. *See* Beer, "Freedom of Expression," *supra* note 7, at 224–26.

311. *Id.* at 225; *see also* Nakane, *supra* note 7, at 34–35, 102–03, 146–51. These cultural traits are also reinforced though active interest group efforts to restrict speech deemed inimical to a particular group's interests. *See* Nelson, *supra* note 14, at 71–84.

312. *See* Haley, *supra* note 4, at 170–91, 195–97; *see also* Nakane, *supra* note 7, at 58–61, 120–24.

313. *See* Ronald J. Krotoszynski, "Back to the Briarpatch: An Argument in Favor of Constitutional Meta-Analysis in State Action Determinations," 94 *Mich. L. Rev.* 302 (1995).

314. *See generally* David P. Currie, "Positive and Negative Constitutional Rights," 53 *U. Chi. L. Rev.* 864 (1986).

315. Fiss, *supra* note 8, at 20; *see also* Fiss, "Why the State," *supra* note 15, at 787, 793–94.

316. *Ono v. Japan,* 15 Keishū 2, at 347 (Sup. Ct., Feb. 15, 1961), *reprinted in* Itoh & Beer, *supra* note 25, at 217, 219.

317. *See* Nakane, *supra* note 7, at 143–51; *cf.* Upham, *supra* note 216, at 223–24 (arguing that U.S. legal formalism, with its reliance on value and content neutral rules, reflects and incorporates the core social values of pluralism and individual autonomy).

318. Indeed, the Supreme Court of Japan could place its obscenity jurisprudence on a sounder philosophical footing by shifting its justification for upholding restrictions from the foreign nature of particular ideas to the lack of a concrete relationship between the speech activity at issue and the project of democratic self-governance. Of course, the results in *Lady Chatterly's Lover* and *de Sade* would still be problematic, because these works advance ideas—albeit unconventional ideas—about proper social values. *See Kingsley Int'l Pictures Corp. v. Regents of the Univ.,* 360 U.S. 684, 688–89 (1959).

319. This value could be seen as related to Meiklejohn's analogy of a town meeting in which a parliamentarian enforces rules to keep order. *See* Meiklejohn, *Free Speech, supra*

note 125, at 22–27. As Meiklejohn puts it, "[t]he First Amendment, then, is not the guardian of unregulated talkativeness." *Id.* at 25. On the other hand, "unwise ideas must have a hearing as well as wise ones, unfair as well as fair, dangerous as well as safe, un-American as well as American." *Id.* at 26.

320. *See* James B. Thayer, "The Origin and Scope of the American Doctrine of Constitutional Law," 7 *Harv. L. Rev.* 129, 144 (1893); *see also* Symposium, "One Hundred Years of Judicial Review: The Thayer Centennial Symposium," 88 *Nw. U. L. Rev.* 1 (1993). As Thayer put it, a reviewing court "can only disregard [an] Act when those who have the right to make laws have not merely made a mistake, but have made a very clear one,—so clear that it is not open to rational question." Thayer, *supra*, at 144; *see also id.* at 148:

> The judicial function is merely that of fixing the outside border of reasonable legislative action, the boundary beyond which the taxing power, the power of eminent domain, police power, and legislative power in general, cannot go without violating the prohibitions of the constitution or crossing the line of its grants.

321. *See* Mark V. Tushnet, "Policy Distortion and Democratic Debilitation: Comparative Illumination of the Countermajoritarian Difficulty," 94 *Mich. L. Rev.* 245, 245–47 (1995).

322. *See* Thayer, *supra* note 320, at 151–56; *see also* Frank M. Johnson, Jr., "In Defense of Judicial Activism," 28 *Emory L.J.* 901, 910–12 (1979) (arguing that the best way to avoid instances of "judicial activism" is to encourage "legislative activism" in defense of civil liberties); Frank M. Johnson, "The Alabama Punting Syndrome," *Judges' J.,* Spring 1979, at 5–7, 53–54 (arguing that judges cannot turn a blind eye on legislative intransigence in the face of proven constitutional violations if constitutional guarantees are to have any real meaning).

323. *See infra* Chapter 6; *see also* Ronald J. Krotoszynski, Jr., "*Brind & Rust v. Sullivan*: Free Speech and the Limits of a Written Constitution," 22 *Fla. St. L. Rev.* 1, 4–10 (1994).

324. Tushnet, *supra* note 321, at 300.

325. *See id.* at 299–301.

326. *See* Thayer, *supra* note 320, at 153–56; Tushnet, *supra* note 321, at 299–301.

327. Kenpō, art. 1 ("The Emperor shall be the symbol of the State and of the unity of the people, deriving his position from the will of the people with whom resides sovereign power."); *see* Okudaira, *supra* note 2, at 1–8 (discussing the Constitution of 1947's shift in paradigm from a sovereign emperor to a sovereign electorate).

328. *See* Meiklejohn, *Free Speech, supra* note 126, at 1–27.

329. *See* Abe et al., *supra* note 12; Beer, *supra* note 10, at 393–99; Beer & Itoh, *supra* note 10, at 7–12; Itoh & Beer, *supra* note 25, at 20; Maki, *supra* note 27, at xli; Beer, "Public Welfare," *supra* note 7, at 210–20; John M. Maki, "Japanese Constitutional Style," *in The Constitution of Japan: Its First Twenty Years, 1947–67, supra* note 7, at 13, 16–18, 35–39; Okudaira, *supra* note 2, at 25–32.

330. Indeed, for many years the Japanese language did not even contain a word that expressed the concept of rights against the state. *See* Kim, *supra* note 7, at 53–54 (arguing that *giri,* or "duty," is far more important to dispute resolution in Japan than any notion of individual rights); Yosiyuki Noda, "Nihon-Jin No Seikaku To Sono Ho-Kannen [The Character of the Japanese People and Their Conception of Law]," *in The Japanese Legal System* 295, 305 (H. Tanaka ed., 1976) (describing selection of word *kenri* to describe the concept of rights); Kevin Yamaga-Karns, Note, "Pressing Japan: Illegal Foreign Workers Under International Human Rights Law and the Role of Cultural Relativism," 30 *Tex. Int'l L.J.* 559, 572 (1995) (discussing etymology of words to describe human rights in Japan); Beer, *supra* note 10, at 45–46, 110–11 (same); *see also* Beer, "Public Welfare," *supra* note 7, at 211–18; Ford, *supra* note 24, at 13–16; Okudaira, *supra* note 2, at 8; *cf.* Okudaira, *supra* note 2, at 27 (describing the enthusiastic and varied use of the term "human rights" in contemporary Japan). Similarly, the word used to express the ideas of liberty and freedom, *jiyu,* has "overtones of selfishness and

license." Abe et al., *supra* note 12, at 207–08; see Inoue, *supra* note 2, at 51–55; Kahei, *supra* note 46, at 5, 7–8.

331. Benedict, *supra* note 6, at 295.

332. *Id.*

333. *Id.* at 314.

334. *See* Zechariah Chafee, Jr., *Freedom of Speech* 1–39 (1920); Zechariah Chafee Jr., *Free Speech in the United States* 27–30, 497–505 (1946); Leonard W. Levy, *Legacy of Suppression: Freedom of Speech and Press in Early American History* 236–48, 258–309 (1960); *see also New York Times Co. v. Sullivan,* 376 U.S. 254 (1964); *Abrams v. United States,* 250 U.S. 616, 630 (1919) (Holmes, J., dissenting).

335. *See New York Times Co.,* 376 U.S. at 273–75, 282; Kalven, *supra* note 112, at 204–10.

NOTES TO CHAPTER 6

1. One of the leading American proponents of this theory is former Circuit Judge Robert Bork. *See* Robert H. Bork, *The Tempting of America* 118–19, 147 (1990) ("[t]he absence of a constitutional provision means the absence of a power of judicial review"); *Dronenburg v. Zech,* 741 F.2d 1388, 1396–97, 1396 n.5 (D.C. Cir. 1984) (Bork, J.) (opining that courts should not recognize or enforce rights that lack a textual foundation). However, the notion that written provisions (and particularly constitutional provisions) somehow elevate particular rights from nontextual rights is relatively commonplace in law. *See Planned Parenthood of Southeastern Pennsylvania v. Casey,* 505 U.S. 833, 980–84, 999–1001 (1992) (Scalia, J., dissenting) (arguing that as a general matter courts should enforce only rights with a textual foundation in the Constitution); *Coy v. Iowa,* 487 U.S. 1012, 1015–19 (1988) (holding that the Confrontation Clause of the Sixth Amendment precludes a state from permitting a minor to testify via closed circuit television); *Hudson v. Palmer,* 468 U.S. 517, 555–56 (1984) (Stevens, J., concurring in part and dissenting in part) (explaining that a written constitution provides a greater degree of protection for enumerated rights); *see also Johnson v. Louisiana,* 406 U.S. 356, 388 (1972) (Douglas, J., dissenting) (argu-

ing that the Court should exercise only the powers given to it in the text of the Constitution); *Griswold v. Connecticut,* 381 U.S. 479, 520–27 (1965) (Black, J., dissenting) (lamenting the Supreme Court's decisions to recognize unenumerated rights and arguing that only the text of the Constitution establishes enforceable rights); *Fong Yue Ting v. United States,* 149 U.S. 698, 737 (1893) (Brewer, J., dissenting) (noting that the powers of the United States government are fixed "by a written constitution").

Several leading British scholars share Judge Bork's view that a written constitution is necessary to ensure the adequate protection of individual rights and liberties. *See, e.g.,* Ronald Dworkin, *A Bill of Rights for Britain* 17–23 (1990) (arguing that Britain needs a written bill of rights); Anthony Lester, "The Constitution: Decline and Renewal," *in The Changing Constitution* 345, 353–56 (Jeffrey Jowell & Dawn Oliver eds., 1989) (arguing that Britain needs a written bill of rights to ensure protection of civil rights and liberties); Jim Murdoch, "The Rights of Public Assembly and Procession," in *Human Rights: From Rhetoric to Reality* 173–82, 193–95 (Tom Campbell et al. eds., 1986) (same); Harry Street, *Freedom, the Individual and the Law* 284–85 (1963) (same). *But cf.* Street, *supra,* at 287 ("Our judges may be relied on strenuously to defend some kinds of freedom.").

2. *See, e.g., Texas v. Johnson,* 491 U.S. 397 (1989); *Tinker v. Des Moines Indep. Community Sch. Dist.,* 393 U.S. 503 (1969); *Brown v. Louisiana,* 383 U.S. 131 (1966); *cf. Barnes v. Glenn Theatre,* 501 U.S. 560 (1991) (holding that state law prohibiting totally nude dancing did not violate the First Amendment); *United States v. O'Brien,* 391 U.S. 367 (1968) (holding that law prohibiting burning of draft card did not violate First Amendment).

3. *Compare Regina v. Secretary of State for the Home Dep't, Ex parte Brind,* [1991] 1 App. Cas. 696, 748–49, 750–51 (appeal taken from C.A.) (recognizing, but not applying, right of free speech) *with Rust v. Sullivan,* 500 U.S. 173, 192–200 (1991) (rejecting speech claim by medical doctors); *National Press Club v.*

Commission on Elections, The Law. Review 36 (March 31, 1992) (Philippines) (holding that Philippine constitutional free speech interest does not protect political speech in newspapers); *R. v. Butler,* [1992] 1 S.C.R. 452, 476–84 (Can.) (holding that Canadian Charter of Rights and Freedoms does not protect certain pornographic materials deemed to demean women).

4. *The Federalist No. 84,* at 575–81 (Alexander Hamilton) (Jacob E. Cooke ed., 1961); *see* James Madison, "Address Before the United States House of Representatives" (June 8, 1789), *reprinted in* 5 *The Writings of James Madison* 370–89 (Gaillard Hunt ed., 1904); *cf.* "Letter from Thomas Jefferson to James Madison" (Dec. 20, 1787), *in The Portable Thomas Jefferson* 428, 429 (Merrill D. Peterson ed., 1975) ("I will now add what I do not like. First, the omission of a bill of rights....").

5. *See* William W. Van Alstyne, *Interpretations of the First Amendment* 47–48, 113 n.73 (1984) [hereinafter Van Alstyne, *First Amendment*].

6. *See infra* notes 106–155 and accompanying text.

7. Human Rights Act 1998, ch. 42 (U.K.) (enacted Oct. 2, 2000) [hereinafter Act]; *see* Clive Walker & Russell L. Weaver, "The United Kingdom Bill of Rights 1998: The Modernization of Rights in the Old World," 33 U. Mich. J. L. Ref. 497, 499, 520–25 (2000).

8. European Convention for the Protection of Human Rights and Fundamental Freedoms, Nov. 4, 1950, 213 U.N.T.S. 222 (1955) [hereinafter ECHR]; *see* Conor Gearty, "Reflections on Human Rights and Civil Liberties in Light of the United Kingdom's Human Rights Act 1998," 35 *U. Rich. L. Rev.* 1, 1–3 (2001).

9. Act, §§ 1(a), 6.

10. Act, § 12.

11. *See* Sarah Lyall, "209 Years Later, the English Get American-Style Bill of Rights," *N.Y. Times,* Oct. 2, 2000, at A3; *see also* Act, § 22(3).

12. Act, § 3(1) ("So far as it is possible to do so, primary legislation and subordinate

legislation must be read and given effect in a way which is compatible with the Convention rights.").

13. Act, § 4.

14. Act, § 10(2).

15. Act, § 21(1).

16. Act, § 19.

17. ECHR, art. 10(2).

18. *See* Frederick Schauer, "The Generality of Rights," 6 *Legal Theory* 323, 328–36 (Cambridge 2000).

19. *Id.* at 336.

20. *Id.*

21. *See* Department for Constitutional Affairs, *Constitutional reform: a Supreme Court for the United Kingdom,* CP 11/03 (July 2003), *available at* http://www.dca.gov.uk/consult/supremecourt/supreme.pdf.

22. *See id.; see also* Secretary of State for Constitutional Affairs and Lord Chancellor, *Summary of Responses to the Consultation Paper on a Constitutional Reform: a Supreme Court for the United Kingdom, available at* http://www.dca.gov.uk/consult/supreme-court/scresp.htm.

23. *See* Department of Constitutional Affairs, *supra* note 21.

24. *See* Robert Verkaik, "New Supreme Court Would Be Harmful, Claim Law Lords," *The Independent* (London), Nov. 5, 2003, at 2.

25. Alison Hardie, "Lords Throw Out Proposals for a US-Style Supreme Court," *The Scotsman,* Mar. 9, 2004, at 2.

26. *See id.; University of Edinburgh School of Law, Scots Law News,* http://www.law.ed.ac.uk/sln/index.asp?page=337; *see also* Constitutional Reform Bill, http://en.wikipedia.org/wiki/Constitutional_Reform_Bill; Supreme Court of the United Kingdom, http://en.wikipedia.org/Supreme_Court_of_the_United_Kingdom.

27. *Compare Brind,* [1991] 1 App. Cas. at 748–49, 750–51 (recognizing, but not applying, right of free speech) *with Rust,* 500 U.S. at 198–200 (rejecting speech claim by doctors).

28. [1991] 1 App. Cas. at 752–56.

29. *See id.* at 711–15; *see also* Patricia Wynn Davies, "Law Lords Uphold Media Bar on

IRA," *Independent,* Feb. 8, 1991, at A10 (discussing the ban and the challenge brought against it by several broadcast journalists).

30. 500 U.S. 173 (1991).

31. *Id.* at 198–200.

32. Or, more precisely, that the existence of a written constitution does not always ensure that the seemingly valid invocation of a right can be interposed to block the application of government proscriptions against the exercise of the right.

33. *See Regina v. Secretary of State for the Home Dep't, Ex parte Brind,* [1991] 1 App. Cas. 696, 748–49, 750, 763 (appeal taken from C.A.); *cf.* Bork, *supra* note 1, at 147.

34. *See, e.g., Regents of the Univ. of Cal. v. Bakke,* 438 U.S. 265, 312 (1978); *Keyishian v. Board of Regents,* 385 U.S. 589, 603–08 (1967); *Sweezy v. New Hampshire,* 354 U.S. 234, 250 (1957); *id.* at 262–63 (Frankfurter, J., concurring); *Young Women's Christian Ass'n of Princeton v. Kugler,* 342 F. Supp. 1048, 1063 (D.N.J. 1972), *aff'd,* 493 F.2d 1402 (3rd Cir.), *cert. denied,* 415 U.S. 989 (1974); *see also Roe v. Wade,* 410 U.S. 113, 163, 166 (1973) (recognizing the constitutional importance of the professional judgment of a physician in making medical decisions); *see generally* William W. Van Alstyne, "Academic Freedom and the First Amendment in the Supreme Court of the United States: An Unhurried Historical Review," *53 Law & Contemp. Probs.* 79 (Summer 1990) [hereinafter Van Alstyne, "Historical Review"].

35. *See Rust v. Sullivan,* 500 U.S. 173, 192–200 (1991); *see also infra* notes 116–155 and accompanying text.

36. *See* Mark Tushnet, "Critical Legal Studies: A Political History," *100 Yale L.J.* 1515, 1524, 1538–39 (1991); Girardeau A. Spann, "Baby M and the Cassandra Problem," 76 *Geo. L.J.* 1719, 1735 (1988); Robert W. Gordon, "Critical Legal Histories," 36 *Stan. L. Rev.* 57, 114 (1984).

37. Gordon, *supra* note 36, at 114.

38. *See* Ronald J. Krotoszynski, Jr., Note, "Autonomy, Community, and Traditions of Liberty: The Contrast of British and American Privacy Law," 1990 *Duke L.J.* 1398, 1399–1400, 1446.

39. *See* P. S. Atiyah & Robert S. Summers, *Form and Substance in Anglo-American Law* 222–39, 408–09 (1987).

40. A particularly good example of this is the *Handyside* case. *Handyside* involved the British government's attempt to suppress "The Little Red Schoolbook" because of its somewhat frank discussion of sexual matters. This effort ultimately succeeded, even though the book circulated freely elsewhere in Western Europe. *Handyside v. United Kingdom,* 1 Eur. H.R. Rep. 737, 740–43, 758–60 (1976).

41. Atiyah & Summers, *supra* note 39, at 227–28, 298–306; Street, *supra* note 1, at 286; *see Regina v. Secretary of State for the Home Dep't, Ex parte Brind,* [1991] 1 App. Cas. 696, 715 (C.A.).

42. Atiyah & Summers, *supra* note 39, at 299–306; Street, *supra* note 1, at 309–11; Colin Mellors, "Governments and the Individual—Their Secrecy and His Privacy," in *Privacy* 93 (John B. Young ed., 1978); Frank Dowrick, "Council of Europe: Juristic Activity 1974–86: Part II," 36 *Int'l & Comp. L.Q.* 878, 888 (1987); *see also* Sheila Rule, "Group Says Press Freedom is Declining in Britain," *N.Y. Times,* Oct. 19, 1990, at 7A; Joe Rogaly, "Why Britain Should Copy Germany," *The Financial Times,* July 13, 1990, § 1, at 16; James Atlas, "Thatcher Puts a Lid On Censorship in Britain," *N.Y. Times,* Mar. 5, 1989, § 6, at 36.

43. Indeed, recent cases suggest that it will afford free speech judicial protection to the extent consistent with the constitutional role of the British judiciary. *See Brind,* [1991] 1 App. Cas. at 748–49, 751; *see also Derbyshire County Council v. Times Newspapers,* [1992] 3 W.L.R. 28, 48, 56–58, 63–65 (C.A.).

44. *See Rust v. Sullivan,* 500 U.S. 173, 200 (1991) (noting that although doctors are required to spout the party line from the Department of Health and Human Services (HHS) as a condition of participation in Title X clinics, participating doctors need not represent the party line as their own professional opinion); Title X Pregnancy Counseling Act of 1991, S. 323, 102d Cong., 1st Sess. § 2 (1991).

45. James Madison, "Address Before the United States House of Representatives" (June 8, 1789), *reprinted in* 5 *The Writings of*

James Madison 370–89 (Gaillard Hunt ed., 1904).

46. Great Britain has a "constitution," albeit an unwritten one. Unlike the U.S. Constitution with its Bill of Rights, the British Constitution concerns itself exclusively with the division of powers among the Crown, Parliament, and the judiciary. *See* A. W. Bradley, "The Sovereignty of Parliament—in Perpetuity?" *in The Changing Constitution* 25, 27–29 (Jeffrey Jowell & Dawn Oliver eds., 1989); Lester, *supra* note 1; Stanley De Smith & Roger Brazier, *Constitutional and Administrative Law* 3–14 (6th ed. 1989); J. A. Jolowicz, "The Judicial Protection of Fundamental Rights Under English Law," *in* 2 *The Cambridge-Tilburg Law Lectures* 5–6 (Dr. B. S. Markensinis & J. H. M. Willems eds., 1980); Street, *supra* note 1, at 11, 283–89; *see also Legislation on Human Rights: A Discussion Document* ¶ 2.01–05 (Home Office 1976).

47. Gearty, *supra* note 8, at 20.

48. *See* Department of Constitutional Affairs, *Declarations of Incompatibility made under s4 of Human Rights Act 1998, available at* http://www.humanrights.gov.uk/decihm .htm; *see also Chaidan v. Godin-Mendoza*, [2004] UKHL 20 (June 21, 2004) (listing cases in which British courts have issued a declaration of incompatibility).

49. *See, e.g., Attorney-General v. Guardian Newspapers* (No. 2), [1990] 1 App. Cas. 109, 156–59, 178 (C.A.). (the so-called "Spycatcher" case); *cf. Sunday Times v. United Kingdom*, 14 Eur. H.R. Rep. 229, 240–44 (1991) (holding that contempt orders in one of the "Spycatcher" cases violated the right of free speech under the European Convention on Human Rights); *Observer & Guardian v. United Kingdom*, 14 Eur. H.R. Rep. 153, 174–83 (1991) (holding that temporary injunction violated Article 10 of the European Convention on Human Rights); *Sunday Times v. United Kingdom*, 2 Eur. H.R. Rep. 245, 266–67, 275–82 (1979) (holding that British law of contempt could not be applied to impose a prior restraint on the *Times*'s publication of articles on the thalidomide disaster, despite the existence of pending lawsuits). The *Sunday Times* cases are examples of litigants with free speech claims taking their complaints to an extranational tribunal to vindicate their speech rights. *See generally* Krotoszynski, *supra* note 38, at 1420–26, 1430.

50. Gearty, *supra* note 8, at 17.

51. 347 U.S. 483 (1954).

52. 5 U.S. (1 Cranch) 137, 162–63, 177–78 (1803); *see* Alexander M. Bickel, *The Least Dangerous Branch: The Supreme Court at the Bar of Politics* (1962).

53. *See Regina v. Secretary of State for the Home Dep't Ex parte Brind*, [1991] 1 App. Cas. 696, 748–49, 751 (appeal taken from C.A.); *see also Derbyshire County Council v. Times Newspapers*, [1992] 3 W.L.R. 28, 48, 56–58, 63–65 (C.A.) (incorporating freedom of speech into the English law of torts to preclude local government from recovering for libel). In particular, Lord Bridge seems to be applying a "compelling state interest" test to determine whether the ban on in-person broadcasts of the Irish Republican Army representatives was "reasonable" for purposes of reviewing the administrative action. *Brind*, [1991] 1 App. Cas. at 748–49.

54. Lord Goff perhaps explained this best in *Guardian Newspapers*:

> I can see no inconsistency between English law . . . and [A]rticle 10 of the European Convention on Human Rights. This is scarcely surprising, since we may pride ourselves on the fact that freedom of speech has existed in this country perhaps as long as, if not longer than, it has existed in any other country in the world. The only difference is that, whereas [A]rticle 10 of the Convention, in accordance with its avowed purpose, proceeds to state a fundamental right and then to qualify it, we in this country (where everybody is free to do anything, subject only to the provisions of the law) proceed rather upon an assumption of freedom of speech, and turn to our law to discover the established exceptions to it.

Attorney-General v. Guardian Newspapers Ltd. (No. 2), [1990] 1 App. Cas. 109, 283 (appeal taken from C.A.). Of course, Lord Goff conveniently failed to mention that Parliament's ability to proscribe speech is unlimited. In light of this fact, his observation is somewhat circular: in Britain, anyone is free to say what they wish anywhere, anytime, unless there is a legal prohibition against the particular speech. However, this proposition is just as true in North Korea or Yemen as it is in England.

55. *Brind,* [1991] 1 App. Cas. at 767.

56. *See, e.g., Regina v. Inland Revenue Comm'rs, Ex parte* Rossminster Ltd., [1980] 1 App. Cas. 952 (appeal taken from C.A.); *see also* Atiyah & Summers, *supra* note 39, at 46–47, 100–12, 267–69; Street, *supra* note 1, at 283–84.

57. *Marbury,* 5 U.S. (1 Cranch) at 163.

58. Atiyah & Summers, *supra* note 39, at 46–47, 269–70, 299.

59. *See* Gearty, *supra* note 8, at 20–21.

60. *See Marbury,* 5 U.S. (1 Cranch) at 176–78.

61. *Brind,* [1991] 1 App. Cas. at 761–62. The British judiciary's use of free speech as a background consideration when considering the scope of parliamentary enactments is entirely analogous to its use of privacy as a legal canon. *See* Krotoszynski, *supra* note 38, at 1413–15, 1425. When faced with an ambiguous parliamentary command, the British judiciary will consider vindicating free speech claims. *Brind,* [1991] 1 App. Cas. at 748–50, 763; *see also* Krotoszynski, *supra* note 38, at 1413–15, 1425. Likewise, in the absence of a clear parliamentary command, the British courts are willing to incorporate free speech values into the common law. *See, e.g., Derbyshire County Council v. Times Newspapers,* [1992] 3 W.L.R. 28, 48–49, 53–54, 56, 64–65 (C.A.). However, where Parliament speaks with a clear voice, the British judiciary will not interpose the community's tradition of free speech to thwart the parliamentary command. *See Brind,* [1991] 1 App. Cas. at 715 (C.A.).

62. The British courts have not yet addressed the applicability of the HRA to claims involving so-called secondary effect. For example, a free speech objection to the content of British libel law might not be cog-

nizable under the HRA. *Cf. New York Times Co. v. Sullivan,* 376 U.S. 254 (1964). The HRA applies to any official government action, but its effect, if any, on private law remains to be seen.

63. *See Attorney-General v. Guardian Newspapers* (No. 2), [1990] 1 App. Cas. 109, 156–59, 178, 203, 218–20, 256, 283–84; [1987] 1 W.L.R. 1248, 1286, 1296–97 (H.L.).

64. *Brind,* [1991] 1 App. Cas. at 759–62, 717–18; *see* P. Van Dijk & & G. J. H. Van Hoof, *Theory and Practice of the European Convention on Human Rights* 10–18, 91–92, 456 (1984); R. Higgins, "United Kingdom," in *The Effect of Treaties in Domestic Law* 123, 124–25, 129–30, 134–35, 137 (Francis G. Jacobs & Shelley Roberts eds., 1987); Krotoszynski, *supra* note 38, at 1415–18, 1420–21.

65. European Convention for the Protection of Human Rights and Fundamental Freedoms, Nov. 4, 1950, 213 U.N.T.S. 222 (1955) [hereinafter ECHR]; *see Brind,* [1991] 1 App. Cas. at 761; *In Re* K.D., [1988] 1 App. Cas. 806, 813–15, 823–25, 828–30 (appeal taken from C.A.); *see also* Krotoszynski, *supra* note 38, at 1425.

66. Article 10 of the ECHR provides:

1. Everyone has the right to freedom of expression. This right shall include freedom to hold opinions and to receive and impart information and ideas without interference by public authority and regardless of frontiers. This article shall not prevent states from requiring the licensing of broadcasting, television, or cinema enterprises.

2. The exercise of these freedoms, since it carries with it duties and responsibilities, may be subject to such formalities, conditions, restrictions or penalties as are prescribed by law and are necessary in a democratic society, in the interests of national security, territorial integrity or public safety, for the prevention of disorder or crime, for the protection of health or morals, for the protection of the reputation or rights of others, for preventing the disclosure of information re-

ceived in confidence, or for maintaining the authority and impartiality of the judiciary.

ECHR, art. 10, *reprinted in Brind*, [1991] 1 App. Cas. at 760. Quite obviously, section 2 creates exceptions to the general rule that could, in the abstract, justify a wide range of restrictions on free expression. Such restrictions would probably not pass muster under contemporary First Amendment standards. *Compare Simon & Schuster, Inc. v. Members of the New York State Crime Victims Bd.*, 502 U.S. 105 (1991) (holding that statute imposing financial burden on speakers because of speech content was unconstitutional) and *Near v. Minnesota*, 283 U.S. 697 (1931) (prohibiting the application of prior restraints on the press) *with Brind*, [1991] 1 App. Cas. at 749, 751, 759, 763, 765 (upholding content restrictions on mass media) and *Attorney-General v. Guardian Newspapers* (No. 2), [1990] 1 App. Cas. at 109 (restraining publication of book) and *Sunday Times v. United Kingdom*, 2 Eur. H.R. Rep. 245 (1979) (overturning prior restraint the United Kingdom imposed on newspaper).

67. Atiyah & Summers, *supra* note 39, at 61–62, 299–300, 322–32.

68. This is also true in the United States. *See Chevron U.S.A. v. Natural Resources Defense Council*, 467 U.S. 837, 841–42, 863–65 (1984).

69. *Brind*, [1991] 1 App. Cas. at 757–59; *Council for Civil Serv. Unions v. Minister for the Civil Serv.*, [1985] App. Cas. 374, 410 (appeal taken from C.A.); *Associated Provincial Picture Houses v. Wednesbury Corp.*, [1948] 1 K.B. 223, 230 (C.A.) (holding that an administrative regulation may not stand if it is "so unreasonable that no reasonable authority could ever have come to it"); *see* Sir William Wade, *Administrative Law* 388–462 (6th ed. 1988); *see also* Atiyah & Summers, *supra* note 39, at 61 & n.72.

70. *Brind*, [1991] 1 App. Cas. at 761–62; Krotoszynski, *supra* note 38, at 1420–25.

71. *Brind*, [1991] 1 App. Cas. at 762.

72. Including Sinn Fein, Republican Sinn Fein, and the Ulster Defence Association, *Brind*, [1991] 1 App. Cas. at 755. Sinn Fein and Republican Sinn Fein are organizations committed to the reunification of Ireland, and historically have not proven averse to the use of force in their attempts to further this objective. The Ulster Defence Association is committed to the continued unification of Northern Ireland with the United Kingdom, and has proven itself equally receptive to the use of force. *See generally* David Remnick, "Reporter At Large: Belfast Confetti," *New Yorker*, Apr. 25, 1994, at 58 (discussing the shared propensity for terrorist violence on the part of republican and unionist paramilitary groups in Northern Ireland).

73. *See* F. W. Maitland, *The Constitutional History of England* 387–405 (1908) (discussing the composition and historical development of the "government").

74. Section 29(3) of the Broadcasting Act, in relevant part, provides:

> Subject to subsection (4), the Secretary of State may at any time by notice in writing require the Authority [the IBA] to refrain from broadcasting any matter or classes of matter specified in the notice; and it shall be the duty of the Authority to comply with the notice.

In turn, section 4(1) of the Broadcasting Act provides:

> It shall be the duty of the Authority to satisfy themselves that, so far as possible, the programmes broadcast by the Authority comply with the following requirements [including]—(a) that nothing is included in the programmes which offends against good taste or decency or is likely to encourage or incite to crime or to lead to disorder or to be offensive to public feeling.

Reprinted in Brind, [1991] 1 App. Cas. at 752–53. Subsection (1)(b) and (1)(f) provide, respectively, that the Authority must provide news programming and that programming relating to political matters is impartial.

Although these media restrictions may initially seem incredible to American eyes, two mitigating considerations apply. First, the provisions of the Broadcasting Act apply to a public entity, not a private concern. Mandating editorial neutrality is at least arguably less odious in this circumstance. *But cf. Miami Herald Publishing Co. v. Tornillo*, 418 U.S. 241 (1974) (holding government requiring or forbidding newspaper to publish specified matter is unconstitutional). Second, insofar as a government subsidy of the speech is involved, it is quite conceivable that the First Amendment would not stand as any impediment to a like scheme of regulation for, say, the Corporation for Public Broadcasting. *See Rust v. Sullivan*, 500 U.S. 173, 200 (1991). Consistent with *Rust*, so long as the journalists were not required to represent that the views they expressed were their own views, *see Rust*, 500 U.S. at 200, the government could most assuredly regulate the content and editorial policies of the publicly owned broadcast outlet. The purpose of setting forth the statute is primarily to show that the Home Secretary seemingly held broad discretion in regulating the content of broadcasts through either the BBC or IBA.

75. Directive of the Home Secretary (Oct. 19, 1988), *reprinted in Brind*, [1991] 1 App. Cas. at 711 (C.A.).

76. *Id.*

77. *Id.*

78. *See* Letter from Mr. C. L. Scoble, Office of the Home Secretary, to the BBC (Oct. 24, 1988), *reprinted in Brind*, [1991] 1 App. Cas. at 753–54.

79. The Home Secretary's Office made this clear in an explanatory letter:

[T]he correct interpretation (and that which was intended) is that [the directive] applies only to direct statements and not to reported speech, and that the person caught by the notice is the one whose words are reported and not the reporter or presenter who reports them. Thus the notice permits the showing of a film or still picture of the initiator speaking the words together with a voice-over account of them, whether in paraphrase or verbatim. We confirmed that programmes involving the reconstruction of actual events,

where actors use the verbatim words which had been spoken in actuality, are similarly permitted.

Letter from Mr. C. L. Scoble, Office of the Home Secretary, to the BBC (Oct. 24, 1988) (explaining the regulation's intended scope) *reprinted in Brind*, [1991] 1 App. Cas. at 753–54.

A hypothetical demonstrates the absurdity of the regulation. Under the ban, a show styled "Gardening with Sinn Fein" would be prohibited if the show were hosted by an official representative of Sinn Fein and the gardening tips were sanctioned by the group. However, if an actor re-created the Sinn Fein programming or a broadcaster used a voice-over to convey the message, the ban would not apply. Likewise, a suitably sinister actor could re-create a terrorist communication, and such programming could be broadcast with impunity. (Although, the actual speaker could presumably be held accountable for threats of violence.).

80. *See Near v. Minnesota*, 283 U.S. 697, 716–720 (1931). Prior restraints are highly disfavored instruments under the Supreme Court's longstanding First Amendment jurisprudence.

81. *Brind*, [1991] 1 App. Cas. at 748, 751, 757–58, 764–66; *see also Associated Provincial Picture Houses, Ltd. v. Wednesbury Corp.*, [1947] 2 All E.R. 680, 683 (C.A.).

82. *Brind*, [1991] 1 App. Cas. at 748–49, 757–58.

83. *Id.* at 757.

Where Parliament has given to a minister or other person or body a discretion, the court's jurisdiction is limited, in the absence of a statutory right of appeal, to the supervision of the exercise of that discretionary power, so as to ensure that it has been exercised lawfully. It would be a wrongful usurpation of power by the judiciary to substitute its [own view], the judicial view, on the merits and on that basis to quash the decision.

Id. For an administrative law analog in the United States, see *Chevron U.S.A. v. Natural Resources Defense Council*, 467 U.S. 837, 842–

44, 864–66 (1984) (deferring to the Environmental Protection Agency's interpretation of the Clean Air Act).

84. A Law Lord is a member of the House of Lords who is appointed for life (he or she is not necessarily a member of the peerage) and who sits in decision over the appeals taken from the lower British courts. The House of Lords, as a whole, does not sit to decide cases. Rather, the small cadre of Law Lords discharge this function. *See* Atiyah & Summers, *supra* note 39, at 269.

85. For instance, an administrative regulation that prohibited media outlets from propagating the advocacy of the reunification of Ireland as treason against the Crown would presumably be beyond an administrator's power in the absence of an express Parliamentary delegation of authority to promulgate such a regulation. *See Brind*, [1991] 1 App. Cas. at 748–49, 750, 757, 763.

86. *See id.* at 751.

87. Opinions of the House of Lords, unlike the Supreme Court, are issued seriatim, with each Law Lord on a particular panel holding forth individually. However, it is not unusual for a Lord to write a short opinion that simply concurs in the opinion of another panel member. *See, e.g., Brind*, [1991] 1 App. Cas. at 749–50 (concurring opinion of Lord Roskill).

88. *Id.* at 748.

89. *Id.* at 748–49.

90. *Id.* at 749.

91. *Id.*

92. *Id.* at 749–50.

93. *Id.* at 748–49 (emphasis added).

94. 485 U.S. 312 (1988). To justify a content-based restriction on political speech, the Supreme Court has "required the State to show that the regulation is necessary to serve a compelling state interest and that it is narrowly drawn to achieve that end." *Id.* at 321 (quoting *Perry Educ. Ass'n v. Perry Local Educators' Ass'n*, 460 U.S. 37, 45 (1983)).

95. *Brind*, [1991] 1 App. Cas. at 750.

96. *Id.* at 751.

97. *Id.*

98. *See id.* at 749–50.

99. *Id.* at 763.

100. *Id.* at 764.

101. *Id.* at 763.

102. *Id.* at 757.

103. *Id.* at 759.

104. *Id.* at 756, 758.

105. *See id.* at 756, 758.

106. *Id.* at 759.

107. Note that Lord Bridge, joined by Lord Roskill, and Lord Ackner refers to a *right* of free expression. *Id.* at 749, 750, 757. However, Lord Templeman recognizes that "freedom of expression is a principle," *id.* at 750 (emphasis added); Lord Lowry also refers to freedom of expression as a "*principle.*" *Id.* at 763. Thus, three of the five Lords on the panel characterized "freedom of expression" as a "right."

108. *See Simon & Schuster, Inc. v. New York State Crime Victims Bd.*, 502 U.S. 105 (1991); *Boos v. Barry*, 485 U.S. 312 (1988); *Minneapolis Star & Tribune Co. v. Minnesota Comm'r of Revenue*, 460 U.S. 575 (1983).

109. *Brind*, [1991] 1 App. Cas. at 748–50, 757–59, 763.

110. *See Beatty v. Gillbanks*, [1882] 9 Q.B.D. 308, 313–14; *see also* Gearty, *supra* note 8, at 13–14.

111. *See D. P. P. v. Jones*, [1999] 2 App. Cas. 240 (H.L.) (appeal taken from Eng.); *see also* Gearty, *supra* note 8, at 14–15.

112. For instance, should the Home Secretary prohibit the media from reporting on the political activities of Sinn Fein, it seems entirely probable that, under *Brind*, the House of Lords would quash the regulation. Such hypothetical regulation would impose more than a minimal restriction on freedom of expression, and would be extremely difficult to justify as serving a "compelling" need.

113. As Professor Gearty has noted:
Since there are no "human rights" guaranteed in any document, it is clear that the health of Britain's representative democracy depends both on the forbearance of Parliament in not legislating to erode civil liberties and on the vigilance of the judges in deploying their powers of adjudication and interpretation to protect civil liberties from legislative and executive attack.

Gearty, *supra* note 8, at 15.

114. *See generally* Schauer, *supra* note 18, at 334–36. Of course, the HRA now incorporates Article 10 into domestic law. Would the result in *Brind* necessarily change as a result? It seems doubtful, given Article 10's express sanction of restrictions on free expression necessary to protect "national security," "public safety," and "disorder or crime." ECHR, art. 10(2). The only real question would then be whether the regulation at issue was "necessary in a democratic society." *Id.* Given the limited scope of the regulation, it could be argued (perhaps successfully) that the social benefit conferred by the regulation is so modest as to render the regulation unnecessary. *But see Glimmerveen & Hagenbeek v. The Netherlands,* 4 Eur. H.R. Rep. 260 (1979) (holding that the Netherlands could prohibit racist political speech without violating Article 10's guarantee of free expression).

115. *See supra* Chapter 5.

116. *See, e.g., Simon & Schuster Inc.,* 502 U.S. at 508–12; *Texas v. Johnson,* 491 U.S. 397 (1989); *Hustler Magazine v. Falwell,* 485 U.S. 46, 55–56 (1988).

117. *See generally Planned Parenthood v. Casey,* 505 U.S. 833, 978–79, 980–84, 999–1001 (1992) (Scalia, J., dissenting) (arguing that as a general matter only rights with a textual foundation in the Constitution should be enforced by courts); *Coy v. Iowa,* 487 U.S. 1012, 1015–19 (1988) (holding that the Confrontation Clause of the Sixth Amendment precludes a state from permitting a minor to testify via closed circuit television set); *Hudson v. Palmer,* 468 U.S. 517, 541, 555–56 (1984) (Stevens, J., concurring in part and dissenting in part) (explaining that a written constitution provides a greater degree of protection for enumerated rights).

118. *See, e.g., United States v. O'Brien,* 391 U.S. 367, 376–78 (1968).

119. *See* Krotoszynski, *supra* note 38, at 1448–49.

120. *See, e.g., Rust v. Sullivan,* 500 U.S. 173, 198–200 (1991).

121. An obvious candidate would be the Due Process Clauses of the Fifth and Fourteenth Amendments. *See Roe v. Wade,* 410 U.S. 113, 152–54 (1973); *Griswold v. Connecticut,* 381 U.S. 479, 481–486 (1965). Professor William Van Alstyne has suggested that free speech values could have been imported into the Constitution through the Guaranty Clause, which provides that "[t]he United States shall guarantee to every State in this Union a Republican Form of Government. . . ." U.S. Const. art. IV, § 4, cl. 1; *see* Van Alstyne, *First Amendment, supra* note 5, at 8–9; *see also* Akhil Reed Amar, "Intratextualism," 112 *Harv. L. Rev.* 747, 748–49, 788–802 (1999) (advocating "intratextual" reading of constitutional text to better inform understanding of discrete clauses and noting also the utility of "intertextual" interpretation that reads constitutional text in conjunction with other foundational documents, such as the Declaration of Independence or the Articles of Confederation); Akhil Reed Amar, "The Bill of Rights as a Constitution," 100 *Yale L.J.* 1131, 1201–10 (1991) (arguing against reading provisions of the Bill of Rights atomistically and urging instead a dynamic, holistic approach to interpreting the Bill of Rights). To be sure, the existence of the First Amendment Speech and Press Clauses most certainly help to ensure that federal court judges will perk up and listen when a free speech claim is presented for review. This does not necessarily mean, however, that such claims would fail to receive consideration on the merits absent the clauses.

122. *Rust v. Sullivan,* 500 U.S. 173, 179–81 (1991).

123. H.R. Conf. Rep. No. 1667, 91st Cong., 2d Sess. 8, *reprinted in* U.S.C.C.A.N. 5068, 5081–82 (1970); *see also* 42 U.S.C. § 300a-6 (1988).

124. 42 U.S.C. § 300a-6 (1988).

125. *Rust,* 500 U.S. at 179–81.

126. 42 C.F.R. § 59.8(b)(5) (1992). On his first day in office, President Clinton repealed these regulations. *See* 58 Fed. Reg. 7455 (Feb. 5, 1993).

127. *See* 42 C.F.R. § 59.8(b)(5) (1992).

128. *Id.*

129. 42 C.F.R. §§ 59.8(b)(1), (5) (1992).

130. *Rust v. Sullivan,* 500 U.S. 173, 183–87 (1991).

131. *Id.* at 204–07 (Blackmun, J., dissenting); *id.* at 223–25 (O'Connor, J., dissenting).

132. *Id.* at 187.

133. *Id.* at 192–200.

134. *Id.* at 192–95.

135. *Id.* at 193.

136. *Id.* at 194–95 & 195 n.4.

137. See *Frost & Frost Trucking Co. v. Railroad Comm'n,* 271 U.S. 583, 593–94 (1926).

138. See *Perry v. Sindermann,* 408 U.S. 593, 597 (1972).

139. *Id.* (quoting *Speiser v. Randall,* 357 U.S. 513, 526 (1958)); see Kathleen M. Sullivan, "Unconstitutional Conditions," 102 *Harv. L. Rev.* 1415, 1421–28 (1989) (defining and discussing the doctrine of unconstitutional conditions).

140. *Rust,* 500 U.S. at 196.

141. *Id.* at 197–98.

142. *Id.* at 200.

143. *Id.*

144. *Id.*

145. *Id.* at 201–03.

146. *Id.* at 201–02; see *Harris v. McRae,* 448 U.S. 297 (1980); *Maher v. Roe,* 432 U.S. 464 (1977).

147. *Rust,* 500 U.S. at 204–20 (Blackmun, J., dissenting).

148. The task at hand is not to establish the general injustice of the *Rust* decision but, rather, to demonstrate that the existence of a written constitutional provision expressly protecting free speech made little difference to the outcome of the case.

149. *Rust,* 500 U.S. at 207–11; see *Frost & Frost Trucking Co. v. Railroad Comm'n,* 271 U.S. 583, 593–94 (1926).

150. *Rust,* 500 U.S. at 209–11 & 210 n.2.

151. 42 C.F.R. §§ 59.8(a), (b) (1992).

152. *Rust,* 500 U.S. at 211.

153. See Robert C. Post, "Subsidized Speech," 106 *Yale L.J.* 151, 170 (1996) ("The HHS regulations plainly discriminate on the basis of viewpoint, if by viewpoint discrimination is meant, as Justice Kennedy meant in *Rosenberger,* to constrain speech on only one side of a disputed subject.").

154. *Id.* at 212–15.

155. *Id.* at 213 (emphasis in original). A hypothetical helps to illustrate Justice Blackmun's concerns. Suppose a law school professor at a state-funded institution teaches the introductory course in constitutional law. Suppose further that the governor and state legislature decide to appropriate funds for the express purpose of providing instruction in constitutional law at the publicly funded state law school. To make the picture complete, we need only hypothesize that as a condition of the grant, which any instructor at the law school is free to accept or reject as she pleases, the instructor must teach that the equal protection doctrine of "separate but equal" as set forth in *Plessy v. Ferguson,* 163 U.S. 537 (1896), is the only correct interpretation of the Equal Protection Clause of the Fourteenth Amendment, and that *Brown v. Board of Educ.,* 347 U.S. 483 (1954) and *Gayle v. Browder,* 352 U.S. 903 (1956), which hold otherwise, were incorrectly decided and reflect the basest form of judicial usurpation. Relatively settled law on the First Amendment and academic freedom would, until *Rust,* have presumably precluded either the federal or a state government from so limiting the professional activities of our hypothetical constitutional law instructor. See *Regents of the Univ. of Cal. v. Bakke,* 438 U.S. 265, 312 (1978) (Opinion of Powell, J.); *Keyishian v. Board of Regents,* 385 U.S. 589, 609–10 (1967).

The *Rust* majority declined to decide whether a medical doctor acting in a professional capacity enjoys the same First Amendment protection of his professional speech as an academician, because the regulations "do not significantly impinge upon the doctor-patient relationship. Nothing in them requires a doctor to represent as his own any opinion that he does not in fact hold." *Rust,* 500 U.S. at 200. Under this rationale, so long as a university professor was not required to represent particular viewpoints as her own—*i.e.,* so long as she could at least marginally disassociate herself from them outside the classroom—the state may force her to abdicate her professional duties and academic integrity. Whether this result well serves core First Amendment values seems, at best, dubious. Cf. *Young Women's Christian Ass'n of*

Princeton v. Kugler, 342 F. Supp. 1048, 1063 (D.N.J. 1972).

156. *Rust*, 500 U.S. at 200; *but cf. Legal Servs. Corp. v. Velazquez*, 531 U.S. 533, 540–49 (2001) (distinguishing *Rust* and upholding First Amendment challenge brought by LSC lawyers against limitations on their representation of clients seeking to challenge federal or state welfare laws and regulations).

157. *Regina v. Secretary of State for the Home Dep't, Ex parte Brind*, [1991] 1 App. Cas. 696, 763 (appeal taken from C.A.); *see also Brind*, [1991] 1 App. Cas. at 757 (calling for "close scrutiny").

158. *Brind*, [1991] 1 App. Cas. at 749.

159. *See Rust*, 500 U.S. at 200 (requiring no justification for the restriction on a treating physician's speech).

160. *Id.* at 212–15. Justice Blackmun quibbles merely with the result, and not with the particular means to the result.

161. *Id.* at 200; *but see Velazquez*, 531 U.S. at 548 ("The Constitution does not permit the Government to confine litigants and their attorneys in this manner. We must be vigilant when Congress imposes rules and conditions which in effect insulate its own laws from legitimate judicial challenge.").

162. This actually implicates two speech interests: (1) the interest of the professional when performing duties to do so in a fashion consistent with prevailing professional standards of care, and (2) the recipient's interest in receiving the information. On the first point, *see Keyishian v. Board of Regents*, 385 U.S. 589 (1967); *Parducci v. Rutland*, 316 F. Supp. 352 (M.D. Ala. 1970), on the second, *see Virginia State Bd. of Pharmacy v. Virginia Citizens Consumer Council, Inc.*, 425 U.S. 748, 756, 757 & n.15 (1976). For whatever reason, Justice Blackmun's *Rust* dissent largely ignores the patient's interest in receiving accurate and complete medical information. *See Rust*, 500 U.S. at 211 n.3, 213–14. Yet, the *Rust* majority's approach entirely discounts the patient's interest in full disclosure with the offhanded observation that "[t]he program does not provide post-conception medical care, and therefore a doctor's silence with regard to abortion cannot reasonably be

thought to mislead a client into thinking that the doctor does not consider abortion an appropriate option for her." *Id.* at 200. This approach is troublesome for several reasons.

First, its factual premises are flawed: why would it be "unreasonable" for a patient who discovers that she is pregnant to assume that her doctor's silence on the question of abortion reflects a negative determination about the abortion procedure in her case? Moreover, if a patient has doubts about the desirability or appropriateness of an abortion and asks about abortion, the treating physician is required under the regulations to tell her that "abortion [is not] an appropriate method of family planning." 42 C.F.R. § 59.8(b)(5) (1992). Thus, if a patient asks about abortion, any doubts she has regarding the possibility of obtaining an abortion are to be answered in a fashion suggesting that the option is not a viable one.

Second, and perhaps more importantly, the government has not been put to any test regarding this restriction on the doctor's right to speak and the patient's right to hear. *Cf. Rust*, 500 U.S. at 200 ("We need not resolve [the First Amendment] question here . . . because Title X program regulations do not significantly impinge upon the doctor-patient relationship."). The Court was prepared to accept the restriction without any substantive justification regarding either its necessity or appropriateness.

163. *Compare Virginia State Bd. of Pharmacy*, 425 U.S. at 756–57 (holding that any First Amendment protection enjoyed by advertisers seeking to disseminate prescription drug price information also is enjoyed by the recipients of such information and therefore may be asserted by the recipients) *with Rust*, 500 U.S. at 200 (holding that the doctor-patient relationship does not justify an expectation on the part of the patient of comprehensive medical advice from a doctor in a government-funded clinic).

164. *See Rust*, 500 U.S. at 200.

165. U.S. Const. amend. I.

166. Whether Congress intended 42 U.S.C. § 300a-6 (1988) to impose the "gag" rule is open to doubt, if the congressional

hostility to the regulation was any indication. *See* Title X Pregnancy Counseling Act of 1991, S. 323, 102d Cong., 1st Sess. § 2 (1991); Family Planning Amendments Act, H.R. 3090, 102d Cong., 1st Sess. § 2 (1991); *see also* 138 Cong. Rec. H 2,822–51 (Apr. 30, 1992) (House debate on H.R. 3090); 138 Cong. Rec. H 10,667–77 (Oct. 2, 1992) (House debate on override of presidential veto of S. 323). Senate Bill 323 passed both houses, but, citing *Rust* in support of his position, then-President Bush vetoed the bill on September 25, 1992. 138 Cong. Rec. H 10,667 (Oct. 2, 1992). Although the Senate voted to override the President's veto by a margin of 73 to 26, *see* 138 Cong. Rec. H 10,667, the House failed to muster the required two-thirds majority to override vote. 138 Cong. Rec. H 10,678 (recording vote of 266 in favor and 148 opposed to override). President Clinton subsequently overturned the ban on his first day in office, Jan. 21, 1993. *See* 58 Fed. Reg. 7455 (Feb. 5, 1993).

167. *See* Post, *supra* note 153, at 153–56.

168. *Id.* at 152.

169. *Id.* at 163.

170. *Id.*

171. *Id.*

172. *See supra* note 155.

173. *See Legal Servs. Corp. v. Velazquez*, 531 U.S. 533, 540–43, 545–48 (2001).

174. Post, *supra* note 153, at 169.

175. *Id.* at 173.

176. *Id.* at 173 n.127.

177. *Id.* at 174.

178. *Id.*

179. Indeed, the Lords held forth *despite* express Parliamentary approval of the Home Secretary's directive. *See Regina v. Secretary of State for the Home Dep't, Ex parte Brind,* [1991] 1 App. Cas. 696, 715 (C.A.) (noting that on Nov. 2, 1988, the House of Commons approved a motion by a vote of 243 to 179 that "this House approves the Home Secretary's action").

180. *Brind,* [1991] 1 App. Cas. at 748–49, 750, 757–58, 763.

181. *See* Graham Zellick, "Spies, Subversives, Terrorists and the British Government: Free Speech and Other Casualties," 31 *Wm. & Mary L. Rev.* 773 (1990).

182. *See* Krotoszynski, *supra* note 38, at 1431–32; *see also New York Times Co. v. United States,* 403 U.S. 713 (1971) (permitting newspapers to publish sensitive government papers on First Amendment grounds; no comparable British decision exists); *New York Times Co. v. Sullivan,* 376 U.S. 254 (1964) (holding that the First Amendment restricts the application of the common law of libel to newspapers; no comparable British decision exists).

183. An easy way to accomplish this object would be through the incorporation of the ECHR into British domestic law, which is precisely what the HRA accomplishes. *See Regina v. Secretary of State for the Home Dep't, Ex parte Brind,* [1991] 1 App. Cas. 696, 761–62 (appeal taken from C.A.).

184. *See Legal Servs. Corp. v. Velazquez,* 531 U.S. 533 (2001) (upholding challenge to limitations on scope of LSC lawyers representing clients seeking to challenge welfare laws or regulations).

185. *See Rust v. Sullivan,* 500 U.S. 173, 200 (1991). Essentially, the majority endorsed the government's position that speech about abortion, in the context of a doctor-patient relationship, was not relevant to the service provided by a Title X family planning clinic. This is akin to saying that speech about God is irrelevant in a church.

186. Post, *supra* note 153, at 174–76, 179.

187. *Id.* at 176.

188. 410 U.S. 113, 171–78 (1973) (Rehnquist, J., dissenting) ("I find myself . . . in fundamental disagreement with those parts of the opinion that invalidate the Texas statute.").

189. *See Planned Parenthood of Southeastern Pennsylvania v. Casey,* 505 U.S. 833, 944 (1992) (Rehnquist, J., dissenting); *Webster v. Reproductive Health Servs.,* 492 U.S. 490, 519–21 (1989) (plurality opinion).

190. *See Webster,* 492 U.S. at 518–20; *id.* at 529–31 (O'Connor, J., concurring in part and concurring in judgment).

191. *See id.* at 529–31 (O'Connor, J., concurring in part and concurring in judgment) (applying an "undue burden" test rather than rationality review to test validity of Missouri abortion statute).

192. *See, e.g., Posadas de Puerto Rico Associates v. Tourism Co.,* 478 U.S. 328, 345–46 (1986) (holding that "the greater power to completely ban casino gambling necessarily includes the lesser power to ban advertising of casino gambling").

193. *See Hill v. Colorado,* 530 U.S. 703, 708–15 (2000).

194. *See id.* at 714–18 (characterizing case as presenting question of "whether the Colorado statute reflects an acceptable balance between the constitutionally protected rights of law-abiding speakers and the interests of unwilling listeners" and noting that given "the competing interests at stake" both sides have "legitimate and important concerns").

195. Ronald J. Krotoszynski, Jr., "Dissent, Free Speech, and the Continuing Search for the 'Central Meaning' of the First Amendment," 98 *Mich. L. Rev.* 1613, 1667 & 1667 n.178 (2000).

196. *See NAACP v. Claiborne Hardware Co.,* 458 U.S. 886, 907–12 (1982) (holding boycott of white-owned businesses was protected by First Amendment, despite threats of violence used to help enforce the boycott).

197. *Maher v. Roe,* 432 U.S. 464 (1977) (holding that the constitutional right to terminate a pregnancy "implies no limitation on the authority of a state to make a value judgment favoring childbirth over abortion, and to implement that judgment by the allocation of public funds" and arguing that "[t]here is a basic difference between direct state interference with a protected activity and state encouragement of an alternative activity consonant with legislative policy").

198. *Harris v. McRae,* 448 U.S. 297, 314–18 (1980) (holding that "although government may not place obstacles in the path of a woman's exercise of her freedom of choice, it need not remove those not of its own creation").

199. For other examples of this phenomenon, *see Plessy v. Ferguson,* 163 U.S. 537 (1896) (holding that statute requiring trains to provide separate but equal accommodations for white and black citizens was constitutional); *Minersville Sch. Dist. v. Gobitis,* 310 U.S. 586 (1940) (holding that state regulation requir-

ing public school students to recite the pledge of allegiance was constitutional); *Korematsu v. United States,* 323 U.S. 214 (1944) (holding that a military order that directed Japanese Americans to leave their homes, which were located in a West Coast military area, was constitutional).

200. *See* Tushnet, *supra* note 36, at 1524.

201. Gordon, *supra* note 36, at 114.

202. Of course, the question whether the determinacy game is worth the candle is open to question. *See* Robert Lipkin, "Indeterminacy, Justification, and Truth in Constitutional Theory," 60 *Fordham L. Rev.* 595, 619–23, 642–43 (1992) (criticizing the determinacy/indeterminacy paradigm as unhelpful to meaningful analysis of constitutional adjudication).

203. Tushnet, *supra* note 36, at 1524, 1538–39.

204. Spann, *supra* note 36, at 1734–39; *see* Mark V. Tushnet, *Red, White, and Blue: A Critical Analysis of Constitutional Law* 46–52 (1988) [hereinafter Tushnet, *Red, White, and Blue*].

205. Spann, *supra* note 36, at 1736.

206. *See, e.g., Bush v. Gore,* 531 U.S. 98 (2000); *see also* Ronald J. Krotoszynski, Jr., "An *Epitaphios* for Neutral Principles in Constitutional Law: *Bush v. Gore* and the Emerging Jurisprudence of Oprah!" 90 *Geo. L.J.* 2087 (2002) (criticizing Justices in both majority and dissent for engaging in unprincipled analysis of merits).

207. *Id.* at 1736–38; *see also* Tushnet, *Red, White, and Blue, supra* note 204, at 197–202; Neil Gotanda, "A Critique of 'Our Constitution is Colorblind,'" 44 *Stan. L. Rev.* 1, 8–12 (1991); Peter Gabel & Duncan Kennedy, "Roll Over Beethoven," 36 *Stan. L. Rev.* 1, 33–41 (1984).

208. Gabel & Kennedy, *supra* note 207, at 33–34. Gabel and Kennedy explain this aspect of the CLS canon as follows:

> DUNCAN
> What do you mean there are no rights?
>
> PETER
> They don't exist. They have no existence. They are shared, imaginary at-

tributes that the group attributes to its members that don't in fact exist. It's a hallucination. Moreover, the group itself is not constituted. There is no constituted group here, that is in fact acting in any way that we should consider. . . . There is no group discussion; there is no shared power among people generating forms of consensus about social reality. Yet there are thousands of classes each year in "constitutional law" that pretend that such a constituted group exists. . . .

[T]he way it happens with lawyers is that lawyers are far down the ladder from the political theory. They are taught the presuppositions of the democratic political theory without ever in fact engaging in hardly any discussion of whether those presuppositions or what they're based on are true. So they're taught at a purely technical level how to manipulate things that are presupposed, such as that the Constitution is a democratic document, based on the will of the people. Nobody gets to discuss that. Instead, you learn constitutional law, which has good things in it like freedom of speech and equal protection. But all of which relegitimizes the idea that there is currently existing a political group, a group in fusion, that is developing forms of shared meaning that is what people want. That is the false consciousness. That does not exist. In fact, it is invented by people in the service of maintaining their fear and anxiety about really developing such a political group, because they choose to believe it, and it's not true.

Id. at 34–35. Thus, under this view, constitutional law is little more than a sham to justify the ruling class's continued empowerment, and the sham maintains itself by representing itself as a reflection of the values of a common culture.

209. *Id.* This criticism of rights includes attacks on the First Amendment Speech Clause. Gotanda, *supra* note 207, at 11. Most recently, CLS adherents have objected to constitutionally imposed impediments, based on First Amendment considerations, to prohibitions against so-called "hate speech" on university campuses. *See* Charles R. Lawrence III, "If He Hollers Let Him Go: Regulating Racist Speech on Campus," 1990 *Duke L.J.* 431; Mari J. Matsuda, "Public Response to Racist Speech: Considering the Victim's Story," 87 *Mich. L. Rev.* 2320 (1989). Indeed, some in the CLS movement appear to reject the utility of written legal rules, even at the constitutional level, believing instead that some sort of communitarian discourse can more effectively resolve disputed matters. *See* Tushnet, *Red, White, and Blue, supra* note 204, at 317; *but cf.* Kimberlé Williams Crenshaw, "Race, Reform, and Retrenchment: Transformation and Legitimation in Antidiscrimination Law," 101 *Harv. L. Rev.* 1331 (1988) (arguing that rights and rights-talk create crucial breathing room for oppressed minorities); Richard Delgado, "The Ethereal Scholar: Does Critical Legal Studies Have What Minorities Want?" 22 *Harv. C.R.-C.L. L. Rev.* 741 (1992) (suggesting that a pragmatic approach to rights discourse will better serve minorities than rejection of rights discourse because of ideological objections to creation and recognition of rights by elites); Patricia J. Williams, "Alchemical Notes: Reconstructed Ideals From Deconstructed Rights," 22 *Harv. C.R.-C.L. L. Rev.* 401 (1987) (arguing that minorities should recognize limitations inherent in rights-based claims, but should not abjure invoking rights when doing so might be beneficial to the group).

210. *Cf.* Tushnet, *Red, White, and Blue, supra* note 204, at 51–52, 197–202, 317.

211. Herbert Wechsler, *Principle, Politics, and Fundamental Law* 20–22 (1961); Herbert Wechsler, "Toward Neutral Principles of Constitutional Law," 73 *Harv. L. Rev.* 1, 12–20 (1959).

212. *See, e.g., Simon & Schuster, Inc. v. New York State Crime Victims Bd.*, 502 U.S. 105, 123 (1991). The Supreme Court decided *Simon & Schuster* in same term as *Rust,* and the result enjoyed the endorsement of a unanimous Court. Likewise, *Hustler Magazine, Inc. v. Fal-*

well, 485 U.S. 46, 55–56 (1988), exemplifies the Court enforcing the First Amendment in good faith. As with *Simon & Schuster,* the Court was of a single mind in *Falwell. See Simon,* 502 U.S. at 123.

213. Cf. Tushnet, *supra* note 36, at 1538–39. Tushnet argues that the real dispute within the academy is not whether indeterminacy exists—he suggests (correctly) that all sides agree that it does—but focuses, rather, on the *level* of indeterminacy within the system. CLS adherents argue that the level of indeterminacy is quite high, whereas the more traditionally minded folks believe that determinate results obtain fairly frequently. *Id.*

214. *See, e.g., Moore v. City of East Cleveland,* 431 U.S. 494 (1977) (invalidating a local ordinance that did not allow certain categories of relatives to live together under the same roof because relevant community traditions encompassed the right of extended family members to reside in the same household); *see also* Phillip Bobbitt, "Is Law Politics?" 41 *Stan. L. Rev.* 1233, 1309 (1989) ("[T]he liberal tradition (taking that to be the tradition of our Constitution and its construction) [ ] not only permits but requires [the] judges and presidents and members of Congress [to] resort to their consciences when, having scrupulously followed the modes that ensure legitimization, [a conflict remains]").

215. The Constitution provides that no state shall deprive any of its citizens "equal protection" of the laws. Thus, if a state attempted to deny black citizens the right to vote, such a restriction would be unlawful even if the state had a tradition of denying its black citizens the vote. *Compare Grovey v. Townsend,* 295 U.S. 45 (1935) (holding that the denial of the right to vote to a black citizen pursuant to the rules of the state's Democratic Party did not implicate state action and therefore did not violate the Fourteenth or Fifteenth Amendments) *with Terry v. Adams,* 345 U.S. 461 (1953) (holding that Democratic Party election machinery denied the right to vote to citizens on the basis of race in violation of the Fifteenth Amendment); *Smith v. Allwright,* 321 U.S. 649 (1944) (holding that

the denial of the right to vote to a black citizen in a Democratic primary violated the Fifteenth Amendment). Turning to the use of tradition, a court presented with a case challenging the hypothesized law would act illegitimately if it upheld the regulation on the basis of the community tradition, the Equal Protection Clause notwithstanding. Recourse to tradition should occur only after the relevant decisional principle has been selected; tradition does not itself provide the decisional principle. *See, e.g., Moore v. City of East Cleveland,* 431 U.S. 494 (1977) (holding that due process of law is the relevant decisional principle); *Griswold v. Connecticut,* 381 U.S. 479 (1965) (holding that various provisions of the Bill of Rights provide the relevant decisional principle).

216. A dubious proposition, at best. *See* Van Alstyne, "Historical Review," *supra* note 34, at 93–97, 112–18; *see also Board of Educ. v. Pico,* 457 U.S. 853 (1982); *Keyishian v. Board of Regents,* 385 U.S. 589, 603, 609–10 (1967); *Young Women's Christian Ass'n of Princeton v. Kugler,* 342 F. Supp. 1048, 1063 (D.N.J. 1972).

217. *Rust v. Sullivan,* 500 U.S. 173, 200 (1991).

218. Perhaps the best example of this kind of turnabout occurred in the flag-salute cases, *Gobitis* and *Barnette: Minersville Sch. Dist. v. Gobitis,* 310 U.S. 586 (1940) (upholding a West Virginia law that required all students in the public schools to participate in a daily recitation of the pledge of allegiance); *West Virginia Bd. of Educ. v. Barnette,* 319 U.S. 624 (1943) (reversing its three-year-old precedent). Had President Clinton not mooted the issue, the Supreme Court would ultimately have reconsidered its decision in *Rust.* A doctor's interest in her professional speech is no less important, and therefore should be no less protected, than an academic's interest in academic freedom. *See generally Roe v. Wade,* 410 U.S. 110, 163, 166 (1973) (noting that "the abortion decision in all its aspects is inherently, and primarily, a medical decision, and *basic responsibility for it must rest with the physician*" (emphasis added)); *see also* Van Alstyne, "Historical Review," *supra* note 34, at 86–87 (describing the origins of academic

freedom as beginning in Germany to protect scientific endeavor from ecclesiastical meddling). The Supreme Court's more recent decision in *Velazquez* limits *Rust* by distinguishing the speech at issue in *Rust* as "government-sponsored speech" and limiting the *Rust* holding to such speech. *See Legal Servs. Corp. v. Velazquez*, 531 U.S. 533, 542 (2001) (holding that "the LSC program was designed to facilitate private speech, not to promote a governmental message"). The net result is that lawyers working in government-subsidized practices enjoy greater free speech rights than do doctors. The Supreme Court seemed to recognize this, and justified the differential treatment by invoking the lawyer's special duties to the courts. *See id.* at 544–47 ("The restriction imposed by the statute here threatens severe impairment of the judicial function.").

219. *Regina v. Secretary of State for the Home Dep't, Ex parte Brind,* [1991] 1 App. Cas. 696, 748–49, 757, 763 (appeal taken from C.A.).

220. *Id.* at 748–49, 750, 763; *see Hubbard v. Pitt,* [1976] Q.B. 142, 178 (Eng.) (Denning, Lord, dissenting); Colin Turpin, *British Government and the Constitution* 91–94 (1985); *see also* Street, *supra* note 1, at 96–97 (describing lapse of press restrictions from 1695 to 1945).

221. *See* Krotoszynski, *supra* note 38, at 1440–42; Edward Gary Spitko, Note, "A Critique of Justice Antonin Scalia's Approach to Fundamental Rights Adjudication," 1990 *Duke L.J.* 1337, 1348–59.

NOTES TO CHAPTER 7

1. *See Universal Declaration of Human Rights,* U.N. GAOR, 3d Sess., 183d mtg., G.A. Res. 17, U.N. Doc. A/810 (1948), art. 19 ("Everyone has the right to freedom of opinion and expression; this right includes freedom to hold opinions without interference and to seek, receive and impart information and ideas through any media and regardless of frontiers."); *see also* International Convention on Civil and Political Rights, art. 19, G.A. Res. 2200A(XXI) (1966) (guaranteeing right of free expression).

2. U.S. Const. amend. 1.

3. *See* Nihonkoku Kenpō [Constitution] [Kenpō] art. 21, para. 1 & 2.

4. *See* Part I of the Constitution Act, 1982, Canada Act, 1982, ch. 11, sch. B, art. 2, § 1 (U.K.) (containing the Canadian Charter of Rights and Freedoms) [hereinafter the Canadian Charter].

5. Grundgesetz [Basic Law], art. 1 (F.R.G.) [hereinafter Basic Law].

6. *See* Ronald J. Krotoszynski, Jr., Note, "Autonomy, Community, and Traditions of Liberty: The Contrast of British and American Privacy Law," 1990 *Duke L.J.* 1398.

7. *See* Friedrich Kübler, "How Much Freedom for Racist Speech? Transnational Aspects of a Conflict of Human Rights," 27 *Hofstra L. Rev.* 335, 375–76 (1998) (describing and discussing the European Court of Human Rights' use of a "margin of appreciation" for local understandings and interpretations of the fundamental rights protected by the European Convention on Human Rights and Fundamental Freedoms).

8. *See* James Q. Whitman, "Enforcing Civility and Respect: Three Societies," 109 *Yale L.J.* 1279, 1295–1344, 1384–94 (2000).

9. Michael J. Perry, *The Idea of Human Rights: Four Inquiries* 64 (1998) (emphasis in the original).

10. *Id.*

11. *Id.* at 65.

12. *Id.*

13. *Id.* at 73.

14. *Id.* at 91.

15. *Id.* at 92.

16. *See supra* note 7.

17. *See* Perry, *supra* note 9, at 91–95 (discussing potential "absolute" rights that should not admit much variation based on differing cultural contexts).

Index

About the Author

Ronald J. Krotoszynski, Jr., is Professor of Law and the Alumni Faculty Fellow at Washington and Lee University School of Law in Lexington, Virginia.